WORKING WITH
UNATTACHED YOUTH

The International Library of Sociology

THE SOCIOLOGY OF
YOUTH AND ADOLESCENCE
In 12 Volumes

WORKING WITH UNATTACHED YOUTH

Problem, Approach, Method

The Report of an enquiry into the ways and
means of contacting and working with
unattached young people in an inner London
Borough

by
GEORGE W. GOETSCHIUS
with
M. JOAN TASH

First published in 1967 by
Routledge and Kegan Paul Ltd

Reprinted in 1998 by
Routledge
11 New Fetter Lane, London EC4P 4EE

Printed and bound in Great Britain

The publishers have made every effort to contact authors/copyright holders
of the works reprinted in *The International Library of Sociology*.
This has not been possible in every case, however, and we would
welcome correspondence from those individuals/companies
we have been unable to trace.

British Library Cataloguing in Publication Data
A CIP catalogue record for this book
is available from the British Library

Working with Unattached Youth
ISBN 0-415-17671-9
The Sociology of Youth and Adolescence: 12 Volumes
ISBN 0-415-17828-2
The International Library of Sociology: 274 Volumes
ISBN 0-415-17838-X

The authors and the Project Committee regard the publication of this Report as a memorial to Beryl Hilton, whose faith and active help in this work were strong from the very beginning until her sudden death on the 19th November, 1965.

CONTENTS

CONTENTS

viii

FOREWORD

The importance of this book, as I see it, is in the definition of un-attachment, and in the perhaps unexpectedly wide range of implications for youth work and the Youth Service that might follow from it.

Unattachment is defined as "a conflict in expectations between those who offer the service (clubs, youth centres and others in the Youth Service) and those—the young people—who want and need it but who are unable or unwilling to accept it on the conditions on which it is offered".

In describing the work that gave rise to this definition, the authors help us to see that the conflict in expectations has its roots in a much wider context than we had been able to see before. They show not only that a wider variety of *services* might be necessary (help with jobs, boy/girl relationships and family problems, as well as recreation) but also that a wider variety of *needs* exists, ranging from those of the twelve-year-olds to those of the married couples under twenty.

The field-work, which is the basis of this book, is seen against a background of the social changes which brought about this conflict in expectations. These include increased social, vocational and edu-cational mobility, and particularly higher levels of aspiration, to-gether with changes in social attitudes about authority, discipline, loyalty, etc. There are also the problems of adolescents attempting to come to terms with themselves and society in situations where we (the youth-serving agencies) are not always able to offer the right kinds of opportunity in the right way at the right time. The authors quite rightly emphasise what they term "the cultural poverty" of much of contemporary social life as it affects youth and youth work, school-ing that "does not make sense", work that is boring, repetitive and "leads nowhere", and the absence, in many cases, of values and standards in the adult world that are either clearly enough defined to be under-stood and acceptable, or are seen by the young people as worthy of achievement. The authors indicate that this is an important field for further study.

Of the many practical suggestions and pointers to the way forward, the most important is the recurring emphasis on the need for "com-munity-centred" attitudes and action. Without minimising the diffi-culties (some of which were experienced in the field-work) the authors suggest a consideration of the structure and function of the local youth committee and the work of the local Youth Service as the starting point for the creation of such attitudes and action.

Suggestions for advanced and specialised training courses are made, including the possibility of bringing together the adjacent social services (probation officers, youth employment officers, adult indigenous leaders, heads of schools, etc.) as well as those directly concerned with youth work. This idea of a community-centred Youth Service, and the training necessary to establish it, is seen as the logical and natural extension of ordinary educational provision. The annotated bibliography is useful in providing further references to this idea.

A good deal of this material, I believe, will be of use to those teaching youth leadership and to their students, as well as to club leaders and management committees attempting to interpret the needs of the unattached in their communities. It should be of help as well to those who are beginning or are already involved in similar work. The role of the worker and his problems in the field are fully documented and discussed. (In this, as in other sections, it is possible to catch something of the actual excitement, stress and frustration that belong to this work.) The comments on the role of the agency, especially as it is affected by the conflicts in values and standards among the parties concerned, are valuable. The interest of this study, however, is not confined to "those directly concerned in the field of youth work". The general public will find many answers to the questions they ask about youth work and the relevance of Christian commitment to youth work.

The book has, I feel, one drawback—its length. I confess I should have been as hard pressed as I know the authors were to find ways of shortening it, or to find the means of dividing it into two volumes without breaking the necessary continuity. However, the length of the book ensures that many aspects of the problem are covered, and that no one or other section of the youth work public is excluded from participation in the discussion which should follow its publication.

This book deserves both careful reading and prolonged discussion —not because it will "solve all our problems", but because it can perhaps help us to develop a broader view of the task we have set ourselves, both in the original Circular 1486, and in the Report "The Youth Service in England and Wales", and offer us an ordered and systematic way of approaching it.

DIANA ALBEMARLE

20th September, 1966

PREFACE

This book is a slightly revised version of the Report of the London Y.W.C.A. Coffee Stall Project as presented in March, 1965 to the Youth Service Development Council of the Department of Education and Science and the Carnegie United Kingdom Trust, who gave generous help. It covers five years of field-work with the unattached in a London borough.

The focus of this youth work enquiry is the role of the detached youth worker, the sponsoring agency and the local community in providing the programme and the services necessary to meet the needs of the unattached. The report suggests possible terms of reference for further discussion in this field.

We are indebted to numerous people, both for their co-operation and contributions to the project, and for their comments and advice in the preparation of this report. Unfortunately, because of our obligation to maintain strict confidence about the persons, groups, agencies and the community with which we worked, the eight field-work staff on whose work and material this book is based must remain anonymous. This also applies to our colleagues in the community, the youth officer, the youth committee and youth leaders, local borough councillors, local youth employment, probation and child care officers, officers of the local Council of Social Service, the local police superintendent and representatives of many other social agencies, without whose help the field workers could not have made contact nor worked with the unattached.

We are glad to be able to acknowledge our debt to:

Dr. T. R. Batten, Senior Lecturer, London University Institute of Education. Ilys Booker, Community Development Worker, North Kensington Family Project. W. A. Cockell, National Training Officer, Methodist Association of Youth Clubs. The Rev. Ian Davidson, Diocesan Youth Adviser, Diocese of Southwark, London. Peter Duke, Principal, National College for the Training of Youth Leaders. Canon Sydney Evans, Dean of King's College, London. Edward Ewing, Development Secretary, Young Men's Christian Association. John Hayes, Lecturer in Social History, Christchurch College, Canterbury. Harold Haywood, Director of Education and Training, National Association of Youth Clubs. Peter Hodge, Lecturer in Social Science, London School of Economics. Elizabeth Irvine, Reader in Social Work, University of York. R. W. J. Keeble, Principal Youth Officer, Inner London Education Authority. Peter Kuenstler, World Youth Officer, United Nations, New York. Janet Kydd, Senior Lecturer in Social Science, London School of Economics. Elisabeth R. Littlejohn, Secretary, Councils of Social Service, National Council of Social Service. Joan Matthews, Lecturer in Social Group Work, National College for the Training of Youth Leaders. Patrick McCarthy, Detached Youth Worker, Portobello Project. The Rev. David Mason, Notting Hill Team Ministry, Notting Hill Social Council. A. T. W. Oxford, Deputy Chief Secretary for Training, National Association of Boys' Clubs. Dr. C. S. Smith, Director, Diploma in Youth Work Course, University of Manchester. Muriel Smith, Department of Community Development London Council of Social Service.

Y.W.C.A. volunteers and staff whom we wish to thank are Joyce Scroxton, Margaret Brown, Dorothy Lea, Pamela Melbourne and Mavis Kentish, and especially Frances Glendenning, who not only served as project chairman during the field work but who played a major part, with the assistance of Sheila Llewellyn, in the preparation of the manuscript for publication.

A special debt of thanks is due to the Gulbenkian Foundation, which assisted the Consultant's secondment to the London Area of the Y.W.C.A. for this work.

The Consultant had the responsibility for the preparation of this work, assisted by Miss M. Joan Tash, Administrator to the project, but both the field-work team and the project committee advised on the preparation and final draft, as well as those of our colleagues already listed. The Consultant would like to take this opportunity to discharge a personal debt to Dr. James Mallon, C.H., formerly of Toynbee Hall, who did so much in the years shortly before his death in 1963 to interest him in the needs of those now known as the unattached and to help him to clarify in his own thinking the nature and content of some of the problems that unattachment represents. He would also like to record his thanks to the late George Devine, C.B.E., and his wife Sophie, whose constant questioning and personal support were generously given and appreciatively received.

INTRODUCTION

The point of departure for this project was the concern of statutory and voluntary bodies in the field of youth work, as well as of a section of the general public, about the large numbers of young people who were unattached to any youth organisation.

The Executive Committee of the London and Southern England Area of the Y.W.C.A. initiated and planned a twelve month 'experiment' to find out whether contact could be made with these young people, through the medium of a mobile coffee stall on a street corner.

A London borough was chosen as the location of the 'experiment' and with the approval and co-operation of the borough council and the support of some of the local agencies, the coffee stall was set up and opened four evenings a week at a busy street corner in a high density, working class neighbourhood.

It was the success of making contact with the unattached at the stall, together with the impact of the Albemarle Report, which encouraged the London Y.W.C.A. to attempt the more extensive three-year field-work project of which this presentation is a report.

The initial assumptions on which the project was based were:

1. That the coffee stall offered a point of contact with the unattached, and that the progress made indicated that the young people needed and would use this contact.

2. That it should be possible to find a way of developing a programme designed to meet their needs.

3. That the programme might include helping them to form groups of ten to twelve persons, which at this point appeared to be the best milieu for offering a service.

4. That one development in this project might be introducing the young people to club life and helping them to make contact with other agencies.

The Ministry of Education, on the recommendation of the Youth Service Development Council, agreed to grant-aid the project at the rate of £4,200 a year for three years (the actual amount allocated was £13,500). A condition of this grant was that the project should be carefully documented, so as to provide information and suggestions on methods of work which might be useful to others attempting to contact and work with the unattached.

As a result the terms of reference of the project became "to contact and work with the unattached in the borough using detached workers, to study and develop methods of doing this, to record the work and

1

to prepare a document based on the records". The Carnegie United Kingdom Trust through a staff member of the London School of Economics agreed to allocate £2,550 over a three year period so that a Research and Training Consultant could be appointed to design and implement the study, train the field workers, and act as a consultant for the overall project. George Goetschius, who accepted this appointment, was seconded to the London Area of the Y.W.C.A. on a half-time basis by the London Council of Social Service with the approval of the Gulbenkian Foundation which was grant-aiding his work with the Council.

The London Y.W.C.A. to which the grants were made, agreed to cover the administration costs of the project, and appointed a Project Committee to guide the policy. Joan Tash, Area Training and Programme Secretary, was seconded, also on a half-time basis, as Administrator/Supervisor, responsible for the overall development of the project.

The Project Committee, on which the administrator and consultant were executive officers, appointed five field-workers during the first year.

The field-work

This report of the three-year project is based on the work of the five field-workers, three men and two women, who at first met the young people at the coffee stall, got to know them and, when accepted by them, moved into the community, to the street corners,' coffee bars, dance halls, public houses, youth clubs, and in two instances into premises in the neighbourhood temporarily rented by the Y.W.C.A.

The programme operated in four ways. We worked with individuals helping them with personal problems related to family, school, work, friends, boy/girl relationships and the law.

We worked with natural friendship groups within the larger grouping of young people around the stall, helping them to plan and carry out recreational activities and offering them the leadership and resources with which to do this. We helped some of these groups to get on with each other, and to plan and do things together, as well as separately. At one point we helped the older boys to run their own 'commercial café'; at another we worked with a group inside an established boys' club in the neighbourhood. We started a special group for the younger girls on probation, who did not find it easy to make friends and join in natural friendship groups, and who needed a special group to help them learn to cope with some of their problems.

We worked with ourselves. The emphasis in the whole project was on the possible methods of contacting and working with the unattached. This meant that we, the staff, were focussing the investigation on ourselves and our ability to assess the needs of the young people, to make contact and develop relationships, to meet needs, to plan and carry out the programme, and to decide how best to do this within the limitations and potential of the resources available. For this purpose recording, in-service training, weekly staff conferences and supervision sessions, were an essential part of the work.

We worked within the community, in association and in co-operation with the individuals, groups and statutory and voluntary bodies. These sometimes included family, friends and neighbours of the young people, or the café proprietor and his wife, as well as other indigenous adult leaders. Often they were probation officers, court officials, employers, youth employment officers, welfare officials, youth leaders and the bodies to which they were attached. Sometimes we shared information with a person or an agency which could thereby do more effective work with an individual or a group. Sometimes we ourselves acted as a bridge between an individual or group and an agency, or between agencies. Frequently we had to interpret the needs of the unattached as we saw them, to the youth serving agencies in the community, and we had to explain to the young people where such agencies were and what they offered. Indeed, it was this last aspect of our field-work, work with the community, that we eventually came to see as the most important area of the whole operation.

During the three years of field-work, at least 326 boys and girls were known to the workers. Of these, at least 236 participated in the programme erratically, and 159 (88 boys and 71 girls) received help individually and in groups for periods of up to three years. Thus, 159 young people could be considered as regulars within the programme. We came to see about 20 of these as 'can copes', 93 as being 'simply disorganised', 35 as 'temporarily disorganised', and 11 as 'seriously disorganised'. The work on which this report is based centred on the 159 young people, but the 326 young people, as well as those who attended the coffee stall earlier, are included in the material about social attitudes and individual and group behaviour.

Although the field-workers varied in the time they gave to the different aspects of the work, on an average half their time was given to field-work, one fifth to work related to the field, and three tenths to training, staff conferences and recording.

The total expenditure for the project was £18,800. Of this amount, £14,850 was allocated to salaries, £3,180 to programme, and £770 to office, travelling and general expenses.

The report

This report is intended for those involved in and interested in the

3

field of youth work, and is written as much as possible from the point of view of the detached youth worker doing the job, and the voluntary organisation supervising the work. It describes the kind of programme, and the nature and content of field-work necessary to plan, organise and evaluate such programmes, as well as the approach and method developed to do the job.

At no point in this report are we suggesting that the specifics of our work are necessarily applicable in other areas, but we do feel that the basic argument of the presentation can be a guide to others in thinking out their own approach to the same or similar problems. The relevance of this report to other similar work in this field (The Bristol Social Project, The Liverpool Project, and the Project of the National Association of Youth Clubs) is discussed in the appendices.

The use of field-work records

The information for this report was collected from field-work records and from staff conferences, supervision and training records. In addition we used notes of committee meetings, and meetings or interviews with community agencies and our colleagues in the field of youth work.

Perhaps the most difficult problem facing anyone attempting to document field-work in any area of human relations is that of confidence. On one hand, for no reason and under no conditions, can the confidence of an individual, group or community, be exploited, or the invasion of their privacy by publication, be countenanced. On the other hand if the material presented is to lend itself to meaningful discussion, and be used as teaching material, it must be factual, detailed and systematic as to incident and context.

We have attempted to reconcile these two imperatives by using only portions of any one record at any single point of presentation in order to make identification impossible, by disguising the names of persons and places, including those of the field-workers, and by re-arranging the order of events where this does not affect the accuracy of the material presented.

In the circumstances, in order to avoid identification, no single profile is that of an actual young person. Each profile has been constructed from records describing a number of different young people. They have been put together to make a composite profile, which when added to the other profiles, forms a picture as representative as possible of the young people in the whole coffee stall grouping.

The question of disguise has proved the greatest problem in relation to the form of presentation. We originally intended to select several young people and several groups, and follow them through the whole period of our contact and work with them. This, we felt, would allow the characteristics of the unattached young people, the role of the worker, the nature and content of programme, and the relevant information about approach and method, to unfold naturally as we followed them through the three years of field-work. We finally agreed not to use any one case history in its entirety, but to use only a section of each relevant field-work record in different parts of the presentation in order to make a specific point. This may be a less successful way of presenting the material, but we see it as the only way of making it unidentifiable. In one instance, that of social group work with the girls' probation group, we felt that the best use of the material would be to prepare a separate publication for restricted circulation, although we do mention this aspect of our work briefly within the report.

Unattachment

It will be noted that throughout this report we use the words 'attached' and 'unattached' in several different ways. At the beginning of the project we use the word to designate young people who had no regular contact with a youth club or other youth serving agency, in fact according to common usage. As our thinking in these matters changed through the development of the work in the field, we came to see unattachment as meaning unattachment to a much wider variety of opportunity and service (even for nominal club members) and to cover a much wider variety of young people.

This recognition affected our usage and we then began to speak of the various 'specific categories' of young people who made up our general category of unattachment—the 'can copes', the 'temporarily disorganised', the 'simply disorganised' and the 'seriously disorganised'. The nature and content of these purely descriptive categories will be explored early in the report.

Finally we came to see the unattached as a community problem rather than simply as a problem of young people unable or unwilling to make use of facilities offered by the Youth Service. Indeed, we came to see the part the agencies themselves played in causing unattachment. For these reasons no single definition of unattachment obtains throughout the whole presentation, but we hope that our attempts to show the changes in our thinking about unattachment at each stage of the report, together with the context in which the word appears, will always make the meaning clear.

Youth work study

The enquiry described in this book was a youth work study. It set out to explore the needs of young people in terms of the possible roles of the detached worker and the Youth Service in a particular community. It can perhaps best be seen as an 'institutional' study which sets out to clarify some of the relations between the needs of unattached young people and the possibilities of meeting them within the pattern of association and service provided by the local Youth Service in its role of social institution, community agency and administrative unit.

The reader may like to know that follow-up study is now being planned which will attempt further exploration of several of the recommendations of this report.

Chapter One
THE CIRCUMSTANCES

1. The young people

During the pre-project period and the first year of reconnaissance, a good deal of the field-work consisted of collecting information about the young people, from which we were able to build up a series of profiles of them as individuals and in groups. Following discussion of this information among ourselves, with the project committee, and with colleagues, we developed observations about the unattached young people in our coffee stall grouping, from which we made assumptions about the nature and content of the service needed, the kind of programme possible and the approach and method most likely to be useful in developing these.

This section includes a collection of these profiles based on records of direct contact with young people on the stall, in cafés, public houses, other premises, the streets, or on expeditions. They are representative of the characteristics of the whole coffee stall grouping—including the girls, with whom contact was made at a later stage. The profiles have been reconstructed to prevent their being identified as individual persons.

When we had accumulated enough information to allow us to be more exact in our observations, we were able to agree on four categories for the young people within the total contact group.

1. The 'can-copes'—the young people among our contacts who were both able and willing to use the resources available to them to do things and be things that they needed and wanted.

2. The 'temporarily disorganised', who were between school and work, in need of information, guidance and support, on a temporary basis only, some of whom, even if we had not been present, would have managed on their own, but many of whom needed help in order not to fall into more serious difficulties.

3. The 'simply disorganised'—by far the largest category of our con-

tacts—who needed information, guidance and support, and help in developing for themselves a recreational programme that met their needs, within the resources available to them. This category contained, as did category 2, many young people whom we saw as easily falling into serious difficulties if this help were not offered them.

4. The 'seriously disorganised'—the smallest category of contacts— who needed the most intensive guidance and support on a long term basis, and who made up the bulk of the serious probation, court work, and boy/girl problem cases.

These categories, to which we sometimes refer in the profiles that follow, are more fully developed, together with the implications they had for our programme and approach in Chapter Four.

Dick

Dick is 16, a short slightly built self-confident and friendly youngster, keen on adventure films, on watching sport, and a collector of information about football.

His father is a skilled, comparatively well-paid carpenter, and his mother a cashier in a café. He has an older brother who is also a carpenter, and a younger sister who is looked after by a neighbour when she gets home from school. Dick's family is solid, working class, an artisan type of family with some overtones of middle-class taste and behaviour. They go to the country on the occasional Sunday and have been to Spain for a summer holiday. Sometimes the whole family goes into the West End to the cinema. The family has strong ties with all four grandparents, and to numerous uncles and aunts. Dick is still at school and is going on to a technical college to learn to be an architect. He thinks his father and older brother are "too much of a pair", and that his mother's main concern is his fourteen-year-old sister who is to stay on at school and have a career as a personal secretary.

Dick liked school and had friends there whom he never brought to the stall because "they wouldn't like it" or "lived too far away". He is not a regular attender at the stall but when he comes he is usually with Sid and Bob. They both like Dick because "he can explain the stories in the films" to them, and because he can make TV sports programmes "almost come alive". Dick is rarely with us at weekends. He spends some weekends with his family, and his friends visit him there. He is often away from the coffee stall group for weeks on end because "he has things of his own to do at home at night". His friends in the coffee stall group do not seem to resent this and explain his absence by saying "he gets very busy but he always comes back after a while".

Dick has no regular girl friend now. He says she turned out to be "unreliable" and hints that this means that his parents did not approve of her. The girl was not from the coffee stall group. He met her through one of his school mates. He sometimes goes to the cinema with the girl companions of his friends in the coffee stall group but never takes a girl on his own. He explains this by saying "he is still looking". He occasionally goes to club dances and to dance halls in neighbouring boroughs and talks about "the girls you can pick up there". He indicates when talking to us that he is really looking for a "girl of the better type" and he seems to expect us to understand that the girls in the coffee stall group are the "poorer" type.

Dick tried several clubs but after his 13th birthday, felt that they were "kids' stuff", and dropped out. His father and brother agreed with him about this but his mother did not. She felt that a club would help to make him a "good boy". Her reiterating this seemed to have been one of the factors that led him to "give the whole thing up". He was with "the boys" one night at a West End cinema when they picked a row with the cinema attendant, jumped the attendant and hit him. This resulted in a court case, because of the use of force and because none of the boys except Dick had admission tickets. Since Dick had a ticket and was not directly involved in the fight the magistrate let him off with a caution. He feels that the police and the probation authorities are necessary but usually "very jumpy", that is, they are quick to make the wrong assumption. The best thing in the end is to avoid being "where trouble happens" because in one way or another people always seem to "get roped in".

Dick seems to need the coffee stall and the friends he has made around it both as a relief from the closeness of his family ties and as an environment in which to gather a few casual friends to whom he can exhibit his knowledge about sport and about the "makings of a really good adventure picture" and with whom he can exchange stories about girls.

He sees himself as knowing what he wants to do and how to do it, and as fairly skilled in knowing what people expect of him. He offered this story of his court experience—"I knew when I went into the court that the important thing was not to deny everything—even though I did not hit the attendant or tell any one else to—but to tell the magistrate I was sorry, that it was all a mistake, and to call him 'Sir'." This behaviour in court did not anger his friends. He had a similar attitude to school. He said "You have to find out what they want you to do and then see how much you can give them".

We saw Dick as a 'can cope' in the sense that he knew what he wanted and had already set about getting it. His uncle had already promised to get him into a firm when his training was over. He was engaged in finding a steady girl friend. He had arrived at his own way of handling the authorities in order to get what he wanted. We saw Dick as being representative of only a small number of the boys we contacted. This is not surprising as we were becoming better known for our help in dealing with court and employment problems. The coffee stall group became self-selecting in that it tended to attract those boys who most needed help, and to become simply a diversion or an occasional entertainment for the 'can copes', who were capable of getting along on their own.

Mac

Mac is 15, one of the younger coffee stall contacts, short, stocky and always 'on the go'. He gives the impression of having a good deal to do and of getting on with it. His mannerisms are decisive, his speech blunt and to the point. He gives the impression of being older than he is. He is a bit of a clown and will do an 'act' on the pavement in front of the stall at the slightest provocation. He occasionally describes himself as "that mad old thing".

Mac's family is large. He has two older sisters, one older brother and two younger brothers. His father is a builder's labourer, well-paid and apparently in regular work with a good deal of overtime. His mother does not go out to work. Mac thinks his father is too heavy handed and favours the girls in the family. He feels his mother still thinks him a baby which he sometimes finds useful, since he can always 'work out' a shilling or two without much effort. Mac's sisters are very strictly supervised by his father. They must be home at ten, which they resent, but there is nothing his mother can do about it. Mac thinks the girls are silly, mostly because they 'cry their way out of things' instead of standing up to them.

Mac's idea of his family is that they are all right if you know how to 'work them'—avoid the old man, steer clear of the girls, lay down the law to the younger brothers. "The best of the lot" is Bingo his older brother who is 23 and an electrician. Mac admires and gets on well with him. Bingo wants to get married but Mac's father is against it "but it will probably come off next month anyway". Mac likes Bingo's girl friend, Sue, and sometimes is allowed to trail around or go to a cinema with them. Mac didn't think very much about school. He thought it was good for a laugh, and liked several of the masters "providing you don't take them too seriously". He did rather well in some subjects "if I do say so myself".

Mac wants to be a motor mechanic and has been doing odd jobs since he was twelve at a garage in the neighbourhood. At first the garage owner didn't want him hanging round but since he was able to make himself useful, he agreed to let him help. On leaving school he was taken on as 'odd man out' to help the two full-time mechanics.

His brother Bingo has looked into this and found that the boss at the garage is willing to keep Mac on and to consider training him as a mechanic if he will take it seriously. Mac likes this and already refers to himself as "Mac the top mechanic".

Mac belongs to a small friendship group of which he could be the natural leader, but he spends so much time at the garage—often late into the night—that he is not with his friends often enough to keep the leadership in his own hands. His friends frequently visit him at the garage "for a giggle", and his boss has warned him several times that he'll "get his cards" if it continues. Several months ago Mac borrowed a motor scooter and drove it about without a licence, knocked up its front wheel and left it in the West End. He was not caught nor does his father know, but his brother Bingo found out about it and punished him. Mac has led a few of his friends in some ill-advised escapades, more for adventure than for any inner compulsion to break the law or for the small financial gain that these petty crimes are wont to provide.

Mac has been a member of several of the clubs in the neighbourhood, for two or three month periods, and feels that clubs are all right "but take up too much of your time: once they get to know you they try to drag you in on everything". Club leaders are all right providing you let them know you are not serious about it (like teachers), "if they think you are they will try and get you roped in and then you've had it". Mac is not interested in girls as he feels they are apt to be like his sisters. "They are good for a laugh." Mac sees himself as very busy getting on with things, capable and headed for a good future in the garage "Some day I'll have a garage of my own", he says.

We saw Mac as being representative of those young people in our contact group who were 'temporarily disorganised', that is, between leaving school and settling in to a work routine. In Mac's case the chance of his continuing with the occasional petty crime is rather slim, whereas in all probability he will settle into the garage, and find a steady girl friend. His interest in his work, his relationship with his mother and his older brother, all indicate that he will probably outgrow any tendency to unattachment. Mac's need for us was simply as a fill-in, a place to meet friends, have a laugh, and lark about. He liked our appreciation of his ready wit and also liked the trips, especially the camping—"anything for a giggle".

Fred

Fred is 16 years of age, tall, with sandy-blond hair, light complexioned, thin and loose-limbed, and wears glasses. He will dance or sing at the drop of a hat, knows all the 'pop' singers and has a good record collection. He is "kind to everyone", avoids fights and even

11

arguments, tries to turn everything into a lark, and often succeeds. He plays the part of the philosopher. His line is always an attempt to show that life is "like that anyway". He has picked up the word "fatalist" and describes himself as one. He reads the horoscopes in the daily papers whenever he can get hold of them. He thinks they are "fixed" but that they have the right idea, namely that things are "that way because they are that way".

Fred has one younger brother of twelve and one sister of fourteen. His mother keeps house, his father is a transport worker. Fred's mother is frequently ill with migraine and spends long periods in bed. She keeps Fred's younger sister, Mabel, home from school, to take care of the house and the men. This has in the past caused difficulty with the school attendance officers, and is now causing difficulties with Mabel who "wants out" as Fred puts it. Fred's father was once in trouble with the police about a stolen lorry but that was long ago and after that Fred's mother took over. Fred says his father "hasn't had a break out since". He drinks at home and not in the pub.

Fred works as a packer at a china and glass ware factory. Before this job he changed jobs "about three times a month" either because he didn't like the people with whom he worked or because they didn't think he took an interest in the job and sacked him. He likes the work, mostly because he likes his workmates and the foreman, who, he says "is a right good George", and takes care of his mates when the boss gets on a "let's straighten things out here kind of kick". The job has no future but it "doesn't break my back either".

Fred has three friends who form a loosely knit friendship group that attaches itself this week to one group, next week to another. They go to the cinema a lot together. They go on frequent half-hearted "bird hunts", or visits to dance halls and occasionally "the singing pub" in the neighbouring boroughs. Much of their time is spent wandering from one coffee bar to another. He has been caught up in several 'rumbles' inside and outside the neighbourhood. "Stands to reason, you gotta support your mates." Fred does not have a steady girl. He likes to dance with girls and "lark about a bit", but nothing serious.

Fred didn't mind school. He thought a lot of it was interesting (not that he went all the time), and appeared to be sorry that it was all over. He read *Kon Tiki* at school and found it very exciting. As a result he is always talking about trips to Brighton and the seaside simply because he wants to see the sea, which he explains is "part of the same sea" since they all connect up, "so from Brighton you can see the same water that the *Kon Tiki* floated on". When asked if he would have liked to continue at school he says, "Well, maybe it's interesting enough" but gives the impression that it is really for children and people who don't have to work. He sees it as a pleasant enough recreation, parts of which he would enjoy if he had nothing else to do. Our suggestion that going to school at night might give him something practical as well as entertaining was not taken seriously.

Fred is on probation for having been with a group that borrowed a car. He didn't think it was wrong. He just went along for the ride. Nor does he think it was wrong for the court to put him on probation. He keeps his probation appointments and will say nothing either against or in favour of his probation officer. "It's all just like that isn't it?" He is suspicious of the statutory and voluntary bodies but he isn't angry about them. He thinks being a policeman is a job like anything else, and says that it is not the policeman's fault if you get in his way. "He has the boss on him as well." The "employment", the "welfare" and "attendance people" are all hired by the borough council "to keep things going" and it is the job of a sensible person to get as much out of them as possible, or to steer clear of the whole lot. Clubs are all right for a night now and then but they get "sticky" and say "why don't you join" and "wouldn't you like to do this or that?". Fred thinks most conditions are "out of your control and there's no point in trying to do anything about it". He does not hide from himself the fact that there may be more trouble, especially with the police, but "why worry?"

We saw Fred as being representative of a large number of the 'simply disorganised' in our coffee stall grouping, in that he lived only from minute to minute. He could follow the lead of either 'can copes' or of the 'seriously disorganised' boys.

Bill

Bill is aged 17, of medium height, slightly built, with black hair and dark eyes. He is "quick on his feet" as his friends put it. He is a rapid forceful talker in clipped sentences. He is sometimes withdrawn and sullen, sometimes argumentative and aggressive. He can be friendly and cheerful, and then suddenly becomes angry and violent for no apparent reason. On some of these occasions he has started fires, smashed equipment and hit his girl friend with a hammer.

Bill's father disappeared some years ago. His mother washes dishes in a canteen, and takes odd cleaning jobs. He has an older brother at sea, two younger brothers 14 and 12 years, and a younger sister of 11. The family lives in $2\frac{1}{2}$ rooms. When he is unemployed Bill's mother alternates between giving him 'hand-outs' and refusing to give him anything, including food.

Bill disliked school intensely. "School was a waste of time. I liked Mr. T. You could talk to him about going to Australia—but he got the sack." (In fact Mr. T changed schools of his own accord.) He has worked in many jobs as a plumber's mate, rarely for more than three weeks. Once he lost a job because he took home some of the material—"It was only fair. The wages were too low". Frequently he left because of trouble with his boss, who was always seen as taking advantage of him; but often he was sacked because of his time-keeping. He talks of wanting to be a plumber and to go to Australia, but "they push me around too much". He says he will be a "builder" one day, because "that's where the money is". He sometimes takes a casual job on a building site.

Bill is the natural leader of the small group of boys around him, usually two or three, occasionally more. He takes the lead in planning anti-social activities, that are sometimes the 'employment' of the group—breaking into telephone kiosks, gas meters, and cigarette machines. He has been fined several times, and is on probation after being in court for carrying an offensive weapon. He guesses he'll be "for it" next time. Bill's friends are not so much friends as accomplices, with whom he needs "to do things", and in order to get the extra money that petty thieving brings. They like him because "he's always good for a giggle". He promises the group "big money one day", and "the right kind of bird in the right numbers", none of which he can expect to provide for them or help them provide for themselves. Petty crime as "regular work" and sexual adventure, seem to be more talking points to keep his hold over the group than actual potentialities of his leadership. What he does provide is a feeling of togetherness, the petty crimes, the occasional lark, the occasional bust up and a stream of promises, suggestions and "laugh talk", that offer the group a protection against boredom and the need to think realistically about their environment. Bill has a girl friend who supplies him with money and tries to persuade him to work, and to keep out of trouble. Sometimes he is about to "give her a ring", sometimes he beats her, sometimes he is very depressed because "her old man won't let me near her".

Bill thinks "the law is a racket", and the police only want to "put you inside". He unwittingly helped us in the early days of the coffee stall by the way in which he interpreted the attempt of the police to move the stall. One evening, the police came by and pointed out that we were too near the crossroads and would have to move the stall two yards along the road. "Stick it out" said Bill, "don't budge". He began a long tirade against the police "who are against us". He included the coffee stall workers in 'us', elicited from the other boys present their own feelings about the police, and in the end crystallised in the minds of the group present, that we (the staff and the workers) since we were being pushed around by 'them' (the police) were in fact part of 'us' (the young people). This cleared away the suspicion that we were in some way connected with the police.

Bill sees all officials as 'them'. They are all part of the 'racket' and "tell each other what they know about you, and try to catch you out like when the school officer came about Betty, and told the probation officer I was at home and not working". Bill has been a member of most youth clubs in the neighbourhood, for short periods. He sees the club leaders as too demanding. "Give them your sixpence, then do what they want. What do they do with that money, I'd like to know."

Bill was one of the smaller number of young people whom we saw as falling into the category of 'seriously disorganised', and for whom special provision had to be made in our programme of service. Bill saw us as 'suckers'—"good for a few bob" but he also had the suspicion that we had the necessary 'know-how'. We could deal with 'them', and if he used us properly we would help him 'go places'. He did find us useful in dealing with 'them' although not always in the way he intended. He became very dependent on us for support with his problems and his depressed periods. We felt that the chances were very remote of helping Bill to see that some sort of compromise with the demands of his social environment was necessary.

Sally

Sally is 18, dark-haired, with a light complexion, a bit above medium height for a woman and slightly chubby. She is an intelligent, pleasant and happy girl. She dresses well, speaks well and as her friend Bob explains "dances well into the bargain". Sally is more mature than the girl friends of Bob's mates and she knows it, though she never makes anything of it. Bob often does. He says to Sweeney or Al "you should get yourself a girl like Sally". He is well aware of the importance of Sally in his life. She sees that he is dressed properly, sometimes washes his shirts for him at her home, helps him to stick to his job, despite his urge—especially in the spring—to "chuck it all up and start again". She deposits some of his salary each week in a post office account, together with some of her own.

Sally has an older sister and two younger brothers. Her father is a skilled lathe operator. Her mother does not go out to work. The family is closely knit, spends some of each weekend together, and always has Sunday dinner together. It is usual for Bob to have Sunday dinner at Sally's house and he often turns up for supper during the week.

Sally liked school but thinks it could have been a bit more practical. She is working as a filing clerk in an insurance company and taking shorthand at an evening institute. She says she wishes she had been helped while in school "to take it all a bit more seriously". She could now be a secretary at the insurance company and making a good deal more money if she had only "done the right thing at school". But she

15

feels she can make it up on her own with the help of her evening classes. She bought a second-hand set of linguaphone records to teach herself Spanish which she has now been doing for the past three months. Bob refused to help her with this, since he objected to the whole idea of a foreign language, mostly because he thought that it might bring her into contact with foreigners. She cannot convince him that it might help in her work, and he is unimpressed with her idea of getting a better job if she has more qualifications.

Sally has a friend, Alice, whom she met at work, and she and Alice, with the help of Sally's older sister make some of their own clothes. Alice designed a sack dress, copies of which they both made up. Alice and Sally shop and lunch together, read women's magazines together and often spend evenings at each other's homes, "washing their hair". Sally and Bob and Alice and her boyfriend never go out together as a foursome. Bob claims that this is because Alice's boyfriend is a snob and doesn't like him because he is not the "clerk type".

Sally tries to persuade Bob to be more enterprising, to go to the West End, or to go to a jazz club, but usually Bob says it isn't worth it. She has collected many pictures of furniture and household decorations in preparation for their flat when they are married. Bob says he is determined to build most of the things "because it is cheaper that way and because they would be better anyway". Sally supports him in this, and persuaded him to make a coffee table as a beginning.

Bob has been on probation for helping some of his mates to get away with a load of material from a construction site. Sally stood by him throughout this difficulty and it is due to her, he says, that he is now "on the straight and narrow". His mates count him out of the jobs they plan because "he won't take it on because of Sally". Yet they still feel themselves to be his mates and he theirs, and although they tease him a great deal, they frequently go out together to wrestling or public houses.

Sally's parents are not particularly impressed with Bob, yet they know he is Sally's choice and are kind and accepting despite their misgivings. Sally's older sister approves of him. Bob works as a second driver on a delivery van but will shortly be running a small van on his own for the same firm. Sally's parents do not think this is a skilled job but they don't attempt to interfere or to influence Sally. Bob's parents are very happy about Sally. Bob's mother loses no opportunity to tell him that "she is too good for you". Bob and Sally take all this good-naturedly.

We saw Sally as a girl who knew what she wanted to do, and usually how to achieve it. Normally she could cope on her own and was well supported by her family, but she saw the stall and the workers as a support for herself in her relationship with Bob, and more especially for Bob himself. She encouraged Bob to come to the stall, and often arranged to meet him there. When they had the occasional row, they passed messages to each other through a worker. If a question arose such as, "Does having been on probation mean difficulty in getting on the housing list?", they came together to discuss it at the stall. She frequently discussed fashions and furnishing with a female worker. She persuaded Bob to go with a worker and a few others to theatres and on other expeditions, to which he would not go with her alone. She saw us as the "right kind of people" to advise Bob—people he liked—who would help him to avoid "getting into trouble again, and regretting it later".

Jane

Jane is 13 years old, with brown eyes and long straggling hair. She is of medium height and very plump. She always seems to be wearing old clothes, usually blouses and skirts, both summer and winter.

Jane is the second of nine children. Her father works only occasionally, is a heavy drinker, given to violence, and has served three prison sentences. Her mother attempted suicide some years ago and received treatment for some time afterwards. The family lives mainly on National Assistance. One of the boys is on probation, another in a children's home. The attendance officer is frequently at the home, which is also visited by a welfare worker and health visitor. The family lives in three rooms, which are in bad repair and have little furniture.

Jane is on probation for stealing jewellery with three other girls— "we'd have been all right but Mavis would go into this other shop to get more stuff". She likes the probation officer—"she doesn't get mad at you—but she keeps telling me I've got to go to school". She thinks school is too strict—"they hit you with a ruler and if you are cheeky, send you to the headmaster". "We have lots of fun there. I like arithmetic, drama, art and playing games. I'd like a school where you could have jokes with the teachers, and where the headteacher wouldn't jump down your throat if you are five minutes late." Jane goes to school on average about three times a week. "It's usually too late to go, by the time I'm ready."

Jane had her first communion at the Catholic church a year ago. She was very proud of it, and could not stop talking about it. "You could be a Catholic if you want to. It's nice being a Catholic." She is in constant trouble for fighting, both at home with her sisters, and at school. She is friendly with three girls, each friendship being 'on' or 'off' with great frequency. She will shout at boys and tease them, but is indignant if they tease her or chase her in return. "They're just cheeky."

Her mother has threatened to put her "in care" several times "but she needs me to look after the kids—our Mavis never does anything". She was invited to join a special group for younger girls but she is often late coming to the clubroom, sometimes with such comments as "I had to get the groceries. Our mum would've spent the money if I hadn't." In the clubroom she mimes and sings beautifully and gets two or three others to make up plays with her. She fights with the older girls and tries to organise the young ones. Her father objects to the club because "it is making her too fast, with make-up", but she usually manages to come. Jane loves outings, and is good at skating and swimming. She likes driving into the country and playing boisterous games on the grass. On one occasion, when everyone stopped to admire the view, she hid her face, saying "I can't look. I just can't bear it."

Jane wants to be a "model or a window dresser". She says she will leave home when she is sixteen. "When you leave home, you don't have any worries about your mum, or brothers and sisters." She will send her mum some money, and "my little sisters can visit me, and I'll send them Christmas presents". She wants to get married when she is 20. She will have two girls and a boy. "I'll buy them nice clothes, and play in the garden with them, and let them have a boyfriend when they are 13. I'll give them a present on their birthdays, and so will my husband."

Jane was representative of a number of younger girls referred to us. One would hope that she was going through a period of temporary disorganisation. She was so affected by her home, that she was unable to get on at school and to work out her problems in that environment. Jane needed the same constant individual support and help as the older more seriously disorganised girl. We provided a small, carefully structured group which could give her the experience of relating to an adult, and to a few girls of her own age. We hoped that within the group she could learn to be and do things together with other girls, and that the experience would help her to work out some of her problems.

Jean

Jean is 17 years old, blonde, with blue eyes: a slim attractive girl who is popular with both boys and girls. Her father is a builder's labourer, and her mother stays at home. She has six younger brothers and sisters, ranging from four to fifteen years. Her father used to insist on her being home by ten but after many battles he now allows her to please herself. She helps to get the evening meal and look after the younger children before she goes out.

Jean says she is a 'mod' and is always attractively dressed with lots of new clothes. She likes dancing, and visits most of the youth clubs and local dance halls for it. At one of these she met Jim with whom she has been 'going steady' for nearly a year. She is expecting a baby in four months time and will be married in three weeks. When she first knew about the baby she daren't tell her parents—"my dad would have beaten me"—so she left home and went to live with Jim's parents for two months. Eventually Jim's parents visited hers, the marriage was arranged, and Jean returned home. Her father won't have anything to do with her "but he'll come round". Jim's mother has offered the pair a room in her home after they are married. Jean pointed out that a friend of hers didn't get married when she was expecting a baby, and "she got everything, baby clothes and even a pram—but it's better to be married".

Jean is a hairdresser and enjoys the work. "The girls are friendly and we have a good laugh." The boss is mostly strict, and sometimes "a bit fresh—but we know how to handle him". One girl at the shop is her "friend" and they spend evenings in her friend's home, listening to records and dancing.

Jean thinks school was "all right", but you "didn't learn much". The teachers were friendly, but you felt sorry for them because "they had to say such silly things". She used to spend most evenings in coffee bars or just "being around". Occasionally she visited a public house with a group of girl friends. "It was a laugh at the time, but we didn't like being sick afterwards. It was a waste of money." She liked the coffee bars—"there were plenty of boys there—some of them used to take purple hearts—but not often, no one had the money". She had a series of boy friends, and occasionally was caught up in a "rumble" but she was "fed up with the boys' spoiling dances with their fights". One boy used to take her on his motor scooter to "Southend and places". She has been to the West End "for a lark" but is not interested in seeing the sights of London. "I'd like to go to Paris— I'd like to travel—but you can't get out of this place." Sometimes Jean is gay and lively, but frequently she will say "I'm bored. What's it all about anyway. What can you do."

Jean is fond of Jim "but I wish he'd get a steady job". He gets her to phone his employer to say he's ill, if he doesn't want to go to work —"but he always gets his cards in the end". Occasionally she shows her bruises—"he got mad at me last night because he thought I was too fresh with the boys". Jim has promised he will get a regular job after they are married. Jean constantly points out that afterwards "Jim will stay with me and the baby—he won't go out. We'll just go out together sometimes," and then she will insist "I know he will— he's promised."

We saw Jean as typical of a number of girls with whom we worked, in that she managed to get along fairly well at home, and stayed in her job mainly because of the people there. Most of her problems were outside her home. She tried anything available, but had little hope of getting beyond the limitations of her environment. She wanted the security and status of marriage, but the chances of her hopes being realised were slender.

Irene

Irene is 17 years old, short with black hair and brown eyes. She is a pretty girl with a pale complexion, and she alternates between making up very heavily indeed, and not making up at all. Irene's father left home some years ago, and she's had more than one 'stepfather'. She has six younger brothers and sisters and one older sister. The family lives in five rooms, which are usually untidy, and sometimes sordid. Her mother lives in a state of disorganisation which does not appear to worry her unduly. She is very fond of the children particularly when they are young, but accepts that they are beyond her control as they grow older.

Irene ran away from home when she was fifteen, and spent some weeks staying in a variety of places, before the police found her working and living in a café. She was in a remand home for a while and then returned home. One year later she was in court for shoplifting. She has been on probation since then. Irene's friendships all form a similar pattern. Frequently her friends are girls, single or married and separated, living in small flats. She finds someone she likes and who, she says, likes her. They become very close and Irene will stay with her friend for a night, or several days. They have parties, and go about together, and eventually Irene moves into the flat. Very shortly there is an explosive situation, and after a series of rows, Irene, in a depressed state, goes back home. She then has more arguments with her mother who says she must get a job or get out.

Irene has had fifteen known jobs since she left school—mostly as a shop assistant. The main reasons for her being asked to leave are "rudeness" or not working regularly. Sometimes Irene leaves of her own accord, and says, "They always pick on me". She usually adds that "everyone picks on me—my mum hates me—no one wants to help''. For some weeks she will spend half of every day in bed, and otherwise will sit in coffee bars saying very little.

Boys find Irene very attractive but her friendships with them are short-lived. The boys are usually older, and she borrows money from the friend of the moment and persuades him to buy presents and to take her to expensive clubs and restaurants. It seems that when he tires of this or is unable to continue, the friendship ends in rows.

Irene didn't like school because the teachers were always "getting at me". She remembers nostalgically a school in the country which she attended as a child—"they were friendly and everyone was kind. We used to collect flowers, and learn about the animals."

Irene loves children, and sometimes takes out her younger brothers and sisters. Sometimes she says she will marry and have a large family, but sometimes says "I'll never marry—pity the poor children". Her comments on the police or the probation officer and on other people who have tried to help her, also change. Sometimes she says, "They are all against me", and sometimes, "They try to help me, but what's the use—I'm no good". She often says she would like to be a model, and once made enquiries about training, but on other occasions she says, "Who would help a person like me to be a model?"

Irene is one of the very few girls whom we knew, who appeared to be in the category of the 'seriously disorganised'. She was referred to us by an agency and needed daily support and help. It was only the time factor which prevented us from accepting more referrals like Irene. They could rarely be contacted through friends or found in a group, and work with them had to be on an individual basis for a very long period.

Jack's group

Jack's group usually numbered from four to five boys between the ages of fourteen and sixteen. Sometimes it was only three in number, sometimes, although rarely, it was as high as six or seven. The membership of the group frequently changed, but although the leadership changed too, Jack was usually the centre of the group. Jack was the person who produced the ideas and believed "you don't need to be bored", "you can always have friends if you find things for them to do".

Most of the activity of the group consisted of sending each other up, a good deal of sex talk, and constant questioning about "what should we be doing instead of standing here" interspersed with long periods of card playing. Sometimes they played cards sitting on the kerb with their hands hidden so as not to attract the police; sometimes they played in each other's houses or in the waiting room of a station; sometimes they sat in a café or stood in a fish and chip shop; if the place was private they ran a dice school.

One of the rules of the group was never to pay to get into a cinema. On the whole this worked well and provided a good deal of activity including the inevitable friction with the cinema managers and attendants.

Another rule of the group was for each member to refer to another only by the "number". These numbers were assigned and used instead of proper names. For a while one of the group's activities was to stop a constable on the beat and ask for directions, and in the course of the conversation to say "my friend here, 52691 says he thinks it is in exactly the opposite direction". An added rule to the game was that under no

c

circumstances should the conversation be about anything save directions (geographical) and that "no, constable", "yes, constable" were the only permissible replies to any question asked by the officer. This and several other similar games gave evidence of Jack's imagination. He and the group, as he reported it, would sit for hours with the TV on and the sound turned off and each boy would take a character in the TV presentation and *ad lib* the lines, which "made for a world-sized giggle".

The group was comparatively 'anti-social' in its recreational activities. These included a club bust-up now and then (their definition of 'club' included cafés and some of the smaller commercial clubs) but for these the group was always part of a larger group. The reasons given for the 'bust-ups' were to teach someone a lesson if he had been too cheeky, to even out a score, and on one occasion, revenge for the way they were treated at the door, "it could not be brought home just by talk". Jack's group never broke into a shop or building in order to steal. Goods were casually taken from the back of a van, or from a counter, and a car was borrowed.

The group often came back with harrowing tales of what they had done in other neighbourhoods, and how "the others are sure to come back here and try to finish us off", but nothing ever materialised. They also told of a "treasure island" at the end of the Metropolitan Line where there were no men at all and the women grabbed you on the street.

On the whole the group's life was boring and they knew it. At one point they said "the stall is a bit of a break since we can always send you two up" (the two workers on the stall). Often at weekends, and sometimes during school holidays, they spent day after day together "doing nothing", preoccupied with raising money for lunch and deciding which cinema to "live in". If they got into a cinema at 1.30 or so, they sometimes stayed until it was closing time. The group tended to keep the younger boys from going to school, the older ones from going to work, and made it difficult for boys to establish worthwhile relationships with girls.

This group was typical of other coffee stall contact groups. They constantly asked us, "What can we do with ourselves?". "How can we do it?" Sometimes a boy would ask a worker about jobs or tell him that he had found a 'steady', but it was made clear that this and any other serious matters discussed were not to be passed on. When the whole group was together the serious discussion was replaced by the usual banter and lighthearted conversation.

The Market Street boys

The Market Street boys were a group of seven or eight boys whose ages ranged from 15 to 17 years. Matt was the leader, who had a personal following of three boys, forming the core of the group. Hal, with two or three of his friends formed a sub-group which usually followed Matt's lead, but which sometimes operated on its own. This arrangement seemed to work well when Matt and Hal were friends, but made it difficult for the group to act as a group when they were not getting on together.

The full group seemed to plan one big activity every two or three weeks. There was usually a good deal of argument about what this was to be, a raid on a youth club, a café, an incident to be created in a dance hall or a prowl in somebody else's territory to "send-up" their "birds" in order to "make the thing go". It was always hoped that they could create an incident that would involve the various talents of the membership—fighting, shouting, delaying tactics, watching for the police and producing obscenities and threats. The discussion about the possibility of bringing one of these incidents to pass sometimes lasted several days, and then word would get around that "it" was to be on "Wednesday".

The plans varied. Sometimes Hal and the other younger boys were to go into a café, club or dance hall "and just wait to see what happened". At the first sign of a slight, real or imagined which could be interpreted as "against us" word was to be sent to the older boys outside, who could come in and "brighten things up a bit". On other occasions full scale 'rumbles' were planned, when many boys of the neighbourhood were to be gathered to beat up groups from other neighbourhoods.

We frequently suspected that many of the incidents never happened, and that those which did were completely spontaneous. Even so, long descriptions and reports of many incidents were faithfully produced. It was difficult for us not to believe that the most enjoyable part of the activity was neither planning the incident nor the incident itself but the elaborate description of it, since the gangs they had "done in", the constables they had "mashed" for life, and the bus conductors who were now but "bits and pieces", neither showed up to demand redress for the dreadful injuries nor asked the police to do it for them. It seemed that exaggeration, over-statement, boasting, phantasy and, dramatisation, were more at play than factual reconstruction of any event. It appeared to us that we had been cast in the part of a discriminating, but appreciative audience. We were constantly being prodded into asking "and then what happened?".

The group's imagination provided entertainment when they invented a girl called Ruby who was supposed to have a car, an Italian sports model, convertible, with buttons to put windows up and down, and according to one account, leopard-skin upholstery. She liked young boys. She used them, among other things, to get rid of 'hot' watches, to circulate reefers and purple hearts. She used them to decoy the police and in a hundred other ways all of which were within the James Bond repertory. Ruby sent birthday cards to everyone stamped "South France". She sometimes gave good advice like "If you are asked to answer a magistrate, always smile and say you are sorry". Ruby came to a bad end in that she had been shot by a 'screw' while trying to help two boys to escape from an approved school—the boys had been wrongly convicted. Ruby had been buried in Ireland. No reason was offered for burying so auspicious a national heroine on foreign soil except that "Ireland isn't part of this place so they can't dig her up". Ruby was an exercise in phantasy, that drew the boys closer together as each contributed to the development of the myth. She was also a link with us since we not only accepted her on the reality level at the beginning, but later entered in as listening participants to the development of the myth itself.

The criminal behaviour of the group was for the most part minimal. They rarely paid on the underground, created incidents on buses as a diversion for avoiding paying fares; and got their cigarettes and small change by removing them from cigarette machines or telephone kiosks. The only serious incident of which we heard, was an attempt to strip the lead from a church roof. The group was organised, strippers and lookouts appointed, tools procured and the job begun. It went well the first time but at the second try a constable was called by a neighbour, who had seen the boys on the roof. Three of the boys were taken in, but the rest got away in time. All three were first offenders (the boys claimed it was planned that way) and were put on probation. By all accounts the church roof affair was the best organised, and the most successful operation the group achieved, but on the whole the group was not sufficiently intent on criminal activity to take on any big 'jobs'.

When one of its members took a job and started to go steady with a girl or developed a private interest such as evening classes, the rest of the group belittled and berated him for a while. But none of this seemed too tyrannical nor did it appear to affect unduly the boy concerned.

Our contact at the stall with the Market Street boys was a useful one for several reasons. It was in the cafés, or on the street corners that their incidents were liable to flare up and the stall was a good meeting point for seven or eight of them, where they could mill around and talk without trouble arising. We also provided an interested adult audience for the reports of their 'happenings', and we had a selection of newspapers and a *What's On*, which allowed us to offer information on horror film programmes anywhere in London, together with a planned itinerary, and on occasion the news of a car or boat show at Earls Court or Olympia. But the real point of contact was the fact that we were "really interested" in their escapades and stories.

Kim and his followers

Kim was a short, thin hyperactive young man, 19 years of age, who had spent most of his adolescence in approved schools and Borstal. His speciality was breaking into small shops and safes.

Kim would appear amongst us either on French leave from an institution or during the short periods between commitments. As a runaway he was entitled, by the rules of the game as played by the boys in the neighbourhood, to all the aid necessary to 'keep on the run'. Kim was a classic case of a 'seriously disorganised' boy whose trade was 'crime'. He came home to the neighbourhood with exciting and adventurous stories about what he had done to the screws, or how he had outwitted the governor, and with specially prepared plans for bigger and better jobs. He seemed to have collected systematically, while inside, all the relevant information about what the other inmates had done and how they had done it, and then applied what he had learned in the neighbourhood.

He pretended to know the ins and outs of the law, how to pull the perfect job, how to get around the judge, and as is usual where phantasy plays a large part in the attempt to avoid reality, Kim was never pressed to explain why it was that he with all his know-how and his reservoir of experience was for the most part 'inside', and had so rarely got away with anything. His stories provided him with the opportunity to be the centre of attraction, and to play the part of a hero. He inevitably seemed to know which boys would go along with him on his next job—and indeed which of the boys seemed to need to do so. He was a natural leader, not without charm, who demanded adherence from those followers of his choice, many of whom were unable to resist giving it.

Kim would spend a night or two outlining a job, working up enthusiasm for it like a patent medicine salesman promising a cure-all, and then offer to let selected boys in on it. It was difficult for us to influence these boys directly as they would merely have labelled us as 'copper lovers'. This might have meant our losing the relationship with the boys who at this point needed us more than ever. We could only support even more strongly the elements within the whole grouping, especially those closely related to the boys chosen by Kim, in their fears and questions about the project in preparation. Sometimes this was a friend who feared for his mate, sometimes it was several of the boys in a small friendship group whose plans for a camp or a weekend out of town would be threatened; as often as not it was a girl friend who stood to suffer most from the likely outcome of the venture—approved school or Borstal for her boy.

Kim was never with us for more than a few weeks at a time. We saw our job as threefold—to plant as many doubts as possible without causing a breakup in our relationship, to support the anti-Kim elements (especially the girls) in the grouping, and to prepare behind the scenes to get psychiatric help for Kim next time he was sent away.

Kim always took the possibility of violence in his stride. On one occasion he planned a job which required stealing a car, getting over a warehouse wall and then into the night watchman's office. He counted on the night watchman not being there. If he were there he would have to be 'handled'. This brought silent disapproval from the by-standers who saw it as too much of a risk. We were able to use this, and to make the job look like a badly planned and impossible venture. This together with a special dormobile outing to Brighton on the night the job was to take place, with preference given to Kim's accomplices and their girls, "broke the back of the job" as Kim put it. Strangely enough, Kim did not openly resent our planning the Brighton trip for the same evening. He seemed to think it fair play in which he had been outwitted, and the boys, although they did not say so, were relieved to have a face-saving device as a way out. The girls were quick, of course, to get us this information without the boys being aware of it.

Dan, a leader of 'can copes', was a great help during these periods when Kim was around. He was known as a person who could "get things done", and had a large following for his entertaining activities. With our support, Dan was a stronger recruiting sergeant than Kim. But when Dan was not around, and Kim was, one or two of the boys would usually find themselves in serious trouble with the police.

Three things emerged as important to our work in this situation.

1. It was important to have a full scale programme of personal service and work with groups, which provided opportunities to 'contain' the 'seriously disorganised' within the programme of activities.

2. The best kind of help any of the 'disorganised' could have was from their friends, who could with the help of an adult who knew how to offer it, create an atmosphere in which "doing that type of thing" caused loss of status instead of gain of it, and who could enforce the recognition of this by way of social pressures within the friendship group or larger grouping. This way was more fruitful than the direct intervention of the worker.

3. Dan and his followers were outsiders just as Kim was. Both Dan and Kim brought ideas, attitudes, ways of behaviour, and skills from outside and tried to implant them within the coffee stall grouping.

We saw the difference as Kim offering the 'wrong thing' and Dan the 'right'. In Kim's case we supported the not so 'seriously disorganised' elements in the grouping in order to alienate Kim's hold over them. In Dan's case we supported him in his attempt to organise entertainment, impose order and keep discipline, which we saw as positive—in terms of helping us to build a programme that would serve the other boys and girls.

2. The borough

The borough, which is within London's inner urban ring, covers an area of 1,400 acres. It is approximately 1¾ miles wide, east to west, 3 miles long, north to south, and shaped like a crescent moon, running north from the heart of the metropolis. Its population is approximately 112,000.

A first impression of the social geography of the borough can perhaps best be gleaned from a glance at the pattern of distribution of income groups and the pattern of social circulation.

The south east of the crescent borders on a superior residential area and a metropolitan shopping centre. The residential accommodation in this section of the borough is distinctly high income with some institutions and offices. The south-west side of the crescent consists almost entirely of residential hotels and institutions, hostels and boarding houses, with restaurants, public houses and night clubs. The remaining residential accommodation in this part of the borough is distinctly high income (with a new block of council flats in the middle). The north east of the crescent is mixed in character, in that boarding house accommodation, small hotels and overcrowded slum dwellings are interspersed with large new office blocks, a large modern council estate and several small shopping centres. This section of the borough also includes some light industry, mostly electrical goods, radio parts and assembly, together with several small firms concerned with the transport of goods. At the centre of this section is a railway terminus. Bordering on this mixed complex, is an exclusive high income residential area. The north west of the borough, its largest section in area and population, is an ordinary working-class community in rows of small terraced houses. The borough has a few small open spaces but it is near to a big London park.

These four sections of the crescent are geographically self-contained. Railway cuttings and major thoroughfares act as boundary lines. Each area is socially homogeneous to such an extent that the group life which normally results from contacts made at school or in leisure time, is restricted.

The borough as a whole has no large scale industry, save a large

27

motor works across the north-west boundary. Work is related mainly to the railway station, hotels, hostels and boarding houses, the assembly and service of electrical and radio parts. Many people go out of the borough to work. The borough has the same health, welfare and recreational facilities as those provided by the statutory and voluntary bodies elsewhere in London. The schools, except for two, are old ones.

The borough is in the top seven of the London boroughs for its high incidence of recognised social problems—children in care, illegitimate births, families and old people on National Assistance, juvenile court convictions and young people on probation, racial problems and a very serious housing shortage indeed.

The overall impression of the borough might well be one of several foreign enclaves, of middle- and upper-class life, together with the amenities to support it, amidst a sea of rapidly deteriorating slums and a working-class society. All this is in a fairly rapid state of change. Large houses on the fringe of the south-east section of the borough are being remodelled for upper-income housing, and office and institutional use, as are some of the fine old Victorian and Edwardian houses in the upper-income south-east section. The slum houses are being demolished and replaced by flats at a lower rate of density. (The former rate of density was 92·5—(1951)—the present rate of density is 86·2 per acre, the future rate of density is planned as 99·0.)

But this impression must be reduced in scale if it is to have any direct relevance to this report. We did not work in the whole borough, but only in two of the neighbourhoods that make up the southern corner of its north-west section. Both these neighbourhoods had a higher proportion than most of the rest of the borough, of unskilled manual workers who were more liable than others to be affected by fluctuations in the employment market. The incidence of social problems in both these neighbourhoods was higher than in other areas of the borough. These included children in care, illegitimate births, family and old people on National Assistance, Juvenile Court convictions and young people on probation. Both neighbourhoods were seriously affected by overcrowding and lack of amenities in housing, a situation which was only beginning to be remedied by the urban renewal programme.

The residents were mostly English with a small number of Irish families and an even smaller number of West Indian, Asian and African residents. Each neighbourhood was seen as a neighbourhood on its own and referred to as such by some of its residents. The natural boundaries were made by the railway on the south, the main road on the north and the 'high street' thoroughfare down the centre which divided the area into two. Many of the young people in both neighbourhoods were known to each other as some of them attended the same schools. They also had a common meeting ground in a New

Town, which they frequently visited as their relatives, boy and girl friends had been rehoused there.

Our coffee stall was between the two neighbourhoods. There were three youth clubs, two boys' clubs, an evening institute, and a settlement serving the two neighbourhoods, with ample opportunity for boys—not so much for girls—if they were willing and able to use them.

The 'posh' areas to the south west and east across the railway bridge provided a host of attractions—cinemas, bright new cafés, expresso bars with exotic and alluring names, night clubs, some legitimate, and some not so, the latter complete with prostitutes and purple heart pushers, jazz clubs and 'queer' joints, with numerous foreign visitors who were an easy touch for a coffee, a drink or even a pick-up. Just as convenient, but a bit more to the north, a large West Indian and overseas community provided opportunities for all sorts of adventure from gang fights with West Indians to break-ins and break-ups of 'black' cafés and clubs.

We found that, unlike the pattern in some east London boroughs, there were few or no close family ties within and between families, nor was there a strongly developed feeling of belonging to a street, a block of buildings or a neighbourhood. Yet there were some signs that these forms of informal association had existed in the not too distant past.

The feelings of neighbourhood were an almost wholly adolescent phenomenon which seemed to develop anew with each new generation of young people and to be based more on the negative feeling of being 'pushed about', closed in, not really getting a chance, and on the camaraderie of boredom and even bitterness—which was not without a sense of violent adventure—than on the positive feelings of identification that spring from the acceptance of the older working-class ethos.

The staff

The background and previous experience of the staff is relevant firstly, because it was a factor in deciding what we could offer to the young people, and also because it contributed to the way in which we saw the problem of field-work and eventually came to define it.

The first member of the staff, Jumbo, was a retired army officer of 50 years of age, who had been educated at a public school and Sandhurst. He was appointed to open the coffee stall and remained throughout the project.

His work with different ranks in the army, both above and below his own position, his awareness and appreciation of the different styles of life in the army, and in the indigenous populations of the overseas territories in which he had been stationed, gave him an

29

ability to accept and empathise with different kinds of people in a non-judgemental way. This, when coupled with his 'upper-class exterior', was an important factor not only in interesting the un-attached young people but also in dealing with some of the statutory and voluntary bodies at a high level, where often a retired service officer was more readily received than the 'ordinary' youth worker. He had no previous training in youth work or social work but was a willing and eager inservice training participant.

The second staff member, Jim, was 38 years of age. He had pre-viously carried out experimental work in an adventure playground and already knew something about the problems and behaviour of some of the young people with whom we were working. He brought to the team a well developed sense of how to observe the young people as individuals and in groups, as well as the community. He was able to introduce other workers to observing in the neighbourhood. It was his contribution during the early days which led us to see employment as one of the main problems to be considered. Unfortunately he had to resign due to illness after eight months' work.

Mary, the first female worker, was a Canadian of 26 years of age. She had a bachelor of arts degree, had experience of settlement work in Canada, and also a certain amount of training in social group work. Her particular contribution was the sense of orderliness which she brought to her work, together with her acceptance of other people's behaviour. Her ability to make no personal demands in her relation-ships, together with her Canadian nationality, made her particularly attractive to the younger girls and boys. As well as contributing from her observations, a large amount of information about girls, she was able to establish work with the younger girls' group before leaving at the end of two years.

Peter, who was 21, was a clerk who had just completed his national service in the R.A.F. He wanted to move into social work and chose to join our team before starting full-time training. He was the youngest of the workers, a Methodist lay preacher with definite values and standards. He, more than any of the other workers, offered the team from his field-work experience, problems that we saw as representative of the younger youth leader working in this way, problems of identity, problems of recognising and using mobility, differences in values and standards between the worker and the young people, questions about 'activities'. He needed to see things in a structured and ordered way and he often rightly demanded that we be more orderly and consistent.

Gerry replaced Jim at the end of the first year. He was 31 years of age, had a social science diploma, and had spent a year on a university youth work course. He was more introspective than the others and more fully prepared to experiment with absence of restraint in dealing with the young people. He helped the staff to understand that 'natural events' and the day-to-day relations between young people should be seen as the basic material for the programme. He was reluctant to rush into interpreting field-work events and was a valuable guard against generalising too quickly. He was suspicious of abstractions and by his questioning of them, helped us to be more realistic about the field-work problems.

Marian was 25 years, had been to boarding school, acquired a diploma in social administration, and had worked in a housing department before joining the project at the end of its first year. Her main work was in supporting girls within a mixed setting. Her ability to accept the boy/girl relationship pattern in the neighbourhood enabled her to develop relationships with individual girls, and she frequently reminded the staff of the individuality of needs, and was able to put forward the girls' point of view in a way that was acceptable to the male staff.

Susan was 26 years when she joined the project at the beginning of its third year to work with younger girls on probation. She had trained as a youth leader, after which she had worked in a New Town. She had been a staunch member of the Methodist church, but a year of work and travel through different countries had made her begin to question some of her own values and standards. Although this meant difficulties at first, Susan was able to use this questioning to help other staff members and in her work with the girls' group. As she was the only worker with a stable group over a long period, her contributions on group behaviour and the role of the worker were useful to the other workers with their constantly changing groups.

John, at 20 years, came to the project as a volunteer from London University where he was a theological student. He was later released from his studies for twelve months so that he could be a full-time student/worker for the last year of the project. His main contribution to the work with the young people sprang from his being in the same age bracket as the older boys and representing to them a different mode of life. He went to University, read books, could make his way around the West End with the minimum of trouble and was going to be a priest. This last item was a particularly good talking point, since the church was seen as one of 'them'. It offered him an identity and a point of contact that was helpful to him while getting to know the young people. It is doubtful if this would have been so had he already been a priest and represented in their eyes a full identification with 'them'. After the termination of the field-work he went to the U.S.A. to take part in a training programme for urban priests. He will shortly be ordained and plans to work in a team ministry in London.

The administrator who was a trained youth worker with experience of youth work in Great Britain and the Middle East, was assigned

31

by the Y.W.C.A. to take responsibility for the project on a half-time basis. She acted as a link between the staff and the project committee and the rest of the Y.W.C.A. She, like the consultant, had come to the task, thinking that on the whole social group work might well provide the answer to the problem of contacting and working with the unattached. It was part of her job as we came to think differently about this and other matters to interpret these changes to the project committee and the Y.W.C.A. She supervised the female field-workers, participated in the in-service training and arranged the staff conferences.

The consultant was an American social worker with long settlement experience, who had worked in Italy and India as well as in the U.S.A., and who had come to the task with a more or less definite social group work orientation. In addition to having to learn about youth work in Great Britain, he was responsible for the in-service training, and for the study of the work being done in the project. He supervised the male workers and participated in the staff conferences and project committee meetings. He was also responsible for the final consultant's report to the Project Committee and the Youth Development Council of the Department of Education and Science.

3. *The sponsoring agency*

The importance of the sponsoring agency, the Y.W.C.A., as a factor in these circumstances is twofold. It was willing to attempt this project using the approach and method developed here. Once it had taken this responsibility it became one of the network of statutory and voluntary bodies in the community. As such, it frequently responded to field-work problems in terms of the values and standards of those bodies, and required the same interpretation from us, about our work, as did the other agencies in the field.

Chapter Two

THE SEQUENCE OF EVENTS

An outline of four years of field-work experience covering the development
of the project from the first contact with the young people, through
the full programme of personal service, group activities and work
with the community, to the termination and final phase.

4. Getting started

After the decision of the London Y.W.C.A. to attempt to work with
the unattached, the help of Y.W.C.A. students was enlisted to make a
survey for a possible location of the coffee stall. Eventually, a street
corner was chosen which had several advantages Five main roads met
at the corner, and covered a large catchment area. Bus stops, a cinema,
public houses and shopping facilities encouraged enough traffic to
make a coffee stall part of the street scene. There was enough room on
the pavement for a small group to stand around the stall. In addition
to this a telephone kiosk and public conveniences were nearby.

Jumbo drove the stall to the site for the first time on June 1959.
He and his woman assistant then opened it on four evenings a week.
The first customer was Tommy, twelve years old, who came night
after night, sometimes alone, sometimes with his younger brother. A
constant stream of adult passers-by used the stall, some of whom
settled in for a chat over a cup of coffee and a sandwich. Some of the
adults returned night after night for coffee and a pie, or to change
money for the meter, and often found it difficult to stop pouring out
their life stories. They included Old Jim, who had been a merchant
seaman and was anxious to have an opportunity to recreate for a
friendly audience, life in a dozen different ports around the world;
Big John, who had broken his back on a construction job and who
had been on the mend for as long as he or anyone else could remember;
Mrs. Johnson who disliked being cooped up in her room and needed
the opportunity to talk of the past when her husband, who had
been a Civil Servant, was alive and "things had been oh so much
better".

Jumbo soon realised that if he were not careful he would build up
a group not of unattached young people, but of unattached adults
from the boarding houses, bed-sitters and small flats in the neighbourhood. This was not within our terms of reference and so regretfully

he began to find ways to avoid developing relationships with them. As he began to make it known by his behaviour that his interests were with the young people, most of the adults dropped off as regular clients and the younger people, who now had all his attention, began to take the stall over.

During the first few months the average number of young customers was about six, although these were drawn from twelve to fifteen boys between twelve and eighteen years, who hung around the stall, and chatted with the workers and with each other. As Jumbo got to know some of the boys better, it became clear that they were suspicious of him. He was too willing to listen, too out-going and interested, too willing to let the occasional adult customer wait in order to continue a conversation with a young person, and it was obvious that he was not particularly concerned with making money. The consensus of opinion was that the stall was a front for 'them'—a vague combination of police and other authorities.

During this period the boys tried the workers out a good deal, not always paying for coffee and pies, making elaborate attempts to steal from the counter, presenting long involved stories about crimes they had committed and of 'rumbles' and fights. The woman assistant especially had to face a good deal of trying out—freely laced with sexual innuendoes and suggestive behaviour. All of this tailed off when in August 1959, the police moved the stall along the road, and Bill came to Jumbo's aid, and defined him, by his defence of him, as "one of us" (the boys), which took him out of the category of "one of them" (the authorities).

Jumbo was prepared, if asked, to say that the Y.W.C.A. owned the stall, but no one asked. The boys came to like and accept Jumbo and reasoned that, since the stall could not be a paying proposition, and was not a "police front" it must be a tax-dodge. They never faced him with this belief, but as we came to know later, accepted it among themselves as a perfectly adequate explanation of his presence and of the presence of the stall and the assistant, and one which put the whole enterprise in a category that was acceptable to them. Once the police incident was accepted by them as proof of our being in the right camp, individuals around the stall opened up, and talked of the day's events, of trouble at home or school or work, of their lack of money, or of boredom. When alone, a boy was prepared to ask for advice on almost any subject—about a job delivering newspapers, the Merchant Navy, driving a car, fishing, sex problems or points of law. Yet when in groups they just laughed and played around.

After four months some of the boys asked what Jumbo did at weekends, if they could visit him at home and if they could 'tag along' when he went out. Jumbo arranged a number of weekend lunches at his flat, followed by a trip to the country, into the West End, or to a cinema. This got the boys out of their neighbourhood, involved them in several bus or underground trips and above all gave them a sense of freedom from boredom for at least part of the weekend. It gave Jumbo an opportunity to know them better, both as individuals and in small friendship groups. The boys phoned or called on Jumbo at any time of the day or night. Sometimes it was just for a chat, but more frequently it was for help with some "urgent" trouble. The group around the stall grew from fifteen to twenty-five, and many of the boys had problems to discuss with Jumbo in the cab of the stall or wanted to meet him at other times.

It was at this stage, after nine months work, that we realised the coffee stall had proved itself as a point of contact, but that if we were to be of real help to the young people we should have to make arrangements to meet the increasing demands for help over and above that which was now offered. We planned an expanded project in which five full-time workers would be appointed at intervals to spend three years in the neighbourhood. In September and October 1960, Jim and Mary were appointed, and were introduced to the boys as assistants to Jumbo on the stall. Mary spent three months at the stall in order to make contact with any girls who might come, and also, as a friend of Jumbo's, so that she could get to know the boys and be a bridge between them and the girls when they materialised.

Jim stayed on the stall just long enough to get to know the boys and for the boys to get to know him and then moved out into the neighbourhood, to coffee bars, public houses, and on to street corners. He ate his lunch and supper in the coffee bars, sometimes spending a whole afternoon or a whole evening in one coffee bar over a period of several weeks. He became known to the proprietors and gradually to the groups of boys who had temporarily settled in the several different coffee bars. At first he remained in the background, but was drawn into conversations more and more frequently. Individuals were easily accepted in this setting and no questions were asked. Most of the boys he got to know in this way were between the ages of sixteen and twenty-two. As he became accepted by the boys, he was slowly able to learn about their work habits, their patterns of recreation and a good deal about their social attitudes, towards the neighbourhood, work, money, petty crime and boy/girl relationships.

At the end of five months of work in coffee bars Jim knew some young people well enough to greet them and be greeted by them, to join in their discussions indoors and on street corners. He also knew eleven out of his whole contact group well enough for them to be able to ask his advice and help in their personal problems. His overall observations emphasised the mobility of the young people, the helpfulness of some of the café proprietors, and the problems of employment.

Mobility seemed to be an attractive and acceptable mode of life for many of the young people Jim was observing. The younger ones roamed from youth club to youth club and, if pressed to say why they had left one club for another, would either say they did not know or give a stock answer—"They tried to make us do too many things". "We wouldn't pay up", or "They get in your hair". Such answers, although they might in some general sense be true, had little or no specific meaning since they were used time and time again by different groups to explain leaving all the clubs in the neighbourhood.

There also appeared to be no particular reason for the migrations from café to café or coffee bar to coffee bar, which were an accepted part of the life of the whole group. The proprietors had learned to expect and accept this mobility as part of the pattern of teenage patronage. Sometimes the migrations were full scale, and included a number of smaller friendship groups loosely-knit into a network of young people, all known to one another. On occasions one friendship group would move out ahead of the others and settle for several weeks in the next coffee bar. Frequently one of the small groups would just be leaving one café to move to another when the small group that had left several weeks before was about to return. Sometimes the movement would be in and out of several places in one evening. All this was considered proper and not requiring any explanation. Often girls followed or were part of the moving groups. Sometimes the girls waited for boys to move in. The area for the migration was noticeably small—about six cafés or coffee bars were the meeting points for the forty to fifty young people. When we understood more about this mobility we were able to see that the point of using a detached worker in this situation was that he could keep contact with the fifty young people in a relatively restricted geographical area, simply by moving around with them.

Some café and coffee bar owners did a great deal to help the young people. They gave free coffee or meals if the young people seemed to need it, advised them on their problems and passed on information about jobs. In one case a coffee-bar owner went to court to give character evidence for a boy. His wife took an interest in helping the girls, and let them use the coffee bar when it was closed on one occasion to learn how to dance.

Employment was a serious problem. Sometimes boys wanted jobs and could not get them. Sometimes they wanted to change jobs they did not like because they felt they were dead-end jobs or did not pay well. To many boys, jobs were a "laugh" or a "lark", to be thrown over for a caprice, to be held on to only as long as the money was absolutely necessary. If boys "earned good money", they could afford to rest for a while, without any consideration of what constant interruption in their employment records might mean, and without regard to what it meant to workmates and the work in hand for someone to pull out suddenly.

It was also apparent that the boys would welcome information and advice about jobs. One of the immediately understood and accepted ways of being of use to them was to help them with constantly recurring work problems. Their attitudes towards the youth employment service and the employment exchange were mixed and often contradictory. "They took too long", "offered no well paid jobs", "didn't like it if you kept coming back", "tried to make you take the job they wanted", were some of the comments made, but on the whole it seemed more that the boys resented having to go to some particular office, and just wanted jobs to 'happen' like most of the other things in their lives. Most of their jobs seemed to be acquired through the grape-vine within the larger group. News of jobs came from brothers, fathers, friends, or from boys within the group, a job here or a possibility there—usually with the name of a man "who could give it you" and the advice to tell him that "Mike, John, or Big Tommy sent you". Of course there were those in the larger grouping who had been at the same job for six months, a year or even more and who cared about their future in that job, were satisfied with the pay and intended to continue. It seemed that most of these boys had fathers, older brothers or even interested neighbours who had "fixed it up for them" and whose authority in the matter was accepted. Some of those who held their jobs were influenced in doing so by the girls with whom they were going steady, or whom they had recently married.

On the whole the job pattern seemed to us to be similar to the mobility pattern in recreational life in the neighbourhood, but an important factor was the number of older boys who showed no signs of settling, who were uncertain of what they wanted to do and be, and who had grown to feel that the "really sweet plums" were not theirs for the picking.

Employment at this early stage appeared to be one of the keys to our contact and work with unattached boys. Jim investigated the possibilities of his working as a 'detached' employment officer, bringing news of jobs to the boys in ways which were acceptable to them in that community, and at the same time working closely with employment officials and employers. Unfortunately he had to resign due to illness, and this aspect of the work had to be postponed.

Finding girls

We had assumed that once we were settled in, known and accepted by the boys and through them by the neighbourhood, the girls would show up at the coffee stall almost as a matter of course. It did not turn out this way. Occasionally a girl arrived at the stall—a sister of one of the boys or somebody's 'steady'—but she rarely stayed long. Sometimes a girl was sent off by a boy who did not feel that the stall was the right place for his sister or girl friend, but usually the boys wanted to be on their own and to monopolise the worker, and so frightened away the rare girl customer.

We already knew from Jim's observations that there were girls in the coffee bars, and it was agreed that Mary should attempt to make contact with them there. She had little success. When girls were in a group with boys, they were suspicious of any other female who was around, and so ignored her. Girls moved so quickly from one coffee bar to another that Mary could not be with them long enough to get to know them, and she did not feel she could follow them without an invitation. In addition the coffee bars opened and closed frequently, due to fights and the breaking up of premises. The greatest difficulty for Mary was that the boys, supported by the neighbourhood system of values, did not accept as "right and proper" that she should be out on her own, travelling from coffee bar to coffee bar. Word got around that she must be a prostitute. Mary was now well-known to the boys at the stall, yet they were puzzled by her behaviour. Jim could move freely as a single man, and his identity was in the process of becoming established through his help with employment and other problems. Mary's only identity was that she was a friend of Jumbo. They could not understand that she would have any reason to meet girls, and therefore she must want to meet men.

We felt that Mary's relationships with the boys were at this stage as important as any that she might develop with the girls, and certainly would affect girls' attitudes to her. She therefore withdrew from the coffee bars and decided to find out how much was known about girls in the youth clubs of the area. She found that youth work was mainly geared to the needs of boys, and that very little seemed to be known about girls. Some girls were to be found in classes, in club canteens, and dances, but leaders seemed concerned that they knew so little about girls, that girls were so apathetic and that they were much more 'difficult' than boys. Through her own observations, and through discussions with boys and with leaders, Mary learned a great deal about girls' attitude and behaviour in the area, but she made contact with very few girls.

We then thought of trying to contact girls in schools—but the Avondale experiment (see appendix) was already producing interesting information on this type of work: by following up those who had left the Girl Guides—but unfortunately none were forthcoming: by approaching firms—but the National Association of Youth Clubs in its experiment was already making contact with girls in factories (see appendix).

Finally Mary attached herself to a boys' club, to which girls were invited two evenings weekly for dancing. The girls were not members and were not known to the one male leader. Mary became a volunteer and settled in, dancing and talking with the girls, taking photographs, and inviting two or three out for coffee. Just about the time that she thought she was becoming accepted by a few girls, the club was closed because of rioting, and when it reopened, new girls arrived. When this was repeated and the leadership changed several times, we knew that in this setting too, we should have only casual contacts. Mary withdrew, but this time she knew several girls well enough to feel that if she had a meeting place they might be drawn together into a group. Preparations were then made to acquire disused shop premises, which could be adapted for use as a meeting place for girls.

We toyed with the idea of setting up a cosmetic stall for girls on a different corner from that of the coffee stall, and providing cosmetic samples, make-up and advice. This would give the same opportunities to meet the girls as the coffee stall did to meet the boys. But at this point girls began to join the boys in their programme of activities which had developed from the coffee stall. The idea of the cosmetic stall did not materialise, as Mary rejoined Jumbo to work with boys and girls together.

Developments on the coffee stall

The attendance at the coffee stall was increasing, and the personal service in the field-work began to loom so large that we began to think that a 'Trouble Clinic' was needed, staffed by case workers, but without the formal paraphernalia that would have made it impossible for the young people to accept the help offered. We had thought that when the young people began to know and accept us, we should continue to help them individually, to work with them in groups, and to provide recreational activities. But we expected to be able to refer them to other agencies for specific help. In the majority of cases this proved to be impossible. Frequently it was because a boy's problems covered such a wide range that no one agency appeared to exist which could help him. Sometimes, as in the case of employment or recreational facilities, any suggestion that a boy should meet the officials concerned meant to him that we were 'passing him on' and to the very people he wished to avoid. This meant that, regardless of our unwillingness to carry a case-load that was too heavy for our resources, or which sometimes required skills we did not have, we had to continue to develop a personal service programme to meet the demand. We felt inadequate for the task and the answer to this problem seemed to be to get some agencies to work with us at the stall, and to help them to make the same kind of relationship with the young people as we had done. But at this stage we had not even introduced all of our field-workers through the stall, and so we had to postpone such attempts.

The second most pressing problem at the stall was the need for a policy regarding the anti-social or criminal behaviour of the boys. How was Jumbo to react when boys asked him to keep stolen goods or a knife for them? What should he do with such dangerous knowledge? He began to meet probation officers at boys' requests. Should he approach them without the boys' knowledge, and how much information could he impart to them without breaking confidence? We were now seen as 'insiders' who could be talked to and trusted, and who were apart from 'them', the authorities. Any handing over to the police or other social agencies of information which could be used against the young people would be a betrayal of confidence. by our behaviour and attitudes we had led the young people to assume that we were to be trusted, in the terms implied by that word within their own set of values and standards. It would have been foolhardy from the point of view of our attempts to contact and work with them to make any move which they could interpret as betrayal.

We decided that our relationship with the young people was our primary concern since it was only through the relationship, that we could offer help. Within the context of a relationship, the worker had to consider the boy's needs first, before his own or those of the rest of the community. But the worker himself had values and standards and represented the values and standards of the larger community by way of the assignment he had accepted from the Y.W.C.A. He could not give information to the police or other bodies to the detriment of the young person, but he could not participate in criminal behaviour nor could he approve of it when it came to his notice. Even so care had to be taken that his disapproval of behaviour did not indicate the withdrawal of approval from the boy concerned.

Moving into premises

We had expected that Jumbo would pass groups on to the other field workers fairly quickly, that he would continue to meet the boys at the stall, and that the other field-workers would move around with them. This proved impossible during the first year. The boys had a strong relationship with Jumbo, and the other workers were not known well enough to be trusted at this stage. The boys at the stall constantly demanded that Jumbo should provide them with a place in which to meet. Jumbo suggested the youth clubs, but this made no impression, They explained that they had joined all the clubs in the neighbourhood and had been thrown out or had left of their own accord—because "they were all so wet", "too bossy", "not open late enough, or on weekends or holidays". They wanted a club like other clubs, but with more freedom in which to eat, drink, dance and do as they pleased.

We had expected to open some sort of 'headquarters' for groups in the neighbourhood, but we had never thought of them as being in any way a youth club. Indeed we had already told the youth serving agencies in the community in all good conscience, that we had no intention of opening a youth club. After much discussion we decided that their need for a club of their own was more than just an attempt to play off the existing clubs against their new-found friends. They needed to try to create for themselves and by themselves the kind of facilities that they saw as best meeting their own needs.

Yet it was with some hesitations that we acquired disused premises —a shop, backroom and basement—which were opened in March 1961. By this time, the other field-workers were able to run the stall, while Jumbo moved into the shop on three evenings a week with a small number of boys. They roughly painted, decorated and equipped the place, and then without warning about fifty boys in the neighbourhood descended on it. They all knew Jumbo and decided that this meant they were entitled to come in. They were entitled to entry simply because of their relationship with the person whose party it was. Abstract rules about membership were an unfair imposition, a kind of wangle, some sort of a cheat.

The first nights were chaotic and in our view dangerous. The boys thought they were very successful indeed—just what they wanted. The tightly-packed small shop was a beehive of activity—pushing, shoving, talking, arguing, playing cards and damaging equipment. We realised that the large numbers made it impossible for Jumbo to get to know boys better and work with small groups. He knew that instead of providing constructive help, he was providing a situation which could lead to destruction. He was able only to circulate, chat a little here and there, and try to prevent serious disorder. There were also indications that one outcome of these gatherings could be a large gang, meeting for anti-social escapades.

We then sent Jumbo, with his approval, a letter stating that, we, the Y.W.C.A. as landlords could not allow such large numbers in the small rooms, and that the club must be closed for a period while he and the boys worked out a solution. Jumbo returned to the stall to talk over the situation with the boys, who decided that different groups should have the premises on different evenings. He moved back into the club after a month, with Mary to help, and a 'committee' of boys who had lists of names for Mondays, Tuesdays and Wednesdays. The committee 'lark' was entered into as good fun, but after returning, the committee made it quite clear that they would not be responsible for enforcing the rules. The result was that after one week, the situation was the same as on the day we opened, and fifty young people—this time both boys and girls—were in the premises. We then agreed that Jumbo was too well known to be in the premises, and that his work must be in personal service at the coffee stall. In September 1961, his holiday was a good reason for closing the premises, and we decided that when they were reopened the new workers must use them.

A new worker

Peter, appointed in February 1961, spent his first weeks on the stall, and moving round the neighbourhood with Jim. He was watching a fight one day, when he casually met three boys of eighteen and nineteen years. Peter talked with them and arranged to meet them in a public house the following night. Soon he was meeting the group two or three times a week, either in public houses or at the home of Arthur the oldest boy who appeared to be 'seriously disorganised.' Occasionally the group met at the premises where they played cards, sketched and painted. Peter attempted to enlarge the group, but this proved impossible mainly due to Arthur's moodiness and general behaviour. He helped the three boys to plan and set out for a holiday in Paris, but as the other two boys had other friends and interests, Peter spent as much time as possible with Arthur, talking with him, helping him to paint, and attending art classes. This continued during the following two and a half years.

Peter also met other boys in coffee bars and on the street, and in an attempt to draw together an independent group, he opened the stall one evening a week, on a site nearer the boys' homes. These boys preferred to continue their casual meetings in twos and threes and so a larger friendship group did not materialise. New customers were arriving, however, and we decided that we must limit the possibilities of making new contacts. Peter then withdrew from the second site.

Peter's arrival at the age of twenty-one re-emphasised the problems of identity. Jumbo's identity had been established easily. Jim and Mary had problems at first, but these had been overcome. Jim had been easily accepted as someone vaguely interested in young people. Mary, after her difficulties in the coffee bars, was accepted as interested in meeting the English, because she was Canadian. Peter was tall and well built. When the boys finally agreed that he was not a policeman, they expected that he would join in their escapades as he was so near to the age of the older boys. The need for an identity was very strong, and eventually Peter said he worked in the Y.W.C.A. office. This had no meaning for the boys for some time, but Peter was more secure with this background.

5. The developing programme

In October 1961 the staff retired to the country for a weekend to evaluate the first year's work, and to make in outline, plans for our second year. Gerry had been appointed to replace Jim, and Marian had been appointed second woman worker. We were now complete —five field-workers, a training and research consultant and an admininstrator/supervisor.

We agreed that by the end of the first year we had a reservoir of information about individuals and groups, and attitudes and behaviour in the neighbourhood. We had made contact with more than one hundred young people, and of those we knew about fifty comparatively well. The first year has shown us that relationship building was a long, slow process, and that although Peter and Mary were now working closely with individuals and groups, it was Jumbo, because of his previous fifteen months on the stall, to whom most of the boys came for personal help.

We realised too that the coffee stall was no longer merely a point of contact for personal service, or a place from which groups would emerge, but had become the centre of a large network of relationships which had existed long before we had arrived among the unattached young people in the neighbourhood. The young people had similar backgrounds. Their fathers were unskilled, semi-skilled or small traders. They went to the same schools and had the same social attitudes. They used the same coffee bars, dance halls, cinemas and streets. They moved around in twos, threes and small friendship groups, and were linked with other individuals and groups through knowing them or being aware of them. The groups were liable to change frequently.

Our presence in the neighbourhood had affected this pattern of association by centring parts of the network on the stall and the activities based on it. The relationships between the smaller groups at the stall were becoming stronger, and these together with fringe groups made a coffee stall network which was emerging as part of the total network. A number of young people were beginning to comment that they 'belonged' to the coffee stall. A group identity was developing, although the network included nearly one hundred young people. This development presented the possibilities of a dangerous situation, and already on one occasion more than half the group had mobilised for a 'rumble'. We had not yet been able to work effectively with the small groups in order to prevent the main group from becoming stronger and we felt we must do so as quickly as possible.

At the same time, we were now accepted as being inside the network, and this allowed us freedom of contact from within. No longer were we in the position of the majority of agencies, of having to make contact and work with individuals and groups from without. It was important for that reason that we should understand and respect the confidence in us shown by this acceptance, by behaving in such a way that we did not violate it.

The most urgent need was to make it possible for individual field-workers to choose two or three smaller groups, from the larger network and to try to work with them, providing more intensive service, and creating within the group an atmosphere within which it might be possible for the young people to help each other. Knowing that pressure was very strong from some of the boys to reopen the premises, we agreed that Gerry, after working on the stall long enough to get to know a few boys, should move into the premises with them. It seemed unlikely that large numbers would demand entrance as Jumbo would not be there. If opening the premises should provide as before, the opportunity to meet girls, Mary would join Gerry. She would work with the girls within the premises, among the boys, and would attempt to find ways of helping the girls to meet separately in the newly acquired girls' premises, in the hope of developing a programme specially designed to meet their needs. Peter would continue his work with individuals, but would be available to draw off a group from the boys' premises if possible and if the numbers should become too great for Gerry to handle.

We now decided that we must limit the numbers of young people with whom we were working. We could not spread ourselves and still give intensive personal service. We discussed in turn all the young people who were now expecting and getting regular personal help from us. These numbered forty boys and ten girls. We allowed for ten more girls, and decided that these sixty young people must be our 'core' group, the group with whom we must work intensively during the next two years. There were many other young people with whom we had made contact casually, and we were aware that more would come to the stall or premises. We knew that it would be important to avoid giving these young people a feeling of being rejected or 'outsiders', although as it turned out later this was not a problem.

We decided that Jumbo was to remain on the stall four evenings a week in order to keep contact and give personal service to individuals and small groups who were not helped by other field-workers, and whenever possible to pick up the 'drop outs' from the groups who were being helped by the other workers. He would not have a group of his own. He would also have to encourage groups or individuals to join the other workers, as his contacts were the strongest. Marian was to assist on the stall, until the girls' work developed, so that Jumbo would be free to talk with individual boys when necessary. It was with these general plans in mind that we set out on our second year of field-work.

Beginning work in the boys' premises

On returning to the neighbourhood, Gerry spent some time at the stall with boys who wanted the premises to be reopened, and then he and Mary moved into the premises with them. There were about twenty boys and one or two girls. Within this number was a group consisting of Frank, Vic, Tommy, Artie and Shortie, who were fifteen or sixteen years old. They had made constant demands for a reopening as they had "nowhere to go" and "nothing to do". They were in trouble with the probation officers as they were not working most of the time. They were too well known to the police for them to hang about as a group on the street corners without being told to move on. They were in the midst of a rash of petty crime—breaking into telephone kiosks, cigarette machines and gas meters. They were talking constantly of a "big job" which they were planning but which never came off. They appeared to be a group more by virtue of being individuals who were not welcome in other groups, rather than because of any intense ties of friendship between them. Yet when the boys were together, which was most of the time during this period, the group exerted a strong influence over its members.

A second group which used the premises consisted of Reg and his followers. Reg was sixteen years old, on the edge of being 'seriously disorganised,' and with a following of 'simply disorganised' boys of fifteen and sixteen. They were a nuisance to the youth clubs in the community, organising fights regularly on any pretext, often simply for a giggle, or to gain status within the coffee stall network.

The remainder of the boys in the premises vacillated between Frank's group or Reg's group. They were mostly 'simply disorganised' boys whom we felt should be prevented from joining either of the groups because of the danger of being influenced by them.

For a few weeks Frank and his group played cards or just talked and larked about, but then they demanded to be allowed to turn the premises into "our club". Plans were made to paint and rebuild the club. It was to have an upholstered coffee bar with cushioned seats, a new sink, wallpaper, a stove, and a small platform for a band. The boys set to work—one as a carpenter, one as an upholsterer, one as a plumber, one as electrician, and one or two as decorators. Gerry acquired the material and money, on their instructions and with certain modifications. Their argument was that the Y.W.C.A. should provide the money and they would supply the labour. Under no condition were they to be told what to do. Gerry was to stay out of it and let them do it all on their own.

The boys could not agree on what was to be done, how it was to be done, who was to do it, with what materials. Each time an impasse was reached they would say, "What shall we do. Tell us what to do, that is what you are here for!" This conflict in wanting complete freedom and not knowing what to do with it, followed by demands that Gerry step in and "give orders", always ended in the same way. If Gerry told them what he thought should be done, they reacted by telling him not to start bossing people around. If he did not do so, they damaged or destroyed work that had been started. The boys' inability to work together or to get on together was ample evidence, if such had been needed, as to why they found life in youth clubs impossible (and why the youth clubs found them unpromising material) and why so few of them were able to hold down a job for any length of time. Work began, stopped, started again, was destroyed, painted over, broken up and begun again. It seemed they were unable to stick even at something they wanted very much to do. They had little self-discipline and little self-knowledge. Accumulated hostilities broke through for apparently little or no reason. Yet during this stage of the work with the boys, their involvement with each other and with the premises sharply cut down their anti-social and sometimes illegal behaviour outside the club.

Eventually Reg and his friends, whose visits to the premises had been erratic, due to their interest in a temporarily popular coffee bar, began to see the possibilities of turning the premises into a club. Reg was divided between his desire to help build up the club with Frank and his group, and his need to keep up his raids on other clubs and similar incidents outside the neighbourhood. As Reg showed interest in the club, Frank grew more resentful and for a while it looked as if the premises would become the scene of constant fights. But Reg was able to out-pace Frank and the two groups joined forces for a bigger and better series of raids in and around the neighbourhood, using the premises as a hide-out and a meeting place.

Gerry continued to give an intensive programme of personal service to individual boys in both groups. He tried to help them get jobs. He worked with their probation officers and helped in family and boy/girl problems. He arranged diversions—a series of trips, cinema parties and outings in a dormobile. These happened in rapid succession and were heavily subsidised. But the outside raids were a setback for us, not only because we were unable to help Frank and his group to follow through with something we knew they wanted to do, but because we were responsible for the two groups joining into what could easily become a gang. Even so by this time we had really got to know the boys, and had no illusions about what they expected from us or what we could do for them. They now knew us and of more importance, knew our limitations and possibilities. This new element of realism in the relationship made it possible to keep contact and continue personal service, while thinking up new ways of helping them to come to terms with themselves and the opportunities offered by the premises.

Dan and company

One evening Dan and his friends arrived from the coffee bar in the neighbourhood, which Reg had frequented earlier. We suspected that Reg had invited Dan in order to show off "my" premises. Dan was eighteen, known for getting things done. He was the victor in several well-known sagas. He had a lively intelligent girlfriend. He had held down a regular job for a long period and had rarely been in trouble with the police. Several of his followers were regular in employment and in maintaining relationships with each other and with their girlfriends. His following rose at times to fifteen boys.

Dan looked over the premises and said they would make "a fine club", especially for regular dances, and he prepared with his followers to move in. Gerry talked about it with Frank and Reg separately. Frank favoured Dan's "coming in on it" since Dan got things done and could "keep Reg in order". Reg was uncertain but reasoned that if Dan could make the club into a "good thing" it might be worth his not taking sides until he saw how it came out. A little later he agreed he would help Dan, if Dan should ask him. Frank and company, Reg and company, and Dan and company formed a management committee. Dan organised the painting and rebuilding and the club opened as a 'commercial youth café' within a week.

We had to admit to ourselves once again that our planning had gone for nought. We had allowed into the premises Dan and fifteen young people, after we had already agreed not to make new contacts, and we could also expect that once more there would be large numbers in the premises. We had to remind ourselves that it was the events in ths field that decided the programme and not our own preconceived ideas of what should happen. Later, Dan and company proved to be so stable an element in our work with Frank and Reg and their groups, that we saw their addition not as an extra set of responsibilities but as an aid to ourselves in helping these groups. Dan and his followers were a contribution which the neighbourhood itself made to the programme by way of the 'healthy elements' they brought in with them. They were able to contribute more, in showing how to get things done, how to get on together, how to manage the dance, and how to keep order, than we could ever have found possible on our own.

The first dance

On the first evening seventy young people crowded into the two small rooms of the premises. By nine o'clock the record player was at full blast. Food and soft drinks were being served and almost everyone was dancing. Vic said, "Well Gerry we've done it at last". Reg said, "Didn't think we could do it did you?" Frank said, "Worth all the work". The sense of achievement was indeed a revelation to the two original groups. They had at last pulled something off. At 10.30 Dan called "closing time" and shortly afterwards without incident the small premises cleared.

The commercial club lasted for seven months. The first month was mainly spent in completing the decorations, planning and organising. The last month, approximately the seventh month, was a period of tailing off. The five months in between provided a period of achievement during which sometimes as many as seventy young people came three times a week to "El Jumbo's"—the name agreed upon—for a dancing session. The management committee was in charge with Dan at the head. It ran the whole venture and was recognised by the young people to be doing so.

A successful enterprise

The success of the venture was largely due to the simple idea that the club was a commercial enterprise. Everyone had to pay a shilling to get into the dance, except the management committee members, who came in free. Sometimes youngsters would pay three shillings a week, and they were often the same boys who complained that sixpence a week was too much for a youth club. The profits went back into the premises. It was successful, partly because it was undertaken on the understanding that no one was doing something out of kindness for someone else or to help anyone. It was from the start a frankly commercial enterprise, and as such the rules of the game were known and agreed upon, and the authority of the management committee was recognised and accepted on a purely rational basis. They were offering for money a service which had no hidden strings, was above board, and fair in the eyes of the people who paid for it. It was seen as sensible to ask someone to leave or to throw them out "because they were interfering with your business" but not to throw them out on moral grounds that were none of your business, as they did in the youth clubs. In short they had defined the rules of the game and agreed among themselves to abide by them.

The dances provided us with what was certainly our most extensive opportunity to get to know and work with young people. We had, with no planning on our part, and with much reservation and occasional trepidation, allowed a situation to develop that seemed to offer the young people what they wanted and which offered us the opportunity to continue work with them as 'persons within the network'.

This is not to say that all went well. Theft or destruction of club property by members, hiding stolen goods, dice schools, recurring threats of violence from within and without, sometimes engendered on purpose from the inside, fights, bust-ups, misappropriation of the takings were common, almost everyday events. But despite this, the young people, not only carried on with the venture, but thoroughly enjoyed the opportunities it provided to get together, and the excitement and the fun offered them.

Early during this period Dan began visiting other commercial clubs in the neighbourhood, trying to interest their members "in a friendly way" to come over to us. This angered the manager of one of the clubs who threatened violence. But two visits from the manager and friends proceeded without incident. Gerry tried to interpret that this was a kind of experimental youth club which the opposition seemed to take simply as a sophisticated ploy.

Reg made the premises vulnerable by fighting expeditions into other territories and tried to provoke retaliation, believing that Dan and company were "at home and could handle anything". Frank and his friends hid stolen cigarettes and other proceeds of petty thievery in the premises, and broke in at the weekends to hide from the police, and to get away from their families. Reg, Frank and others organised dice schools in corners of the dance or broke in after hours to run them.

In short, some of the boys were using Dan and the club as a cover for continued disorganised behaviour, although they were in less trouble with the police during this period than either before or after the successful run of dances. This was not surprising since the amount of time, energy, and ingenuity it took for Frank, Reg and their followers, to keep up with the share in events in the premises, was time and energy taken from anti-social behaviour on the outside. Breaking into the premises, stealing club equipment, collecting door money without returning it to the committee and running their own dice schools might not have been 'nice things to be doing' but they happened within the network, without the intervention of outside authorities.

The boys' behaviour was the occasion for Gerry to try and get Dan to help to work with them. Gerry reasoned with Dan that since Frank and Reg were here and were part of the management and had some followers who paid shillings, everything possible should be done to try to help them instead of just throwing them out. Sometimes this worked, sometimes it did not. Sometimes Dan made allowances, and with Gerry's encouragement had a chat with the culprit or culprits and tried to 'straighten things out'. On one occasion however there was real danger that Gerry's support of Frank might mean his own exclusion. One weekend Frank and a friend broke into the premises, spent two days there, stole the record player and sold it, and destroyed some equipment. They were known to have done this but denied it. Dan and the rest of the management committee wanted to beat up and expel the two boys, and were extremely angry with Gerry who tried to intercede. It looked as if Gerry might be told to get out. As it happened, everyone calmed down after Gerry offered to replace the record player from Y.W.C.A. funds. Frank was allowed to stay. If he had been put out with his group we should have had to follow them into the community to work with them, instead of being able to do so within a relatively stable situation.

At the same time Dan was able to see that the behaviour of these boys, if it continued, would mean that the police would close the club. Indeed on one occasion they threatened to do so. Gerry and Dan had to organise a deputation to the police to interpret their difficulties, and to negotiate. During the planning of this deputation some of the boys demanded, "Tell them off", "Say we'll fight it out", "Don't give in". The success of the deputation both in negotiating, and interpreting that negotiation to the boys was proof of Gerry's ability to work with Dan, and to support him so that he could work with the others.

The same problems had to be solved in the case of the neighbours, to whom noise in the premises and on the pavement outside, lights on in the premises when boys broke in at midnight or over the weekend, and the loudness of recorded music, were often a real nuisance. Deputations had to be formed and sent to negotiate, and an attempt made to keep the noise in the premises and annoyance to the neighbours at a minimum.

In all of this activity, Gerry's functions were numerous. He had to help Dan to learn how to negotiate with the rest of the community, and how to interpret the negotiations to the other boys. He had to support Dan and the management committee. Dan was known as the man who could beat anyone, and at first kept order through his physical strength. Gerry had to help him acquire other skills in leadership. He had to take care that his support of Dan would not result in the other boys seeing him as "one of Dan's men", and so find an excuse to reject the help he was offering. For Gerry's main responsibility was to work with Frank, Reg and their groups. He knew that he must support them, but learned not to overprotect them when Dan put pressure on them to behave properly.

The regular work of personal service continued throughout the seven months. In addition, Gerry was aware that too much concentration on the premises would mean a large gap when the interest waned, and he encouraged the management group to organise numerous trips to the country, sea, bowling alleys, theatres and a variety of other places of interest. Sometimes the trips involved one small group and provided an opportunity for more intensive work. Sometimes forty to fifty young people went out together.

These then and others like them were the main events in a lively six months.

Working with girls in this setting

At the time when the premises were being turned into a 'commercial youth café' Mary moved out of them in order to work with girls referred by the probation officer. Marian replaced Mary in the premises and found she had a big part to play in this mixed group. Girls came along in larger numbers than we had ever been able to contact before. Boys brought the girl friends who were never allowed to visit the coffee stall, and girls who had always been on the fringes of the larger coffee stall group came along.

It was obvious to us at this point that contacting unattached girls required a large mixed setting in which either the boys were willing to bring them or they were able to come on their own. They needed some assurance that a modicum of order prevailed and that if necessary there would be help available if the boys abused them. They came on the tacit understanding that boys and workers would let them alone until they felt at ease, got to know some of the other young people and settled in. This whole process, learning that the place was there and open, and attending the dances to get the feel of it, lasted several weeks. We did all we could to encourage the boys, who at this point did not need the encouragement, to keep up the good work because we knew what it meant to the girls for this kind of service to be available to them.

Marian was offered by the management committee (the boys) the job of buying, preparing, serving and selling the food, which was seen as a girl's job. Later the boys even set up the necessary kitchen facilities in the basement, which gave Marian a place of her own to meet girls and to get to know them individually. Competition between the boys over girls, and between girls over boys, gave most of the girls a good deal of much needed and appreciated attention. This in turn began to give them status in their own eyes. With the knowledge that they were needed and with Marian to fall back on for advice, guidance and support, they began to take an interest in getting the boys to improve the kitchen, and even suggested a powder room just for them with comfortable chairs and a mirror "a proper ladies' room in pink and gold".

The whole pattern of boy/girl relationships within the larger dance grouping was becoming clearer to us. The girls often supported the boys with money, cigarettes, bus fares and entrance to the dance, and even subsidised occasional trips out of the neighbourhood, made excuses to employers, phoned probation officers to explain why the boys could not keep an appointment, spoke to Mums, tried to prevent 'runs in' with the police, and on the whole accepted their status as girls in that neighbourhood. This included being pushed about a good deal and on occasion physical violence.

Marian continued for many months to be just one of the group of girls in the premises, listening, talking and advising, and often comforting. Any attempts on her part to intervene and actually help girls in boy/girl relationships, was seen by the boys as a threat to their own status as 'men'. It was not until the dances had been going successfully for two months that Marian tried a small breakaway. On a non-dance evening, she invited three or four of the girls to meet her at the girls' premises, to look at the facilities there. The boys heard about it and were furious. It took a good deal of persuasion to prevent the boys from going after the girls and "taking them out of that place" and banning Marian from the dances. It was not only that the boys feared the girls would start something on their own which would interfere with the smooth running of the dances, but of more importance, they felt it was for them to say what the girls got, when, how and where, and not the girls themselves. Nonetheless Marian was able to continue to meet with a small group on non-dance nights just to wash their hair, make coffee and talk things over. Once it became clear to the boys that no excessive demands were to be made by the girls as a result of their going off on their own, they reluctantly accepted the idea.

Marian's role was a particular one. She was not a 'club leader for girls' work' in a regular club where her authority extended from her employers, the management committee. The club was a commercial enterprise, run by the boys themselves and they set the pattern within which she had to work. That pattern demanded that she behave just like the other girls in the premises. Once we understood and accepted this Marian was able to contact and work with the girls. It made for definite limitations since there were many things we should like to have done to help girls, but acquiescence in the role assigned to Marian by the boys prevented her from doing them. Even so, it had a big advantage. Marian was seen as inside the network and if she kept to the rules of the game, was free to work within it. The situation had a positive side for the girls as well. They now had an environment within which to pick and choose. They had a place in which to meet other girls and to make friends, discuss girls' problems among themselves and with Marian. She brought information and knowledge, which the girls did not have on their own, into the discussion and through Gerry, she could always manage to get the girls' case heard by Dan and the management committee. The girls now had a new status within the coffee stall grouping.

Dan leaves

The six months of successful dances gave Reg and Frank and their followers an activity, interesting and exciting enough to make them cut down their anti-social behaviour on the outside. It offered them an opportunity to be part of something, but it also gave them a taste of discipline, not discipline enforced by 'us' (the staff), but by the whole dance environment, a discipline that Dan, Frank, Reg and all the young people had created together. The club gave the girls a chance to meet one another and boys in a fairly trouble-free atmosphere, and it gave Dan a chance to exercise his leadership.

At the end of six months the club began to fall apart. This was partly because Dan, with this experience behind him, was beginning to think of bigger and better things. The dances had been successful financially, as well as in terms of the recreational service it offered and Dan began to think of the possibilities of running a larger enterprise. The second reason for the falling apart was that Dan, and the others in his group had come into regular contact with the same girls several nights a week during the six months and as a result boy/girl relationships were strengthened. They were pairing up and moving off, and so had less interest in making personal sacrifices to keep the dance going. Dan came less frequently to the premises and to the dances, began to be less interested in the details of management and was less willing to see that discipline was maintained. His girl friend, Ann, had been with him through most of the six months, and had supported him through many of the difficulties of building up the dance. But she was now encouraging him to spend more time alone with her.

This was all well and good for Dan and his group, including the girls associated with it, but it made difficulties for Frank and Reg and their followers who needed the protection, adventure and chance to participate that the club had offered under Dan. It was also difficult for the girls who were now attached to the club and who had established no on-going relationships with boys. As Dan withdrew, Frank and Reg began to differ among themselves about management details, and were unable to provide a proper service—a man on the door, the latest records, arrangements for coffee and food. They were also unable to keep discipline among their own followers. The dance following dwindled to thirty, and then to twenty. As Frank and Reg, without Dan to help them get on together began arguing among themselves, destruction in the premises increased. We had to find a way of closing the premises for a short summer period and the workers relied on the neighbourhood and outings for meeting the various groups.

A group of younger boys

While Gerry was with the larger goup in the boys' premises, Peter was meeting a group of younger boys. They were nine in number, and still at school, their ages being thirteen and fourteen years. Most of them had been in and out of the youth clubs in the area, and they had called at the coffee stall on several occasions. In the early days of our work in the premises they managed to get in regularly. They became followers of Frank or Reg who ordered them about and tended to exploit them, within the struggle of their two groups.

Peter, who already knew the boys, was asked to pick them up in the premises, get to know them better, and begin a series of trips with them, in order to distract their attention from the premises. Peter thought that three of the boys in this group might benefit by a regular club experience and would probably be able to fit in if special arrangements were made to help them do so. He visited one of the boys' clubs in the neighbourhood and talked with the leader, who agreed to Peter's attending the club with the boys for a few weeks. He and the three boys then visited the club a number of times. On the first occasion the leader and Peter had coffee with the boys, and the leader described the club and its programme to them. Peter stayed on for full sessions, joining in activities with the boys or sitting around with them. At first the boys tended to stick together, moving from group to group and from activity to activity. When after six weeks Peter left them on their own, they separated, followed their own interests and settled into friendship groups within the club.

Meanwhile Peter organised a series of trips for the other six boys to cinemas, the circus, exhibitions, wrestling, and the airport, and later longer expeditions and camping trips. At the circus the boys finished up in the ring teasing the clowns, after which they changed round the 'ladies' and 'gents' signs and retired. At the wrestling they left Peter inside, found expensive seats for the performance and returned to Peter at the end. Outside, they removed a temporary bus-stop sign and persistently provoked assistants in shops and coffee bars until they had to retreat. When visiting an exhibition, Peter for the first time did not produce tickets. The boys had agreed to pay for themselves, but after a long discussion at the gate, realised that they had not enough money. They arranged for Peter to pay his own entrance fee while they slipped successfully through the back door. The longer expeditions gave Peter time to know the boys at leisure. He talked and played games with them in the dormobile while another adult drove them to the coast or camping site.

After several months of meeting together, the boys began to demand a place of their own. This was not a simple matter since we could not take on another shop, which would probably mean a repetition of the programme in the boys premises. The group and Peter considered building a shack, or meeting in the backroom of a shoe-repairer as they had previously been allowed to do on occasions. At last we were able to borrow a room to use one night a week in a boys' club in the neighbourhood.

The room of their own turned out to be more an idea of what they thought they should have, than what they wanted. They had no idea of what they wanted to do in the room, and for some time suggestions from Peter were ignored. Partly out of frustration and partly because it was fun, they broke up equipment, attempted to set fire to the place, turned on the water one night just before they left hoping it would flood the club, and painted the walls with rude slogans. They were unable and did not want to settle in. It was only after several weeks that their destructive behaviour was interspersed with theatrical make-up, dressing up, photography, card games, making sledges, and making plans for outings and camping trips. Peter's occasional attempts to interest the group in the club programme in the rest of the building—the same club into which three of their friends had settled—ended unhappily each time. They visited the canoe building group, disrupted it and tried to walk off with the tools. They erased the scores of the table tennis players, rushed, pushed, shouted and generally made life unpleasant for the regular club members who were interested and enjoying what they were doing.

It seemed to us that the group members regressed a good deal once they got into their own room. It was true that their behaviour outdoors on trips and outings was usually far from what the general public might expect of them. But they had grown into a group recognisable to themselves and outsiders, and had managed to arrange and actually carry out a wide variety of trips and to enjoy doing so. Their premises, the room in the boys' club, seemed to offer them the opportunity to act out being younger than they were. They played at being children when they were thirteen and fourteen years. This was partially because the group had no natural indigenous leader to rally them and create the group atmosphere in which growing up was rewarded and regressive behaviour punished by social pressure from within the group. Leadership passed from boy to boy several times in an evening. Outside the clubroom, however much they acted up, however much they did things for a giggle, it was always with an eye to the audience of adult strangers about them who exerted social control. In public they learned to know how far they could go. In private, in their own room, anything was possible, and, they felt, permissible.

Unfortunately the room was not entirely their own, and much of Peter's time and energy had to be given to preventing damage and behaviour which would affect the rest of the club, and result in their being turned out. If the room had been isolated, and they had been able to meet together for a longer period, it is possible—as with a younger girls' group—that they would have been able to come through their period of regression to the point of being able to get along together, and with other groups and adults. In the circumstances, Peter felt that he must find some alternative meeting place, before they were asked to leave.

During the period in which Peter worked with them, they visited on several occasions an open youth club in the neighbourhood. They usually managed to get in and stay in for a whole evening. Peter talked with them about this club and they agreed that it was a good club if "the bloke in charge wasn't always on to us about paying subs or doing something". Peter opened negotiations with the club leader who knew the boys well. He agreed that Peter could move into the club to work with the group there, and also that he would not press the boys for subscriptions for the time being. Arrangements were made for Peter to be exempt from being a 'club authority' with the group, and in return, if the boys were turned out because of their behaviour, he would be turned out with them. As it turned out, after five or six weeks of attendance the group began to break up, and members joined other larger groups in the club. They came together occasionally to 'send up' Peter or to meet him after the club closed for a cup of coffee. But after a while, the boys became part of a network of several changing friendship groups, which used a coffee bar for periods, and the club at other times. They visited the coffee stall occasionally and continued to use Peter, and later a student-worker, John, to help them with their personal problems.

Factors in working with this group

A number of factors emerged from our work with this group. We had picked up the group at the stall and later again in the older boys' premises at a point in their lives when one day they were 'grown up' "we're not kids any more—you don't tell us what to do—we can make out on our own", and the next day had gone back to being children, "What should we do. You tell us Peter", "You take us out Peter". "Why don't you stop us when we do the wrong thing Peter?" One day they wanted support and understanding from an adult and on another to take him down a peg, make unreasonable demands, send him up or even hurt him physically and emotionally.

In this period of their development they were in conflict between wanting to be a compact group "our gang", "a place of our own", "keep everyone out", and a need to show others what they had, to invite people to share—as on expeditions—and a need to keep up with the older boys.

The worker was seen by them in part as a father or an older brother from whom attention and affection was needed, expected, and demanded; in part a comrade who was expected to be one of the boys and "to do things with us". Both roles could be required of the worker on the same evening by the same boy, while at the same time the worker was expected to be both figures at random to all the other boys in the group and to the group itself. On one occasion they might all gang up on him to send him up and try to hurt him "just to see if he can take it" and perhaps on the same evening they would offer him cigarettes. Problems with fathers, older brothers, school teachers or even the older boys of the neighbourhood were worked out on Peter. This ambivalence to the adult worker, so integral a part of the young person's attempt to come to terms with growing up, required that Peter should allow the projection onto himself of both sets of feelings—the need for affection and support and the need to show independence.

None of this was very different from the behaviour of most adolescents faced with the same problems of growing and in the same stage of development except that many adolescents in other circumstances and in other communities often have families, relatives or neighbours, on whom they are allowed to work out their growing up problems. In this case due to a variety of family and neighbourhood background factors, Peter was useful as the adult available for them to use in this way.

An important factor in working with this group was the variety of facilities needed, which were *an older boy's group* with premises for them to attach themselves, react against, emulate, and finally from which to be separated; *a worker to help them* get about on trips and outings and from whom to get attention, support and guidance while they were trying to 'define themselves' as young adults; *a room of their own* to destroy, and in which to be children again; *money to share*, argue over, lie about, spend and misspend, (both because, springing from large families with serious economic difficulties, they needed it, and because it provided them with a chance to do things they found exciting and real); *planned activity to react against*, someone to plan it, equipment for it which could be broken, stolen and destroyed; *help* with family problems, the occasional school problem, with jobs, and with boy/girl relationships, the occasional small handout for supper, a new tie, or a birthday cake; *a mixed club setting*—an informal kind in which they could learn to get along with others, with some support while they were doing so; *a continuing relationship* with an adult worker, who could go through the whole process with them, helping them to see their problems, and to make choices and decisions; *the coffee stall as a point of contact* to set out from or return to and a place to meet and talk with Jumbo who could always help if one got "sick and tired of Peter" or just didn't want to tell him about a particular problem.

Probation referrals

Early in the second year of field-work, before we had been offered the opportunity to contact and work with girls in the numbers provided by the success of the 'commercial youth café' we contacted community agencies to ask for suggestions from them as to how we might find girls who would need what we had to offer. As a result the probation officers began to refer to us girls on probation who were in need of support as individuals and who needed the opportunity to be part of a group.

The first referral was that of a girl of seventeen years, Monica. She had left home, and had many problems. Mary agreed to meet Monica, and spent an average of one and a half hours daily with her for many months. Eventually Mary was able to help her find a job, and to help her through crises within it. Mary was also introduced by the probation officer to five girls of twelve and thirteen years. They met in the girls' premises, every week to sew, cook, and amuse themselves as they wished. Every second week she took them on an outing, to Hampstead Heath, the zoo, to Southend or for swimming. After three months the number in the group was increased to thirteen. At this stage, the end of the second year, Mary returned to Canada and Susan replaced her, to work with Monica, and with this new younger girls' group in the girls' premises.

Five other girls of fifteen years were referred by the probation officer, and this time it was Marian who met them individually, first at the probation office and then at their homes. She followed this up with visits to the cinema, shopping expeditions, or meals in restaurants. Marian hoped that she would be able to work with the girls as a group, but each one needed a great deal of support, attention and time individually and was unwilling to meet with the others. After a while Marian was able to take out two or three together, but never more. Two of the girls refused several invitations and Marian decided not to press them and visited them only occasionally. The other three, after several individual visits to the girls' premises, and after several months, finally became part of a group of nine girls meeting regularly with Marian.

The number of girls with whom we now had a relationship was approximately sixty, including those first contacted in the boys' premises, and those referred to us by the probation officer.

The coffee stall continues to be the focal point

For a time, shortly after the premises were opened and in full swing we began to feel that with the commercial youth café being the centre of activity, Peter's group in a room of its own, and trips and outings occurring three or four times a week, the coffee stall might lose its central place in the programme. This did not happen. With the exception of the younger girls' group, the coffee stall remained the focal point of contact for the young people with whom we were working. They met each other there and kept in touch with individual staff members and the whole coffee stall grouping. We felt this happened for several reasons. The young people now knew what the stall was for and how to use it. They knew the Y.W.C.A. supported it and that in some way Jumbo, although he was not one of "those people in the West End" was responsible to them. They knew that information, advice and guidance were available without obligations, especially without "red, white and blue tape". They knew that this could be without involvement with other statutory and voluntary bodies if they did not want to be involved, but that contact could be made with these bodies if they did. Jumbo would make the first move for them and would keep an eye on 'them' while things were being sorted out.

Jumbo's programme of personal service now covered probation, police court work, employment, approved school, Borstal and prison visiting, contact with family case work agencies and social welfare services as well as with parents, older brothers and sisters. The stall had become a kind of youth information bureau. It provided information and advice not only from Jumbo and other field-workers, but from a legal aid volunteer, a youth employment officer and several other specialist volunteers, and later in the second year from a voluntary group established for holiday advice and planning. The boys understood that the stall and its personnel would be constantly available if they needed help on an evening. If the stall were not there, or before and after it had opened or closed, they could always contact Jumbo by phone. If they missed him they could usually get on to another of the field-workers.

Groups going out on trips often met at the stall and returned to it to have a cup of coffee and tell Jumbo about their adventures. Jumbo, who had known most of the young people longer than any other of the field-workers, had become a key person in the eyes of the young people. If they were having difficulties in getting what they wanted from other staff they spoke to Jumbo. The field-workers also referred to him difficulties for consideration. Drop-outs from groups —young people who for any number of reasons left their groups— were not completely 'out' since they always felt free to return to the stall, sometimes to be persuaded to go back to their group, or sometimes to be helped to start again in another small friendship group within the network. Much of the personal service work for those in the small friendship groups was done by the worker who was working with that group, but not all. Some of Jumbo's old contacts preferred to use the group for "fun and games" and to come back to Jumbo for personal service. On occasions field-workers did not want to make a second contact with statutory and voluntary bodies when Jumbo had already made one, and so they referred a boy to the stall for Jumbo's help. Jumbo had to have an assistant each night, because he had to be free to go out and phone or meet a boy "around the corner" or in a pub, or had to be able to spend time in the cab of the coffee stall for a personal interview. The field-workers, who assisted on the stall, on nights they were not working elsewhere with their groups, were able to keep in touch there with their own groups, as well as with the other boys and girls in the larger network.

Although there might at first appear to be negative elements in this set up—that the young people could so easily play off the workers at the stall one against the other, and that several workers could be in contact with one individual—they were not as negative as they seemed. They provided us with an opportunity to help the young people see the usefulness as well as the hazards of such attempts, and this could be helpful to them in their life 'on the outside'. The young people had a choice of adults to whom to relate, which they valued. Some of them felt that in coming to the same person over and over again might mean being under an obligation they wanted to avoid.

6. *The full programme*

By the end of the second year we were involved in a full programme, covering four aspects of the field-work—a full programme of personal service—help with work, probation, police, family and boy/girl relationship problems; work with groups—trips, outings, cinema parties, a wide variety of activities in the boys' and girls' premises with workers acting as resource persons to the smaller friendship groups within the network; work with ourselves—coming to terms with the patterns of mobility and associations, learning how to assess social attitudes, change some of our own and develop the skills necessary to use the opportunities we saw the field-work events as offering; with the community—the probation officer, the youth employment service, the youth clubs, borrowing equipment and facilities, helping the community agencies to see what was needed and how it might be offered, helping the young people to learn how best to use what was offered. At the same time we were keeping field-work records, discussing and thinking out together what work with the unattached was about, and how the information we acquired could be passed on to others facing the same problem.

Premises in the full programme

With the coffee stall as the hub of a wheel, and activities radiating out to the rim in all directions—the boys' premises, the girls' premises, clubs, public houses, coffee bars, dance halls, homes and on the street corners, the shape of the programme began to emerge as well as its content.

A group could be in four or five places in one evening, or could settle in the same place for several weeks. A group, apparently settled in a coffee bar, would suddenly decide to go to a cinema, or to the chip shop, to a club, or out for a drive. A small friendship group could change its membership with equal rapidity, although by this stage in the project, more groups were identifiable for longer periods. The sudden change of plan, the sudden departure of an individual, or the sudden change to different premises were all part of the accepted unpredictable pattern. Even during the period when the dances at the 'commercial youth café' were the main attraction, members of the coffee stall network were still erratic and unpredictable in their other leisure time activities. Beyond the movements of a single evening was a broader pattern. For two or three weeks part of the larger coffee stall grouping would be centred on a particular café, coffee bar, or commercial club, while another would be centred on a second, and another on a third, in the same neighbourhood. One group would leave its base and move on to another. Possibly the crowd in the new café would move on to their next hangout and so the migration continued. Sometimes a coffee bar could be almost completely empty for weeks until some group returned to it. Thus, a recognisable pattern emerged of mobile individuals, of numerous small friendship groups, sometimes constantly changing, sometimes more stable, some within larger groups, all within the larger network connected with the coffee stall, and all constantly moving around within the neighbourhood.

By this time the field-workers were equally mobile, and understanding and accepting the pattern, they went along with it offering service at any place, at any time. As a result we were able to allow a programme to develop that not only met the needs of the young people in terms they understood and accepted, but met them where they were. The shape of the programme, like its content, was a response to the behaviour of the young people.

The field-workers not only followed the pattern created by the young people, but they learned to use it in order to be more effective in their service. Firstly, they became a part of the pattern in order to observe the young people, on the stall, in a café, coffee bar, or on a street corner. They observed their behaviour, attitudes and movements. Then they talked with them, argued with them, fooled about with them and eventually were accepted by them. Secondly, they used the casual meetings, on the streets or in a public house, to hear how Tom was getting on in his work, or to listen to the grape-vine news. Frequently a worker planned the 'casual meetings'. He would make sure he met a group which he knew was planning a 'job', or if he wanted to develop his relationship with a group he would casually be in their coffee bar when they arrived.

Sometimes a worker was able to arrange meetings. He would ask two boys from a large group to meet him for a discussion that he could not expect them to have with the whole group present. He would also use "will you be here Tuesday?"—or "Friday?" frequently in order to reach a stage of regular meetings between himself and a group. Later the group would ask him, "Will you be here Tuesday?". Eventually any worker could become one of a group wherever he happened to be, and he could meet a group wherever it happened to be settled in at the moment.

With this pattern each worker offered personal service, help with school, family or employment problems, offered to help them plan interesting things to do, outings, camping, cinema parties, bowling, wrestling, or exhibitions at Olympia or Earls Court. He offered help in organising or subsidising these activities. He helped to keep the small groups in contact with the other groups within the larger network. He carried messages to and fro, helped make plans for several groups to go out on the same trip, was available to help with difficulties between and within groups, and to help the groups explore what the neighbourhood and the larger community had to offer.

We saw all this leading to the idea of the whole neighbourhood being the 'premises', within which were the patterns of mobility, the patterns of association within the larger grouping, our recognition of these patterns and our willingness to work within them. The coffee stall as a fixed point, and the workers moving out from it and returning to it, and the programme happening 'all over the place', meant that the whole neighbourhood was the premises in much the same sense that the club building was the premises of a youth club. Even when we met the demands of the older boys for a place of their own, and opened the shop as a meeting place, and later when we found a room within a boys' club in the neighbourhood, and when we opened the girls' premises, we saw each of these as temporary meeting and activity points, within the larger neighbourhood premises. They were expendable as the groups tired of them, grew through them, or lost interest in them, and were no more and no less important than the café, coffee bar, public house or street corner.

Indeed we realised that if we had continued for say, five instead of three years, a series of shops for different purposes at different places would probably have been necessary, opening, carrying on activities of one sort or another, and then running down and closing. In short, we saw the buildings as 'an activity within the programme', sometimes here, sometimes there, within the larger neighbourhood premises, opened or closed in response to the needs of groups and the larger network.

Activities in the full programme

During the period when the programme was developing, when Gerry was beginning work in the boys' premises, Peter making contact with the younger boys, Marian and Mary looking for and finding girls, and Jumbo at the centre of the network, one of the questions was "What could the field-workers offer groups?" When workers suggested activities at this stage they were turned down. When they inferred that they were open to suggestions, the usual requests were for visits to the cinema or "going out for a lark".

Sometimes we were distressed at the apparent aimlessness of the young people's activities, and the dearth of adventurous activities in the area. Many of the boys wanted to do things which were exciting and new, and yet the only possibilities seemed to be all night drinking parties or breaking into a warehouse. They talked of going to the south of France, or a West End club, as if they would do it next week and yet they knew that they were extremely nervous as soon as they stepped out of their own neighbourhood. There were the two extremes, the day-to-day aimless activities, and the dreams of exciting adventure. The workers had to learn to live with the aimlessness, and to use all the ingenuity they had, to make the exciting happen, and help the young people to the point where they could enjoy it.

We recognised that activities were always happening. Meeting people, talking, discussing, arguing, going out to the cinema or up the road together were just as much 'activities' as were table tennis tournaments or highly organised sports. In fact breaking up an old piano could be an evening's activity, which could give the same opportunity for relationship building as planning for a weekend camp. The opportunities for learning about each other, and learning to participate in a group were just as great. A worker could have ample opportunity to help individuals in groups by sharing in any of these activities.

But it was not always as simple as this, since boys considered antisocial behaviour to be fun, exciting, and a natural activity in that environment, and wanted us to join in this too. While recognising that the boys could learn a great deal while participating in any activity social or anti-social we had to try to show them that in the end they were apt to lose more than they could possibly gain from anti-social behaviour.

On one occasion Peter and Marian took a group to a New Town.

As they neared their destination, out came a tool kit. The boys asked Marian to stop at a cigarette machine, and suddenly Peter realised that their idea was to remove the machine, put it in the dormobile, bring it back to London, and open it for the money and cigarettes. Marian firmly drove past every machine while Peter argued with the boys.

PETER: You know you can't use the van to get away with the machine don't you?

BOYS: There would be no risk. If you and Marian would keep quiet, nothing could go wrong.

PETER: The van could be traced if someone got the number, or the police could stop us.

BOYS: If they stop us you and Marian can say you are youth leaders and we would say it is our machine, and we are taking it to the mechanic to have it fixed.

PETER: The prisons are full of people who tell those kind of stories. It's too great a risk for you to take, and it's not fair on Marian and me, and anyway, if we used the van that way it wouldn't be fair on any of the others.

So it went on, Marian trying to avoid cigarette machines on the route, Peter attempting to keep them talking until they were near enough home to stop at a fish and chip shop. He knew that this would occasion a change in the 'activity' from "Let's take the cigarette machine" to "Well you didn't let us take it. Now we have no money for chips. You will have to stand the treat." The 'activity' then became could Peter stand the treat, and if he could, should he.

Once we relaxed and accepted the material presented by the young people as activities, the talking, larking about, the occasional tip, and spontaneous interests, a full-scale programme developed, wider in scope than anything we had anticipated. Activities frequently started with a sudden idea—a trip to the West End, pronto, right away, now. Any attempt to stop and plan it was resented as interference, and caused a long drawn out argument that took up most of the evening, "We want to do it now. We will find out what to do when we get there. It's no use our waiting until we have the cash or tickets—we won't want to do it then." The field-workers soon learned to "get going was good". They had to be on the alert to answer the group's demand for spontaneous action. On one occasion a group wanted to paint—"why not paint on the walls" said the workers, and everyone was absorbed painting the walls for two hours. When the boys wanted to make sledges, the only wood available was an old ladder, so this was immediately used. When a group wanted to build a coffee bar, the worker had to get as much material as possible within a few hours. When he wanted them to make the place attractive they played around for weeks; when they wanted a smart youth café it was finished within a week. If an outing were successful, other groups wanted to do the same thing and there was a run on a particular outing.

As it became apparent that the field-workers were not trying to push this or that way of spending an evening together, and were willing to do "what we want to do when we want to do it", the worker was able to throw in a suggestion or two which had more chance of being taken up, and ideas about new places to go and new ways of doing things were more acceptable.

Indoor activities included cooking, sewing, handiwork, hairdressing, make-up, theatrical make-up, dressing up, modelling, acting, tape recording, painting, upholstery, plumbing, carpentry, dancing, billiards, table-tennis, short story writing, film making, and planning expeditions and parties. Activities out of doors included tobogganing, bowling, skating, swimming, weekend and afternoon trips and outings, parties to theatres, cinemas, restaurants, clubs, coffee bars, camping and holidays at home and abroad. These were not planned but either happened spontaneously or slowly developed over a period of weeks or even months. Sometimes only two or three young people joined in, sometimes twelve or thirteen, sometimes a number of small groups together, or as in the case of the commercial youth café and some of the outings, much larger numbers.

When the workers accepted spontaneity, some groups were prepared to consider planning ahead, and preparing for more adventurous trips. Sometimes it seemed that plans for an outing were one activity and the outing a completely different one. The worker played along with this, and sometimes was able to bring the two together so that the second was the outcome of the first. The longer adventurous trips had to be planned far ahead, and knowing the apparent remoteness of the trip, the worker had to help the young people there gradually. A group decided to go to Jersey—so first they tried out visiting the West End. Visits to restaurants and to the national film theatre helped them to gain confidence. Gradually they could mix easily with new people. Then followed a two day camping trip in some caves. Eventually they knew that they would get to Jersey. Some girls went through a similar process which ended in a holiday in a work camp in France. The most important factor for them was that they should feel confident about their appearance. Complete wardrobes were prepared by each girl, following discussion on what they would need. Advice by a West End hairdresser was given on holiday hairstyles.

These were simply the externals of the activity programme, underneath, beside and within the trips, the cooking, swimming and other 'activities', the 'real activities' were taking place. Boys and girls were getting to know one another better, learning how to get along together, having opportunities to lead, follow and learn new skills. These activities gave the worker the opportunity to offer advice, guidance and help to individuals and to groups. The externals were only important in so far as they were the occasion for people to do and be things together.

As the programme developed, so our work and co-operation with statutory and voluntary bodies increased, including especially the police, the probation officer and the youth employment service.

The police

Our first contact with the police was in applying for a license to operate the stall. We explained what we were attempting to do and met with sympathetic understanding. It was agreed that the matter should be kept at superintendent level, and that the men on the beat, for the time being at least, should know nothing about it. During the early stages of the work we had little or no contact with the police save the occasional request to move the stall. We were of course constantly in indirect contact through the boys, but it was not until the boys' premises were opened and dances in full swing, that direct contact with the police became part of the programme.

Awareness that there was occasional gambling and drinking in the premises, the complaints of neighbours to the police about noise and rowdy groups on the pavement, the occasional fights outside the premises, all occasioned police intervention. This was usually met by our explaining the situation to the superintendent, letting the law take its course by way of the necessary action of the policeman on the beat, and using the incident to help the boys learn how to look at and cope with the legitimate demands of the law. Several times when we were expecting trouble from outside the neighbourhood we asked for a policeman to make himself known to be in the vicinity. Several times without a request from us a policeman looked in, and we had to help the boys explain to them what was happening. On one occasion when the club was in danger of being closed we organised a deputation to the police. We discussed it with the superintendent first, so that he was prepared for the boys and then we helped the boys to state their case. The boys were allowed to reopen the club on certain conditions agreed by both police and boys.

Our relations with the police over the three years were mutually advantageous, being based on two 'principles'. The first was that of separate but related roles. The police knew that we sometimes had information about the criminal behaviour of individual boys or groups but would not be able to work with the boys if we passed it on to them. They understood that we could not 'control the boys' in the usual sense of the word, that our role was to help and support and if we were successful in helping individuals and groups we were in fact helping the police. But they also knew that direct action to help the police in any particular instance was impossible for us. The second was that part of the work was attempting to interpret the needs of the boys to the police and the legitimate needs and behaviour of the police to the boys.

The probation officer

A good number of boys were on probation. Often our first service to a boy, at his own request, was to "get on to my probation officer", as often as not with the request to tell some tall story about his really being employed, sleeping home every night, or being away at his grandmother's house for the weekend. Our job was to contact the probation officer, pass on the message as just that—a message from Jack or Bill or Harry and an offer to talk things over with the probation officer. When there developed several of these three cornered relationships, between a field-worker (most often Jumbo) a boy and the probation officer, an informal understanding grew up between us and the probation officer. This often allowed us to keep track of a boy for a week or so during one of his "I'm not reporting moods", and it sometimes gave us the opportunity to patch things up between the probation officer and the boy.

It was understood that we could never give information about the boy that might be to his detriment. Nor could we discuss a boy who had not asked us to 'represent' him. Nonetheless we were also to help the probation officer in many cases by supporting the boy while he was trying to carry out recommendations of the probation officer about school, work, or living at home. We could work with parents, relatives, or sometimes even neighbours to enlist their help in supporting the boy in the same way. We could also work with other boys in a friendship group around the stall, to enlist their help in supporting the boy. This was a crucial matter since a boys' mates could often make or break a probation officer's recommendations, especially as regards getting and keeping a job. We were also able to give the probation officer information to help him in his decisions on the advisability and possible effect of treatment, based on information about the boy that the probation officer could not be expected to have acquired on his own.

As in the case of the police we were able to work out this separate but related role for ourselves in relation to the probation officer. We saw ourselves as supporting the boy in meeting the recommendations from his probation officer by working with friendship groups and the neighbours, and in the relationship between the boy concerned and the field-worker. But our support of the probation officer stopped short of passing on information of detriment to the boy. It was agreed between us that while we would co-operate to the limit in helping the probation

67

officer to decide what should happen to a boy in court, we should be in support of the boy when in court, and if necessary would speak for him. It was understood that we had to maintain our supporting relationship with the boy so that on his return to the neighbourhood there would be someone to whom he felt he could turn.

The youth employment service

Employment was a problem for the young people and to us during the whole of the field-work. The difficulties included finding jobs, keeping them, giving them up, getting the sack when they didn't want it, not getting the sack when they did, deciding on reasons for keeping a job, wanting to work and not being able to, having to work and not wanting to. These and a hundred other variations on the employment problem were the largest single activity in working with the boys.

Employment gave us the point of contact with the boys that most often deepened into their asking for other help, advice or guidance. It was our ability to deal and/or help with employment problems that provided the strongest link between the boys and ourselves. On the whole the boys disliked the set-up at the youth employment service, and normally refused to ask them for help. This attitude was both the cause and effect of using the grape-vine to get information about jobs.

At the beginning of the second year we approached the youth employment service to explore the possibilities of joining forces with them to handle a problem which was too great for us to shoulder on our own. After several discussions it was agreed that two youth employment officers should work voluntarily on the coffee stall two nights a week. Once on the stall, the officers were introduced as friends of Jumbo, but they were quickly recognised also as youth employment officers. This recognition presented none of the problems we had anticipated. The fact that they were friends of Jumbo's and were willing to meet the boys on their own territory gave the officers a place in the network which allowed them to help boys to get jobs, to hold the ones they had, to change over, and to think about how to get more pay in the one they had. They were able to do employment counselling on the stall in a way that was beyond our ability and resources, and which the boys were able and willing to accept.

This was an important point in the project since we were not only able to offer a better service to the young people through the youth employment officer, but it was our first attempt to introduce into the network 'one of them', an outsider who was an official of a statutory body, and he became accepted as 'one of us'. The employment officers not only helped with employment problems, but joined in the discussion and general playing about at the stall, through which they became 'people' and not officials. The boys believed that the officers were interested in them, and some began to phone them at their office, and to recommend to other boys that they should do the same. "He's all right. He'll help you." Eventually some boys were able and willing to visit the office itself. This, for a time, led to new difficulties since the behaviour of some boys once inside the office was often impolite and even aggressive. They refused to speak to anyone except the officers they knew. "No ruddy clerk or anyone is going to tell me what to do." For a while the old insecurity of hostility and resentment about 'them' returned. In most cases the officers and Jumbo together learned how to handle this transition from the officers at the coffee stall to the use of the employment office for guidance and job placement.

Youth Service

The borough youth committee and the youth officer supported us from the beginning of our field-work both in principle and financially, more as an act of faith than from any knowledge of what we would or could do, since we ourselves were unable to be specific about where it all would lead, or how we would work with the unattached if and when we succeeded in making contact. We had begun by seeing ourselves as on the periphery of the Youth Service, attempting to help the young people to 'get into it' on terms they could understand and accept. We had begun by thinking that our contacts would be outside the youth clubs. As the project developed it became clear to us that many of our contacts were already known to most of the club leaders in the neighbourhood and had been in and out of most of the clubs. We came to see that trying to get young people into clubs was often beside the point in terms of their real need. Even when the club offered something they needed and would accept, the form and content of the programme would have to be modified to meet their needs and expectations.

Three sets of expectations were at play:

1. The young people. They thought the clubs were too "square", "kids' stuff", "too demanding". They were unable or unwilling to attend regularly, take part in organised activities, participate in the management or even to pay subscriptions but nonetheless they saw the club as a place to try to get into on the odd night, especially if it were a rainy one, somewhere to start a lark or even a bust-up. They also thought the idea of a club as a place of their own, which they ran themselves and in which they pleased themselves, was a good one. They felt that the existing clubs were impossible because of the unreasonable demands of those in charge.

F

2. The club leaders. The club leaders tended on the one hand to see us as workers concentrating on those young people whom they knew from experience would not make good club members, as lowering standards, giving things away (cinema trips, bus fares), condoning anti-social behaviour, starting a club in the boys' premises even though we had said at the outset that we would not. On the other hand they saw us as working with the boys who gave them the most trouble, and providing a necessary service to the young people they could not help because of the shape and content of their own programme.

3. The project staff. We tended to feel that on one hand the young people were mistaken in the expectations they had of club life. Their requirements could not be met within the clubs in the neighbourhood without sacrificing the service to the young people who wanted, needed and participated in the programmes already offered. But on the other hand we felt that it was the responsibility of the Youth Service and the youth club leaders to see the conflict in expectations, and to help the borough youth committee to devise ways and means of meeting the expectations of the unattached by providing a service different from that of the clubs.

Of course as we set to work more precisely on this problem we realised that we too were responsible for doing something about this conflict in expectations, because we had been given the opportunity of acquiring a more direct knowledge of the needs of the young people, their patterns of association and expectations, as well as the needs and limitations and potentials of the youth clubs. One of our functions was to attempt the reconciliation of these conflicts by attempting to interpret each side to the other and to suggest possibilities for contact and service within the willingness and ability of each side to understand.

Our co-operation with youth leaders worked in several ways. On one occasion Mary helped in a boys' club. Although her main job was to make contact with girls, she tried to help the boys, the volunteers, and the club leader to see what the girls wanted and how they could help to provide it. At another time, as previously described, we used a room in a boys' club to work with the group of younger boys, three of whom had been successfully helped to join and stay in that club. Among other things, we attempted to give the group a taste of club life from the inside, and to help the club leader to see the problems that his programme would have to face if his club should help this type of boy. The leader accepted wild behaviour, rudeness, damage and theft in an effort to accommodate us. Another leader allowed us to work in his club with boys who were sometimes in, sometimes out. We were able to co-operate with the leader and the management committee in working out a modification of the club programme in order to provide the setting needed by some of the boys.

It became apparent to us that a variety of types of youth work were necessary to meet the different needs of different kinds of young people in the neighbourhood. Youth leaders in the area recognised this too. We were in agreement that the project's function was to provide facilities for the unattached, and that except for individual cases and also for the one open youth club, the youth leaders' function was to provide facilities for the numerous young people who were prepared to participate in traditional club programme.

Other agencies

Our co-operation with other agencies was spasmodic, and mainly in relation to the needs of a particular individual at a particular time. These contacts included school teachers and officials, children's officers, welfare workers, the family service unit, mental health officers, almoners, psychiatric social workers and the clergy. At one time we thought of trying to get a psychiatric social worker to work with us on the stall to act as a bridge between several of the 'seriously disorganised' young people and the treatment agencies, but we found that both lack of funds and our inability to state the problem within the terms of reference of the professional outlook of the psychiatric social workers made this impossible. We were able to get one boy to a youth consultation centre in north London, but he would not return after a second visit. We agreed that a field-worker should visit the centre in the boy's place in the hope of his being able to work more effectively with the boy as a result.

This pattern in our work with community agencies included three variations. We tried to support the work of an agency, as in the case of the probation officers. We tried to help the agency offer the service within the network from the stall, as with the youth employment service. We attempted to go into the agency with the young people as we did in the case of the youth clubs, acting as a bridge between the young people and the agency, interpreting the limitations, problems and potentials of each to the other. If this worked at least to some extent, we withdrew, allowing the contact to develop on its own.

Jumbo was always available to back up an agency in its suggestions, to support the young people in attempting to take up the service offered, or to pick a boy up again at the stall if he had 'broken off' with his probation officer, or the youth employment officer, or had left the youth club. He would then begin again, without reference to the boy's failure to use the help offered.

Indigenous leaders

We worked at first within the network of the unattached and their families and friends, and later within the network of the statutory and voluntary bodies whose services were needed by the young people. There was a third network, that of the indigenous leaders and autonomous groups, within the neighbourhood. They were as important as the network of established community agencies, in that they offered a 'natural' service needed and used by the young people. We should have been helping and supporting them but never got around to doing so. A café proprietor and his wife knew and cared for the young people. He helped with finding jobs and talked to the boys about trying to keep them. She talked with the girls and allowed the younger girls to use the café on a Saturday morning when it wasn't open, so that they could practise dancing. He had on occasion given a reference for a boy in court. This was early in the field-work before we recognised the full significance of their work. They had so much trouble with groups from the outside, breaking in and breaking up the café, that they closed. If this had happened later in the project we might have seen our way clear to giving them a detached worker to help in their work with the young people, in much the same way as we put a youth worker in a youth club.

The fish and chip shop proprietor, the shoemaker, the newsagent, and a dozen other indigenous adult leaders whom the young people knew and accepted, should have been helped to do a better job. Some way should have been found to pass on the necessary help and support to them.

7. The final months

During the last year of the project our main concern was to prepare for our gradual withdrawal from the neighbourhood, and at the same time to carry on the necessary programme.

As it turned out this termination phase of the work was much more important than we had anticipated. Despite our determination from the very beginning of the enquiry to 'make termination a part of the day-to-day operation in the field', we left the whole process until much too late because we did not appreciate either its full significance or the amount of work and kind of knowledge and skill it would require.

Facing the problem

In the early stages of the work we saw the problem of termination mostly in terms of the moral responsibility we had incurred by developing relationships between the young people and the detached workers. During the opening months of the final phase of the field work it became clear to us that our responsibility was indeed a much larger one. We needed not only to pass on individual and groups but to pass on, if possible, actual sections of the functioning programme to other community agencies. We had to interpret to the agencies concerned, that they could do what we were doing, in the way we were doing it.

We had to see termination not simply as 'withdrawing from the community without letting the young people down', but as an exercise in community organisation as well, and it was during this phase that we no longer saw the problem merely as one of contacting and working with the unattached, but understood that work with the unattached and work with the community agencies were two halves of a single complex problem.

We were not prepared for the task in terms of the time it would take, the work it would involve (meetings, conferences) or the skill and knowledge it would require. But as a result of our work with the community the following programmes of service were developed by agencies to serve our contacts after our withdrawal.

1. A hostel for unattached boys.
2. A special worker from the Family Service Unit to work with 'seriously disorganised' boys.
3. The acceptance of one of our boys' groups by the social council of a neighbouring borough, with a detached worker programme.
4. Continuation of the girls' probation group under the sponsorship of a community-based committee.
5. The addition of a specially designed programme for the unattached in one of the neighbourhood youth clubs.
6. A committee of concern for unattached girls.
7. The operation of the coffee stall by a voluntary group (temporary).

The group work in the final months

Peter and Marian reopened the club premises at the beginning of the third year (September 1962) for those young people who requested it. Attempts were made to see which of the original management group wished to continue.

Dan was no longer interested and by this time was moving round, with a large following, into coffee bars, commercial clubs and dance halls. Gerry moved out to meet Dan. If we had been continuing the field-work Gerry would have helped Dan to find a place to begin again, since the experience he already had in the running of the dances made it almost certain that he would have been able to start again and develop a self-programming youth facility in the community. As it was, Gerry spent his time with Dan and his group helping them to make contacts with people who might be able to help them—a vicar with an empty church hall, the borough youth officer, commercial club managements. He helped Dan and his group to state their case, and helped the people contacted to see the need and to appreciate the group's sense of responsibility.

Meantime Reg, Frank and their groups, with a few other boys and girls on the fringes, talked of having a good 'club' with table tennis, darts, and billiards. They wanted to redecorate the premises and run dances again. The groups and individuals could not co-operate, destroyed their own work, stole their own record players, argued, fought, agreed again and started again. Reg and Frank had seen the possibilities of the club under Dan's leadership, but did not have the social skills to achieve the same success on their own, nor were they yet able to use us to help them achieve it. Nonetheless, we went on, offering suggestions, providing the premises and some of the money, and supporting them in their effort to 'go it on their own'. Numerous outings were arranged in which many groups and individuals participated. During all this the personal service aspect of the work continued—jobs, courts, probation, problems with family, friends and boy/girl relationships, were still a sizeable part of the work involved.

As was usual in this neighbourhood the girls had played little or no part in the split-up of the group, but were 'penalised' nonetheless, since it was only within a well-run dance atmosphere that they had the opportunities they wanted, to meet together and to meet the boys in a relatively ordered environment, and they missed it. But Marian was there to pick up the pieces and was able, now that she knew most of the girls, to go out with them and meet some of them in the girls' premises.

Eventually Frank and his friends attended only occasionally and preferred to spend some of their time at the coffee stall, and to join in with "whatever was going on". Two of the five boys in this group left it, and settled down in regular jobs, joined other groups and found girl friends. Frank was left with two other boys, and all three returned to excessive dependence on Jumbo. Peter concentrated his work on Reg and his group, continuing to meet with them in the premises, and joining them on outings. He went round the public houses with them, and it was during these days that the idea of a film emerged.

A film group

Going to cinemas was naturally a regular activity throughout the three years of field-work. It gave us the opportunity to draw small friendship groups together, to break up larger ones into three or four person groups (just for the evening) in order to get to know individual boys and girls better. Most of the young people had been avid cinema goers long before our arrival, and we saw the small cinema group as offering innumerable and invaluable opportunities for us to take part in discussions about values and standards that arose naturally and spontaneously during or just after most films. Sex, money, the law, marriage and family life, why people commit crimes, why governments behave as they do, were all possible points for discussion when related directly to the experience of seeing a film in which these were elements, actually or inferred in the plot and the action. It was often the occasion for the worker to state his own values and standards about murder, sex, the law, marriage and family, in support of what had happened in a film or in contradiction of it.

Reg and eight of his group arranged with Peter, in one of their efforts to 'keep the club going' to have a film show in the premises. This was a show for a limited number, and afterwards Peter attempted to get the group to discuss the film. They found it difficult to do so. But Peter felt from their comments that they might be interested to have more film shows and even to make their own film. He consulted a film director who agreed to co-operate and if the group asked for it, to help them make a film. The group then went to see the film *This Sporting Life*, after which they met the director, and in discussion decided to have a series of film shows. The first films were *Rififi* and *The Killing* and were shown in private houses. In discussions following the films, a "film of our own" was demanded. The group agreed to go to the National Film theatre for private showings of several films before deciding what their own film would be about. These included *My Darling Clementina*, *Singing in the Rain*, *Les Quatre Cents Coups*, *The Saturday Men*, *Kanal* and others. Meantime the group went to see the film director on several occasions to discuss their own film and script.

They decided that the film was to be about themselves and their various everyday activities—meeting, talking, drinking in a public house, picking up girls, going to a dance, starting a 'rumble'. By this time they were able to discuss techniques as well as plots and action. The film making lasted several months with discussion during the week and 'shooting' at weekends. Since the end of the project, the film has been completed and shown to an audience.

The cinema programme at the National Film Theatre and the making of their own film that followed it, was an important incident in our field-work. This was not principally because it kept Reg and his group together until we could find a place for them and some adult help with which to build again, for we could probably have found other ways of doing this. It was because it highlighted once again the crucial importance of finding ways of helping this type of youngster to develop a 'language' in which to express feelings about self and society, and in so doing to create an occasion for stating to themselves and others, what they wanted and how best they thought it could be obtained, as well as providing the kind of informal situation in which this could happen.

The holiday

Before the film had got under way, Reg and his group had begun to talk of holidays. Jumbo was taking three boys from the stall to Scotland the following summer and Reg and his group talked of Spain, the South of France and Naples as places where there was sun, and girls. Their first idea was to get assistance from the Y.W.C.A. on a *per capita* basis so that the numbers could be overquoted and those who did go would reap the benefit. Peter had to produce a letter from the Y.W.C.A. making it clear that tickets would have to be produced before a grant was made. They arranged to have the dormobile so that they would avoid the expense of a hotel. The aim of the holiday was never just to camp. The whole idea was that this would be an enjoyable holiday, with the same kind of activities as they enjoyed at home, drinking, dancing and girls.

In the event, everyone enjoyed a trouble-free holiday, except for Reg who could not go as he was sent to prison for a brief period at that time. It is possible that his absence was one reason for the lack of serious incidents. After the first week of drinking and looking for girls, the group members said they were fools to be wasting their money, and might just as well be at home, so they started to spend time on the beach, swimming and rock-climbing. They came home with a real sense of achievement, to make plans for a holiday in Spain the next year.

Intensive work with girls

The final year of the project gave the two female workers, Marian and Susan, the opportunity for the first time to work with the same girls over a longer period. Marian worked with girls of fifteen years and over, while Susan worked mainly with the girls of thirteen and fourteen years originally referred by the probation officer.

Marian, in her work with the older girls had three main functions. She worked alongside any male project worker who was working with a mixed group, she was able to offer more intensive help to some girls within the mixed group, and she worked with several girls who had difficulties in making relationships or in joining any group.

When working alongside a male worker, Marian could be in the boys' premises, or on outings, where she supported the girls and acted as a bridge between the boys and girls. She now knew the rules of the game and was able to support a girl without the boys feeling that the girl was "demanding too much or going too far". She also knew the boys well and they now accepted her and did not resent her intervention on behalf of the girls as they had done earlier during her attempts to work with girls in a mixed group. Marian was able to be a go-between without raising the anxiety or hostility of either party, and to avoid giving the boys reason to take out any misgivings they might have, on the girls concerned. But in her work with the girls Marian was rarely able to change the boys' attitudes. A boy's status among his mates often depended on how he treated girls. Any change in this would have meant changed status among his mates, which was more than could be accepted.

Within the larger grouping of girls, Marian was constantly looking out for girls who needed more intensive help. This was not as simple as it was with the boys, who were quicker to ask for, or even demand help once they knew and accepted the worker. Marian often had to spend many weeks just chatting and being around before she could encourage a girl to talk about herself. Sometimes it turned out that she needed a new job, sometimes help with a drinking problem, but most frequently help with boy/girl relationships, especially when sexual intercourse was part of the relationship. The problem could be that a girl was unable to get a boyfriend, or had difficulties in having too many. It could be that parents disapproved of a boyfriend, or that she envied her girl friends, or they envied her. A few girls were going steady for long periods with boys who seemed 'seriously disorganised,' with the result that they were often acutely unhappy. In such relationships girls often had to take a good deal of violence and brutal exploitation. Although the boys seemed to talk much more about sex, it appeared to be a greater problem for the girls. They were often confused about how to behave, about the contrast between parental expectations and those of the neighbourhood, as well as about knowing who was to be pleased. In this situation it was difficult for Marian to know how best to help the girls. The one thing however which none of these outside expectations seemed to take into account, was that a girl had feelings and emotions, with which she had to deal. It was in recognising this that Marian was usually able to begin to help.

There were several pregnancies among the girls, and these on the whole were taken as a matter of course. Sometimes the boy and girl married and sometimes they did not. One girl was seven months pregnant before her parents knew about it. They ignored the pregnancy, and her boyfriend did not allow her to go to the clinic or seek any kind of help. She was his, and "it's my kid". On the other hand it was at these times that a girl's friends became very supporting, and even if only for one evening at a time, would move closer together as a group. Marian's help had to be extremely practical, and she was able to talk with boy friends, parents, welfare workers, doctors, youth employment officers, and neighbours, attempting to act as a bridge between a girl and the adults in the environment in which she was having the difficulties. As Marian became accepted as a person to whom one could talk freely, and a person who could give practical help, each girl developed an individual relationship with her, which meant her telephoning or demanding help or outings at any time. Marian had to extend her service beyond sharing in the mixed activities, indoors and outdoors, and to meet with one, two, or three girls on different occasions.

This work linked up with another of Marian's functions in her work with girls. There were three girls remaining, from the five fifteen-year-olds who had been referred by the probation officer, and there were two or three others with whom she had made contact, but who had never been in a group. These girls had more serious difficulties in making relationships. They demanded almost an exclusive worker/girl relationship in which to work out their problems, and objected to Marian's meeting several at one time. Marian went along with this, and in between working with the larger mixed group, she would meet girls individually or take two to a dance, three to a jazz club, two to a restaurant, one to an art class, two for a drive. Several of these meetings could happen within one evening. At the same time, Marian let it be known that she was in the girls' premises on the same night every week. For months two to four girls came, although they were often different girls.

It was the suggestion of a holiday which brought nine girls together to meet regularly for several weeks. Two girls suggested the holiday, and discussed the chances of going abroad. In the interests of economy a working holiday was suggested, and a voluntary group was able to make arrangements for a fortnight in a work camp in the South of France. In the preparation for the trip, difficulties over money, saving fares and finding the right clothes for everyone, presented problems which required and brought about the full and interested participation of each girl. The attitude of adults interested in the trip, and the other young people in the neighbourhood gave the group confidence and a feeling of importance. It was when the group found itself in strange surroundings, and within a large international group, that the slenderness of the ties between the girls showed itself in tensions and dissensions. They were unable to form a united front, and to support each other in the confrontation with strangers. Towards the end of the fortnight several girls had learned to adjust to the situation and to enjoy the contacts with other individuals and groups. Marian had to support, protect and encourage the others throughout the holiday. Even so, the girls returned with a sense of achievement, and suggestions for returning the following year. The group continued to meet regularly for some weeks, and eventually several of the girls were able to join evening classes, art classes, and other groups without too much difficulty.

The younger girls' group

During this same period, the last year of the field-work, Susan continued her work with the girls' probation group, which Mary had begun earlier in the project. This was the group of thirteen girls all of whom were under fourteen when they joined the group. The girls came from large families, most of which were multi-problem families known to the Family Service Unit or other welfare agencies, and mostly living in cramped inadequate flats, five, seven or nine people in two or three rooms. Almost all the girls in the group were known to the probation officers. Some had been in court for stealing and others for non-attendance at school. Each member of the group had some problems in her family, and usually with teachers and other adults too. The group included two pairs of sisters and one set of three sisters. Most of the group members had difficulty in their relationships, and the rivalries between the sisters added to the tensions in the group.

During the first few weeks in the club, the girls were very quiet. They were delighted with the premises (a shop and back room) and spent their time sewing, making coffee and trying out different kinds of handwork. Very soon, as they relaxed in the new premises, they realised that they were not forced to 'do' anything, nor were they told to be quiet. The activities became individual, washing hair, cooking, sewing, playing records, making-up, or cleaning. At the same time they almost ran amok. They argued, fought, broke equipment, stole from each other and from Susan. One girl Jean remained completely withdrawn, and two or three others joined in only occasionally. But almost all the girls demanded Susan's individual attention constantly. Susan tried to make sure that everyone got attention, provided diversions, and intervened only to prevent physical harm.

It was during this period that the girls showed their anxiety about the club. "Will we come next week?" "You will be here won't you?" "Is this a club for bad girls?" "Do you like us, Susan?" "You won't go away Susan?" Susan arranged a series of fortnightly trips and outings. The girls made lists of all the places they would like to visit, and after much argument would choose one. They wanted all the outings at once and apparently found it difficult to believe that they would continue meeting long enough to cover all the expeditions. When they went out, they were at first extremely nervous, but as they became experienced they became wilder, and Susan allowed them to take the consequences of their behaviour from bus conductors and other officials.

The meetings and outings began to give the group an identity. They talked of "belonging to a club", and "not missing the club". The club never had a name—it was just "The Club". The group was recognised as a group by cinema attendants, by conductors, or fun fair managers and the public. The 'outside world' made the girls draw closer together in mutual support and some of their hostile behaviour was directed outside the group instead of to each other.

Even with the growing recognition of a group identity, and even though the physical fighting decreased, the tensions within the group continued. Christmas came, and for the first time everyone worked together making decorations and preparing the tree. But afterwards the fighting and arguments started up again, and Susan arranged one or two special trips as a new year diversion.

One evening Susan put on a Mozart record and a few girls began to mime and dance to it. This led to the idea of acting and the group divided into two parts, and made up and acted plays. Susan and Jean were the appreciative audience. The older group acted out mainly imaginary incidents in the neighbourhood, in which sex played a prominent part. The younger group acted hospital and family episodes. For a whole year (this group continued one year after the project ended) acting, miming, singing and modelling played a prominent part in the activities, and the girls were gradually able to compete with, judge, and applaud each other.

Meantime Susan experimented in taking out the two sub groups separately on different types of expeditions. The older group after their acting, were able to discuss sex problems with her, and to ask direct questions, which brought many of their fears into the open. Some months later, this same group became anxious to meet boys, and began to use the club as an assembly point. The interest in boys resulted in new tensions between parents, daughters and the club. Susan, after long discussions with parents was given permission to take the older group to a mixed youth club, and spent evenings there with them, but only one girl was prepared to return without the group.

The behaviour of all the girls within the group began to change. They became interested in the premises, in keeping them clean, in planning meals, in buying the food, in cooking, and in cleaning up. They were able to plan their outings, to reach decisions and to decide what was fair and what was not.

Although in the early stages they had asked constantly for more money, more food, more gifts, more time, more outings, now after a year, they were able to accept limits with arguments from only one or two. Whereas stealing from each other, from the club and from Susan, and in public places was a problem for Susan for twelve months, it slowly disappeared within the club without comment. After a holi-day, when they spent a week by the sea, meeting by day and staying with different families by night, the girls came back to the club as a closely knit group. They were able to co-operate, to enjoy their programmes without too much argument, to plan ahead, and to talk freely about themselves, their problems and their ideas. They depended very much on the support of the group, and instead of talking only about "the club", would talk at home, at school and to probation officers about "my friends". At the time of this report the 'friendships' have lasted almost two years.

It was a few months later (after the main project had ended) that new tensions arose, this time between the older and younger group. Susan asked if they would like to meet as separate groups, and with very little comment they agreed. The separation caused no difficulties. The older group, five in number, started out on an 'adult' programme —expeditions to restaurants and to clubs, dressmaking, or just playing records and talking. They became a unit that moved around together whether or not Susan was present. The younger group accepted new members, and although they were still interested in expeditions, for the first time they became interested in children's and party games.

During this whole period the attendance of the girls was very regular, and only two girls left the club. The first girl moved away from the district, and she was the only girl to be in trouble with the police again. The second girl appeared to be 'seriously disorganised', and to have many more problems than the others. Eventually the hostility towards her was so strong that Susan had to suggest her leaving. When she did so, some of the tension in the group dis-appeared. Susan spent time separately with her and was consulted constantly by her welfare officer. Finally, on the basis of her not going to school, she was taken to a children's home. She enjoyed being there and although she found school attendance difficult. Susan visited her regularly, and on her return several months later she was accepted into the older girls' group without difficulty.

As this programme for girls on probation developed, the role of the worker developed too. At first, she had to get to know the indi-vidual girls in the group, accepting their demands in their relation-ships with her, and recognising that they must be individual. Secondly, she had to help them in their relationships with each other using both conflict and co-operation in the process. Thirdly, she had to offer a setting in which the group could develop a positive identity in its own eyes. Fourthly, she had to help each girl to come to terms more realistically with her own problems, through the girl's relationship with the worker, and through her association in activities with the other girls.

Within this context the worker had to know when to set limits, for sometimes the girls were afraid of their own behaviour, when to leave a decision to the group, and when to help them make one. She had to know when to allow conflict and when to create a diversion, when to support an individual and when to support the group, when to suggest a particular activity and when to abandon one. She had to remind herself constantly that her first priority was that of a group worker. The problems of the girls were so intense and so numerous that she could easily have become a case-worker, thus intensifying her own relationship with a girl in preference to helping the girl in relationships with her peers. This recognition of her function helped her co-operate more realistically with the probation officers and other welfare workers who worked with the girls individually, and her own identity as a group worker became recognised by other agencies as she did so.

Even so, her function as a group worker did not limit her work to group meetings. First she was able to help girls in their relationships within the group by meeting them in ones, twos, threes and fours outside the group. She did this in order to encourage friendships, to help girls support each other, and to have more opportunities to discuss problems. She also used this to help the girls to see for themselves that they were individuals. They could see that although she didn't have 'favourites' she could still behave differently towards each girl. Gradually a girl understood that although she would not have one particular 'treat', she would have a different one.

The worker was also concerned about the girls' relationships at home and at school. She visited all the homes regularly and knew mothers and sometimes fathers very well indeed. She had to accept hostility from the parents on occasions, when a mother was wary of the worker's relationship with her daughter, or when a father blamed "the club" for his daughter's behaviour. But on the whole the mothers welcomed her as a visitor, and were glad to have the opportunity of expressing their own fears and worries. The worker was frequently able to act as a bridge between mother and daughter, and to a small extent help strengthen their relationships with each other.

School was the most difficult problem, and the worker spent time talking to teachers, and sometimes taking girls to school herself. But it remained a problem for most girls throughout the project. Several were able to attend more regularly but at least two were in court a second time for non-attendance, although the probation officer stretched her powers to the limit to prevent it. One girl said "If only we could have small classes like the club".

After eighteen months there were changes in all the girls. The most obvious was in Jean, the girl who had been completely withdrawn. She was now able to attend school fairly regularly. She could visit the probation officer alone. She could act and sing in front of the group, could argue and defend herself, had several friends including a boyfriend, and had taken a new girl who was withdrawn, under her wing. Out of doors the behaviour of the group had quietened down, and girls checked each other if they behaved 'badly'. They now reminded themselves of the early days "Do you remember when we used to fight?" "Do you remember . . . ?" and laugh at their earlier behaviour. The problems at home were still numerous but the group, their status and the new experiences seemed to have given them a bit more strength to cope with them. The comments about leaving home were not quite so strong or so frequent. Two mothers were now meeting regularly and supporting each other. The parents came to accept the club as helpful instead of showing hostility towards it as several had formerly done.

Termination-individuals

During the final phase of the field-work we met regularly in staff conference, to review systematically each individual contact and to read the records of work with groups, in order to assess the ongoing help needed for the young people and to find ways of providing it for them. It was during this series of staff conferences that we developed the categories, *can copes*, *temporarily disorganised*, *simply disorganised*, and *seriously disorganised*. It was as a result of these discussions of the needs of individuals and groups that we were able to develop some idea of the kinds of the help that would be needed for the different types of young people, once we had withdrawn.

The first priority was to find continuing help for the 'seriously disorganised' boys who numbered about seven (and included Frank and his two friends). They needed and would take continued intensive support, and would continue to need a worker almost to themselves. There were several others who appeared to be almost as 'seriously disorganised' but who would not take and could not use intensive support. They would show up for the occasional informal chat and ask for advice and information. We thought that an intensive relationship might be possible for them after a long period. The second priority was to find a continued point of contact that would offer for the boys in the other categories ('temporarily' and 'simply disorganised'), 'emergency help and support' above and beyond whatever provision for recreational service could be provided in the community after our withdrawal.

The Family Service Unit

We attempted to meet these needs in the following ways. First, we consulted the Family Service Unit, with whom we were already co-operating in some of the field-work related to family casework. We explored the possibility of their using the approach that they were now using with families, to reach out and support the 'seriously disorganised' individual young person, work with whom might or might not involve the Family Service Unit with the whole family.

After discussing a number of individual cases and considering the various pros and cons, the Family Service Unit decided to allocate a special worker to work with the seven 'seriously disorganised' boys who could use and would accept continued support. We created circumstances in which these boys could get to know the Family Service Unit worker, to accept him and the service he could offer, and then we set about transferring the relationships. For a while some of these boys had two workers helping them with work, probation, police, and family problems, until they could accept the same help from the Family Service Unit worker that they had received from the project worker. For a while this was a delicate situation since the boys tended to play the workers off against one another—not entirely a bad thing since it gave both workers a new dimension of contact with the boy.

The hostel

The second provision was a neighbourhood hostel to help with the ever recurring problem of the boy thrown out of his home for the weekend, or the one who had left home for several weeks, or the boy who returned from the approved school, Borstal, a construction job in the North, or a stretch at sea, and found that his home was not ready for him, or that he did not want to go back to it. We had sometimes provided lodging ourselves (in the homes of staff members), and the probation officers with whom we worked often talked to us about the need in this neighbourhood for short-term accommodation.

Basic to our idea of a hostel for short-term accommodation was (a) that it should be neighbourhood-based so that the boys could continue in their present employment, or seek employment under familiar circumstances and in familiar ways, keep up their friendships, and be near their homes and in contact with their families and neighbourhood; (b) that it should have an open-door policy so that the relatives and friends of the boys in residence could visit them, have the occasional meal, and talk to the warden and other adults concerned; (c) that the hostel could be a point of contact for the 'seriously disorganised' who could, or would, not take up the offer of intensive help from the Family Service Unit, but who would be more likely to 'drop into the hostel for a chat' in much the same way that they showed up at the coffee stall for a chat.

In short the hostel was to be more a type of boarding house in the neighbourhood than 'an institution'—a bed and breakfast hostel linked as closely as possible to the boy's roots in the neighbourhood, and linked as closely as possible to the services of the voluntary and statutory bodies who would have the opportunity to offer their services in its informal atmosphere. This we hoped would be especially helpful for the youth employment officers, the probation officers, and psychiatric social workers.

The chairman of the local council of social service was approached. She gave her support immediately. A committee was formed which included the senior probation officer, the youth employment officer, the director of the Family Service Unit, the chairman of the council of social service, Jumbo and at first, the project administrator and consultant.

A young people's hostel association is now in operation, and has purchased a house which has beds for fourteen boys and a lounge for informal contact with the non-resident boys in the neighbourhood. Jumbo has been appointed warden. This has meant that some of the relationships with 'seriously disorganised' young people, whom we were not able to pass on to the Family Service Unit were not disrupted. He is now beginning a programme of open evenings at the hostel, for boys who want and need help, but who otherwise might have remained unserved after our withdrawal.

Termination—groups

Our third priority was to find ways of providing help, after our withdrawal, for groups which had formed within the coffee stall network as a result of our presence. We saw of as special importance the needs of Dan and his followers, of Reg and his group, and of several fringe and younger groups.

A neighbouring social council
and Dan's group

First there was Dan's group which Gerry was supporting in its attempts to establish its own club. In his search for adults who would help this group, Gerry met a detached worker, Jack, who had recently been employed by a social council in a neighbouring borough, as a result of their concern for the unattached. Dan and some of his followers lived across the borders, and it was agreed that Jack should start his work with this group. We met with members of the council several times, exchanged ideas and discussed possible approaches. Gerry then introduced Jack to Dan, and both Gerry and Jack met with the group until it recognised that Jack was acceptable and would be able to help them. The social council is now responsible for the group which is running a successful youth café on its own.

The youth club, the younger boys
and Reg's group

During the final year John, a theological student released to work
in the project for a year, made contact with all the younger boys from
Peter's original group, and with some of the fringe groups who had
attended the boys' premises regularly. They frequented coffee bars on
some evenings and visited a youth club on others. Peter had been
given permission to work with the boys in and out of the youth club,
and John was able to continue this work. He took boys on several
trips around London, or in the dormobile, spent many hours in the
coffee bar, and played billiards or table tennis with them in the club.
He continued to offer personal service to the boys, and occasionally to
girls within these groups.

Meantime, Peter and Reg and his group having returned from holiday were preparing enthusiastically to complete their film and wonder-
ing where they could meet. They had now become a more closely
knit group, and Peter hoped to find someone who would help them
to continue as a group.

It was at this stage that the situation worsened in the open club
where John was helping. More and more of each night was taken up
with fights at the door, breaking equipment in the club, and finally a
series of break-ins, after which the club was closed. The boys who
could have used a traditional club programme, but were not willing
to stand for continual chaos had left long ago. These events were
interpreted by the leader and committee as a failure in working with
young people, and yet the young people returned again and again.
This was the one club which was willing to provide facilities for the
non-conforming boys, and had been able to work with them for long
periods. The problem seemed to be that of confused expectations. The
leader and committee wanted very much to open their doors to the
young people who most needed them. At the same time they felt
pressured to expect the kind of programme and behaviour in the club
which were unrealistic for the kind of young people they were
attracting.

It became possible for our problems and the club's problems to
be discussed by the club's management committee and ourselves. We
agreed that Peter, John and Marian should move into the club premises
with their groups for three months, during which time some of the
difficulties could be discussed.

The idea was put to Reg, that his group could use the club premises.
It was received with caution, but they moved in, enjoyed using it as
a meeting place on four nights a week, and delayed making any
effort to attract more young people.

The girls were not welcomed in the premises, and eventually

Marian retreated with the girls to the girls' premises to await an opening of the club for dances, when they would return. The younger boys wandered in and out of the club, and eventually left it altogether and joined another youth club. Here they disrupted the club programme to such an extent that the leader came to see us after the project had ended, to ask for suggestions.

Meantime, we discussed the following points with members of the club management committee.

1. The kind of programme most likely to attract and keep this type of young person was an informal programme with less organised activity, a programme in which a good deal of activity was outside the premises, in the neighbourhood, or in the larger community; a programme which put less emphasis on payment of subs, on registration, on regular attendance, on club loyalty and formal participation.

2. The obstacles that the management committee of the club could see in introducing such a programme were that they would need to explain spending money on things that did not look like 'activities', especially if they were outside the premises. They would need to find ways of explaining to their supporters why they thought this was a job they should be doing at all. They would need to consider whether or not working in this way would lower standards for work with 'attached young people'.

3. We had to consider the kind of help we could offer—support and supervision to the new leader if necessary; a part-time girls' leader seconded for a few months; our two male workers to overlap with the new leader for a period; partial subsidy of the activities until the committee was able to find the necessary financial support; help in interpreting the need for this kind of work, and the problems to be faced in doing it, to present and potential club supporters.

4. The management committee had to consider the implications of taking on a leader who was willing and able to work both inside and outside of the club, and of giving him as much support as possible in thinking out the criteria for work with the unattached.

In the end it was decided that the management committee would take on a club leader who agreed to attempt both aspects of the programme and that we for a short period would provide a woman leader (half-time) and a male leader (full-time), some financial assistance, and supervision and support for the club leader. At the time of writing this report, the club is functioning, having had structural alterations and redecoration, carried out by the boys with the support of a new leader, and a part-time woman leader. Reg and his group, some fringe groups and younger boys, together with some of Marian's contacts among the girls are using the club and the leaders. The final sequence of the film was completed in the club premises, and holidays are being planned for Spain and a resort in this country.

A contact point

Even though we hoped that this club would provide a meeting point for the unattached we realised that it would be only one of the meeting points, to be used either temporarily or alongside the use of other places. The mobility of the new leader would be an asset for the young people, but there would be need for other contact points. There were also other 'temporarily' or 'simply disorganised' young people within the coffee stall network for whom help should be available if and when they needed it.

At first we thought of trying to get a community agency to take over the stall as an information centre. We contacted the Citizens' Advice Bureau hoping they might see their way clear to operating the stall, not in order to continue our full programme, but simply to offer the young people an advice service geared to meet their needs. They were unable to do this. The Citizens' Advice Bureau in the community was already overtaxed. Finally the stall was taken over by the voluntary group, which had worked with some of the young people within the project, helping them arrange expeditions, camping trips and holidays. They were prepared to use the stall to offer information to the unattached about interesting and adventurous activities, and to help them carry out these activities.

A committee of concern

At this point, we saw the value of a 'committee of concern' about the unattached in this community, which would consist of those statutory and voluntary bodies who had a direct interest or definite concern in the problem. We felt this would offer a solution to two problems. Firstly it would keep in contact the various community agencies that had been involved in the field-work, some of whom had taken up parts of the programme, and secondly it would provide a discussion group that could think about and plan future work with the un-attached.

We discussed the idea with colleagues in the community who felt it was not yet the right time for the agencies concerned to come together in this way. The agencies taking up parts of the programme would have to think out and evaluate their own efforts separately before they would be in a position to come together to think out anything more broadly conceived. Also the community as a whole was perhaps not yet ready to see more effort going into this particular social service. This was not surprising considering the extreme pressure on the existing services in this particular neighbourhood. In the end we were able only to help set the stage for a possible coming together of those concerned at a later date.

The special concern for girls

Towards the end of the project field-work we became more concerned about the girls than about the boys. We had been able to arrange for some continuing help for the boys, but we realised that gaps in meeting the needs of girls were greater than those of the boys.

The girls' need for personal service was equal to that of the boys but the behaviour of the boys frequently made their needs appear more obvious. Their proximity to violence, to petty crime, and their ability to dramatise their needs, was supported by the neighbourhood's system of values that encouraged the boys to see their needs as more pressing and more important than those of the girls. The girls' problems seemed to be non-attendance at school, occasionally drinking, problems in relationships, particularly with boys. They were 'quiet problems' in the sense that the girls tended to accept them almost as inevitable. It is possible that in some instances, they had grown to expect the adults in their environment to see the problems as unimportant. It took us a long time to make contact with enough girls to allow us to assess the problem, and to develop relationships with them which could provide us with the information on which to base a programme. This delayed our ability to assess how we could arrange continuing help for them.

Girls of fourteen and over moved around in twos and threes, sometimes sharing their problems with a close friend, sometimes keeping them to themselves. Their main preoccupation seemed to be that of finding boys. They moved around in the fringes of the boys' groups within the coffee stall network, attaching themselves for short periods to one group of boys and then moving on to another. Sometimes they went to dance halls and sometimes to the youth clubs in the neighbourhood for dances. One boys' club leader volunteered the information that the girls were invited in only because the boys wanted them and the management thought it might be a good idea to "have them in occasionally". The girls had come to accept that the clubs were for boys and that the leaders were for the boys as well. "Even where they let you in when there isn't a dance, they only do boys' things." Personal help, group activities, opportunities for interesting things to do were difficult for a girl to find unless she had initiative and strong support from her family and friends. This was rare as the values and standards of the neighbourhood did not recognise initiative on the part of the girls in these matters as being 'the right thing'.

The probation officers recognised the value of our younger girls' group, which offered the opportunity of doing interesting things in a small group where individual attention was a priority. We felt that it should be continued, not only for this reason, but because of the information it was likely to provide at a later date about the needs of this type of young girl and possible methods of helping her. We felt that this would be useful to other community agencies working with the same type of girls as well as to those working with less 'seriously disorganised' young girls.

The older girls too had to be considered. There were many in the coffee stall grouping and on its fringes. We agreed that they needed a great deal of support and help and that this could well start within the youth clubs they visited. We were already working with one of these clubs, helping them to rethink their programme to meet the needs of the unattached boys and we supplied Marian to continue work with these girls who would sooner or later follow the boys into the club. We saw this as did the club leader and the management committee, not only as an opportunity to do mixed work with the unattached but as an attempt to build a job for a female worker whom the club would provide once we had withdrawn. But even then we were aware of the almost pitiful progress we were making in finding continuing help for the girls.

During the last months of the project, we approached several agencies concerned with girls. The chairman of the council of social service agreed to call together a group of women to form a committee of concern for girls. Those who came included probation officers, a youth employment officer, a headmistress, a worker from the National Association for Mental Health, and representatives of the child care committee, the Moral Welfare Association, the Family Service Unit, and the Y.W.C.A.

The Y.W.C.A. agreed to provide a worker for an extra year for the younger girls group, in order to give continuity until the committee of concern could take over. Suggestions were also made for a hostel, similar to that provided for the boys, and for the employment of a detached worker based on the hostel. We hoped that in the future the work of this group would develop and become linked with agencies and individuals whose immediate concern was the boys.

The final phase

The field work of the project was due to end on August 31, 1963, but Gerry and John were the only two who had fewer responsibilities by that time, and even they continued to visit the neighbourhood occasionally or talked to the young people on the telephone. Marian continued to work part-time in the youth club until a new woman worker was appointed in January 1964. Peter worked an extra month in the youth club to support the new leader. Susan continued for an extra year with the younger girls, and Jumbo moved in for an unlimited period as warden of the hostel. Our contacts with the different community agencies who had been involved with us in the field, or who had taken over parts of our programme continued.

With the completion of the field-work project, the work entered its final phase, that of putting the records in order, and drawing out generalisations about the nature and content of field-work as a basis for a statement of the problem and of the approach and method used within the project. Finally, we had to attempt to evaluate the work and to write this report.

Chapter Three

THE PROBLEMS OF FIELD-WORK

8. The staff workers under strain

Work with people is often a great satisfaction, but at the same time it can be a strain. We were working with the young people, our colleagues in the field and our own project committee as well as with ourselves, and the kinds of strain with which we had to learn to cope were numerous. The first was simple physical weariness after being out night after night, on street corners, in cafés, public houses and on the stall, in all kinds of weather. The second was being constantly available to young people at night, and to young people and adults for personal service arrangements in the daytime. The third was the strain of working in unknown ways and having to think out most moves anew, because the rules, regulations and methods of working with the unattached were not 'given' but had to be worked out in the field. The criteria for success or failure in our work were also not established and had to be evolved from the field-work experience. The fourth kind of strain was that of constant interpretation at three levels at once, to the young people, the agencies, and the committee, and in three different 'languages', sometimes when we were not even sure ourselves of what we were doing and why.

Finally, the study had to be carried out at the same time as, and as part of, the project field-work. This meant that not only were we doing the job, but we had to document why, where, when and how we were doing it. Often all these kinds of strain were operating at the same time, and sometimes over long periods.

This section is a description of some of the particular problems with which the field-workers had to contend. The material may at first seem strange, since it is mostly concerned with the introspective detail of the worker's response to field-work events. It may seem that such matters are the concern of the individual worker, and do not need to be brought constantly into the open. A moment's consideration might suggest that even in the traditional club the same 'introspection'

takes place, in the minds of the club leaders, the management committee and even the members. But where club work is traditional, the
need to examine and use the internal happenings as well as the external
ones is not so apparent, since the language and logic of the work is
established and accepted by those concerned—the young people as
members, the leader and his assistants, the management committee,
the borough youth organiser and committee.

It is because the rules of the game in work with unattached young
people are not established and accepted, that this kind of introspective
material, and the discussion of it, is a necessary part of the development
of this approach. It is through its examination and the discussion of
its implications for the role of the worker, together with the detailed
material of objective field-work experience that agreement about the
nature of the work can best be achieved.

Learning to observe

Fundamental to the work of the project was informed observation.
All walks of life, all fields of endeavour have their preconceptions and
prejudices, which often tend to prevent the observer from seeing
'what is there'. This problem was constantly with us, especially in the
early days when it was so important that we should understand our
job. What were the needs of the young people and how did they meet
them or fail to meet them? What did they want, and what would they
accept from us? How and why should we offer it to them? What did
they reject from us and other agencies, and why?

This might seem a peculiar problem for a group of adult and
reasonably mature youth workers to have been facing at this stage,
but our experience soon showed us both as individual workers and
as a team, that we had much to learn about informed observation as
a technique in detached youth work.

The first aspect of our learning was what to observe. We began by
seeing the need to observe the young people, their behaviour, their
patterns of association, their characteristics as individuals, in groups
and as a 'class' (the unattached) in order to build up some picture of
their needs, and to consider how we could help. Although this was the
place to begin, we soon realised that it was only a small part of a much
larger field of observation.

The second aspect of our learning was how to observe. In the early
days we were concerned with unattachment simply in relation to
clubs. We gained a picture of club life in the community but this
approach seriously narrowed the range of observation, and tended to
define the problem, and so suggest the solution, in terms of degrees of
'clubability' only. This in turn tended to condition the kinds of things
we looked for in the day-to-day events in the field. Once we could see

the youth club as only one of the factors, and a very small one at that in unattachment, we were able to see the necessity of observing the larger pattern of association of the young people. This covered their relations with school, work, the neighbourhood, the larger community and especially with each other, in small friendship groups, in large recreational groups and in boy/girl relationships.

In short, we began to see the advisability of allowing the field-work events themselves to suggest the pattern of observations, by simply recording all events as they occurred, and reading, rereading and discussing the records, to see what generalisations emerged that could be guides to more informed observation. This had its drawbacks, as a mass of records was produced, a large part of which was not used. This was sometimes because we did not have sufficient skill to see their relevance, and sometimes because so much information covered factors over which we had no control. The information was noted, but could not help us in working more effectively with the young people. But, from this general observation we were able to build up a reservoir of material from which to choose the pertinent points at which further observations would be advisable. By the second year we had evolved a recording system that gave us the information necessary, not only to define our problem, but to plan the day-to-day and long-range work in the field. Of course, this was not as neatly arranged as set out here. It often went wrong for a number of reasons.

1.   At first we felt ill at ease at recording opinions as well as facts.

2.   We tried to avoid recording the social attitudes that lay behind the behaviour of individuals, groups and social institutions.

3.   Once we saw the need to record opinions, feelings and subjective material as well as facts, the fear arose that the field of observations might become too big to handle.

4.   At one point the relationship between different types of observation could not easily be seen, especially the fact that behaviour was conditioned by social attitudes which reflected values and standards. This meant that the interpretation of observation was at this point impossible except at the most elementary level.

5.   We tended to be shy of recording the effects of our own participation in events, (the documentation of which was vital,) if we were to be able to suggest methods of dealing with them.

6.   We tended to try to avoid documenting some conflict situations especially between social agencies and the young people. This was a serious difficulty because so much of the work included interpreting the needs of the young people to the agencies and vice versa.

7. Sometimes we were more concerned with the meaning of the facts for ourselves than with what they meant to the young people, the neighbourhood, or the statutory and voluntary bodies.

8. Occasionally it became an 'observation for observation's sake' routine, unrelated to the possibilities of action in the field.

9. The speed of the work was such that recording could have reached huge proportions, and workers had to choose between records for training and supervision purposes and those for the overall project.

10. Frequently when the most useful records could have been written, a worker was so involved and pressured by the crises with which he was dealing that none were written at all.

11. Sometimes if a worker appeared to become too introspective or worried, a supervisor would ask him not to record for a while.

These difficulties were resolved by the way in which we finally agreed to record the field-work and by the use we made of the records in supervision, staff training, staff conference and interpretation. Once we could see clearly how we would use the records, we were able to clarify and then handle the difficulties. The nature of our success or the extent of our failure in learning to observe in the field and to prepare this report, can perhaps be best assessed by an appraisal of this whole presentation since it is the result of three years of our recorded observation in the field.

Identity

Identity was a constantly recurring problem. We had to say repeatedly who we were and what we were doing, in terms that were acceptable to the young people, the statutory and voluntary bodies, the project committee, and ourselves. We were never able to interpret completely who we were and what we were doing to all the young people with whom we had contact. For the first six months we had to avoid any of the stereotypes in the minds of the young people, that would have made contact impossible We were not the police, not the probation service, not law-breakers on the run. Obviously we were not club leaders as we did not have a club building nor did we ask anyone to register and pay subscriptions. The coffee stall had no identity, but we were prepared to answer questions. It was months before questions were asked, mainly because everyone assumed that Jumbo owned the stall and that the new workers introduced were friends lending a hand. The Y.W.C.A. was known to give money and premises but no one knew or asked what the letters Y.W.C.A. stood for. This we saw as typical of one of the aspects of social life in that community.

They could not ask us who we were because under the rules of the game, as they played it, we in turn could then ask who they were, and information about probation, national assistance and jobs could, to their way of thinking, be legitimately solicited by us. If on the other hand they asked us no questions, we could ask them none.

It was only through day-to-day and prolonged relationships with individuals and groups, doing things together in the community, that a worker could establish an identity. Only by helping to find young people jobs, by being willing to speak to a probation officer, a court official, a teacher, a school attendance officer or housing official for a young person or his family, by being there on the corner, in the public house, in the café, and above all regularly on the stall, ready to talk, to go places, to do things together and to help, could we establish an identity that avoided stereotypes and had more than an abstract meaning for the young people.

This was both a subtle and an important aspect of the identity problem. Each worker had to be aware that if he showed he could help with, for instance, a probation problem and phoned the probation officer, met him and succeeded in getting what was interpreted as 'results' for Johnny, this same success in helping Johnny, who now accepted the worker, would keep Ken, another boy in the group, from asking the worker's help, since he would interpret the worker's ability to be successful with the probation officer, as a sign of the worker's being 'in with Them'. This would give the worker, at least temporarily, a negative identity. The same was true of working with groups. If we helped Fred's group to get into a club we might be seen as being 'in' with the club people, which Fred's group might appreciate. Keith's gang, however, with whom we were just beginning to work, would interpret this as our being in league with the club which had just expelled Pete and his gang. Timing in the unfolding of identity had to be slowly and carefully phased so that while we were becoming known 'for what we really were' to one individual or group, we were not at the same time preventing other individuals and groups from asking and taking our help.

Identity was always a more pressing problem for the worker than for the young person. The security of a title as a club leader, teacher or priest and the paraphernalia of an established institution gives so much support that it might be said that they give the worker an identity in his own eyes as much as in the eyes of the young people in the community. Endless staff conferences, supervision sessions, and informal discussions, centred on the worker's identity, and they were always resolved by reference to the basic principle of this approach: "It is the ability of the worker to make relationships with individuals and groups, that they can understand and accept, which gives him an identity." The club leader, the teacher, the caseworker, the priest, all have identities thrust upon them which both help and hinder them in making relationships. The detached worker at first has only himself.

Identity had several aspects. Firstly, in the eyes of the young people: Who is he (the worker)? Why has he come? What is he doing? How is he doing it? What can I or we get out of it all? Secondly, in the eyes of the agencies: How will his (the worker) work affect us, our members, our programme, our method of work? How can we help him? How can he help us? What is he doing that might threaten our service or our approach? Thirdly, in the eyes of the worker himself: If I am not acceptable as a club leader, or social worker, what is my identity? Fourthly, in the eyes of our own project committee: What is a detached youth worker? How does his work differ from that of a youth worker in a club or a youth centre? All these, and other aspects of the problem of identity, we came to see as soluble only in terms of the worker's function in the field. The identity of the worker in the eyes of the young people, the agencies, the project committee, his colleagues and himself, came from the practice of detached youth work, not from his function as defined by the established social institutions. The young people recognised it in terms of his usefulness to them. This identity had to be interpreted to the social agencies and the sponsoring committee in terms they understood and which were related to their needs as social institutions, which were often different from the needs of the young people. The worker's identity in his own eyes was a composite of what the young people saw him to be as a person and of what he did for them, together with what the agencies saw him to be and allowed him to do.

The interesting factor about the whole problem of identity was that it was not a problem for the young people (provided the test of being one of 'us' rather than one of 'them' had been passed). It was a problem of the worker, who wanted an identity to lean on; it was even more a problem for the committee and the agencies who felt it necessary to be "open about it", that it might "be dishonest" not to state one's identity from the very beginning. Even a partial recognition of our relation to the Y.W.C.A. enabled the committee, the agencies, our colleagues and ourselves to relax and feel that at last there was no more hide-and-seek about the work. The important fact was that it was the 'authorities' who were relieved, and not the young people, who neither understood nor particularly cared who the Y.W.C.A. was or what it did. They simply felt that it must be 'O.K.' since we (the field-work staff) were part of it. In short we gave the Y.W.C.A. its identity, not the other way round.

The need to offer ourselves

The pressing question which had to be answered before we could get on with the job was what were we offering of ourselves, and how were we to offer it? We began to clarify this question by finding out what we were not offering. It was not a full-blown relationship, like that of a parent or a friend, nor was it a relationship without limitation wherein for example young people could expect us to be party to a criminal act. It was not the type of relationship in which we knew what was best for them and would work towards helping them see this by passing on a particular political or religious outlook, moral philosophy or set of values and standards. It was not a formal teaching situation wherein we knew what games to play, which 'right and good' activities we would attempt to train them to do 'properly'.

It was instead an enabling relationship, the purposes of which were to pass on information, to pass on simple social skills, to show acceptance, and to give recognition and support. At first this was difficult for us to grasp. If we had come to help, how could we have nothing definite to give that was particularly our own—our own religion, our own particular values and standards, our own particular preferences in activities? It took a while to realise that the very things we had thought we needed to give, were already available in the club or the school or elsewhere. We needed to give ourselves in a definite and limited way, ourselves as persons in a relationship, to be used in terms of the young people's needs.

This meant that a field-worker had to develop new skills, new attitudes, and a new awareness of what he had to offer as a person rather than as a club leader, a teacher, or a recreational instructor. It meant having to interpret to the agencies and to the project committee that the real work was done in relationship between the worker and the young person, and had to be seen and judged in that context, and not in terms of the traditional pattern of youth work activities.

But the need to give oneself, and the temptation to impose or demand acceptance and conformity in the guise of giving oneself, was a continuing field-work problem even after we had come to recognise its character and to know how we should deal with it. The importance of supervision was that it should help the worker to be more objective about what he gave of himself, under what conditions he did so and for what reasons and how.

9. Mobility

It took us a long time to come to terms with the natural patterns of mobility that were woven into the life of the young people. At first we tried to stabilise small friendship groups and knit them into larger groups. For a time we attempted to plan activities and to think of ingenious ways of trying to make sure that they did take place. We worked towards helping the young people set up committees of their own, programmes of their own devising, and activities that they could accept as having been self-programmed, always with the aim in mind of slowing down what we saw to be the furious, almost frantic haste with which they jumped from place to place, activity to activity, broke dates and rearranged arrangements. We developed elaborate theories of how to increase 'stickability'. We even on occasions withdrew our leadership and support when carefully planned events which had cost time and money were abandoned before they could take place. But we soon learned that no amount of pretence about self-programming in the sense that we would suggest and guide before the event, would stabilise anything.

After long and heated staff discussions, much disappointment and discontent, we came to see that it was our own urgency about wanting something to happen that caused our difficulties. The young people were not willing to be 'advised' into anything. We had to relax and await developments and be ready to use what happened and not what we had attempted to make happen. Dances, trips, parties, cinema outings, all happened when the young people wanted them to. Our job was to suggest possibilities, show how choices among possibilities could be made, provide some of the resources, and be at their beck and call, if and when they wanted to do something.

In short we came to see that mobility was a problem not because the young people moved about too much, lost interest too quickly and changed their minds too often. It was that we had attempted to create an artificial pattern of events instead of being flexible enough to use the actual happenings, which were, once we were able to see them without preconceptions, rich, meaningful, and full of programme possibilities. In short it was within the natural events in the lives of the groups and individuals that we had to find the material from which to try to help their social development, and from which to help to construct the activities by which we hoped to achieve this. Perhaps the most important implication for the project was the need to help the detached worker to see that not having a fixed schedule of activities, following instead of leading, using the natural pattern of activities instead of attempting to create an artificial one, required a different set of skills, different attitudes, a different approach and a different set of criteria for judging his success or failure.

Sometimes workers were discouraged and tended to feel they had failed when activities did not happen. It took time before we could all see that the real need was to bring the same insight, knowledge and understanding to bear in what we found happening in cafés, on street corners, in the public house, on outings and trips, and at the coffee stall, as would be brought to bear on any activity suggested by us. For the detached worker the whole area was his 'club premises', with ready-made activities which he could use with his group or single individual as required. We were careful not to imply that mobility in all things was to be accepted. In employment, boy/girl relationships or in friendship group relations for example, mobility was not of necessity the best thing. We abandoned any attempt to keep the premises going as a youth café once the group concerned had lost interest, but we went to great lengths to keep a boy in a job, or to keep small friendship groups together long enough for their members to find the opportunity to do things together that they could not do on their own. Nor did we see these patterns of mobility as a totally good thing for all the young people all the time. We kept the younger girls' group separate from the larger network of relationships, and in order to help with this their worker did not get involved with any of the other young people. The girls badly needed a small self-contained group, and it was eighteen months before they wanted and were encouraged to move out of it.

To the young people our recognition of their pattern of mobility was an added indication of our acceptance of them as they were, a hint of our growing understanding of why and how they found us useful. But most important it really gave credibility to our statements about not wanting to get them to do anything. On the other hand it tended to confirm several of the voluntary and statutory bodies in their suspicion that we were lowering standards, "going a bit too far", not playing the game, increasing the indiscipline of the young people. These suspicions, when seen from inside the structure and programme of these agencies, were justified, in that the young people with whom we worked might well expect a similar recognition of their natural patterns of mobility under circumstances—in the club or youth centre —where it could not be legitimately recognised if the regular membership were to be adequately served.

This meant that we had to interpret the need of our young people for mobility to the agencies, while assuring them that we saw why they could not be expected to meet this particular need, but why it was imperative that we should. We also tried to interpret to the young people why the club could not be expected to stop everything it was doing—organised activities, regular times and places for dances and outings, registration of members and subscription paying —simply to provide for them.

Our recognition of the pattern of mobility was a problem for the project committee in the same way that it was for the statutory and voluntary agencies. They at first felt that "a regular organised programme of activity" would help stabilise the young people and make them more responsible. In our work with the committee we had to help them to see what we had learned—that to observe the pattern of mobility, to help the young people to see what these patterns are and to explore them, their limitations and potentials and then use those patterns as the basis of the programme, meant abandoning preconceptions about where, how, why and at what time things should happen. It meant just being ready for things to happen all the time and using them together with the young people to the best advantage.

But that is not the end of the story because even when we saw all this and were willing to accept it, it did not occur to us until the third year that the very recognition of mobility that allowed for free-flow of events might partially result, as it did, in some of the very stability we had agreed to forego. The natural pattern of association, intensified by the young people doing things together more often and over a longer period, produced a tightening up in the network of relationships. It gave an identity, that is, a sense of 'belonging' to the coffee stall. This in the end made planning outings, trips and holidays a smoother, more organised, less chaotic process.

10. Values and standards

Just as we had to spend time thinking out the problems of identity and mobility and deciding how best to deal with them, so we found ourselves at a later stage having to concentrate on the question of values and standards. We realised that these together with the social attitudes and expectations to which they gave rise, created the problem underlying all our field-work.

Within the scope of our field-work, three sets of standards and values about school, work, authority, money, sex and the law, were at play. One set was held by the young people—amorphous, undefined, often contradictory, sometimes complying with the neighbourhood society, sometimes at variance with it. The second set was the values and standards of the neighbourhood society itself, not stated as a rational, coherent system but demanding and persuasive nonetheless, and most of the young people in one form or another subscribed to it in part or fully. The third set of values and standards was that of the larger community including the voluntary and statutory bodies, a set that was overtly reflected in the formal institutions—the school, the church, the police, the youth club, the welfare services. This set made specific demands which included particular expectations, compliance with which could on occasions be enforced by the officials representing the institutions—the school attendance officer, the national assistance official, the probation officer, the policeman. Obviously these three sets of values and standards were not separate, isolated each from the other, but were overlapping, interrelated and interacting. Some individuals, groups and sections of the community participated in all three sets, or publicly subscribed to one and lived by another. Nor was each set totally self-consistent. Internal contradictions and conflicts abounded. This was just as true of the third set—the public morality of the statutory and voluntary bodies—as it was of the other two.

We now saw the complex interaction between these sets of values and standards as one of the fundamental problems of field-work. Every field-work event was in one way or another concerned with values and standards. To which set were we as detached workers to subscribe? Which set were we to attempt to get the young people to understand? By which set were we to evaluate and interpret our performance?

Three points soon became clear to us. Firstly, we had to recognise, and to let the young people know we recognised, their own values and standards. But we could only partially accept them, and we showed this by reserving the right to reject certain behaviour. In doing so we were careful never to suggest disapproval of the person concerned. Secondly, we realised that in all our work we would have to be perfectly honest in bearing witness to our own values and standards which for the most part were related to the third set (statutory and voluntary agency-middle-class). This could not include demanding their acceptance by the young people, but would mean helping young people to accept and trust us as persons with different standards and values in much the same way as we accepted them. Thirdly, we understood that we had to use the ever-present conflicts in values and standards to point out the choices available and to help individuals to see how choices were made. It became a matter of policy never to suggest to a young person what value choice he should make but instead to suggest how he could go about making it.

With these points in mind it was possible to see more clearly other aspects of our job in this field. Certainly the worker must not preach or moralise. The formal institutions in the larger community, with more skill and resources at their disposal, had already failed or only partially succeeded with the unattached. Our job was to show what choices were available within the young people's experience and understanding, and to attempt to mediate between the three sets of value systems and standards in order to keep communication between them open. It was to help the young people to understand the behaviour and expectations of those within the third set (statutory and voluntary bodies) to know how to choose whether or not to meet those expectations and if so, how to do it. On the other hand, our job was, when possible and necessary, to explain to those within the third set, the standards and values underlying the behaviour of the young people (in so far as we could ascertain this), their expectations and their attitudes, and even on occasions to suggest how in terms of service offered, a reconciliation of expectations could be arranged.

Obviously, this was a very difficult thing to do. We ourselves were at first seen as one of 'Them' (the agencies) by the young people and the neighbourhood. We were in danger of being seen as one of 'Them' (the young people) by our colleagues in the statutory and voluntary bodies, by our committee and on occasion by ourselves. Our constant attempts to mediate, to interpret 'Them' to 'Them' often resulted in either or both parties feeling that we had "gone over to the other". We soon realised that we had to have a foot in each camp, while attempting to keep the dialogue between the camps open and productive. This was especially difficult for our younger workers, who often felt in danger of coming down on one side or the other and who most felt the strain of having to be both while being neither, and at the same time to be themselves.

We realised that the cause of unattachment was in part the conflict between different sets of standards and values and their different expectations. Working towards a reconciliation of this conflict in so far as it concerned the unattached, gave rise to a series of problems concerned with interpretation among ourselves, between ourselves and the young people, between the team and the project committee and between ourselves and the agencies.

Giving things away

One of the most pressing problems, especially in the early days of field-work was the need to give something away, money, equipment, a place to meet, things of all kinds. This need arose partly from the insecurity of the worker who felt himself out on the streets, without an identity, and with none of the traditional paraphernalia of the youth club to offer. When faced with giving only himself, in relationships, he tried to establish his identity by giving things away. Once the young people saw this they asked for things as proof of acceptance, and the situation tended to become one-sided, the young people asking and taking and the worker giving. If this were carried too far the worker's identity as 'a giver of things' tended to keep the relationship between the worker and the young person from taking a 'proper role', that of an enabling relationship, covering a far wider range of needs, in which the worker offered his knowledge, his skill, understanding and acceptance as an adult, as well as things.

Even so, we had to accept that while a relationship should not be focussed only on giving things, it had to include giving things. Sometimes we felt that things were legitimately needed, legitimately asked for and legitimately given—bus fares to work, or cinema money for the plumber's apprentice to spend on his girlfriend when he was struggling to convince himself that he must complete his apprenticeship. But we also had to learn that from the young person's point of view giving things was an important part of the early stages of a relationship. It was the part of a relationship which he understood. It could be used to test out the worker in many different ways, and was one of the conditions which the young person imposed. This meant that we had to stop generalising. We had thought that giving things was not good because it might endanger the development of the right kind of relationship. Now we realised that each request had to be thought out in its own context, and the important factor was not what we gave, but how and why we gave it. At this point, giving things away became an accepted part of our approach.

But even though we could accept this for ourselves, it had to be interpreted to our committee and to other agencies. Giving things away could all too easily be seen by others as "undercutting the accepted standards" or as "giving in to unacceptable demands" or "as not being an aid to proper character training". This faced us with the problem of explaining under what conditions and for what reasons we gave things away.

We explained firstly that we would give to cover a need that was not met by another agency in a way that was acceptable to the young person. Whereas a youth club might provide gymnastic equipment, table tennis or billards, we might pay for a group to have a meal in a West End restaurant. Secondly, we would give to show acceptance, support or recognition in a relationship with an individual—it could be a birthday present, or advancing money if a boy had to work a fortnight before collecting wages, or money for a haircut before an interview. Thirdly, we would give to help an individual or group to learn how to use a relationship. When a group redecorated and rebuilt a clubroom it learned how to negotiate through the worker with the Y.W.C.A., so that it received financial help on terms acceptable to both sides.

But while we decided the bases on which we would give things, we also had to consider what this would accomplish in the relationship, what would be its repercussions on group life, and what it would mean to the whole programme. We provided three kitchen sinks in a short period in order to support a group and prevent frustration and violence, even though we felt it was not helpful to the person responsible for smashing or removing them. On another occasion we gave all the members of a younger group the same amount of money for an outing knowing that some could afford more, because at that time more financial help to one would be interpreted as "liking her more". In each case, the worker had to be able to explain to himself the need for his particular act of giving, in order to be certain that it was not just an easy way out.

These explanations were not at first easily accepted by those outside the staff team. The giving of money particularly ran counter to certain elements in Protestant and middle-class tradition or to certain elements in social work. It could be mistaken for charity, or it could be considered a way of evading the real problems. Also we had not allowed for such expenditure in the budget. This was another example of a conflict in expectations. The expectations of the young people were to get something for nothing sometimes as a lark to show up the worker as an 'easy' touch; to get something from the worker believing this to be a sign of his approval; to take as a right the reappropriation of Y.W.C.A. funds, and put them to any use "we see fit" since 'they' will never know (if you don't tell them); that if a worker has more money than the others in the group, he must not let 'us' know, or he must share it with 'us', or expect to lose it by every means of 'our' devising.

The expectations of the field-worker were that he must use money as an 'activity' in relationships with individuals or with groups (although before this realisation he had difficulties in understanding the place of money in the relationship, or the expectations of the young people); that money must be available quickly, to be used as equipment, at the discretion of the worker; that those responsible for administration should understand this and help the worker express it so that it could be included in the budget; that within a relationship money should eventually be substituted by something else.

The expectations of the committee and other agencies were that the use of money should be planned in advance; that 'giving money' should be a last resort as the recipient could well consider it 'charity' or a 'clever move' on his part.

In order to help resolve this conflict in expectations we reminded ourselves, and our committee of the 'giving' which was acceptable in other situations. In certain instances it is known that a case worker will pay a mother's fare when she needs to come to an agency for help with problems. It is customary to give prizes on speech day—a mark of approval for effort and achievement. (Some such system was needed for our young people, without the competitive element, by which they could be shown approval of their achievement even if it might only be keeping a job for a week.) A youth club might hire a projector and films to show to members free of charge (compare taking a group to a cinema). These we felt were only a few of the examples in which gifts and money were used as support, recognition and approval, or even education.

Once our committee was able to understand the various ways in which we felt we must use money, and to recognise the expectations of the young people, the field-workers were able to relax, and within the limitations of a sum allocated, to use money as one of the natural materials of programming. As the work developed we realised that many of the young people no longer concentrated on gifts or money but found other factors in relationships which were important to them.

Dealing with growing self-awareness

At one point in our work, after we had recognised and come to terms with the problems of identity, the need to offer ourselves, the problems of mobility, of values and standards and interpretation, we began to show the strain of dealing with our own growing self-awareness. We tended to become self-conscious, to lose spontaneity, to think out each field-work event before participating and acting in it, to spend more time on 'self-analysis', to brood over mistakes and to feel discouraged easily.

The crisis in self-awareness which was at first an individual matter reached by each worker separately, became a team problem some time during the second year's work. In retrospect we saw the problem of growing self-awareness as implicit in the attempt we were making to extend the traditional approach to youth work. In making this attempt we recognised the need to change our attitudes about the problems of identity, mobility, values and standards, and this meant that we had to find new resources within ourselves, to meet this challenge. We saw that it was this need to develop new inner resources which occasioned the crisis in self-awareness. The crisis was characterised by over-awareness of our own motives ("Am I only trying to help these young people in order to get them to see things my way?"), over-sensitiveness to rejection ("I react much too sharply when the young people don't like me"), too great a fear of acceptance ("I think too much about why they like me").

Most of the things troubling us were real and deserved considerations but we had become over-sensitive in our reactions. We were afraid to show anger when we were angry, discouraged about our ability to help the young people and unable to say we were discouraged, unsure of what, how and why, we were observing and recording. We were feeling swamped by pressures over which we could never hope to have any control, pressures upon the neighbourhood, the young people and ourselves. We were perplexed by questions arising from our work in the field, to which we could never know the answers.

Although it was of little help, we had to remind ourselves at this stage, that by the very nature of this work, there invariably occurs a period during which things have to be thought out and experienced from the 'inside' and that during this period confusion and discouragement are part of the game. We managed to get through this crisis for the most part by changing emphases in supervision and training. We concentrated on the need for the field-workers to be themselves, to be angry, discouraged, rejected—the lot—but simply to be aware of it. We also tried to relieve the pressure during these periods by encouraging the field-workers to look outwards, to concentrate on the young people and the field-work as a whole.

The analogy that seemed to help us in this was that of someone who hears Beethoven's *Eroica* for the first time, is carried away by the wonder of it and spontaneously and freely reacts to it. He then begins to read music criticism, listens to it again and finds that with his new knowledge he is aware of a host of different aspects of the work, and that he has lost the essential, natural pleasure of listening. He then forgets about the whole thing, comes back to it again later and simply listens. At the third listening he finds that what he has learned from his analysis of the work is still a factor in his listening, but it no longer prevents him from full spontaneous participation.

We found that after we had passed through the analytical stage we too could gradually return to being ourselves, without being too self-conscious about the theoretical implications of what we were doing. So we were able to regain a good bit of our original spontaneity and self-trust. It was a great help to be a team, in which we could support one another, and see the humour of many of our most serious predicaments.

In our case the crisis in self-awareness was not only engendered by the nature of the work but was complicated by the need to carry on an enquiry into what we were doing, and how we were doing it, at the same time as we were doing the field-work.

11. *Assessing needs—legitimacy of needs*

One of the problems that was a constant ingredient of field-work was assessing needs. We had begun by thinking that we had only to assess the needs of the young people. It soon became clear that we had also to assess the needs of the neighbourhood, our sponsoring agency, the statutory and voluntary bodies and ourselves. We then had to see the needs of the young people within the context of all these separate but related categories of need, before we could arrive either at practical possibilities for programme or criteria for priority. This meant being as clear as possible about the different sets of needs.

The first set was that of the young people who, on the whole, needed to be accepted as individuals and in groups as and where they were, and helped in terms and in situations that they were able and willing to understand. They needed help to state what they wanted to do, and to find ways of doing it. The second set was that of the neighbourhood, which needed to know who we were, to be sure we were not collecting information for the police, the national assistance board or other authorities, and which needed to be accepted as it was and judged, so far as it was possible within its own terms of standards and values.

The statutory and voluntary bodies also needed to know who we were, and that what we were doing did not threaten their programme or approach. They needed to be helped to define the problems of the unattached in terms that would make them willing to meet them within their own service. The sponsoring agency—the London Y.W.C.A.—needed to feel it was doing the right thing, yet not going too far. It had to be helped to see what structural changes in the relationship of the committee and the staff had to be worked out in order to accomplish the agreed ends. It needed to see how and why this work differed from its usual work, especially in the allocation and use of resources. It also needed to develop new criteria for the evaluation of the work.

We, the staff team, had needs. We needed the support of the statutory and voluntary bodies, the recognition of the neighbourhood and the support of each other, and of our agency. The needs of the larger community were also important. It had to know that its money was being spent in the best way, that the law was not being infringed and that something would come of the project.

We felt that all these needs were legitimate, and yet we had to see those of the young people as primary. It was our responsibility to attempt to tip the scale in favour of helping the young people to meet their needs, while attempting to interpret these to the other parties concerned in terms of possibilities of service. We came to see the needs of the young people as for the most part legitimate, and ourselves as agents, appointed by a statutory and voluntary body—our committee —and the larger community. We had to be recognised and accepted by the young people to represent their needs within the community. Once we saw this, all else hinged on how we defined the legitimacy of need.

We had at first thought that once we had agreed on the needs of the young people and found ways of helping them to meet these, the problems of 'assessing needs' would be for the most part solved. This was far from being true, because our acceptance of a particular set of needs was not necessarily seen as the right assessment by our committee, the statutory and voluntary bodies or even, on occasion, by the young people themselves. Consequently what seemed to us a reasonable way of meeting a need, was sometimes questioned or rejected by the committee and the agency.

This led to a discussion of why, how and under what conditions a need could be seen as legitimate. We discussed biological and social needs, first in terms of the individual's own growth and development, in the context of the family, the peer group, school, work and the neighbourhood. We then considered how each need was seen by the individual himself. Did he or she fully recognise the need and its implications? Did he want to satisfy it? Did he feel guilty about it? Did he feel frustrated at not being able to meet it?

Then we looked at the same need as seen by the authorities, parents, teachers, leaders, social workers, police. How did they see this particular individual's need. Did they recognise it as deserving of fulfilment? Did they see it as needing to be thwarted, or repressed or diverted for the good of the individual, the groups to which he belonged or of the larger community? Who was to help with the fulfilment, the repression or the diversion? Was it to be the individual himself, the group concerned or the social institutions and their appointed agents? This was a long and at some points fruitless discussion, but we recognised that individual, group and community were usually seen and judged by groups and institutions from the point of view of their own function and their own particular programme of service. Needs which did not fit within the function of a service tended to be considered illegitimate by that service

Part of our job then was to explain these needs of young people, which we saw as legitimate, so that the groups and institutions could recognise them as coming within their own terms of service. As it turned out much of our work was just that—finding out ways of legitimising the needs of the young people, first to ourselves and then to our committee and the statutory and voluntary bodies.

12. Never enough time—frustration

One of the problems of field-work was that we never had enough time; enough time to accomplish what we set out to do in our day-to-day work; to record, to discuss and plan the work; to interpret the work to the other statutory and voluntary bodies, and to our own committee.

This resulted in our thinking that we needed more field-workers, new work schedules, different work responsibilities, and more clerical help, and also in a general feeling of urgency that we at first saw as indicative of our own 'high sense of commitment'. In reality it was nothing of the sort, but arose from our inability to see our own limitations and to accept them. We came to see this complaint not only as a sign of unresolved conflict about priorities, but also as an indication of our own inability to resolve the conflict in expectations that was part of the problem of working with the unattached. If we followed the natural pattern of association, and the natural patterns of timing among the young people, our work had to meet these requirements instead of the artificial requirements of administrative patterns. If we followed the natural pattern of association and timing we could not meet the expectations of the statutory and voluntary bodies who had developed their criteria from work in more formal institutional settings. This meant abandoning the attempt to work one way in the field—following and using the natural pattern of events—and another in the 'office', attempting in our evaluation of the work to force the pace.

Thus we saw the need to rethink the role of the administrator and the consultant, who were to become more 'servants' of the staff than they had been, as it was the staff evaluation of the field-work events that should set the pace, and not the needs of the agency. This led to a new approach to interpretation, both to the statutory and the voluntary bodies and the project committee, in that we could now say what we were doing and evaluate it with fewer preconceived notions of what should be done and with a greater sense of the reality of what was happening.

With our awareness of the complexities of the field-work, it became almost inevitable that we should become conscious of the frustrations of the work to an almost 'dangerous' degree. Well planned (by the young people), long anticipated programmes of events which had taken much time and sometimes much money were often allowed to lapse. Individuals who had shown much 'promise of improvement'—with six months or a year of intensive support—had a 'relapse'. Individual workers who could have gone faster than other members of the team could not do so without endangering the work of their colleagues. Hoped for results and interpretation to statutory and voluntary bodies were not realised. The pressure of events outside our control—housing, unemployment—often appeared to undo many months of work.

These factors tended on occasion to create in individual staff members and the team a sense of acute frustration which we had to learn to handle through self-knowledge. We had to try to see frustration itself as one of the natural events in this type of work, to be accepted and used as part of the detached worker's response to the field-work. Even at its most negative, frustration, anger, anxiety and desire to 'pack it all in' had to be seen as ingredients of field-work that could be used as material for our own growth and development. The fact that we had to recognise and accept for ourselves the same kind of frustration that the young people with whom we worked experienced every day, made us more realistic in our approach. Perhaps after some months of work with a young boy, helping him to keep a job and develop some work discipline and a sense of accomplishment, he was given his cards because of retrenchment and not through any fault of his own, or perhaps the family of one of the young people was evicted because of rent manoeuvres. The worker then shared realistically in the consequent frustration, although no solution was at hand.

In the main, the problem of frustration (whether in programme work with individuals and groups, in staff working with each other, or in staff working with agencies and committee) was at root another aspect of the same problem that underlay our sense of insufficient time. It was the problem of not being able to respond directly enough to field-work events because of preconceptions of where, how, when and why things should be done. These preconceptions could stem from our own training, experience and attitudes, from the committee, from our agency, and from colleagues and other organisations. It was not that the frustration was caused by any wilful imposition of preconceptions, but simply that the parties could not know what was necessary beforehand, and so had to make do with the available traditional approaches. When events in the field suggested the need for changes, and new procedures were evolved the frustration was lessened. Even then individual worker's sense of frustration was the opportunity for the more informed use of supervision, training, and team work.

Chapter Four

OBSERVATIONS

These observations are based on five years' thinking about our work with the unattached; one year while only the coffee stall was in operation, the three years of the main project, and the year during which the report has been written. The information collected during this time came from our direct contact with the young people, from our staff discussions, and from our colleagues in the community. Some of it was discussed with and verified by a variety of youth workers in different positions in the youth service. Much of our contact with the latter took place during the final year when we consulted them while preparing our report.

The observations apply only to the particular young people (a comparatively small number) whom we contacted during the project in a particular community. Some of the gaps, particularly those relating to school and families, were mainly due to the nature of our work, which precluded attempts to make direct contacts with adults except with the approval of the young people concerned.

The observations are also limited by our angle of observation. We were youth workers with the preconceptions and sometimes the prejudices of youth workers, and we were observing in order to do something within the terms of reference of the youth service.

13. The young people

The categories we agreed upon to describe the various groups within the larger coffee stall grouping were not meant to indicate separate, mutually exclusive classes of young people. We worked them out as an aid to understanding the shape and content of the programme needed not as 'pigeon holes for people'. We were aware from the beginning that they were moving points on a continuum that overlapped, interchanged, and interacted, with boys and girls changing over, and growing through, sometimes appearing in one category at one time to a particular worker and at the same time in another category to a different worker. Nonetheless the categories we developed served as points of departure for discussing groups of young people within the larger grouping.

In this context the word 'disorganised' refers to the behaviour of the young people (in our contact group) as it was evidenced by their inability or unwillingness (for whatever reasons) to cope with the everyday problems of friendships, school, work and recreation, in comparison with the apparent ability and willingness of the 'can copes' to do so.

The 'can copes'

The 'can copes' were the young people among our contacts who were both able and willing to use the resources already available to them in the community.

Family On the whole the 'can copes' were from families which followed a fairly constant set of standards and expectations, which operated within a fairly well known and agreed upon system of rewards and punishments, and in which the roles of the mother and father were defined and accepted by members of the family. Above all they were families in which the young person could count on at least one adult for support when in difficulties, even if it were a grand-parent, a close relative or a near neighbour "who was part of the family anyway". It did not seem to be so much a question of 'happy family life' as of the young person knowing where to go for help, and under what conditions it would be given.

School Most often the 'can copes' had come to terms with school, not perhaps as model pupils—but they had found out what was expected, given as much as they felt they wanted to or as they thought necessary, and had settled into 'taking out' what interested them. Many appeared to be uneven learners, but some had found subjects in which they became interested. Most felt that school was a dreadful necessity which could sometimes be fun. One or two valued relation-ships which they had made with teachers.

Work Most of the 'can copes' liked their work, were sticking it out in order to get on, or were biding their time until they would change over to "something better". They had only the occasional periods of discouragement at not getting on fast enough or wanting to do something else.

Friends The 'can copes' tended to be able to keep up their relationships with boy and girl friends over relatively long periods, and to grow through them rather than break them off. In many cases these relationships were outside the coffee stall grouping.

Recreation Many of the 'can copes' had tried youth clubs, and occasionally they visited one or several for dances, but they preferred to choose from a variety of meeting places. They tended to be more sure of what they wanted to do, more able to do it, and to have a more varied recreational life than the young people in other categories.

Social attitudes The attitudes of the 'can copes' towards marriage, sex, money and future possibilities seemed to be a mixture of the older working-class attitudes and those evolved by their adolescent grouping. Marriage to the boy was more about "having kids and a family" than about relationships and companionship, and to the girl was freedom, security and status. Sex was for the boy to get where and when he could, at least before marriage, and for the girl was frequently a conflict situation, that is an uncertainty as to who should be pleased, the boy, herself or her parents, and doubt as to which attitude or action would please whom. Money was not a thing in itself, but was useful for what it would buy. Saving large amounts for future use did not enter into their calculations. Future possibilities were within known bounds, marriage, a better job, a flat outside the neighbourhood, a motor-bike, a car, lots of good clothes, and perhaps holidays abroad. Status came from the approval of families, relatives, neighbours and friends and was mostly related to work with good wages, spending money rightly and not getting involved with the police. The rules by which status was achieved were known and agreed upon, and were only "common sense". Apart from housing and wages, things were not too bad as they were, but it was wise to look out for 'number one', even if it meant being an inch or two on the other side of the law.

Service The help we gave to the 'can copes' was on the whole unplanned. Nonetheless it was valuable to them not because of any direct service, but because of the incidental opportunities it offered to be part of the larger coffee stall grouping. It was valuable to us in that they were necessary as a 'control' in the group. We should probably have attempted to contact more of them and to offer them more prolonged opportunities in the programme both because of what their presence offered the other young people, and because of their own needs to belong to something larger in their own community. We should also have collected more information about this kind of young person in these circumstances. All in all the 'can copes' tended to 'come and go' more often than the other categories and to give more to the programme than they took away.

114

The 'temporarily disorganised'

The 'temporarily disorganised' were those among our contacts who were between school and work and in need of information, guidance and support on a temporary basis only. Some of them would have become 'can copes' on their own, but many of them needed help to prevent their falling into more serious difficulties.

Family The 'temporarily disorganised' did not appear to us to have any particular kind of family background in common. They appeared to come from a wide variety of family types.

School On the whole the 'temporarily disorganised' tended either to be anticipating leaving school with great relief, or having left school, were enjoying their new-found freedom. In most cases they saw school as something to get through quickly and saw leaving school as the proof that they were grown up. They neither strongly resented school and the school authorities, nor considered school "really worth while". It was seen as "something kids had to do until they grow up". In only a small number of cases did they indicate that they would have liked to continue at school.

Work The 'temporarily disorganised' rarely knew what job they wanted to do, and were unable or unwilling to set about doing anything definite about employment, a trade or a career. They sometimes said they were disappointed at not being able to "walk right into the right job". Sometimes they had outsized expectations about the rate of pay, the conditions of work, and their status in a job. Disappointment at the discipline or boredom of the work routine caused many of them to change jobs often. Sometimes the inability or unwillingness to know what they wanted, or how to get it prevented them from taking a job at all.

Friends The 'temporarily disorganised' frequently had friendship problems, because their school friendship groups were breaking up. Sometimes they were separated from their friends who had stayed on at school, or who had found good jobs and had more spending money. New friendships sometimes grew up between boys who were not working and spent time just 'hanging about'. Boys or girls often made a friend of the opposite sex more for status value than because they were ready for boy/girl relationships.

Recreation The 'temporarily disorganised' had mostly been in youth clubs and had left them. They often attempted to get in with the older boys in the coffee stall grouping to prove they too were grown up. For a while after leaving school they were very serious about their recreational life. They had to do something, anything and everything, now, tonight, tomorrow, the night after, and the weekend. If they were working and had the money they stayed out late or all weekend. If they did not have the money they were resentful at not being able to do so.

Social attitudes The 'temporarily disorganised' as might have been expected often held two sets of views on most matters, each in conflict with the other: "I'll never get married, it's not worth it" and the same boy a day later, "If I had a good job, I'd find a good girl and get married now." "If you work hard and show the boss you are interested and really do a good job you can get ahead" and the same boy a bit later, "They have the whole thing sewn up. You can't win. It's all their show." "Money is the only important thing, people take notice when you have it and you can do anything you want" and later, "The high pay is no good if you don't like your workmates or the work". The same ambivalence about getting ahead, "You can go where you want and do what you want" and then later from the same boy, "If you are from this place you've had it, you can't get out. If you do they will push you back again soon enough."

In general the 'temporarily disorganised' seemed to be in a period of feeling let down after school, for the most part because they expected too much of their new-found freedom. At the same time they did not want to settle down until they had made the best use possible (in their own minds) of their freedom. In this transition period, they were above all in a difficult employment situation, because of the differences between their expectations and the opportunities offered by the community.

Services The 'temporarily disorganised' tended to have specific needs at specific times and often required intensive work for short periods, and like the 'can copes' they left the project when their needs were fulfilled. In one way this was all to the good, since they no longer needed us or the coffee stall grouping, and often had become able to manage on their own in the neighbourhood without contact with us. But that they left when they 'got what they needed' was perhaps not always a sign that it was time for them to leave. It could have been an indication that we were not providing the right environment for their continued development.

The 'simply disorganised'

The 'simply disorganised' were by far the largest category within our contact group. They included many young people who appeared to be heading for serious difficulties if they were not offered help.

Family Many of the families seemed to have a struggle to manage on their incomes. Frequently this appeared to be due to low incomes, and sometimes to an inability to plan realistically. The ongoing life of the families seemed to be dull, undemanding and unrewarding, with only the occasional crisis. Some parents had apparently "given up hope" on behalf of their children, expected little, and gave little in return by way of support, encouragement, affection or approval. Many of the young people seemed to have resigned themselves to being "involved in the family" while seeing the involvement as without purpose. Family life was seen as a bore, not helpful or potentially so, but useful for bed and breakfast. Frequently it was a place to leave as soon as possible. In many cases there was not an open conflict, simply a lack of common interests, and a gap between the young people and their families which made them unwilling or unable to communicate.

School The 'simply disorganised' had found school a place to go to, something to do, less of a bore than just doing nothing. Most had attended comparatively regularly for some periods, but not during the final years. Some had found a subject interesting at the time, but did not show an interest in its after leaving school. They did not resent discipline nor did they take it seriously. School was inevitable, but was not meant to be taken seriously. If you did you were in for a disappointment because "things aren't the way they say at school".

Work On the whole, the 'simply disorganised' were in two employment groupings. In the first were those who had jobs and were not looking for others. This sometimes meant holding on to a job with no real future, and doing uninteresting work because it was safe, and less trouble than changing. It could also be an indication of a feeling of responsibility to contribute regularly to the family budget or could be related to the desire to have a 'steady' girl friend. Within the second grouping were the 'job hoppers' (mainly boys) who changed from job to job at whim, or because their misbehaviour resulted in dismissal. To many of these boys work was a necessary evil. They tended to prolong periods of unemployment, and to live on money from mums, older brothers or sisters and girl friends, or from petty thievery.

Friends The 'simply disorganised' tended to have one or two friends with whom they would circulate within the coffee stall grouping, moving casually from group to group, depending on what was happening, who had a good story to tell, a good lark to organise, money to spend, an interesting place to visit or something exciting to do. They were attracted by the activities of the 'can copes', sometimes grew tired of their nomadic wandering, and were frequently drawn to the 'seriously disorganised' who promised "big things".

Recreation They seemed to float into their recreational pursuits because "there was nothing else to do". On some occasions they were 'pushed' by the opportunities provided by the 'can copes' or the activities provided by the 'seriously disorganised'. They called on

I

youth clubs more often than the 'can copes', who "did not want to have things done for them" or the 'seriously disorganised', who "did not want to have things done to them". They seemed on the whole to like the clubs when and where they "let you alone" or where you could just "be", and would probably have used youth clubs more if the clubs had been less demanding.

Social attitudes The 'simply disorganised' appeared to accept without discrimination and apparently without undue concern the prevalent neighbourhood attitudes (whether traditional or peer-group) about marriage, work, the family, sex, money and education.

Service The 'simply disorganised' were most easily contacted, were the largest grouping, and in some ways were helped more than the other young people. They were helped with individual problems, and were able to participate in a wide range of recreational activities. In this way we were able to provide them with some opportunities for social development. But it seemed that our offering failed to develop the full potential of some of these young people, in that we were able to do so little in the area of cultural deprivation.

The 'seriously disorganised'

We termed the smallest category of our contacts, the 'seriously disorganised'. They were the young people who needed the most intensive guidance and support on a long term basis, and who provided the bulk of the more serious probation, law, employment and boy/girl problems.

Family Their family backgrounds were on the whole as seriously disorganised as the individual young people in this category. Most were multi-problem families, that is, they were liable to have economic, social, emotional and health problems. There were often difficulties in relations between husband and wife, between parents and children, and between children, trouble with school attendance authorities, landlords, the police, relatives and neighbours. The economic difficulties of the majority of these families were frequently due to their being unskilled, at the bottom of the labour pool, with a backlog of real poverty over the years. Most of them were known to several of the welfare agencies. These families provided two distinct kinds of problems to the young people in this category. They offered no moorings that could help their young members with the problems of adolescence, no constant agreed upon system of rewards and punishments, no ordered roles within the family, no incentive to achievement in order to win status. They tended to see the young person almost as an economic unit to be "sent out to work" as soon as possible without regard to educational opportunities or the nature of the employment.

118

None of this necessarily meant a lack of love, and many of the parents were concerned about their families, and a mother or father would work long hours at monotonous unskilled labour. Frequently a love/hate relationship between parent and child was one of the factors in the situation.

School The attitudes of the young people towards school were mainly those of resentment and hostility. School attendance was seen as an irrational demand on the part of adults in the community who had the unfair advantage of being able to "force you to do what they want". It was unnecessary and unfair, and more important, it was useless. Work was unpleasant, but at least it was rewarded by a weekly pay packet. But school offered nothing. Even though it could be a lark to 'send up' one of the teachers, better larks were possible outside. A master or headmaster might be a "good bloke", but there was little he could do for you as he had to do as he was told, and contact was limited to the school setting.

Work On the whole, work was a necessity only when one couldn't get money any other way. The good jobs were taken by "the boys at the top". Accepting work routine was "going soft" or "letting them have it all their own way". Dreams of making a 'pile' or some fantastic scheme either side of the law, were often seen as more realistic than trying to get on in a particular job or trade. Hostility to adults in authority beset these young people and was one of the major causes of their not getting on at work. They entered each new situation with a chip on their shoulders and it grew larger when the whole situation was repeated on the next job.

Friends Friendships were unable to offer these young people the opportunities and support that they gave the 'can copes'. Fear of exploitation by others and exploiting others in mistaken self defence, being over demanding, wanting control, asking for more than could be expected by way of loyalty, constant availability and personal devotion, characterised the friendship pattern of the 'seriously disorganised'. Short-lived intensive friendships were broken in the heat of conflicts which neither party understood. The 'seriously disorganised' frequently had a current best friend and/or a group of small followers. These usually came from among the 'simply disorganised' to whom they used to show off, and whom they led into a variety of larks, laughs and often petty crimes. It might be said that the 'seriously disorganised' boy tended to attempt to define himself to himself by way of the image he was able to evoke from his followers, having no meaningful attachment to a reference group (family, school, work) that gave him acceptance and from which he could evoke status rewards. He tended to develop a reference group of his own in which to seek a reflection of his own identity and status.

119

This often led the boy to overplay the role of the 'villain', first in phantasy, then in talk to the group, eventually in external behaviour, sometimes in petty crime, in order to have the objective material with which to support the charade. Often the play fell apart, either because he overacted and frightened off his followers, because he lost interest, or because he was "taken in by the police". Friends and followers deserted, parents and older brothers and sisters were too busy, too tired, or had been "through it all before", and the boy was left on his own, sometimes acting out his unhappiness to the police and the courts, who took the only recourse at present open to them and put him inside.

Recreation As individuals and as a group within the larger coffee stall group, the 'seriously disorganised' took little part in relaxed leisure time activities, having fun or just doing things for the sake of doing them, or in organised activities for achievement, such as games or sport. On the whole, almost everything they did was actively purposive, an almost hectic attempt to solve problems with which recreation alone could not help. By their antics they may be said to have provided recreational activity for others in the coffee stall group, especially for the 'simply disorganised' who welcomed tall tales, bragging and larks at other people's expense as a kind of barrack-room jesting.

Service The service that we first developed at the coffee stall—jobs, probation, the courts, the law, family difficulties—was 'problem orientated', which attracted the 'seriously disorganised', because they could get the service they needed and wanted on terms they understood and could accept. Our success in doing this we now feel 'distorted the programme', since an undue proportion of time and money was spent on the most difficult young people. This was not a mistake in terms of their need—they were the most needy—but in terms of our service to the other groupings in the programme. Our limitations in helping the 'simply disorganised', the 'can copes', and 'temporarily disorganised', were mainly due to this bias in the way we allowed the programme to develop.

14. The unattached needing help

The characteristics of the unattached, who seemed unable to cope on their own, could be described as follows:

Their interests, both as individuals and in groups, are most often limited to the present. It is the immediate situation that gets the attention, that is seen as important, such as asking for one's cards at work, simply to show off to one's workmates, or to achieve temporary ascendance over the boss, or simply out of momentary pique or discouragement. This attitude, this commitment to the present (especially if it causes a 'giggle' or a 'laugh') causes difficulties for the young people. The choices and decisions they could make are severely limited, as they cannot consider the morrow, the implication of a particular act, or the probable consequences of the sequence of events of which it is a part.

Their extreme mobility is characterised by rapid change of interest in events, things and people. This means that their participation in school, work or friendship group changes on an almost week to week basis. Interest in anything—events, situations, people, seems to lack even the most rudimentary perseverance. As a result there appears to be a little sense of achievement, little organised experience of doing and being things together, and few, if any, long term objectives to accomplish.

Interest seems to be severely limited by low verbal ability, not necessarily related to low intelligence (at least so far as we could ascertain) but to an inability or unwillingness to think abstractly. This often prevents the young person from being able to state to himself or to others what he feels his needs to be or what his problems are. This inability "to define himself to himself" prevents him from "protesting" in terms that can be recognised or discussed, and, of course, severely limits his own ability to do anything about it as well as other people's ability to help him.

They have a decided and generalised distrust of whatever is seen to be authority, and a constant inability to come to terms with it even when coming to terms with it is well nigh inevitable. This is particularly true of the police, but is sometimes true even when the authority is recognised by the individual and the group as legitimate, that is, the recognised indigenous leader of the friendship group. They are unable to use the services offered by the statutory and voluntary bodies because their conditions are felt to be unacceptable (e.g. clubs—subscriptions, registration—or having to take part in an organised programme of activities).

They lack the simple social skills needed to make the best use of opportunities at school and at work, in friendship groups or in boy/girl relationships. This results in boredom, resentment and frustration which often means that violence is just below the surface and will sometimes erupt with little or no apparent reason.

The young person is often demanding, aggressive, liable to overstate the case or impugn the motives of other people, unable to judge what the other person is feeling, unable to understand or unwilling to take into consideration the limitations of another person's position (headmaster, probation officer, youth employment officer).

There is a decidely high rate of involvement with the police, rapid turnover in employment, long periods of self-imposed unemployment frequent difficulties at home with parents and family, broken friend-ships and broken boy/girl relationships.

They have a distorted view of the opportunities offered by the larger community to get ahead, to get out of the rut, to achieve some-thing, or to be something. Most often "getting on" in any direction, in even a limited way is seen as well nigh impossible because it is "who you know", or "how well you avoid getting caught" or just "plain luck" (which you have no part in attracting) that does the trick—not effort, self-knowledge or perseverence. Both of the above points are equally applicable to the 'simply disorganised'.

Society is seen, from the bottom looking upwards, as an intricate, irrational network of rules and regulations devised by 'them' for 'us' and designed to keep 'us' where 'we' are, and there is nothing 'we' can do about it except the occasional 'lark' to out-smart 'them'. A 'job', breaking into a phone coin box or a gas meter is fair play con-sidering the way the cards are stacked against 'us'.

The unattached girls have similar characteristics with few excep-tions and complications. The girl is even less articulate than the boy, and it is more difficult for her or for others to understand her prob-lems. She is less liable to be in trouble with the police, or to change her job, but her problems in her relationships at home and with her peers are much greater. Her parents' attitude to her behaviour is either strict, over-protective, critical or fatalistic, or sometimes a com-bination of all these attitudes. Frequently she wants to live away from home, but is afraid of the consequences. Her world is smaller than that of the boy, and eventually the boy (and the boys as a group) becomes her authority. Although she can influence him in many subtle ways, she has to accept the role assigned her by him. She has to be at his beck and call, a ready playmate, sometimes the recipient of his violence, and always a loyal supporter. She does what he wants when he wants it. In his role, the boy is supported by his friends and many of the im-peratives of the sub-culture prevalent in the neighbourhood. The girl has to achieve what she can by way of status and fulfilment within the bounds of this relationship. Not only is the girl at the bottom, looking upwards to society, she is also in the position of a 'minority' group at the bottom.

Of course, not all of these characteristics were true of every boy or girl, and where they did apply they varied in degree and from time to time. Nor did we see these as observations of the unattached as a whole but simply of the unattached among our contacts whom we saw as in need of help.

The help needed and the help we gave

Our programme within the project was designed to contact and work with those unattached young people who showed signs of not being able to cope on their own with the problems of growing up. We saw their main problem as being the unavailability within the family, at school, at work and in the neighbourhood, of relationships comparable to those which supported the 'can copes' to the point where they could work out most of their adolescent problems; and the consequent inability or unwillingness of the unattached to use relationships if and when they were available.

In order to offer a programme which they were willing and able to use we had to find ways of making and maintaining relationships with individuals, wherein a worker could serve as a bridge between the young person and the help he needed. The unattached, individually and in groups needed an informal and accepting adult whom they saw as being on their side, seeing things their way; a person who could offer help in terms they could understand; a person who could "reflect reality" by pointing out consequences or suggesting alternatives within the possibilities open to the young people in that community. The coffee stall and the detached workers were in a good position to make these relationships since they were not included within the stereotype 'them' the authorities. The young people did not seem threatened by the offer of help from the workers.

We had numerous kinds of help to offer. They included support, guidance and the offer of social skills directly related to their needs as young people in that community, help in getting along with each other, with parents, at school and at work, in getting to know about services and facilities offered and in learning to make use of them.

We gave information about jobs, how and where to get them, how and why to hold them; about the processes and procedures of the law and probation; about boy/girl relationships; about many different aspects of their work, school and personal life. This information had to be factual, practical, understandable and acceptable.

We offered guidance on how decisions and choices were made; on how to say what they needed and wanted to themselves and to other people, on how to get what they needed and wanted. We helped groups to find adventurous things to do together, and to find the necessary resources, personal and financial, within the community.

The whole grouping

There can be little doubt that we were more successful in offering a service to the whole coffee stall network than we were to any one of its constituent parts. Where we often failed in the separate categories of young persons, we in large part succeeded in filtering the necessary resources into the network. As a result of our presence, contact and concern, the network tended to become more closely knit, that bit

123

more stable, offering a more settled environment in which individuals and groups could meet in a wider variety of activities, than had been the case before we intervened.

This slight but significant increase in stability gave the opportunity for individuals and groups within the network to come together more often for longer 'sessions', and to stay together for longer periods of time. This gave the members of the network an identity (we belong to the coffee stall), which was at first simply accepted, then sought after, and finally seen as an advantage by the participants.

Within the network we were able to provide a much wider variety of recreational opportunities, together with some of the physical and social resources necessary to make the most of these opportunities. A much wider variety of services were also possible and although these included services from the 'outside' (the probation officer, the Family Service Unit, the youth employment officer) they were seen and experienced by the participants as being within the familiar and acceptable pattern of association in the network.

But perhaps most important of all, after the first year or so of contact with us, the coffee stall group came to feel that there were adults who were accepting and understood some of their problems, even though they could not always do something about them. Whether or not many or indeed any of them saw this as indicative of the concern of the larger community for the welfare of its members, is a moot question.

15. The neighbourhood

These points about the neighbourhood are relevant to this discussion in several ways. Firstly, the neighbourhood itself was in part the origin of many of the social attitudes held by the young people. Secondly, the neighbourhood partially defined the potentials and limitations of the opportunities and the services available to the young people, and thirdly the neighbourhood was the focus of our endeavour, the point at which we made contact and for the most part the physical location of the programme.

A neighbourhood in transition

The traditional working-class neighbourhood with the extended family (sometimes grandparents and often uncles and aunts) and the solidarity street block or small group of streets, tended to provide an ordered, reasonable and agreed upon system of relationships and standards and values, which in turn were largely shared with the rest of the 'working class'. It had a status system of its own, and it provided a 'natural environment' within which the young people could find their bearing, relate themselves to a recognised system of rewards and punishments, responsibilities and privileges and known criteria for achieving adulthood. This pattern of family and neighbourhood life often made available to the young people support, guidance and control from a variety of interested and accepting adults within the neighbourhood, whose authority the young people accepted. Uncles, aunts, grandparents, neighbours next door, or round the corner, occupied positions of friends, guides, or disciplinarians.

In short the neighbourhood had a system of support, guidance and control exercised from within, unquestioned and seen as a natural part of it, and requiring only the occasional intervention of officials who were also allowed to act only within the strict limitations already set down by the neighbourhood itself.

In the neighbourhood in which we worked only the barest minimum of that system now survives. It was in an area in which the large Victorian or Edwardian houses were no longer occupied by single families but were divided and rented to a number of households, which sometimes came from different neighbourhoods. The inadequacy of the physical amenities, and the conflict resulting from overcrowding, and joint use of bath and toilet, sometimes even of cooking facilities, militated against growth of the old kind of 'neighbourliness'.

In the redevelopment of the neighbourhood, the families which left the area first, to move to a new town or estate, were frequently the more stable families. In addition the nearby railway terminal and goods depot was a contributory factor in attracting individuals and families from the north, Ireland and overseas, who brought different traditions with them. Although some of these families settled in the neighbourhood, the atmosphere became one of transience, and sometimes of disorganisation, contributing to a neighbourhood pattern in which it was difficult for the young person to get his bearings. The network of a system of privileges and responsibilities, the network of the extended family, friends, and neighbourhood was no longer there to support, guide or control. To all intents and purposes the young person was left to his own resources and those of his family and friends.

Small pockets here and there, mostly families of skilled workers tried to and often did succeed in maintaining the old ethos. But our overall impression of the neighbourhood was one of a working-class community, made up mostly of families from elsewhere who had not moved in to an already structured, well-developed community life which had a 'place for them', and who were not able to reconstruct communal life in the new environment. This may perhaps seem overdrawn but it outlines that aspect of the neighbourhood that most

OBSERVATIONS

occasioned the need for this work, namely social transition. It was within the limits and potentials of this particular situation that we had to find the ways and means of contacting and working with the young people.

16. The statutory and voluntary bodies

The statutory and voluntary bodies are relevant to this discussion in two ways. Firstly, as they were seen by the young people, and secondly, as they saw the problems of the neighbourhood and of the young people. These bodies, seen by the young people as a composite 'them', were the schools, social work agencies, clubs and recreational organisations, probation and law enforcement bodies and occasionally the medical services.

As seen by the young people

The attitudes of the young people can be described as an indiscriminate lumping together of the various bodies, seeing them as a single entity "all in it together", and inability to differentiate between the various functions and services. They saw the voluntary bodies as departments of the borough council. The health visitor would be asked to get Johnny a job, the school attendance officer perhaps to help find a "disappeared husband", the probation officer to "move us up on the housing list". If an official had to pass on a request for help to another official, it was interpreted as "passing the can", the "brush off", or "the usual thing". The young people believed that each official told all the others whatever he knew about them, so that asking for help from the health visitor might "put you in bad" with the housing people or even the police. They also saw an opportunity to play off one official against another in the hope of confusing them, and perhaps getting the same help, particularly material help, from several agencies.

They often had outsize expectations of the different services which led to excessive demands, "If you're supposed to help me give me some money; that's what would help me most". Disappointment led to hostility and then withdrawal. "You're supposed to get me a job that pays what I want, not what you want." "Who are you keeping all the good jobs for?" "I don't go to the youth employment, they don't want to help me."

Not all these attitudes were held by each individual to the same extent, nor by all the young people together in the same way. A variation of these attitudes was held by the whole contact group. The 'can copes' were often not serious about them, the 'temporarily disorganised' were only occasionally concerned, the 'simply dis-

126

organised' accepted them but were not concerned, and the 'seriously disorganised' were deeply involved in believing and propagating. Another factor was that simply ignoring and avoiding contact whenever possible was the general attitude overlaying all the specific ones. These attitudes owed little to individual experience. They were held by the reference groups in the neighbourhood, and were shared by the whole coffee stall network. There was little evidence that they saw politics as being one of the ways open for changing the attitudes or services of the statutory and voluntary bodies whose behaviour they mistrusted or resented. Nor was there a coherent suggestion as to an alternative of any kind. Those who were able to make contact as individuals in a face to face relationship, were able to bypass, at least after the opening stages of the relationship, the negativism represented by these attitudes. The youth employment officer on the coffee stall, the odd teacher or headmaster, the probation officer who had coffee in the café with the boys, were exempted if they "produced the goods". When one of these officers, or workers, was at least in part exempted from the general stereotype because of his behaviour, and the help he offered it was often explained that he was "a good bloke" who had somehow got involved with the wrong people.

There are several general factors concerning the statutory and voluntary bodies which affected the situation in the neighbourhood. Many voluntary bodies began as charities and had their roots in Victorian times. On occasion they still include in their approach and conditions of service, moral overtones based on values which are no longer universally accepted, and which in part at least are concerned with social problems, the content of which has been transformed by widespread social change. They tend to demand a particular cultural conformity (usually middle-class) in exchange for the services given. In youth work, there are preconceptions about programme content, time, place, and conditions, frequently based on a reasoning that youth work is about character training which includes being made to meet the conditions of service. Subscriptions, organised activities, rules and regulations, and ideas about loyalty are either not understood or are resented by the young people. This creates a conflict in expectations.

Ideas have changed as to who should be offered service. It is no longer offered to the 'needy' only, but to all groups in the community, by the community. Sometimes statutory and voluntary bodies pay only lip service to this changing conception and even if they accept it, find it difficult to use in offering service.

The use of social studies (individual and social psychology, sociology and social anthropology) has contributed towards the formulation of old questions in new ways, and has suggested different solutions, implying the need for different kinds of training. In response to the increasingly complicated and diversified nature of the social problems, the social services too, tend to become diversified, each defining its particular concern in a particular and technical way. This makes communication between agencies difficult, and in some cases, rare. It also leads to other difficulties. For example, the recipients are affected because help can only be given on the condition of visiting the agency office, or a worker can offer service only within the specialised category agreed by his agency's policy.

Perhaps the main problem with which the statutory and voluntary bodies have to contend, is co-operation in order to provide a planned service. There appear to be many reasons for this—the traditional differences between the bodies, which on the whole are kept under the carpet where little or nothing can be done to resolve them; the outmoded agency structure that gives priority to traditional practice and traditional status systems; the departmentalisation of the various services due to historical chance, administrative convenience or professional preconceptions; value and standard differences between the agencies; and the lack of accurate information about current neighbourhood problems.

Consequently the bodies concerned, singly or in small groups define the problem in different ways, suggest different solutions, use different methods and different criteria for evaluation. This situation makes it very difficult for the statutory and voluntary bodies to contact and work with the indigenous leaders and autonomous groups as partners in youth work, and means that there is no acceptable language of community affairs shared by the different elements in the community, whose responsibility it should be to create the conditions of community effort.

These observations have not been made as a criticism of statutory and voluntary bodies. Some of them arise from contact with our own agency (Y.W.C.A.) Others arise from our own participation in the community—as a voluntary body.

Although our early preoccupation about the nature of the problem of the 'unattached' was not completely limited to the young person/youth club, it was as it turned out, too narrowly conceived. It caused us to focus too much on service to individuals and groups only, and more or less to ignore community aspects of the work. This naturally affected what we chose to do and how we chose to do it, which in turn conditioned the kind of information our recording produced. It was only when the demand for help to meet a variety of needs visibly outdistanced what we had to offer, that we came to see the need for resources beyond our own. Once it occurred to us that it was necessary to work with the youth serving agencies in the same way as we worked with individuals and groups, we panicked, because we did not have the know-how or the skills, and we were not at all certain that it was our job, or even that the agencies would appreciate our attempting to do it. The attitudes of other agencies to our work were, as could have been anticipated, mixed, ranging from immediate acceptance of ourselves and our efforts, to resentment about 'outsiders' coming in to attempt what "we could do if we had the money and the personnel". Most of the statutory and volunatry bodies with whom we were concerned saw our work solely in terms of its relevance to their particular service. At first this often created difficulties, since we could not always say what we were doing and why, as we were still in the process of working that out for ourselves. Our attitudes towards them were in many ways as uninformed as theirs about us, partly because we had to look at their services and the conditions on which they were offered through the eyes of the young people.

These mutual misunderstandings led to a number of problems of interpretation and communication in the earlier phases of the work. As the programme in the field developed, day to day contact with the statutory and voluntary bodies became part of the field-work and the opportunities this provided for discussion, co-operation and joint planning, resulted certainly by the termination phase in a much broader basis of understanding.

17. The staff

The field-workers (apart from replacements) were appointed at agreed intervals The first, Jumbo, was already working on the stall when the larger project started. The others were appointed after one, two, six and twelve months. This seemed a good idea as the young people were able to get to know a worker gradually, and the neighbourhood was not invaded by a team of people. It also meant that the developing programme determined the kind of worker to be appointed.

It appeared to us that the training and/or experience of field-workers were not as important as their characteristics, although it is doubtful if we should have agreed on this if in-service training had not been available. Nor did it appear that age, class, physical characteristics or intellectual ability were as important as the worker's willingness and ability to deal with the differences of values and standards in work with young people, colleagues and agencies. An important factor was that he should get along with adults as well as with young people.

The following therefore would seem to be basic questions to consider when appointing field-workers. What signs are there of a recognition of legitimate differences in systems of values and standards between individuals, groups, and institutions within the community? What signs are there that in addition to this recognition, the person has a value orientation that for the most part makes sense to himself and which he is willing to stand by, modify, or share as the occasion may require? Is he willing and able to share in in-service training?

The variety within the project team of field-workers together with the observations on the young people and the programme, seemed to point up the value of having a balanced team. Different personalities appealed to different individuals and groups. A worker of one personality could more easily contact and work with one group of young people than another. Different occasions and activities required different kinds of participation from the worker. The quiet unassuming steady person could bring continuity and stability to the programme. The more active, open type could contribute excitement and adventure. Each was able to make a different contribution. Male and female workers offered different things that fulfilled different needs of individuals and groups. Untrained 'naturals' working together might have created chaos, whereas fully trained workers, although offering stability and continuity, might have developed too settled a programme.

The differences also affected the work assignments, and the content of observations offered as a basis for interpretation and further programme planning. They also meant that the in-service training was enriched by the variety of personal experiences brought into it.

Variety in the team made the work more interesting and enjoyable for the workers themselves, which meant that they had more to offer the young people. Nothing can be more deadly than a group of highly trained and serious 'anything', or at the other extreme an undisciplined collection of 'one man shows'.

That some people worked too hard and too long, that some people didn't always pull their weight, that some were meticulous about recording and others somewhat evasive, that some workers occasionally went off on their own to plan their work, that some worked best with individuals, some with groups, that some worked by thinking out and others by feeling, were all in the end, we believe, of little importance. It was important that having recognised their need to work in the way they did, they eventually came to see in a similar way why it was necessary and how it was possible to work as a member of a team. We believe that this was largely due to the way in which we agreed to organise and run the staff conferences and the in-service training. It is our belief that the kinds of people needed to do this work, trained or untrained, are perhaps not available in large enough numbers. For this reason we make specific suggestions as to recruitment and training in Appendix V.

Consultant and administrator

The roles of the consultant and the administrator were not as clear as their titles indicated (and became less so).

The administrator and the project committee had been responsible for the original work of the coffee stall. It was when a project on a larger scale was envisaged that the need was recognised for ongoing advice and help, and for more in-service training for the field-workers. The consultant was appointed to meet these two needs, and when it was suggested that the work should be studied and documented, he agreed to undertake this assignment also. The administrator was responsible for the development and administration of the project, for providing continuing support for the workers, and for providing a link with the sponsoring and other agencies.

Inevitably the several roles of the two workers were shared at different points as the work developed. By reason of his other roles, the consultant could not remain an adviser from the outside, and he became involved in the overall planning. By reason of her concern for the welfare of the staff, and her supervision of the female field-workers, the administrator became involved in the training. In sessions these shared roles became noticeable in specific terms. The administrator was responsible for the staff conferences, but the consultant had sometimes to act as a bridge between the needs of the field-workers and the needs of the agency as presented by the administrator. The consultant was responsible for the training sessions, but the administrator asked questions or made comments on behalf of field-workers as well as herself.

The complexity of the roles, and the sharing of these at different points had both advantages and disadvantages. The consultant was frequently able to see the wider implications of the project, but he knew the danger of passing on insights before the staff or the committee were ready to receive them. The administrator could see the point of view of the sponsoring and other agencies. At times she was at the point of pressure between the agency and the field-workers. The consultant had to recognise this, and to try to find ways of relieving the pressure.

Although in some ways it would have been easier if the roles had been reassigned, and divided between more people, we knew that this was not economically possible for this and other projects, and therefore we believed it was more important to recognise, share and switch the different roles, even though this created problems for ourselves and for other people.

The project committee which was a policy-making body, had to rely on the staff more than was usual, partly because of the pressure of speedily changing events in the field, and also because the criteria which the committee brought to the work came from its own past experience, which was largely that of the more formal youth work setting. This was at times a useful situation since it offered both staff and committee experience in interpretation when working out the difficulties of changing attitudes in relation to new problems and new approaches.

18. Generalisations

We see the following generalisations as emerging from the observations outlined above.

1. The unattached in our contact group, on the whole, did respond to opportunities offered them, providing they were able and willing to understand and accept them, and providing the opportunities met a 'real and apparent need' as experienced and defined by the young people.

2. The largest number of the unattached we contacted did have something to gain from contact with youth serving-agencies of an unconventional kind which were flexibly adapted to their attitudes and demands (or the conditions they imposed).

3. Within our contact group the unattached as individuals tended to fall into one of four categories:

   a. the 'can copes'
   b. the 'temporarily disorganised'
   c. the 'simply disorganised'
   d. the 'seriously disorganised'.

This we took as an indication of the different levels of intensity on which a programme designed to contact and work with the unattached would have to operate.

4. That the unattached did not accept what was offered in the traditional youth work setting, was either due to the content of the offering or the manner in which it was offered (as seen from the point of view of the unattached) and could not be taken as an indication of the absence of need. This was especially true of categories c and d, who were in need of a wide variety of services and opportunities.

5. The unwillingness or inability of the young people to participate in the programmes of the established agencies, and of the established agencies to provide programmes that the young people would accept, had their roots in a misunderstanding which might best be seen as arising from differences in value orientation. These differences in value orientation were reflected in the differing attitudes towards work, education, sex, authority and mobility.

6. The differences between the systems of values and standards and social attitudes to which they gave rise created a conflict in expectations. The young people saw themselves as needing and wanting services and opportunities which the statutory and voluntary bodies

132

either offered in a form unacceptable to them, or which the agencies felt were not appropriate youth work concerns.

7. The recognition of a conflict in expectations between the young people and the youth-serving agencies suggested that the objective of any programme to contact and work with the unattached, should be a reconciliation of conflicting expectations within a given community concerning the needs of the unattached.

8. It also indicated the approach and method, namely detached work, where in the detached worker was outside the recognised and established institutional pattern, and could meet expectations by offering the necessary service at times, in places and on conditions they were able and willing to accept.

9. The first step in any suggested programme must be to make contact with the unattached young people on their own terms, to help them state their own expectations and to work with them in finding ways and means of meeting them.

10. In the process of helping the unattached to define and articulate their expectations and to find ways and means of meeting them, a programme should develop determined by the felt and stated needs of the young people rather than by the form and content of the existing services offered by the statutory and voluntary bodies.

11. Such a programme should be characterised by the use of the natural patterns of association, and informal opportunities for contact and service within the pattern of expectations and behaviour of the unattached, rather than by supposition about where, how, under what conditions, and how and with what expected results the service should be offered.

12. Such a programme requires a wider variety of services than the detached worker singly or as a team would be able or want to offer, so that ways should be found of interpreting the needs of the unattached to the statutory and voluntary bodies.

13. The programme should include not only work with the unattached and the statutory and voluntary bodies concerned but also with indigenous lay leaders and autonomous groups which offer help and support to the unattached, but often need recognition, help and support for themselves.

14. At this point the problem becomes one of working with the community, and requires special knowledge, a different approach and different skills from that of the ordinary youth worker or detached worker, and must be seen as the job of a community worker who would

    a. together with the detached workers decide what were the legitimate needs of the unattached, what kind of service they required, in what form and in what time or place;

  b. interpret this to the statutory and voluntary bodies in terms of concrete service possibilities and suggestions as to how these services could be organised, planned and carried out;

  c. at the same time interpret the legitimate potentialities and limitations of the youth-serving agencies to the detached workers, so that they might explain this to the young people with whom they were working.

15. Taking these points together, we see the solution of the problem of the unattached as lying in a community-wide network of services which would provide points of contact, conditions of service and opportunity which the young people could accept by

  a. developing the network of relationships among and between the unattached in the community, through a programme of activities resulting from the presence of the detached worker;

  b. developing a network of informal points of contact for offering help and support for the unattached by using the recognised indigenous leaders and autonomous groups;

  c. developing a pattern of service among the statutory and voluntary bodies to meet the needs of the unattached, which would mean partially changing the form and content of certain services;

  d. overlapping these three networks on a community wide basis.

16. Such a programme should considerably reduce the number of young people in any given community designated as unattached, in the sense that unattached is taken to mean needing service but being unwilling or unable to accept it.

17. Such a programme, even if it is only partially successful, can be expected to have beneficial side effects for the community as a whole. An attempt to build a community wide network of points of contact, service and opportunity around a particular problem (the needs of the unattached) might well create the community atmosphere, the channels of communication, the processes and procedures and the reservoir of goodwill which could be helpful in dealing with other community problems. It might suggest a pattern for the community care of the mentally ill or suggest one approach to dealing with juvenile delinquency.

18. This solution requires working with individuals and groups and the community concurrently, in order to affect a reconciliation of expectations in the field of service to the unattached, using the tools and techniques of informal education. The method might best be described as social education.

  It should be noted that the above observations are included in the report, not only as solutions we found for our problems but also as suggestions for others who might wish to work in a similar way. The implications of some of these will be explored in the rest of this report.

Chapter Five
APPROACH AND METHOD

This part of the report does not attempt to provide a scientifically based conceptual theory: instead it describes with copious illustrations from our records, how we set about our work with individuals, with groups of young people, and with the community. We have described this in detail in the hope that it will be of interest and use to students and youth workers with less experience, as well as to trainers, administrators and those responsible for policy within the youth service and in adjacent fields. We have also presented the general thinking behind our work and training, not in order to claim that this is the only or necessarily the best method of work, but as part of the record of the 'how', and the 'why' of our particular project.

In the previous sections we described our project which involved working in different ways with individuals, groups and parts of the community. These were not seen in isolation but were integrated within the total project. In this section, purely for the purpose of clarity, the three aspects of the work have been separated. Obviously no field-worker could work with one aspect in isolation, nor could one single field-worker do the total job. Nor would we suggest that the whole project is on the one hand an extension of individual work, or on the other an extension of group work. We see the need for several multi-purpose workers, who can understand and practise each aspect of the work.

19. Work with individuals

Work with individuals was the primary task of the whole project. Even when we were working with groups or with the community, our concern was how the group could help the individual or how the neighbourhood and the community could contribute to his growth and development. We saw ourselves as offering a relationship within which the young person could be given information on jobs, schools,

the law or recreation; the services of a go-between, between the young
person, and his family, friends, employer, or the statutory and voluntary bodies; the 'know-how' of simple social skills; and advice,
guidance, acceptance and support in his endeavour to hammer out
of adolescence the identity of a young adult.

What is a relationship?

A relationship is a connection between two people in which some sort
of exchange takes place. This connection and exchange may be verbal,
emotional, physical or intellectual, and is often all of these. It may
include an exchange of ideas, skills, attitudes or values, or even the
exchange of things—money, tools or food. Relationships 'happen'
at all times, in all places, in all parts of society, and in all phases of the
development of individuals. We are all involved in relationships all
the time.

The concept of relationship is of special value to those in the
'helping' professions because it is through relationships that people,
and in particular, young people, learn to seek and get satisfaction for
their basic human needs, social and emotional as well as physical.
They are also means by which the young person learns 'the rules of
the game', how he defines himself to himself and others, and how he
sees his life chances and the opportunities open for their fulfilment.
In tracing the growth and development of a boy whom we shall call
Johnny, it is possible to list some of the relationships in his life and
the opportunities provided by them.

Johnny

Family Food, shelter, protection. A chance to learn to walk and talk
in a protective supporting atmosphere. A chance to relate to adults in
authority, mother, father, older brother or sister and to other siblings
(rivalry, competition, co-operation). A chance to experience love,
affection, anger, frustration, or aggression in a meaningful way in
relation to his own needs in a known situation. A chance to relate to
the outside world—friends, neighbourhood, school and work—and
still have 'background' support and acceptance, to encourage, to
praise success and to buffet failure. A chance to learn numerous social
skills, from how to mix the sugar in his tea and tie his shoes, to what
to wear the first day at work, or to a wedding or funeral. A chance to
learn social attitudes to money, work, school, sex, marriage and
family life. In the process of doing all this Johnny acquires some idea
of who he is, what he wants to be, and how he can go about doing
and being it.

Early playmates A chance to learn to play with, be with, and do things together with youngsters of his own age, outside the family. A chance to develop and use physical skills in play, games, or fighting. A chance to experience and learn about feelings of rejection, acceptance, like and dislike, with people outside the family. A chance to develop and use social skills in getting on with people, to develop and use his ability to talk and to communicate A chance to learn social attitudes to things, people, events and situations.

School mates and teacher A chance, with his early school mates, to settle in to school, to learn to read, write, add and subtract, and to behave in a classroom—a non-family, non-neighbourhood playgroup situation. A chance to relate to the teacher, who is an adult in authority but not a parent nor an older brother or sister, and who must be shared with others. A chance to accept or reject what the school setting offers in subject matter, standards and values, social attitudes and the role of the teacher. A chance to acquire ideas of "why they are trying to teach us?; what they are trying to do for us?; why they are doing it?; what I can get out of it?" He acquires some idea of what is expected of him by family, friends, school, and larger communities during the teenage stage of his development.

Adolescent friendship A chance to have an intensive, sharing, relationship outside the family (the best friend) with all its emotional overtones, including learning to handle the inevitable tensions that arise from disappointment. A chance to have a partner in trying out new things, in sport, games, recreation, sex, petty crime, the first job, the first girl, the first night away from home, the first trip to the seaside without an adult; a chance to have support and companionship in these as a co-operative adventure, and to work out in thinking, discussion and action, to accept, reject or 'invent' and above all to experiment with standards and values.

Groups The same experiences but less intensive in small adolescent friendship groups and less intense again as the group grows larger.

Girl friend A chance to learn to play the masculine role as it is played in the culture or sub-culture of which he is a member. A chance to learn to accept another person and be accepted by her, exchanging confidences, recognising mutual responsibility, and a variety of physical, emotional and social giving and taking. A chance to form an image of himself as a man in relation to work, and as a lover, husband and father. An excuse to lessen the intensity of family, friendship and group ties in preparation for founding his own family.

Workmates A chance to learn about what he is doing, to learn how to get along with other people on the job, the rules of the work game, how and when to avoid work, how and when to take responsibility and do the job well, behaviour towards the boss, or the foreman. A chance to try out new roles as the 'good worker', 'the indifferent or bad worker', 'the good workmate', 'the trouble maker'. A chance to make new friends, often not connected with family or neighbourhood, to learn to get on with them, to brag, or argue—to be in a 'man's world'. A chance to accept or reject the standards and values within the world of work—being on time, working in a team, workmanship, taking responsibility. A chance to assess his life possibilities in terms of profession, vocation, future promotion, or increased salary.

Detached worker   A chance to relate to an adult, who has something to offer and is outside the family, school, friendship or work setting. A chance to test out a number of ways of being or doing things with an adult, acceptance, rejection, hostility, aggression. Someone to talk about himself, his life conditions and chances as he sees them. A chance to find someone from whom he may get things that he needs on conditions which are acceptable to him. A chance to see yet another set of values and standards at play, those of the worker, and by reflection, those of the worker's agency and a section of the larger community.

Johnny's relationships as described were of three types:

1. Primary (as in the family).
2. Secondary simple (teacher, club leader, detached worker).
3. Secondary intensive (adolescent friendship, best friend, girl friend).

The relationships took place in three different kinds of setting— face to face (family, best friend, boy/girl), in a small group, (family, playgroup, friendship group) and in larger complex groups, or a group or groups (school, work, neighbourhood, the coffee stall network). Dividing and subdividing the kinds of relationships and the settings in which they occur, in order to explore the concept of relationship, are simply convenient ways of handling the description of a complex social observation, and are not meant to be representative of social reality 'as it happens'. Relationships between people cannot be said with an accuracy to fall into any set constellation of forms.

It can be said that Johnny's relationships as described here (including his probable marriage and parenthood) are the context within which Johnny is offered the opportunity to satisfy his basic needs, food, shelter, and physical, emotional and social growth and development, including his needs for acceptance and status. We can also glimpse from these illustrations something of the importance of relationships, and the manner in which the different kinds and level of relationships become the context for Johnny's learning more about himself and about others, about ideas, values, physical objects, the neighbourhood and the community. They also provide the opportunity for learning the physical, emotional and social skills by which he becomes 'a person'.

This of course is more complex than we can hope to indicate here. Nonetheless we can assume that at least half of the difficulties of many of the young people with whom we were working were due to the absence, at crucial periods in their development, of satisfactory relationships with adults who could have offered the ideas, attitudes, social skills, guidance and support that would have helped them in their social development. This assumption (and it can only be an assumption), indicated not only the difficulty, but what could be done about it, that is, we could offer a relationship which the young people could understand and accept, and which could in part compensate for the absence of understanding adults in their social environment.

The role of the worker

The worker's role when using the relationship between himself and the young person can be listed under five headings:

1. *Information giving* He offers and gives information in such a way that the young person is able to understand and use it. He tries to offer it at the right time and the right place and in a logical sequence that will make sense to the young person. He tries to explain the source of the information, its limitations or potentials, and where the young person can get more of it on his own. He usually tries to make clear if possible the difference between facts, opinions, a surmise, a guess or a hunch.

2. *Acting as a bridge* He offers his services as a go-between, between the young person and his family, school, work, friends, and the statutory and voluntary bodies, always with the knowledge and consent of the young person.

3. *Passing on simple social skills* He helps the young person to learn how to say what he wants when talking to various kinds of people, how to ask or answer a question in different situations, how to make a request, or let it be known he is grateful for something done for him, how to write a letter asking for something, how to make an appointment or an introduction, how to use the library or other local services, how to behave in the West End, how to say what he thinks to the boss and still keep his job, how to argue with the police and still stay out of the 'nick'.

4. *Advice and guidance* He offers advice and guidance whenever asked. Advice should never be offered until asked for either directly or by implication. Ideally advice should never tell a person what to do but how to find out for himself. Guidance should never be a direct indication of what action to take, but an indication of how to take action, not what decision to make, but how to make decisions, not what choice to make but how to find out how choices are made.

140

5. *Acceptance and support* Ongoing acceptance and support is the underpinning of a relationship with a young person—the acceptance of differences, support in being the same as others, support in being different from others, support in trying to change, to think or feel in a different way, in being what he is or in attempting to be what he wants to be. There are two principal considerations here. The first is the acceptance of the person, regardless of his past or present behaviour, even when it must be made clear that the behaviour and its consequences are rejected. The second is that never, except in an emergency, should a pat answer be given. Instead, the young person should be helped to get the answer for himself, and given the necessary information, and the necessary know-how and support while he tries to work it out by himself.

Stages of development in a relationship

After the initial contact is made, most relationships include an opening stage or testing out, followed by expressions of feelings, the appearance of strong feelings, and then the gradual decline of intensity and tailing off in the relationship. Primary relationships, as in the family, are supposed to and often do, maintain the strong bond of feelings, and allow possibilities for their expression over a long period, sometimes for life. Others such as the adolescent relationship between friends, or the love affair, go through the whole cycle from testing out to tailing off in a relatively short time. The type of relationship we are discussing here is different from both of these, since its function is to offer help of a much less intensive kind. Even so, such may be the deprivation of some individuals that the relationship may give the appearance at different times of being primary or intensive. It is the worker's recognition and skill in meeting the immediate need of the young person, and at the same time looking upon the relationship as a temporary one, which will help to keep the balance. The young person sees the present, but the worker sees the present and something of the future, and uses his skill to help the young person to recognise the limitations of the relationship as and when he is able to do so. The worker should always keep in mind that part of his endeavour is to move the young person from 'testing out' to 'tailing off'. Each stage in the relationship cycle has characteristics of its own that offer the worker the opportunities to develop, work through, and finally to terminate the relationship.

Making contact

There are more than likely to be several adults in a boy's immediate environment, the teacher, the club leader, the doctor, the priest, the social worker—who could offer him a good deal more help than the detached worker. Why has the boy not been willing or able to accept it? More often than not he has reacted against the institutional setting and its expectations and demands, rather than against the person, against the official rather than the individual, and he has interpreted the 'formality of the situation' as a demand, an imposition or an expectation that he could not or would not meet, or even as rejection. As often as not both the boy and the official have been hampered by 'the institutional aspect' of the service and the institutionally induced conditions under which it has been offered. The detached worker has the opportunity to try and make a direct relationship with the boy outside the institutional situation against which he has been reacting. He can afford to reach out further than most of his colleagues to the young person, to demonstrate his acceptance. This enables the boy to respond to the worker's offer without his response being too heavily coloured by his preconceptions about 'them'.

In making a relationship in this way there is a paradox. On the one hand the relationship necessary to help the young person must be allowed simply to 'happen'. On the other hand the detached worker will need well considered terms of reference within which to allow the relationship 'to happen', as well as the know-how with which he and the young person can make the most of 'the happening'. The relationship can only be of real value if it is spontaneous, and yet it has to be thought about if it is to offer what it should to the young person, and thinking about something as intangible as a relationship is certain to curtail its spontaneity. The worker needs to recognise that thinking about the relationship and his participation in it is part of the work, and to accept the fact that this might temporarily hamper the spontaneity, but he must realise that part of his job while being objective, is to stop thinking, allow the spontaneity to take over and the relationship to take its own course. The only advice that anyone can give the worker is that he should learn all he can in abstract ways about relationships in general, the settings in which they take place, the levels of intensity they should or should not include, check what he has learned in this way with his own experience, accept and reject what he will, forget all about it, and then relax and allow things to happen.

Testing out

In the opening stages of a relationship, the young person more often than not is trying out the adult, wanting to know how far he can go, what demands he can legitimately make, how much acceptance he can manage to illicit, what he can get out of the relationship that will be of use to him. The worker is expected to take all this in his stride, not only by good-natured acceptance but by being able to show that he does accept the young person despite the rigours of testing out. In the opening stages of the cycle, being able to 'prove' acceptance is of paramount importance. This is not an unrealistic or untruthful acceptance. The worker must be perfectly honest in reacting to things of which he does not approve while continuing to accept the young person. Since we cannot like everyone it is of great importance that the worker avoid continuing a relationship with a young person whom he knows he does not like and to whom he feels he cannot show an honest acceptance.

The expression of feeling

The expression of feeling is apt to be the second stage in a developing relationship. The young person now feels free to express his feelings about the worker, and usually and quite naturally they are mixed. He dislikes or he 'hates' the worker. He likes him very much, he likes him better than 'Y' or 'Z'. He thinks he is too tall, too short, too smart, too green, of the wrong religion or political outlook. He is useless, a good 'touch', or "the only person around here who is any good". It is at this point that the worker can point up the meaning of the relationship, "I may be a vegetarian, a Roman Catholic, a voting liberal, short and really rather stupid, which might indeed be very silly things for me to be, but that's me, and the fact is that if you want me to help you with a job, or with this or that, I can do so". It is also at this stage of a relationship that the worker can help the boy to overcome his resistance to being accepted This is often very important since many of the boys we work with 'defend themselves' against the idea that any adult does like them and is willing and able to help them. Sometimes they actually believe this, and sometimes it is an easy way out of having to change their opinion that everybody and everything is against them. But it is also during this period of the relationship that the worker can go wrong by offering or implying that he will offer more than he can or should by way of emotional support.

The appearance of strong feelings

If the worker is able to maintain the relationship through the first two stages there usually comes a time when strong feelings appear. The young person makes excessive demands for time, attention or things. He becomes too attached, too affectionate, too aggressive or hostile. This is a pivotal stage since the young person can learn a great deal by the way the worker helps him to handle these feelings and by the way in which the worker is seen to handle his own. These are often

143

difficult times for the worker. He may feel that the aggression is a sign that he is not really helping the young person. This is often untrue. The young person may need to challenge and use the worker as a butt for his strong feelings, in a way he could not use his mates or adults in his environment. This may be complicated by the fact that the boy's feelings are not related to the worker but to his parents, older brother, teacher, boss, probation officer. Even so these are feelings the detached worker must recognise and use. He must see them as the material which he and the boy are learning to handle as part of the process of the boy's social development. It is at this stage of the relationship that its possibilities are the greatest, as are its dangers, and the worker needs as much help in knowing what to do as does the boy. It is at this time that supervision is often most valuable. From this phase of strong feelings the boy can be helped to learn how to relate to adults and to make choices and decisions and act upon them, the experience of which may help him in similar situations elsewhere. It is also the stage in the relationship through which the young person can learn a good deal about how to create an identity.

The decline in intensity

Through all the phases of the relationship the worker should be preparing himself and the boy to transfer the relationship to other individuals, groups, or agencies in the community. He should have been able by now to have helped the relationship through the strong feelings stage so that it has offered the young person some opportunity to know more about himself and to reach out and do new things. The young person may not want to or be able to see why or how the decline in intensity is happening but if the worker has been successful, the boy's new interests should allow him to withdraw slowly, leaving the psychological and social space necessary for the boy to attempt to cope on his own. During this stage the worker may have for a while to enter into the new activities with the boy and even to a limited extent associate himself with the new relationship, with friends, with groups, with a girl friend, a teacher or an employer. He certainly has to support and encourage him in his new adventures. He needs to be definite in his acceptance of the boy's new activities so as to encourage the boy's continuance of them. The worker should realise that the young person will from time to time backslide and relapse into dependence in order not to have the responsibility for 'going it on his own'. This waning stage in a relationship cycle should be seen by the worker as a time on the one hand to allow the person to get on with it himself and on the other hand to make it known he is available if and when things go wrong.

Tailing off

By the fifth stage in the relationship, if the worker has been successful he should be able to continue giving support by only occasional direct contact with the boy, leaving most of the work to be done by the boy's new social environment and by the worker's supportive contacts in that environment. The worker at this point is supporting the boy's friends, putting the boy's case to his employer, supporting the girl in her relationship with the boy, or interpreting the boy to agencies with his knowledge and consent as required. After a time the worker must decide whether or not to continue. In one case a follow up might be advisable, because, by approving a boy's accomplishments in handling the new job, making new friends, or finding new interests, he can further strengthen him in his new pursuits. In another, it might not be advisable because the boy might see himself as having grown through the relationship and might resent a follow up as an intrusion.

Obviously relationships don't fall neatly into the phases we have outlined. Yet such a general description of their possible development can help the worker judge his progress in helping the young person.

Exploring the potential

An important aspect of working with an individual is that of helping him to explore the potentials of the relationship, both in terms of what each person has to offer the other, and in terms of its value to him in helping him to find out what he wants to do and how to do it. An important aim of the relationship is to help the young person to make choices, resolve conflicts and to make decisions. To make a choice implies thinking out the possible alternatives for oneself, and forming some idea of where such alternatives might lead. One then has to decide which alternative to choose and how to act on it. In most cases this is almost a natural process. We are helped by our own past experience, by the examples of those around us, by the awareness of our needs, by the social attitudes and skills we have picked up in our family, friendships, school and work life. For most of us choosing is almost an automatic process, except in unusual circumstances, on grave occasions or in grave emergencies.

But we sometimes overlook the complex set of expectations that are projected onto the adolescent by contemporary society during a relatively short period in his development. He faces the choice of a job or a career, leaving school or continuing further education, of going steady with a girl or even getting married, as well as numerous less important decisions. In short, for a variety of reasons, our society makes adolescence a period of many very important personal choices.

145

In some communities the young person is helped with these choices by the norms accepted by his family, school, friends, the church or the whole community. But in the community in which we worked the norms were not always seen, known, or agreed upon, on occasion did not exist, often those which existed were not accepted by the young person. He had few resources from which to make choices that would affect his future.

Much the same can be said of resolving personal conflicts. The adolescent faces the problem of accepting an identity thrust upon him or creating an identity for himself, although the nature and variety of material offered him to help him may be woefully insufficient to his needs. The worker enters into the relationship with the young person in order to help him learn how to resolve some of these conflicts and how to make his choices and decisions. The young person offers the worker the status of an adult who is a point of reference. He is a particular person to the young person with whom he works.

The choice may concern a job, a school problem, a value and standard choice, a question of whether to lie or steal, a question of "shall I get married now or wait?" The worker's job is to provide within the relationship the tools whereby the young person is helped to answer the question on his own. Frequently however, the incident is presented to the worker, not as a choice but as an accomplished fact, or one about to be accomplished. "We were on a job last night" or "I am getting married next month". The worker learns, in listening to such comments, to distinguish between a presentation of information, and a request for help. It is frequently the young person's inability to ask directly for advice and help, which has handicapped him in his previous contacts, and the worker heeds to be in tune to the underlying requests in the statements made.

Frequently the worker's responsibility is 'to reflect reality'. When the young person talks of "planning a job" the worker might be able to point out the size of the police force, the vastness of its resources (finger-print experts, forensic medicine, identity kits), and might list the number of "our friends already on the inside". In short he avoids preaching or moralising but offers realistic information that the young person can understand.

Workers have to learn how to explain to young people that they (the young people) have to make their own choices for instance about whether or not to become involved in a dice school but that for the worker the choice has been made. The worker has constantly to help the young person to see the limits of the relationship in terms of the worker's values and standards about the law, sex, money or violence, always trying to do so in a way that will not break the relationship. He continues to accept the boy but is able to reject a particular item of behaviour and to say why he did so. The worker is there to offer only certain types of service, and lending his driving licence so that a boy may steal a car, for example, is not one of them. If an incident involves agencies, the worker might point out that they too have 'bosses' who make rules and regulations and that the attitudes of those bosses have to be taken into consideration if their service is wanted. The worker can explain the terms on which the service is offered so that a young person may decide whether or not he will accept or reject it.

New difficulties arise when the reality is openly and obviously a bad situation in the view of both the young person and the worker (as could sometimes be true of housing, unemployment, or police action). The worker has to admit that he believes these are bad and sympathises with the young person, but in doing this he tries to reflect the complexities of the adult world. Obviously he has to admit openly that his standards and values are different from those of the rent racketeer or the detective sergeant who allows his underlings to use violence. The worker's values and standards have to be seen to apply to the behaviour of himself, his colleagues, the statutory and voluntary bodies, and to the community as well as to the behaviour of the young person.

The worker has a system of values and standards which are 'all his own' in the sense that he accepts and acts upon them as a person, and they are also shared at least to some extent with other people, his colleagues in the field, the agency for which he works, or the church to which he belongs. He was not born with these. He has acquired them. The process by which he has acquired them and acts upon them could be a useful subject for discussion within the relationship. Above all, the worker is aware of the points at which he is not absolutely sold on this or that item in his own system, and the points at which he himself experiences conflict. He might be able to show the young person how he lives with, attempts to resolve or uses this conflict. For example a married worker might feel he should be at home more often with his wife and young children. But he has to balance that feeling and the particular values and standards on which it is based, against his desire to do this kind of work. For a variety of reasons, he likes doing it. He likes the young people. He wants to help with the problems he sees. He thinks it is important. It gives him status. It helps him to learn things about himself and other people. It will further his career. Sometimes he is not at all sure why he is doing it. All of this should somehow be part of the material available in response to the questions from the young person, "Why does she let you out so often?—Do you work here to get away from her?—Why don't you spend more time at home in the evening with your kids?"

The worker after all represents a section of the larger community and the society that pays him to do this work. This in itself is an important point to try and make to the young people, if we remember the distorted ideas and attitudes of some of them towards adults and the larger community. The worker is one of 'them' and much depends on how he helps the young person to resolve the differences between seeing 'them' as exploiters and accepting the worker both as one of 'them' and as a person. How this conflict is resolved will in some measure affect how the boy sees the world beyond his neighbourhood. The potential of any relationship is as broad and varied, or as narrow and restricted, as the personal resources the two parties bring to it. The use of its potential as a resource for the young person is the reason the worker has entered into the relationship.

Difficulties in limiting the relationship

We have already suggested that although our concern in this work is to some extent with the success or failure of primary relationships, we cannot offer the young person primary relationships or even secondary intensive relationships, but simple secondary relationships, like those of the teacher, the club leader, the vicar, the knowledgeable adult neighbour, or the understanding librarian. A worker cannot be mother or father to the young people, nor boy friend nor girl friend. The relationships into which workers enter, have definite limits, and the most important of these is the help which a worker believes is necessary for the social development of the young person, in relation to the help the young person seeks from the worker. The analogy here might well be to the teacher. The same limitations, the same potentials, the same possibility of mutual exploration are involved in the teacher/ pupil relationships, though they are within the school setting, and on the whole are directed towards a different objective. They include the need to pass on specific subject matter, and enforce standards, and this frequently limits the teacher's effectiveness in helping the young person to deal with problems of social development, not directly related to school.

Problems frequently arise when the young person who is an isolate or who is emotionally deprived, attempts to use the relationship with the worker to satisfy emotional needs that should have been met by other types of relationships. Some individuals are liable to become over-dependent on the worker and find ways of getting attention and monopolising the worker's time. This again is similar to the problem of the teacher. The worker needs to see that prolonged over-dependence is a failure in a relationship, and that his job is to offer the young person other possibilities for satisfying the same need elsewhere. Exploitation in the sense that the young person demands unrealistic amounts of time, kinds of attention, or money from the worker is often simply a trying-out phase early in the relationship. But if such demands continue the greatest skill is needed in understanding what lies behind apparent 'exploitation'. What are the boy's expectations? At what point is the worker more helpful by limiting the demands than in accepting them? A relationship can break down because the young person 'loses respect' for the worker, loses interest in the relationship, or feels guilty about his behaviour. On the whole we should see exploitation as an opportunity to help the young person find legitimate outlets for his need to exploit, and to learn in the process how to handle that need. The other side of the same problem is the need of the worker to exploit the young person by solving his problems for him and appearing in the relationship larger than life, protecting the young person or over indulging him, things we are all liable to do and which we have to learn to understand and accept in ourselves before they can be avoided.

A constant factor in every relationship must be the worker's recognition that the relationship is temporary and he must attempt to let the young person see this as and when the young person is ready. The relationship is always in transition from worker/young person to young person/others, whether the transition be initiated by the young person or by the worker. In natural transition the relationship tails off because it has accomplished its purpose, the boy has a job, is keeping it, and he has the money, friends and status he feels he needs. The worker becomes only one friend among several and is greeted casually or consulted in emergencies. But the worker might terminate the relationship for other reasons. He might feel that someone else can help the boy more adequately, or that the boy is now able to cope reasonably well on his own. Or it could be that the worker is leaving the area and must arrange a phased withdrawal and attempt gradually to transfer the relationship to another adult. In each of these situations the worker must find ways of letting the individual know what is happening in terms he can understand.

Perhaps the primary difficulty in the termination is the young person's feeling that the worker is attempting to 'pass the can'. Some of this would be normal in any case since no one likes to feel that he is being helped to outgrow a relationship. Change of any kind is often seen as threatening or worrying, even when the change itself is a welcome one. But this difficulty is emphasised in our circumstances by the fact that the 'passing the can' suspicion is so firmly established as an attitude towards the statutory and voluntary bodies, that it compounds the normal dislike or fear of change in the nature or content of the relationship. This complication makes for the possibility of disappointment, anxiety, hostility, even aggressive behaviour, being part of the young person's response to the worker's attempt to terminate the relationship. It is not so difficult when the disappointment is vented on the worker, since he must see it as part of the helping

L

process. The real difficulty comes when the young person directs his disappointment to the new party in the relationship, at school or at work, in the friendship group, or the new worker. The worker then has to help the new party in some way to understand what is happening, and to be at ease with it, so as to be able to offer the necessary help and support.

The same difficulty can be reflected in the follow up when the worker attempts to understand what kind of continued help and support are necessary to the young person in the new situation. He may find the 'I don't want to know you' attitude either because the individual has grown out of the need for the kind of help described above, or because he feels he has been 'turned over to' or 'pushed on to' someone else, and interprets this as rejection on the part of the worker. The worker may find either that the young person needs no help in his new situation or that the same old problems have come to the fore in a new environment in which case he may have to start all over again.

Obviously the pace at which any of these things can happen is dependent upon the needs and capabilities of the young person, and the conditions and circumstances with which he has to contend, as well as the services and opportunities available to him. The 'can copes' on the one hand might be able and willing to 'use the worker' on a very short term basis indeed, while on the other hand a seriously disorganised boy might need constant support over long periods, indeed almost indefinitely.

Illustrations from records

People who work only and intensively with individuals, in a special setting designed to accomplish specific ends would perhaps find it comparatively easy to produce ordered developed case records, illustrating their work. Their approach and method includes meeting the individual regularly by agreement at a specific time and place and for a specific reason.

As detached workers, we had to expect sessions with individuals in many different circumstances and almost always the time and place were of the boy's own choosing. A session could consist of two sentences of casual conversation in passing, a long chat on the telephone, or a lengthy 'full-scale interview' between the boy and the worker in a crowded café. It often occurred in the presence of other people, which partly determined the content of the meeting. In addition to this the worker recorded his contacts with a large number of boys and girls individually and in groups, and this in turn affected the nature and content of the resulting 'case records'. The information available for recording was that which the boy wanted to give and our own observations of his behaviour. The worker had no 'official status' and for the most part was not in a position to question a boy in order to complete a record.

The illustrations that follow from our field-work records are therefore not 'cases' in the classical sense that all the information desired can be included—nor are they in any way 'absolute guides to the helping process'. They are used as, and can only be seen as, minimum indications of the help being offered in relationships, in respect of the needs of the young person and the possibilities open to the worker.

'Temporary support'

Shorty was fifteen when he first came to the coffee stall. He lived with his mother and father and a young sister. When he was ten the family moved out of the neighbourhood, and during the period in another district, he left school and started work as a decorator. When he was fifteen the family moved back into the neighbourhood, and Shorty, on joining his schoolmates, became the instigator of a series of petty crimes and planner of larger "jobs" which never came off. His father became sick and the family lived on national assistance, moving house several times. After a few months with his old friends, Shorty gave up his job, which he had held for fourteen months. He was then unemployed for sixteen weeks after which he worked for a few weeks at a time.

Shorty was always around the stall or in the club premises, but no one seemed to know other than his nickname. He was uncommunicative and apparently uninterested in what was going on. Although he had been known within the coffee stall network for some time, it was not until he had been out of work for several months that he turned to a worker for help.

Worker's record (Gerry)/20th May/club premises

Billy and Shorty were very quiet most of the evening, looking and obviously feeling "very fed up". It was just before closing time when they started to talk. Shorty said they had tried to steal a van and Shorty was caught but Billy got away. Shorty said he had been threatened by a policeman and told it would be Borstal unless he gave the name of his friend, so he had said it was Billy. Billy was angry about this and said that he would never have given way. I tried to say that under that kind of pressure it was not surprising. Don, who was listening in, would not agree and took Billy's side. The conversation turned to what attitude they should adopt in court next day and they both agreed to plead not guilty. Both boys thought they would be convicted but hoped by arguments they might lessen

151

the fine. They were genuinely frightened they would be sent away. I agreed to go to court with them.

May 30th Shorty stopped me as I was going out, to say he had a job with a builder.

Record summary/June

Shorty constantly telephones on every possible pretext. Frequently he talks about himself, about the boy he used to be, about his keeping his job fourteen months. He often talks about Dennis' sticking to his apprenticeship, sometimes saying Dennis is a fool, and sometimes that he knows what he is doing. Frequently I just listen, but I also ask questions in order to encourage him in his obvious wish to get a job and settle down.

Samples of daily contacts from Worker's Records

July 3rd Shorty phoned and asked me to find him a job. Said he wanted to work as a decorator and didn't mind a low wage. I helped him find a firm where he was given a lengthy interview and promised the first available vacancy.

July 24th Shorty was anxious to enquire about the Marines. We went to their office but Shorty was told he could not apply until December. He was not interested in the other services.

August 3rd Wrote a letter to Shorty's old employer asking if he would provide a reference.

August 3rd Shorty phoned and said he and Frank had broken into a neighbour's gas meter. He thought his parents knew about it and was afraid he might get thrown out. I interpreted this as a possible invitation to go and see Shorty's family and thought my presence might prevent a family row. No one mentioned the gas meter, but I was welcomed by both Shorty and his parents. Paid several visits and eventually helped with the family's removal to another flat.

Worker's summary/January

During October Shorty found himself a job through the youth employment office with the decorating firm at which Don works, and he has to date been working very hard with lots of overtime, and consequently earning very good money. He has become rather a lonely figure as a result of this, not going around so much with his previous friends. It is probably because of this that he has become more responsible in outlook and held his job as long as he has. He is still very reserved and withdrawn and difficult to get to know. I feel that he depends very much on the relationships with the project staff and this seems to be one of the anchors which he needs in order to keep his job, and to keep reminding himself that he has rather more potential than some of his friends. Now that he seems to have settled down once more to work, one hopes that he will gradually work through the instability which showed itself during the summer months. His home life is more settled now that his mother is house-keeper to a business firm on the fringe of our area. This provides an adequate standard of living for the family and this was reflected on my last visit, in the obvious comfort and the neat orderliness of their new home. Shorty was much more at ease, more willing to talk, more open and considerate, and very interested in his work.

Youth Employment Officer/March 31st

Shorty could be regarded as a success. He came from North London where for fourteen months he had made extremely good progress with a decorator. Another job was found for him eventually by our bureau with a local firm. For some reason the boy, after agreeing to take the job, failed to start and for the next six months he proved particularly awkward. He found himself four jobs which he left on the slightest provocation and on more than one occasion he came close to quite serious conflict with the police. I had several talks with him at the bureau but could make no headway. I felt most unhappy about this as prior to his move to our area his record had been all that could be desired. When in October I met him at the coffee stall it seemed that because I was meeting him on neutral ground and in an unofficial capacity, he might prove more responsive. I had long talks with him and persuaded him to call at the bureau, when I was able to submit him to another firm. He was duly engaged and has been there ever since and is making first-class progress. He is now seldom seen at the coffee stall, and I think he can safely be assumed to have settled into a new job and new interests.

Comments

The worker's contact with Shorty was through small groups in the network and never developed into a close 'deep relationship'. None-theless, Shorty was able, even in this almost casual relationship, to work out some of his problems. Often it is not the depth of the relationship that is important, but its availability at the right time and place, as well as its usefulness to the boy in terms he can understand and accept.

The use of the telephone is relevant since it emphasises the same facts, that availability is important, and that the young person is in charge of the intensity of the relationship. Shorty may have been using the telephone because he was shy, or he may have been using it as a device to keep the relationship with the worker at the distance at which he wanted it to function.

When Shorty showed mixed feelings about himself, wanted to be the boy he used to be, the worker sensed that this might mean helping him to hold on to a job and concentrated on giving him this support. He could have seen the boy's wish simply as a desire to regress, in

153

which case he could have done little or nothing about it except to try to induce him to go elsewhere for help. But he thought he could best help by supporting the possible positive aspects of Shorty's ambivalence.

So he supported Shorty while he tried to work out his employment problems and helped him find and use the opportunities and facilities with which to do so. Within the project as a whole he could offer things to do with friends and acquaintances, in small groups, while working out his problems, and opportunities for contact with the youth employment officer.

We saw Shorty as a temporarily disorganised young person who needed a temporary tiding over that his parents could not provide during this period, and who could have possibly got into serious trouble, had not help been available at the time and place he needed it.

Ronnie: 'short term intensive support'

Ronnie was sixteen years old when he first came to the coffee stall. He lived at home with his parents and sisters. He was intelligent, highly strung, and given to outbursts of uncontrolled violence. He was on probation for causing grievous bodily harm, and carrying offensive weapons. He often came to the coffee stall and was well known to Jumbo who listened to wild stories of his escapades. Occasionally he mentioned his interest in the Merchant Navy, and Jumbo made enquiries about the possibilities, and tried to impress upon him the need for a clean record and regular employment if he wanted to get in. Ronnie joined two or three other boys on expeditions with Jumbo and sometimes visited the club premises where he became known to Mary, the woman worker, and eventually to Gerry.

Record/Gerry/June 10th

Ronnie came to the stall for the first time with John. There was some argument about the amount they had been paid for their part-time job. This led to talk about wages generally, and the "disgusting wages" which they said always resulted from a job found by the youth employment office. Ronnie quoted the instance of a chap of twenty who was earning only six pounds ten shillings a week as a waiter. Jumbo pointed out that this was made up by tips, but Ronnie declared that he would earn more than that if he worked in a hotel. Ronnie sat talking for quite a while. He told me about gun fights in the area. He related local legends of a thousand B—— boys battling with five hundred from C——. He displayed a bandage which he said was the result of being caught up in a fight in a local cinema. He described the whole operation in detail, ending with the whole row of seats being torn up and himself being trapped underneath them. He described how a crowd of fifty got into the wrestling without paying

He claimed to have contacts in some smuggling concern, which he had visions of joining when he left school. Among other things, he knew the people who had organised a recent hundred thousand pound diamond robbery. He spoke of "the underworld" with great reverence. He had the latest model car, and had done 120 mph in it on the M.1.

June 12th Ronnie arrived with Jim at the stall. They got in the front with me and shared my cigarettes. Ronnie said they would give me a packet of twenty as they would be loaded with cigarettes tomorrow. They had a friend coming back tomorrow with 15,000 cigarettes, of which they had booked 600. Seeing my unwillingness to accept the gift, they explained that it was quite legal. They had not 'nicked' the cigarettes themselves, they had just booked a few hundred from a hoard someone else had 'nicked'. This led on to thieving in general. Ronnie marvelled at the trust of a church he had visited which had left a drawer full of coppers open at a bookstall. He went on to explain that though he might be the biggest thief under the sun, he never stole from churches. He preferred nicking things that were locked up anyway.

Record/Jumbo/October/afternoon

Ronnie arrived in an excited state saying he was on the run, that his mother had told the police he had assaulted his father. He said he must go to France or Ireland or to sea, as his probation officer had warned him that it would be approved school for his next offence. Although he was obviously distressed I had doubts as to the facts presented, but after some discussion suggested that he should consider one of three possibilities:
a. we should go together to the police;
b. we should consult the probation officer;
c. we should try to effect a reconciliation with his family.
I emphasised the need to try *c* first. Ronnie calmed down considerably and agreed to think about it. I phoned Mary who was expecting to meet Ronnie with some of the other boys and asked her to reinforce my suggestions.

Evening I waited at home for the expected telephone call which duly came. Ronnie suggested we meet at H——— station. We did so—he brought Tom along with him—and we went to a nearby barbecue to talk. We covered the old ground and I continued to point out the unreality of his schemes for running away. I managed to get Tom's support in this. I worked the conversation round to the three solutions which I had earlier asked him to think over and stressed the desirability of the third on the list. I could see he was wavering so I suggested he let me first ring up his family and he could be in the booth and hear both what I was saying and what was being said. He finally agreed and we all went into a public call box and I asked to speak to his mother. It appeared that she had only said what she had about the police to frighten him and that in fact there had been no report to the police at all. As I expected it had all been a bluff which had worked

155

only too well. I then got Ronnie to speak to his mother and eventually it was agreed that he should go home and try to get on better with his parents.

Record/Mary/Sunday November 12th

Ronnie phoned at 9.30 p.m. He told me that he had been moved out of his room and had nowhere to go. I wasn't too sympathetic and told him that perhaps he should go home. He said that his father wouldn't have him. I asked if he couldn't stay with some of his friends until he got things straightened out. He said that no one would have him. He said, "Can I stay at your place then?". Knowing Jumbo was away I said he could come if he had nowhere else to go. He arrived about an hour and a half later. He said that the place he had been living in belonged to a friend who was only letting him stay for the week for a favour, and had only charged him a few bob, but he had known that he was going to have to leave on Friday.

Monday I woke Ronnie at 7 a.m. because he had told me that he had to be at work at 8 a.m. About half-way through breakfast he told me that he wasn't going to work today. He had thought of a new idea last night. He was going to go down to the labour exchange to get some new cards saying that he was eighteen so that he could get at least £12 per week, preferably in a factory. He said he would put on an Irish accent, which he can do very well, say he had just come over from Ireland and give a false name. He started thinking up some names. I asked him if he thought he would get away with it. He said he had known lots of people who had done it. I mentioned that if he should happen to get picked up for an offence, and they thought he was eighteen, he would have to go to adult court. He said that it would be better to go to adult court, where he would probably only get three months, than get three years in Borstal if he had to go back to juvenile court. I managed to persuade him to use his own name if he were planning on going ahead with it. He dreamed up a phony address and birth date. He said that after he had been to the labour exchange he was going out to look for a job with more money. If he couldn't find one he would go back to his old job tomorrow. When we met later at the club, Ronnie still hadn't found a job. He claimed that he had fainted today while he was eating his lunch. He was very moody all evening, getting a bit annoyed at the horseplay of some of the other boys.

I have suggested several times that he ask his probation officer to help him look for a place to live because he probably knows of some places where he could start looking. However, he blows up every time the probation officer is mentioned, tells me that the probation officer hates his guts and won't help him get a job or a place to live.

After the club we went to a Wimpy Bar. When we had parked the car and got up to the door, Ronnie said he was not allowed into this Wimpy Bar, because he had been barred for throwing tomato sauce on the walls. Gerry said it would probably be all right as he was with us.

I think he was a bit uncomfortable, especially as there were few people around, and the waitresses were standing talking, and looking at people. At one point he sank down in the seat until you almost couldn't see him above the table. He mentioned to me that he didn't think he should bother me by staying at my place anymore and that he would stay out tonight. I said O.K. and asked him where he was going. He said he didn't know. I mentioned again that perhaps he should go home but he said no, he couldn't go home. A little later he asked Gerry if he could have the keys of the club so he could stay in there. Gerry said he couldn't stay in the club. He then said he would come home with me again. He made a phone call before we left, apparently phoned home, told us that he had been talking to his sister, and his "old man" was being difficult again and making things miserable for his sisters and mother. He reported his sister had said he would make it worse if he went home.

We talked to him about finding a room and offered to help him if he would take the responsibility of keeping a job to be able to pay for his room. He agreed to this and said that he wanted us to help him find a room. Gerry and he came to an agreement that if Gerry could find a place that would give him room and board he would be willing to pay £3.10s to £4 a week, which would leave him about £2 a week pocket money. He had heard about jobs in the "biggest plumbing firm in town" where you could make £18 a week and he was going around to see about them tomorrow. He remarked again that if he didn't get this job he would go back to his old job.

Gerry and I tried to talk to Ronnie seriously about what he was going to do. I told him that it would probably be quite a while before we could find him a room that would be permanent and what did he think he could do until then. He said he would stay in the club. We said he couldn't. He said, "Of course I can, why not?". We argued for a while, he being quite insistent that he could, Jumbo would let him, etc. I finally said, "Don't be silly you know Jumbo will not allow it". He accepted that. I told him that the best person to give him a few ideas about where he could start looking for a room would be his probation officer. He agreed. I suggested that he go with Gerry to meet his probation officer and they could talk about getting him a room. Ronnie looked at Gerry and said, "Who, him?" I said yes, and he said, "Oh, all right". He was quite surprised at the suggestion, but seemed to think it was a good idea. He said he was supposed to see the probation officer tomorrow evening but was going to phone him instead because he wanted to go to the films with us. I suggested that he phone the probation officer during the day, arrange to meet him early in the evening, say six o'clock, and then phone Gerry and arrange to meet him. He went along with this. Gerry gave him his phone number and told him to call between 11 a.m. and 1.30.

Tuesday Ronnie said he was going to the doctor to get a certificate saying he had been sick the last two days, and then was going in to work, but didn't think he would be able to work because the van would be gone by the time he went in. I made him promise he would go and see if the van were there, and check if he still had a job or not. I suggested that he phone the probation officer from my place, but he said he would phone him later. I asked why he couldn't phone him before he left. He said he would phone him later for sure. I suggested that he have Gerry phone him, but he didn't reply to this. A few minutes later I said again that he could let Gerry phone him, but he didn't reply. I reminded him that he was supposed to phone Gerry. He said he would, and he promised he would go in to work.

Gerry reported that Ronnie had phoned him, but had not phoned the probation officer. Gerry is to get in touch with the probation officer and is meeting Ronnie at 5.45 p.m. to go with him to his office.

Later Ronnie said he had got a doctor's certificate and had gone in to work but the van had already gone out so they had told him to go back tomorrow.

Thursday, November 30th Ronnie has now been back at home two weeks, and started his new job. He is still very tense, and frequently angry.

December 5th—Jumbo Ronnie came to see me and said it was not any good trying to live at home and he definitely wanted to join the Merchant Navy. After discussion with Mary and Gerry, I took him to the P & O line in the city and arranged for an interview with the personnel officer. I went with him to this interview and discovered that it was possible for him to go straight to sea on a long voyage starting the following week if he agreed to do the necessary training on board as a substitute for the sea school (they normally insist on a six weeks' course as a probationary period), and provided the parents agreed. His parents had already indicated they would be glad to see him go away, so it only remained to get his probation officer to agree. I had had several previous contacts with his probation officer, who now said that no obstacles would be placed in his way, and if he remained at sea for three months he would have the probation order rescinded.

Comments

This field-work record could be considered from several different angles, and for training purposes it might be useful to challenge the workers' actions in several of the situations recorded. But the following is a summary of what the worker was trying to do.

Ronnie and Jumbo had a relationship that included 'talking things over' and doing things together, as well as in a group. It had the appearance and content of an ordinary, casual, friendly relationship. As a result Ronnie was willing to turn to Jumbo when in trouble, which might not have been the case if the worker had been attached to an organisation and seen as one of 'them'.

Ronnie presented immediate problems in that on two occasions he had nowhere to live. Each time he indicated that he wanted to "get away from it all". The first time he was "on the run", the second time he wanted a different kind of employment, and accommodation. On the first occasion Jumbo overtly accepted Ronnie's statements, as presented, and consequently could not offer the help required to get away. He therefore had to point out the problems of running away, and to suggest alternatives in dealing with the situation, offering his support. While Ronnie was considering the alternatives Jumbo was able to get Mary's support in talking to Ronnie and emphasising possible solutions. When Ronnie agreed on the third solution—to attempt reconciliation with his family—Jumbo acted as a bridge between Ronnie and his mother, and the immediate problem was solved.

The 'real problem', which we saw as one of family relationships, still remained, but since neither Ronnie nor his parents asked for help in this, we did not offer it. The difficulty arose again, and this time in the absence of Jumbo, Ronnie turned to Mary. She offered practical help—a bed—in the hope that she could help Ronnie sort out some problems while he was with her (keeping or getting a job, and finding accommodation). While meeting the immediate requests, Mary and Gerry attempted to act as a bridge between Ronnie and his probation officer. They also continued to try and 'reflect reality' to Ronnie without much apparent success.

Ronnie's need as he saw it was to remove himself from the environment with which he was unable to cope. This could well be interpreted as running away but when Ronnie presented a realistic way of attempting to solve his problem—joining the merchant navy—Jumbo supported him by making enquiries, accompanying him to his interview and again acting as a bridge between him and the probation officer.

We saw Ronnie as a 'simply disorganised' young person who needed an accepting, knowledgeable adult, who could offer information and guidance in an informal setting.

Monica: 'long term intensive support'

Monica was seventeen years old when referred to us by the probation officer. She had a mother and several brothers and sisters but her father was unknown. After leaving school at fifteen, she had had twelve jobs, lasting from one day to three months. Monica was on probation for stealing jewellery. The probation officer had helped with several jobs, and also with accommodation after her mother turned her out. She had stayed with several friends and in lodgings, and was in a hostel when referred to us. She was an attractive girl, fond of children and interested in drama. She frequented many clubs and dance halls, and made several friends, although the friendships seemed short-lived. At the time of referral she was very depressed. The worker saw her role first as that of a friend, helping Monica with jobs and accommodation, encouraging interests and helping her make friends. This was to be a supportive role, with authority coming only from the probation officer. During a period of eight months the worker made contact, at Monica's request, with four hostel wardens, three youth employment officers, a modelling agency, two youth leaders, six employers, a doctor and a psychiatric social worker.

Schedule from worker's record, of direct contacts with Monica

March	14th	Interview at probation office
	15th	Lunch
	23rd	Visit to hostel
	24th	Lunch and afternoon (talking and drinking coffee)
	25th	Dinner and cinema
	26th	Afternoon meeting (chat)
	27th	All day (visited new hostel)
	28th	Afternoon meeting (shopping)
	29th	Lunch and dinner
	30th	Afternoon and evening (walking, talking and meal)
April	2nd	Dinner
	3rd	Evening (coffee and chat)
	4th	Evening (coffee and chat)
	9th	Dinner (M. very miserable)
	10th	Afternoon and evening (meals, walk, psychiatrist visit, cinema)
	11th	Coffee (M. cheerful)
	12th	Dinner (M. very miserable)
	15th	Day out (M. relaxed in morning, lots of worries in evening)

Holiday

April	30th	Dinner (discussed job)
May	2nd	M. stormed in office. Angry and unhappy. Long talk.
	4th	M. phoned to say couldn't come. Had a friend.
	5th	All day (M. had to leave hostel. Angry and unhappy. Arranged new hostel)
	6th	Lunch (M. many complaints and very worried)
	7th	Afternoon at hostel (M. allowed to stay 1 more night)
	8th	Lunch and visit to youth employment office (M. childish and very sullen)
	9th	All day (move to new hostel)
	10th	Dinner (long discussion)
	11th	Dinner
	14th	Afternoon meeting (M. not well, very unhappy and angry)
	20th	Afternoon (M. had visited relative and upset)
	22nd	Coffee (M. depressed)
	25th	Lunch (M. cheerful. Wanting to do something)
	29th	Interview in children's club
	30th	Visit to children's club

June	5th	Dinner
	12th	Coffee (M. wanted holiday job) Depressed.
	13th	Theatre (Introduced another girl)
	14th	Afternoon meeting (M. worried about job)
	19th	Helped at children's club. (M. enjoyed it)
	22nd	Coffee (M. brought gift)
	25th	Coffee (M. nowhere to live)
	26th	Youth employment office and theatre
	27th	M. phoned—(no job. Made enquiries)
	29th	M. phoned—(not got job)
July	2nd	M. phoned and then called (wanted money. M. agreed to go to National Assistance Board)
	3rd	All day (new hostel arranged and move in)
	10th	Visit to hostel (getting on well. Visit to youth employment office)
	11th	M. called (wanted money)
	12th	Lunch (M. wanted money. Visit to youth employment office)
	13th	Interview for job
	16th	M. phoned re latter
	18th	M. phoned—(visited modelling agency)
	25th	M. phoned (needed money)
August	1st	M. called (needed money)
	7th	M. called (trouble at work)
	8th	Visited M. (sorted out difficulties)
	16th	M. phoned (wanted money for court)
	25th	Shopping expedition for clothes
	29th	M. phoned (needed money)
Sept.	3rd	Evening (started making and remaking clothes)
	5th	M. phoned (needed money. Evening—made dress)
	10th	M. phoned (needed money)
	12th	M. phoned (needed money)
	13th	M. phoned (about shoes)
	18th	Evening (Visited M. to check she was all right)
	26th	Arranged with warden to subsidise M's income for period.

Comments

During the first three months, Monica was mainly unhappy and depressed and spent many hours talking to the worker about this. The worker, apart from arranging accommodation, and taking her out for meals and entertainment, spent most of the time listening and occasionally attempting to reflect reality to her. During the fourth and fifth months Monica became more active and the worker supported her. Her efforts were short-lived, and she was unable to become seriously interested in a job. Again the worker supported her efforts and helped with arrangements for work. Another upheaval, being

161

turned out of the hostel, upset her efforts again. At the beginning of the sixth month the worker got her into a hostel where the warden was helpful and made considerable allowances for her behaviour. As she settled in the hostel, she became less dependent on the worker. The warden found her a job and the worker took her to it. She made friends in the hostel and although for a while she depended on the worker to get her out of trouble, eventually she contacted her only for financial help. The worker accepted this, and used the relationship over the money in order to see her regularly until she was sure that Monica could manage. Monica remained in the hostel and her job for more than a year.

Significant incidents in the relationship, from the Worker's records.

Testing out

March 14th I mentioned again about meeting her for lunch and she agreed, telling me that I was mad to spend money on her, and watching my reaction to this very carefully. She was quite pleased when I said I wanted to go to lunch with her. After arranging to meet her for lunch tomorrow I decided to terminate the conversation and said I thought I had better be going as it was getting late. She said, "Do you want me to go", implying by her tone of voice that she felt I was trying to get rid of her. I said that she didn't need to go if she didn't want to. She appeared to think it over and said that she too felt that it was getting late and picked up her bag. We exchanged goodbyes. I mentioned again about the date for lunch tomorrow and we parted. *March 28th* (Having moved into hostel) I suggested we should buy her some stockings as she hadn't any. I asked if she had any pyjamas. She said, "No", so I offered to buy her a pair. She said she needed shoes most and would I buy some. I didn't take the suggestion as I thought I ought to discuss it with the probation officer first. She tried to convince me, but then she saw a pair of pyjamas she liked. We also got a bra, suspender belt and two pairs of stockings. She was delighted with them, said that the probation officer would be after me for getting them and that I was mad to spoil her.

Expression of feeling

April 3rd I told her I had been talking to the probation officer who said she didn't have to report this week, but she'd like to see her if she cared to call in. Monica remarked that she missed the probation officer.
May 2nd Monica stormed in during the afternoon and asked where I had been yesterday. I explained that I had phoned but there had not been an answer. She said she often didn't bother to answer the phone.
May 6th I said we couldn't find another hostel at the moment, and if she didn't stay here, I didn't know where she could stay. She was

angry at this remark, and said she would look after herself. But she calmed down quicky and persuaded me to call a taxi.

May 11th Took her to dinner and told her I wouldn't be able to see her this weekend. She was annoyed and said, "Well, what am I going to do then?" Suggested she should return the borrowed magazines to her friend and could write to her Irish boy friend. She said she would return the magazines and maybe her friend would take her to the pictures. I suggested she should contact me on Monday. She was annoyed but accepted the fact.

May 30th Monica was to meet me between 2 and 3 p.m. She arrived at 3.30 and apologised for being late.

June 5th She asked me if I thought the children (in the junior club) would like her. I said that they had seemed quite interested when she was there, and that children usually liked people who liked them.

June 12th I asked her what she needed encouragement about, and she said, "Oh, about getting a job and that". She then said, "I'm not getting any encouragement and that's the root of the whole problem". I said, "Oh".

Decline in intensity

Monica asked me to meet her at the office. I was early and Monica called me over. She looked terrific. Her hair was the right length and simply done. She looked clean and glowing, and wore a blue cardigan that was just the right colour for her. She introduced me to two girls of her own age, with whom she seemed very friendly, and also to the manager. At the hostel she said she was waiting for a phone call from D. She sees him twice a week. She said she would like an evening job as a baby-sitter. I suggested we should ask the warden if she knew of anybody. We had a meal in a restaurant from which she was going to call on a friend. She asked how the probation officer was and I told her and then said that the probation officer was very pleased with the way she had been able to look after herself for the last few months. She said, "Well, I've changed a lot—then I was a scruffy schoolgirl—now I'm a scruffy woman". I remarked that at the moment she didn't look a bit scruffy.

She walked with me to the underground and hinted that she needed money. I gave her 6s and she complained it wasn't enough. I said if she had no money she could call me and I'd send her some. Monica seemed to be becoming more and more independent of me, except for the fact that she does need money. She seems to have security in her job and at the hostel, and has friends. Her main problem at the moment is lack of money and boredom with her job, which I hope won't lead to anything serious.

Incidents from worker's records illustrating the role of the worker.

Giving specific help

March 23rd Found vacancy at a hostel which may be good. We went

163

for lunch and the first thing Monica asked me was if I had found a place for her. She said the probation officer had said I would find her a place to live. I told her I had a hostel in mind. She seemed pleased and asked if it was one where she didn't have to be in until 12 o'clock. I said I wasn't sure of the regulations, but the warden was very nice and there were a lot of young girls living there. She asked if we could look at it this afternoon.

The warden was very pleasant, talked to Monica for a few minutes, told her times of eating and that she would have to be in by 11.30 p.m. Both Monica and I thought this reasonable. She showed us round the building and the room which Monica was to share with three other girls. Very pretty, and Monica very pleased. I gave Monica soap, shampoo and cream, my phone number, and directions on getting back to the hostel and said she would have to leave Marble Arch at 10.45 p.m. to be back on time.

April 2nd She asked if I knew of any modelling lessons she could take. I said individual lessons would probably be too expensive but I would try to find out about classes.

June 10th Monica came in and the first thing she said was she'd like to try to get a job at a camp for the summer looking after children. She asked me to phone them. The firm was not open that day, but I learned the name of the responsible person and we wrote a letter straightaway.

Reflecting reality

April 19th She said nobody has mentioned getting a job lately to her. I think this surprises her and that she wants a job both for something to do and for money. I doubt if she could get one on her own. She said, "life's boring, there's nothing to do, and you do the same things day in and day out". I suggested if she found a job she might not be so bored. She remarked, "but its the same thing when you're working. You have to do the same thing every day."

April 19th She told me heatedly that the girls at the hostel were snobs, they never even said, "Good Morning" to her. I asked if she spoke to them, and she said she smiled and said, "Hello" all the time but nobody even asked her to sit with them at mealtimes. I said maybe they were waiting for her to be friendly and she said, "what do you expect me to do, go over and say, 'hello darling' how are you today?'."

July 18th Monica said she would stay in this job. I agreed it would be a good idea to stay at least until she could get a good recommendation from them and had a chance of something better.

Acting as go-between

March 30th I asked her why she wasn't at the clinic. She said she was feeling all right and didn't need to go. She said she was voluntary and could stay away if she wanted. I said as the doctor still wanted to see her perhaps she should go today and arrange it with him. She didn't

164

seem too happy but said maybe . . . She came in shortly after 6 p.m.
and later casually remarked that she had been to the clinic.

July 9th Monica didn't contact me. Will go to hostel tomorrow to
talk to Monica, and the warden, and go to the youth employment
office. I don't particularly want to go to the youth employment office,
but don't know how much of an effort she is making to get a job,
though any effort at all is a step forward for her.

August 16th Monica phoned at 11 o'clock. Said she was at court and
wanted 4s so she could take out a summons for assault. Insisted.
Later, asked probation officer's advice. Said Monica could always let
summons drop. Court didn't take kindly to assault cases as both
parties often to blame. She said, "You mean they'd think it was as
much my fault as his". I said, "They sometimes look at it that way".
She was not upset or indignant but said that she would just try to
phone man and get him to pay for repairs to her suit.

September 13th We started making the dress. A French girl joined
us and I left them together, the French girl having said she would
help Monica with the sewing.

May 8th I told her she had an appointment at the youth employment
office at 10. She said, "Why didn't you tell me?" I reminded her that
I had told her but she said I hadn't. She told me to make another
appointment for 2 p.m. I said I would try. I phoned the youth employment officer and they were able to see her at 2 p.m.

Comments

This illustration highlights another aspect of the project in that
Monica was not contacted through the coffee stall, the network, or in
the neighbourhood, but referred to us by a probation officer because
it was felt we as 'outsiders' might be able to help her more adequately.

She was unwilling for us to introduce her into the coffee stall network and its programme of activities. We had to work with her as
an individual where and when it was possible. This deprived us of
the opportunity of using contacts with other boys and girls in the
network as part of the content of the relationship.

Our work with Monica illustrates the role of the detached worker
in long term support, as a bridge between the probation officer and
Monica, approving, informing, supporting and reflecting reality—a
kind of catalytic agent who offers an opportunity to use the relationship to make it possible to 'put some of the odd bits together'.

The illustration also appears to confirm once again the need for
this kind of service, supplementing the services of the other statutory
and voluntary bodies.

Artie: "constant ongoing support"

The following illustration is of work with an individual, where it was clear to the worker that he did not have the expert knowledge to understand the boy's problem, nor to help him adequately, except in constant and ongoing support.

Extract from worker's summary/Gerry/January

Aged seventeen, Artie is the youngest of a family of seven children. One hears a great deal from Artie about his brothers' infamous past. "Everyone at the nick knows my family," Artie is always saying. His father is supposed to have thrown many a policeman out of the house in consequence of which the police never come alone now. All this is typical of Artie's phantasy life, for he lives in a "dream world" of his own creation. Not only does one continually hear about the misdeeds of his family, but more so of the delinquent ambitions for himself. Seldom does he in fact get into trouble with the police. Artie threatens more than most, but acts least. He is always at the back of any ganging up for a fight or plans for a 'job'. His phantasy world extends beyond violent acts to his supposed possession of many luxuries, a gay time with girls and a benevolent treatment of all his friends. His intelligence is high. He passed his 11-plus, but refused grammar school. Often his phantasies take the form of short stories.

Most of his life is so removed from reality that it is no wonder that he cannot settle for long in any one job. There is no doubt that his work is of a high standard. In the club when there are jobs to be done, Artie doesn't need to be asked twice. He thrives on hard work for short periods. But his jobs last only a very short time, mostly under a week. Recently he has been out of work for twenty weeks. In the last twelve months he has been with fifteen firms. He always leaves because of an argument or a fight. Timekeeping does not seem to be difficult for him. At work he likes to be given difficult things to do, and thrives on responsibility. He always demands the highest possible wage and gets it. He is on the whole very frank with adults in whom he confides. He will talk in front of them of the 'jobs' he is planning to do, or of the things he has stolen. If he takes anything from one of the workers he is likely to admit it afterwards. This attitude has made trouble for him among the other boys. At a club party he hid the drinks, admitted it and needed adult protection from the threat of violence from the other boys. He is honest with his parents about not working and gets into more trouble because of it.

Artie's temper is quick and unpredictable. On two occasions he has quite suddenly, after a long period of apparent enjoyment of girls' taunting, laid into them very violently. He has not behaved like this with boys of his own age group, but presumably he has done the same to adults at his places of employment. Girl friends are a great trouble to Artie. The girls like him, but he seems incapable of showing them real affection. For whole evenings when he has been out with a girl in a mixed group he has ignored her in favour of the other boys. He never keeps a girl for very long. Relations with adults who are not in positions of authority over him are comparatively easy going. He is on good terms with all the field-workers. He particularly likes the female staff, and will fuss and do things for them. He is very dependent on the men and telephones them a great deal, at all times of the day and night for any reason. Any excuse is good enough to have a "chat". He carried dependence to the extent of insisting on knowing the full movements of a worker and his family.

Artie has a strong relationship with both Jumbo and myself. He uses us in turn and occasionally tries to play off one of us against the other. But he apparently sees himself as related to all the workers (and is the only boy who has visited Susan in the separate younger girls' group). At one time he tried to borrow 2s 6d from each of the six workers, and managed to get 5s in the evening from two of us. We have to confer frequently about Artie so that we can co-operate in working with him.

Record/Gerry/March (example of help in employment)

We arranged to meet outside the club at 10 a.m. As usual the boys telephoned my home after I had left, to check that I was on my way. Artie had a note of a decorating job which he wanted to try. On the way I explained that a Mr. —— of the firm had said that for a seventeen year old he could only promise a junior rate of pay. Artie took this pessimistically. "I'm not taking any junior rate. You had better come in with me 'cos I shall tell him what to do with his job." He said he would not take less than 3s 9d an hour because he had taken 4s 1d at his last job. Any suggestion I made that he needed a job rather than a high wage was ignored. At the firm's office Artie asked me to go in with him. The wage was announced as 4s 3d an hour, surprising us both. Artie filled in the application form with a little help from me. He was taken on, and given instructions to report tomorrow. Outside the offices we quickly worked out that a forty-eight hour week meant at least £10 gross. I arranged to see Artie later in the evening to give him 10s to get to work since he will not be paid for another week.

Worker's record/Jumbo/June/Letter written to court on Artie's behalf

Dear Sir,

Mr. Arthur —— is known to us through our youth work in ——. W know his circumstances at home, and his relationship with his father is a peculiarly difficult one. The father appears to us to be unduly authoritarian. We feel that this might be the cause of the boy's reacting to teachers, employers, court officials, etc., in a way which might be misinterpreted as directed against these persons. We believe that it would help if people working with him were aware of this.

We are trying to help Artie with some of his difficulties. He is a member of our youth club and we see him several times a week. We feel that the boy's circumstances should be taken into consideration.

167

Artie has a job for next Monday and we shall try to help him to see how he can pay off his fine with regularity.

Yours faithfully,

P.S. We shall be pleased to provide any further information that any Official of the Court may want about this boy.

Worker's summary record/Jumbo/July

Artie has now been in work for the last three weeks as a van boy working at the same place as John ———— and at the moment seems to be very happy in the job. He works hard and regularly and is keeping up with his payments of the fine, for which I think we have to thank the imaginative pressure by the probation officer who seems to have struck just the right note for Artie. Initially he was very resentful of the pressure that the probation officer was putting on him to work, yet appreciative of the efforts of the youth employment officer to find jobs for him, although he didn't avail himself of this and found his own eventually via his friend John. Artie is a very regular attender at the club and the coffee stall and I think would be very lost without them. He said the other evening about his way of life "all get up, work, go to the coffee stall or Jumbo's club and then bed and get up again". He still seems divorced from reality and still will not face up to taking a job which is compatible with his talents and ability. This may come if he can learn to hold his present job for a reasonable period as this will give him a decent work reference which has been very hard for him to get in the past.

Staff case conference/September

The following are points presented at a case conference (after one year's constant support) in another attempt to consider how to help Artie.

Very unsettled in job	Gets into fights at work. For two months has had no full week at work.
Excursions into phantasy	Most nights goes on at length of school-days' exploits. Talks a good deal about what he would like to do to police, to 'spades', etc.
Violence	Always carries weapon, mostly a gun, as yet no bullets. Throws things about—says the boys are going to do something serious soon.
Says he is bored	
Home upsets	Mother's recent hospitalisation. Doesn't seem to 'idealise' older brothers as he once did.
Treatment	Consideration has been given to persuading Artie to accept treatment,

and attempts made to draw a psychiatric
social worker into the project, but
none of these have been successful.

Recommendation from
case conference

To persuade Artie to accept psychiatric
help through introducing him to the
youth consultation centre from which he
might proceed to treatment. It was
agreed that when Artie next discussed
his work problems Jumbo or Gerry
should suggest taking him to the centre
where they would explore with him his
work problem.

Worker's record/Gerry/October

Artie said that he needed money quickly and also a job but if he
couldn't find a job with good money he would just have to find the
money somehow. A job with £6 a week was not good for him. I
suggested to him that he didn't seem to know what kind of job he
wanted and he agreed. He said that he had not gone to an interview
today because he wanted first to get "some gear", by that he explained he meant new clothes and for this he would need some money.
I told him about a friend of mine who might help him decide what
sort of job would be best for him and asked if he would come to
meet him. Artie asked me if I could get this friend to come down to
the club and I said that I would try but didn't think it likely. He said
that he would be prepared to come with me on Saturday morning and
I agreed to do this. Pressed about coming that night he said that he
had to meet a girl at 7.30 at the coffee bar and he would not come with
me as he would later feel a fool turning up at the coffee bar alone. He
remarked "the others won't wait for you". I gave him 2s 6d for
cigarettes before leaving.

Worker's record/Gerry/one week later

Worker reported that Artie had stopped going to the consultation
centre and then reported on the 3rd visit to Mr. A. of the consultation
centre.
    Visited the consultation centre and explained the situation to Mr.
A describing Artie, his background, his behaviour and attitudes.
Took Artie and friend to the centre where he was able to walk straight
into his interview without waiting. He said afterwards that Mr. A
was a "good geyser" and that he wanted to go again. He apparently
liked the frankness of the conversation about jobs, knives, guns,
fights, the club, Jumbo and girls. He asked Mr. A to "come and see
our youth night club".

Worker's record of supervision session/Gerry

Reported on third visit to Mr. A of the consultation centre. Mr. A proposes that I should not go on trying to take Artie to the centre since he is already maintaining relationships with both Jumbo and myself. He felt a third might well be beyond his means, especially one that was totally 'treatment centred'.

Mr. A suggested instead that I continue from time to time to visit the centre and report to him (Mr. A) on Artie's progress, in the hope that we could talk things over and suggest how Jumbo and I could be of more help to Artie.

We agreed (the worker and supervisor) that this would be a good plan since I could use what I get from my visits to the centre and filter it back into programme.

The supervision session ended by our outlining the limitations inherent in the situation and clarifying the fact that our function was only to build bridges, to act as the go-between, and to offer whatever the probation officer, the youth employment officer, the psychiatric social worker or the analyst suggested might be helpful, but not to take these roles in full on ourselves.

Record of next supervision session/Gerry

I explained that Artie could not pay his fine and that the probation officer had said that since this had continued for so long beyond the statutory requirement, he had no recourse except to order that Artie be picked up for non-payment. I said that I thought that in Artie's present state this might end in violence and suggested that we discuss a way of persuading him to pay. I reported that Artie had said he wouldn't even pay a halfpenny since he wasn't going to let them make a fool of him and added that he would rather "go inside than give in". We discussed contacting parents, asking the probation officer for one last extension, none of which really seemed workable in the circumstances. In the end we decided that I would attempt to interpret paying the fine as a way of "getting round the law". I would suggest that we might find out what was the least they would accept as a partial payment on instalments. I should try to get Artie's friends at the club to support the idea of his making a minimum payment. We agreed that our attempts to interpret this as Artie "outwitting the law" would create a situation in which Artie could avoid feeling that he had to hold out, or that he had weakly given in and would lose status in his own or their eyes.

Tentatively we agreed that I would make an attempt to "pass the hat" to pay Artie's first instalment and include the staff in a request for contributions. We agreed that this might present Artie with a way out since he could not only pay part of the fine and save face, but if he wished he could see the contribution from his friends and the staff as a sign of acceptance and approval both of him and his action (of which at this point we felt he was in need) or if he was in one of his moods, he could see himself as having outwitted all of us as well as the law—but in either case he would have avoided being picked up.

We agreed that Artie could be offered the opportunity to look at the "kitty" as either an outright gift or a loan. If he looked at it as a loan, we could suggest to him that he could repay the club by bricking up a wall which was in need of being done.

We agreed that if all went well, we could discuss at the next supervision session how we might be able to interest Artie's employer and his latest girl friend in helping him.

Worker's record/Gerry/club premises/a week later

Artie called me outside. "Gerry, will you write to me when I am in the nick?" He said that he had not any money to put towards his fine and that a warrant officer from the court had been around to his house on the previous day. I suggested to him that he should go up to see Jumbo on the stall. He was not very keen. He decided instead to go across to the coffee bar and I went in to talk to Dan and the others. I told them about his plight and asked if they thought that the others would chip in to help him make a start and secure extra time for payment. Dan said he thought they might, although there was not much money about in the middle of the week. I gave him 10s from Marian and myself as a start and then said that I would take Artie up to the stall while he made the collection. Artie had come back from the café and when I said I would go with him to the stall he came quite willingly. Jumbo took him aside in the van and promised that if he found any money for the fine he would go to the court with him to ask for extra time.

Back at the club, Dan had collected a total of 30s and given it to Marian before leaving. I gave it to Artie and it looked as though Dan had had a whip round while we had been away. He beamed a smile and said, "I didn't think Dan liked me. I will take it up to Jumbo for the fine." He asked Tommy to go with him and he said he would. Tommy then said that he and Shorty had fines and nobody had collected for them. I reminded him that his was a smaller fine and he said that even if they had collected he would not have accepted it. I shouted at him as he went out of the door, "Don't say anything like that to Artie". I don't think he did.

Comments

It should be noted that the attempt to interest Artie in psychiatric help was not explained to him in terms of our concern for his 'mental health" on the basis of his excessive phantasising or inability to cope, but simply as helpful in the search for work. When Artie would not continue to use the expert help of the analyst, the worker attempted with the analyst's help to make his own relationship with Artie more effective.

The whip round to pay the fine is an example of how the worker can help the group to help the individual by offering its concern and support. Artie exemplified the type of young person who needs constant, intensive and ongoing support, with no foreseeable tailing off point.

20. *Work with Groups*

The group is a natural and basic element in the social environment. Man is everywhere committed to social life, a commitment which involves him in a wide variety of social relationships on three different levels. The first is person to person, the second is as a member of a group and the third is as a part of a wider community. In this section we are concerned only with the second level of association, the group.

The group is not a recent social phenomenon but is an intrinsic part of the way man seeks to satisfy his biological and social needs in association with others of his kind.

Kinds of groups

In its simplest form a group is three or more people in association. For example, three people are standing at a bus stop. An observer sees them as three apparently separate individuals, with nothing happening between them, no pattern, order or sequence indicating any kind of association or interpersonal relationship. Then a bus draws up and immediately some kind of visible interaction takes place. They board the bus in a mutually agreed order. They now appear as three people with a common aim, they have organised themselves to achieve it and one can observe the rudiments of group formation. If the bus is full and they are left on the pavement, they may develop an identity as a group in their own eyes "we are left behind by the bus". The recognition of this common predicament in itself draws them more closely together and might even cause them to talk to one another, criticising the bus service, complaining about getting to work late, or speaking of the conductor's impoliteness or the weather.

Let us suppose that these three people have met more or less regularly at the bus stop for the last three weeks and that being frequently left behind has led them to decide to get up a petition to the local transport authority. They might decide to form a local bus-users association with other dissatisfied passengers. One member might agree to write the letters, another to arrange a visit to the authority, and all might agree to take turns in lending their homes for meetings. In short our three bus passengers have become a group in the sense that we mean to use here.

We are dependent from birth on a closely-knit, intensely personal group, the family, which is a kinship group. The family, in turn, is dependent on a wide variety of other formal and informal groups for its identity, structure, function and survival. The influence of groups on our growth and development does not decrease as we grow up. Neighbourhood play groups, school and teenage friendship groups and later work groups influence us throughout our life. A society tends to provide the groups which it considers necessary to the 'proper functioning' of its members.

There are many ways of classifying groups but we need only differentiate between two main categories. The first is the 'compulsory group' such as the school or army, into which people are 'put'. Membership is required, demanded and/or enforced by a 'superior authority'. The second is the 'voluntary' group, which a person joins and leaves of his own volition and which is free to make its own choices and decisions, and to set its own conditions of entry, membership and expulsion.

We are concerned here almost entirely with voluntary groups, which like other forms of group life, are universal in human society. They often exist within the structure of compulsory groups (as friendship groups in the army or in the school). They are infinite in variety, but for the purpose of this discussion can be divided into two categories, the voluntary friendship group and the voluntary interest group.

Friendship groups can be extremely casual or informal, neighbours meeting for a morning coffee or an evening drink, boys and girls meeting on the way to school or on the street corner in the evening. Some groups can last for many years. A friendship group beginning in school could continue and become a group inside an old boys' association. Obviously most people belong to a number of different friendship groups both simultaneously and at different points during their lives.

Interest groups are usually more formal, although here too it is a matter of degree. An individual can belong to a sailing club, a dance club, a parent/teacher group, a church or professional group, and a group on the local council. He remains in any one of these for many years until his interest changes, or the purpose of the group alters. Some interest groups are highly structured, with a chairman, and meetings with agendas, while others might consist simply of a few people coming together to discuss or do things together informally.

Whereas in friendship groups people are drawn together primarily by their interest in each other as persons, in interest groups they are drawn together by the interest itself. But this is obviously over-simplified because within friendship groups there are often special interest groups, and because interest groups tend to produce friendship groups. One can easily develop into the other. A group of neighbours might meet for coffee, find a common interest in their children and continue to meet to discuss child care. Members of a sailing club might decide that they want to meet just to be together, apart from their sailing. The more one studies groups and their behaviour the less one will want to define or classify them in any rigid way. A group forms to meet the needs of its members if their needs change, the structure and functioning of the group change too. Voluntary groups come into being, exist for a time and eventually break up, all in response to the changing needs of their members.

Why people join groups

Throughout this section we need to keep in mind much of what we have said about basic human needs in our work with *individuals*. We shall now consider these needs and their satisfaction through association in a *group*. But in both cases the objective is the same. Some of these needs are reflected in the following reasons which prompt young people to join groups.

To make friends and have companionship.
To do things one cannot do alone.
To gain acceptance and achieve status.
To find an identity.
To exercise leadership or have the experience of being a follower.
To be part of something bigger than oneself.
To learn or to teach skills.
To express opinions.
To have fun and to do adventurous things.
To be free of adult control.
To get to know and learn to adjust to the opposite sex.

All these (and many others) can be seen as directly related to the satisfaction of the individual's physical, emotional and social needs.

Groups would have comparatively few problems if all their members joined them for the same reasons and if each of these reasons were related to the stated purpose of the group. But the chances of this happening are extremely rare, for although individuals might give one reason for joining a group they frequently have others as well. A man might join a rotary club in order to serve the community, or a woman a dressmaking class in order to learn to make clothes, but both could also be joining for reasons of status, to make friends, to develop an identity, or for any of the other reasons listed above. The woman's real motivation may be to learn how to make clothes, to please her husband by saving money, to dress her children better than those of her neighbours, or to make friends. She may be aware of all or any of these reasons for joining, or she may think she has joined for one reason when she has joined for another. If we were to probe more deeply we might even find that she had personal 'problems or difficulties' which prompted her to join the group, but all we need note here is that individuals often have more than one reason for joining a group, and of which they may not be aware.

This inevitably affects the group's behaviour. Nine people might join a drama group, saying that their prime reason for having done so is in order to act. But if one has joined because she likes the producer, two because they feel belonging to the group will give them status in the community, and one because she is looking for a boy friend, it will require a good deal of skilled leadership by the producer if he is to resolve a conflict in expectations that will result from the interplay of these various motives, and then produce a play. If young people want to use a youth club as a place in which to meet and make friends, to be accepted and to do together things of their own choosing, but are asked to take part in a ready-made programme they are liable to lose interest, to withdraw from participation, become 'trouble makers', or stay away altogether.

Of course this is not the whole story. Just as individuals want and need to join groups, so groups want and need members for the skills, interest, loyalty, knowledge and understanding they can bring to the group, and simply because they bring new opportunities for friendship. Groups often compete among themselves for members, especially in the early stages of group development. As intensive group feelings (loyalty and solidarity) emerge, competition subsides, and may give place to an exclusiveness wherein membership itself becomes a privilege, sought after by the outsider rather than the reverse.

If a person joins a group either for needs of which he may or may not be aware, and the group does not meet them, three possible courses of action are open to him. He can leave the group, he can 'fight' to change the group's aims and objectives, its behaviour or his place in it, or he can co-operate with the group to achieve its own objectives. In practice of course each individual will do now this, now that. If a boy joins a carpentry group to be with his mates, he is liable to leave if they do. If he joins a friendship group in order to satisfy a need to exercise control over others he is liable to challenge the indigenous leader. If he joins a group that is known for its gang warfare in order to impress his girl friend or defy his parents, he is liable to conform to its anti-social pattern of behaviour. The effect of a particular group on any one member is not wholly predictable, nor is the effect of any one individual on a particular group, but we are fairly safe in saying that every group modifies the individual's behaviour, more or less extensively and that to some extent an individual modifies the behaviour of the groups to which he belongs.

Johnny

In the section on working with individuals we discussed Johnny as a representative but hypothetical case in terms of some of his social relationships, including relationships in groups. It may be helpful to consider some of the ways in which these may have influenced him. Johnny at this point is eighteen years of age, a member of several friendship groups and a youth club, and works locally as a plumber's mate.

Obviously the physical environment, the climate, the soil, the natural resources that support life on this island, had a part to play in what Johnny has become. Just as obviously Johnny's physical inheritance, height, build, intelligence and blood type, played a part. But why is he not a Frenchman? Why is he *pro* hanging and not interested in the history of Ceylon? Why does he intend to marry at 19 and not 25? Why does he want to get on in his job but refuse to consider "going over to management"? Why does he think leather jackets, not togas, are proper street wear? Why does he prefer draught bitter to saki, and think himself a tough guy who doesn't need to "read books to get ahead" and who says, "nicking money is wrong, nicking things is not"? Why does he say that he could work harder than he does at his job but that he won't "because my mates would think I was trying to get in with the boss"? Why does he agree with his Dad that even if he tried to get ahead and to 'be somebody', 'they' wouldn't let him? Why does he say religion is a lot of 'bilge'?

We cannot answer any of these questions fully. But we can assume that somehow some of these attitudes have been passed on from the larger society to Johnny partly at least by his participation in groups.

A list of the areas in which group membership may have influenced the development of Johnny's attitudes about himself, his life chances and the society of which he is a member, might include:

Learning Johnny's learning in the family as an infant, to smile, to eat properly, to control his bowels—as a child in school or on the streets, to play, to read—and later as a young adult to learn a craft.

Attitudes Johnny's attitudes towards work, play, marriage, hanging and war, his attitudes towards clothes, food, sexual experience and the arts.

Levels of aspiration Johnny's levels of aspiration could have been pushed upwards or brought down by any of the several groups of which he is a member. His family might not have wanted him to continue at school despite his native intelligence, and their friends and neighbours might have agreed. His friends might have thought book learning a waste of time.

Habits of living and working Whether he smokes, drinks, gambles, goes to work on time, eats regularly, is an efficient worker or bathes every day or on Saturday only, is to some extent influenced by the groups to which he belongs.

Self image His picture of himself, his idea of his own potentials and limitations, and how he plays out this image in work, recreation and

176

love-making have been in part conditioned by his experience in playing different roles in different groups. The mother's boy, the joker, the tough guy, the serious bookish type are all self images which partly originate or are supported by participation in a variety of groups.

Feeling of support The support or lack of it from family, friends, workmates, and the other groups of which he is a member, is a decisive factor in strengthening or weakening his ability to make a choice or decision on his own. Johnny's decision to be a plumber's mate could not have been uninfluenced by the 'reference group' to which he belonged.

Standards and values Johnny's standards of fair play, of what is cheating, of what is not, what is important in life, what is worth planning, saving or fighting for, his idea of the rules of the game, are to a great extent conditioned by the values and standards of the groups.

Performance Johnny's performance at school, work or at play, the way he uses his natural endowment to do things, to achieve things, is affected by the classroom groups, the workshop group, the club or recreation group.

Feelings of security Johnny's emotional security, the amount of stress and strain, trouble and frustration he can take, his way of behaving in a personal crisis are to some extent dependent on the emotional support he gets from the groups

Self control Johnny's self control, his urge to power, to silence or submissiveness, his sense of having gone too far, his idea of how far he can or should go while still keeping the acceptance of affection of those for whose opinion he cares, are equally conditioned by these groups

Similar factors would have been at play if Johnny had been a solicitor's son or the son of a peer. The groups themselves would have been different, but the kinds of effect they had in either situation would have been substantially the same.

We have not 'explained or defined' Johnny, and we cannot do so. There is no suggestion that Johnny is 'only the result of his group experiences'. Our object is simply to draw attention to the importance of one of the factors that have influenced Johnny's growth and development. If we reduced Johnny to a preconditioned result of a predetermined social process (which we do not) we could never account for his creativity or the uniqueness of his personality. But with these points in mind, we can still admit that Johnny's membership in a variety of groups had a deep and lasting influence upon what he is.

It should be noted that Johnny's influence on the groups to which he belonged and on their individual members was on occasion as great as their influence on him. Just as he learned from others in the group, so he taught. Just as he accepted attitudes from the group, he passed attitudes on to it. Just as his levels of aspiration were affected by his participation in a group, so his presence and behaviour influenced the levels of aspiration of individual members and of the groups themselves. Just as to some extent what he thinks of himself has been influenced by the group, he has participated in the formation of the self image of its other members. He added to or took away from the psychological support the group offered. In short he 'did as much to the group' as the group and its members did to him.

Group behaviour

Although every group, like every individual, is unique, there are generalisations about group behaviour that can indicate factors common to most groups. Some of these are of interest to us here— groups can be said to have an activity or a task; group behaviour can be said to be concerned with interpersonal relations; co-operation and conflict are important elements in group behaviour; groups have values and standards; groups pass through 'stages' of growth and development. All these factors help us to see more clearly what is happening in the groups with which we work and what part we play in helping them when the occasion arises.

The activity, or task

It could be said that every group has an activity or a task although it may not be always recognisable. An interest group can easily be seen to meet in order to do carpentry, to put on a play, to learn to sew or to carry on some known and agreed-upon activity. It is often this activity which gives the group its identity, motivates members to join and shapes their expectations. In these groups the 'interest' is the activity. The activities of an interest group are often well planned and organised in advance, and may continue over a long period of time. Indeed an interest group is sometimes considered to go on though its membership changes completely ("We have had a canoe building group in this club for the last three years") whereas a friendship group tends to break up as the friendship patterns change.

Friendship groups differ in that they often lack a stated interest and the identity that it bestows, but they are nonetheless engaged in activity, of a less obvious kind. Gathering at the coffee bar for coffee, talking or arguing on the street corner, larking about, discussing, planning an outing, are activities in the same sense as rowing or carpentry. Friendship groups merely acquire different activities. They tend to be more spontaneous in their choice of activities, which are frequently of short duration. But every group engages in 'activities' whether spontaneous or well planned or not, of long or of short duration. Activity is a 'natural process' that takes place in all groups at all times.

Interpersonal relations

During a shared activity relationships in the group are developing, each member has attitudes, feelings and opinions about the others. A wide variety of interactions result (among other things) in sub-groups—partnerships, threesomes and other groupings. Sally is 'drawn' to Mabel but dislikes Susan and Mary, and never even notices Kate. John and Tony are close friends. Tom and Dick are 'sworn enemies' and maintain a close relationship on that basis. Sally and Mabel and John and Tony make a foursome. Bert has three followers slightly younger than himself who make up a sub-group. Kate is on her own and says she often wonders why she bothers to come. Ken is disliked by all the members of the group. He and they seem to recognise and accept this. He has no thought of leaving. Sub-groups are constellations that may last a night, a week, months or even longer. In all cases they affect the nature of what happens in the group.

The attitudes, feelings and opinions of group members towards each other can be positive or negative, and determine the ever-changing pattern of conflict and co-operation which is seen by the outside observer as group behaviour. This is somewhat less true of adult task-centred groups (say a management committee), which are more concerned with the accomplishment of the task than with the inter-personal relations between the members. Yet even here we must assume that conflict and co-operation, based on personal feelings of members about each other, plays a part. But with the kind of adolescent groups described above, the most dominant force underlying group behaviour is the personal likes or dislikes, feelings, attitudes and opinions of the young people about each other. That these are often simply reflections of other events in their own lives or the life of the community is not here an issue.

It seems that adolescent groups are frequently more able to accept conflict as an overt element in group life than are older people, and it can certainly be seen that they enjoy this conflict more openly. Strong arguments, prolonged bickering, threats and physical fights are just as acceptable ingredients of adolescent social life as are pleas to 'make it all up', patch up our differences, stop fighting and get on with it. This is probably because one of the reasons that adolescents join friendship groups is to have a chance to test themselves in relations with their peers, learn to express aggression and hostility and learn to accept it in others.

179

If we accept then that happenings in groups are around conflict and co-operation, we can see why these can be referred to as 'natural elements' from which a programme grows. Ordinarily, whereas co-operation is generally accepted as a very good thing indeed, conflict is not. As a result conflict is often denied, attempts are made to hide it, or to force its resolution from outside and above. Although occasionally this may be necessary in order to achieve an objective in an adult task centred group, it is usually a very unwise procedure in working with adolescent groups. In seeing conflict as a natural and necessary element in group life, as essential as co-operation if change is to take place, we are providing both the group and the worker with essential material with which to work out the problems of activity and inter-personal relations. In this sense a fight is as natural and acceptable an event, and presents the group and the work with the same oppor-tunities, as does a compromise. We can say that both conflict and co-operation are aspects of the same programme, each with a per-missible part to play in the everchanging pattern of group behaviour that we call the group process.

Just as sub-groups develop as a result of interpersonal relations, there also develops a series of roles that a group allots to its members and that the member 'takes from the group' and plays out as one of the conditions of his membership. The most obvious role is that of leader. The leader may be 'called' to the leadership by the group who recognise his skill, ability or way of life, or he may take the job be-cause no one else is doing it and it needs to be done (even so he needs their agreement) or he may become leader only when after a long struggle he has wrested the leadership away from someone else. Every group has at least one leader. The nature of his role and the kind of person who is given or assumes it, depends upon circumstances particular to the group. Other such roles are the good mixer, the one who helps to ease situations, the scapegoat, the clown or joker, the one who provides the ideas, or the mouthpiece who can be counted on to speak for the group. Often a role is given to the individual by the group, because his behaviour has already indicated that he wants it or will accept it. If on the other hand the group forces a role, say that of scapegoat, on a member who does not want it, this might force him to leave the group.

We have seen that every group is engaged in some kind of activity, formal or informal, and that interpersonal relations are also an im-portant factor in any group. It is unwise to ignore either of these aspects of group life. In an interest group the activity (or task) is often of immediate importance, but interpersonal relations also need to be considered.

Sometimes the activity or task is seen as so important that the individual members are willing to set aside differences in order to

180

complete the task (e.g. raising funds for Oxfam). In this kind of situation, interpersonal relations are secondary to getting on with the job. Sometimes the indigenous leadership is so skilled at helping the group to get things done that the task and the interpersonal relations complement one another and both develop smoothly. Sometimes the task is imposed from the outside and from above, and the group loses interest and breaks up. On occasion, when a group has completed a self-chosen task or project successfully, the group itself continues in existence, either as a friendship group because of the deepened interpersonal relations occasioned by working together, or having undertaken another task for the sheer pleasure of achievement.

In a friendship group, the interpersonal relations are of primary importance to the participants, and the activity or task is often simply a way of helping or supporting these relationships. But this may be true of interest groups also, since the agreed activity may be a screen for many other interests. The question for the worker then becomes "do I help the group to achieve its task (say, to produce a play) or do I help the individuals in their personal relationships at the expense of the task?". If, for instance, the canoe building group gradually changes into a friendship group during the building, and then decides to "pack the canoe in" in order to spend time together doing things outside the club, should the worker press for the completion of the task or help the group to function better as a friendship group? These kinds of questions can only be answered in relation to a particular group at a particular time in its development, taking into consideration the history of the group, the needs of its members, its limitations or potentials (although sometimes a worker has to consider the expectations of his agency).

We have noted that interpersonal relations affect the task or activity and that this in turn affects the interpersonal relations, and that the worker can help with one by helping with the other. An activity that more nearly meets the expectations of the members (their reasons for joining) can provide a situation in which interpersonal relationships are more satisfying. Help in working out conflicts between members can help in accomplishing the task and carrying on the activity.

The distinction between activity and interpersonal relations is only a conceptual device. In reality they are aspects of the same process. This is often referred to as the group process and one definition might be the interaction between people in a group occasioned by the interplay of the two aspects of group behaviour, the activity or the task (people doing something together) and the interpersonal relations (the thought, feelings and other behaviour that arises from this interaction). It is the nature and content of the group process that determines what groups choose to do, how they choose to do it, how and when sub-groups arise from within the group, what roles are assigned

N

to whom, when and how the group achieves its identity and how long it continues to function as a group. It is these elements in interaction one with the other which suggest the kinds of help a group may need, when they may need it, how it can be offered, and the role of the worker.

Values and standards

Both the activity and the interpersonal relations within a group affect and are affected by the values of each member and of the group as a whole. Every member (including the worker) brings his own values into the group. He has acquired these from his experiences outside the group, ideas about 'good and bad' behaviour, about 'attractive or unattractive' people, about useful skills and useless skills. Inevitably he judges other members of the group according to his own ideas, whether in terms of money, intelligence, skill, behaviour or appearance. Almost inevitably his own evaluation of other group members is eventually modified by his participation in the life of the group.

In a football team it is probable that most of the group will rate skill on the field very highly, although in some football groups 'sportsmanship' or the ability to 'share in a bit of fun' could rate equally. A criminal gang often gives a high rating to a 'good organiser or jobs' or to someone who is successful in evading the police. A girls' friendship group might give a high rating to a girl who has several boy friends, to one who is successfully keeping her 'steady' or to one who dresses well. In this way the values of the neighbourhood and the larger community are brought into the group as well as the personal values of its members.

As the group draws more closely together it tends to evolve an agreed system of values and standards for rating its members. In a group whose activity requires skill (an interest group), the rating is likely to be related to the activity, but even then other criteria of rating will continue to apply in the interpersonal area. In a friendship group the criteria are not always so obvious or so easily agreed upon, but that ranking does occur is obvious by the way indigenous leadership develops in such groups. We must assume that in a voluntary friendship group some consensus involving ranking exists for the leadership to be acknowledged. A group enforces the agreed standards and values of its members in several ways—in the way in which it accepts or expels members, allots tasks, ignores a member or assigns to him the role of scapegoat. In short, every group after a time develops a system of rewards and punishments which are the outward signs of its rating and ranking system. It might be well at this point to define a group more technically. It follows from what we have been saying here that a group is a persistent and recurring pattern of interaction in association between three or more people. It has a definite and observable system of overt interaction among its members (verbal and non-verbal, talking, arguing, laughing, gesturing), and evidence of interpersonal identification in the form of group loyalties (a sense of belonging to the group), and a common set of values and norms in setting its own task, in agreeing about the purpose of the group, and what, where, why and how things should be done.

Stages in development

We have observed that people join groups for different reasons and that each one brings different standards and values, that individuals join a group, are influenced by and influence it, that each member acts, reacts and interacts in relation to all the others, and that this interaction is occasioned by their doing and being things together, that the interaction is expressed in terms of conflict and co-operation. We have called all this together the group process. This process obviously has different results in different cases and is seen in its different aspects at different times in the development of a group. Relationships between individuals constantly change, values, standards and social attitudes are modified, and the form and content of the group process alter. Nothing within the group is ever 'static'. But as inter-action between members of a group occurs more frequently and more regularly, so the members develop a sense of belonging, a kind of group loyalty and as a result the group develops an identity which the members experience as a feeling of solidarity. In our field-work young people often said, "I belong to the coffee stall". This was technically impossible in the sense that members belong to the Athenaeum, but it was the expression of a social reality, of a feeling of identity by way of association recognised by regulars and by the neighbourhood.

If the members of a group enjoy a sense of identity, feel that it gives them a status and mutual support, these in turn become factors in strengthening the group ties, and in continued development. If the form and content of group life is determined by the needs and resources of its group members, the stages of group development can be seen as an objective indication of how well the group is meeting its members' needs, how successful it has been in allocating its resources to that end. A group that has been successful in some self-chosen activity, a holiday, a dance, an outing, will from the experience of this success develop a stronger identity. This in turn might bring greater co-operation between its members in choosing, planning and organising activities. It may strengthen the group's confidence in its ability to get things done.

The constantly changing pattern of interpersonal relations in the group in relation to the activity, facilitates change in the form of the group, which we are describing here as stages of development. It moves from the early stages in which members are just getting to know one another, to the emergence of feelings of belonging (the development of sub-groups and the assignment of roles) through the development of a distinctive identity, on to a decline in interest in the group, as the interests of members themselves change, to the final stage where the group meets less frequently.

The role of the worker

These characteristics of groups and the elements of group behaviour are the 'natural' attributes of group life. They happen spontaneously as part of the group process and are not consciously contrived by the participants. A voluntary group may assign the roles of scapegoat or joker. It may have pairs, threesomes or other sub-groups. Its members rank one another. But there is no point in the life of a group when its members or the indigenous leader say, "Today we shall assign the role of scapegoat, make up the sub-groups or do the ranking and rating of our members". Those things just happen naturally without special thought or attention as a result of the natural give and take when people try to get on with each other and do things together.

Within this 'natural' process, many voluntary groups are able to function adequately and effectively without the help of an outsider, some cannot. These considerations bear on the role of the outsider (the worker) in trying to help such groups. The worker needs to be a knowledgeable and skilled adult who knows something about the way in which groups operate. On the basis of this knowledge he can participate helpfully in the life of the group.

But this participation is not exactly the same as that of the other members. It is controlled and purposive in view of his special function. This is to help the group to help individual members, to help the group itself, and to help in its relations with other groups, with the neighbourhood and the community. As in work with individuals, he must not impose his values and standards on the group or its members, nor manipulate the group or its members for his own ends or those of his agency. This is one example of the difference between the worker's participation in the group and that of other members. They must be assumed free to exploit each other and the group, to manipulate and to attempt to impose values and standards, for this behaviour is part of the content of the conflict and co-operation of group life. It is the extent to which the worker seeks to avoid this behaviour himself that defines his controlled participation. He is not after all, one of the boys. His aims are different from theirs, and so is much of his behaviour. He must always be aware of this and help the group to be aware of it and accept it.

184

Acceptance by a group

The worker's first responsibility is to become accepted by a group. He may do so by meeting a group regularly, or by meeting individuals and helping them form a group.

In the first instance the worker may frequent the place where a group meets, get to know them and become accepted as one of the group members. During this period he might offer his services in numerous ways—by listening, by suggesting ideas, by helping with problems, by providing equipment, a vehicle or tickets for an outing, or information as to where to get them. He thus develops a relationship with a group on the same basis as with an individual, using similar means and techniques. Meantime the boys are testing him out, exploiting him, expressing feelings, sometimes intense feelings, exploring the potential of the relationship, and later reducing or extending their demands. This process is liable to continue throughout the worker's membership of a group, as it does in a relationship with an individual. There comes a time however, when by way of his offerings the worker becomes accepted as a group member, and is given his identity and his role in the group. Both he and the group recognise that he is also in contact with other groups and individuals, and responsible to some authority, which is also liable to provide facilities to help the group. So both the worker and the group accept that he is a participating member with a particular function.

In the second instance the worker may help a group to form. He could observe two boys moving around together, occasionally meeting three other boys, larking about, occasionally going to the cinema together. Sometimes they might say they are having a good time, sometimes they might complain they have nothing to do, nowhere to go, and that they are bored. The worker might suggest activities to the five boys in order to draw the individuals together and to provide opportunities for the development of a group. He doesn't do this because he wants to "adjust people to groups", or because "everyone else is in a group", or because it's easier for him (the worker) to work that way. He does it because he believes adolescent boys profit from being together in a group in a way that they could not on their own. In drawing these boys closer together and offering them opportunities to meet, he is helping them to decide what the group will be about—an interest or a friendship group—how it will be organised, what it will do, how it will do it and why. In the course of doing these things, the group is able to develop a more closely-knit pattern of interests and an identity. It is able to provide an opportunity for the use of their skills and knowledge, to make friends, to lead and follow, and the chance for new experience. Sooner of later the worker will find that he has helped the group to "go it

185

on its own" with only the occasional bit of advice from him. His aim is to pass on the necessary social skills and let the group get on with it.

In both these examples the worker becomes accepted by the groups by way of the services he offers. In the first instance these might be an audience, information, advice, ideas, problem solving, material goods or help in achieving objectives. In the second, he also offers the means for individuals to meet together in order to form a group. In neither case is there a particular moment when the worker can say, "This is when I was accepted by the group". His offerings are accepted at specific moments, but his acceptance as a participating member is part of the ongoing process of giving and taking by all concerned.

Helping individuals

The worker's main concern is to help the individual in his participation in the group by way of what he gives and takes, and also to make the group experience an opportunity for the individual's social development. This may include making the individual more aware of his reasons for joining the group, and helping him to see he has other expectations which the group may or may not be able to fulfil; helping him to see what the group expects from him and how to give or withhold without giving up his membership; to see what skills, knowledge, and understanding he has that the group could use, and how he might best contribute them; to understand the conditions of leadership in the group and how he can achieve leadership if he wants to; to understand the conditions of membership and how he can work towards modifying them to his own needs. In short the worker helps the individual to see the group as an opportunity he can use, and to understand how he can use it.

The worker might do these things in various ways on many occasions. He does them by getting to know an individual boy, and his needs as the boy sees them, and then considering his own interpretation of these needs. He observes the response of the individual to the other members of the group and theirs to the boy. He seeks to observe, understand and accept his own feelings about the boy in the group and then to act as a bridge between what he sees as the boy's need and the group situation. His aim is not to help a group to adapt entirely to one individual disregarding the needs of the other members (which would be an unrealistic demand) nor to try and make the individual a 'good group member'; but simply to create the atmosphere in which the individual and the group will learn to work out their difficulties without either party's being too drastically exploited. If the group learns to accept something of an individual's demanding behaviour and the individual something about how to seek acceptance, there is some hope of getting it, and each party will have contributed to the social development of the other.

There is another aspect of this process that seems to be important here. When a worker moves into a group, inevitably he affects relationships between individual members. Firstly, he is another person who participates in the group. Secondly, he is recognised as being both within and without the group. Thirdly, he is an adult with resources which the other members do not have. The group members have to learn to relate these three factors so that eventually they are able to accept the worker as a person, and also understand the role he will play.

Although in some groups, the members will unite to test out the worker during these early stages, more frequently, individual members may attempt to develop relationships with him. In some groups members compete in attempting to form an 'emotional tie' with the worker. The individual's behaviour may be friendly, hostile, or ambivalent, but it is directed to the worker. Sometimes he has to accept very great individual demands if the members need to form strong individual relationships with him before they are able to relate positively towards each other. But even as he accepts these demands, he needs to find ways of helping the individuals to get along with each other. He may encourage sub-groups, meeting two, three or four members together, and in various ways encourage friendships, help individuals to support each other, and provide opportunities for them to discuss problems.

As the worker becomes accepted by the group, and understands the pattern of their relationships, so he is able to strengthen sub-groups, to draw out leadership, to help boys take on new roles, giving them opportunities to be important to the whole group. Sometimes he draws new boys into the group, or helps a boy to leave the group for another one. Sometimes he is able to help the indigenous leader to understand different techniques of leadership and to adapt better to individuals in the group. In this way, unpopular boys who need help in their growth and development, can be given the support of an indigenous leader. By helping an individual to relate to himself, to others and to the whole group, he uses his role to meet the basic needs of the individual to get along with friends and with adults, and to learn how to reach agreement and achievement together.

Conflict, co-operation and the worker

We have seen that conflict and co-operation are present and necessary in any group, and it is in this aspect of group life that the worker needs to use much of his skill, and knowledge of individuals and groups. The conflict and co-operation are the expression of needs, values and interpersonal relations, and they happen around and within the activity of a group—or they can be the activity of the group. In order to resolve conflict the worker helps individuals to express and handle the conflict they feel, and the groups to accept and use the conflict. His role changes frequently. He has to know when to mediate, arbitrate, or create diversions. He has to know when to make a decision for a group, when to help it make a decision, and when to leave the decision entirely to them. He has to know when he must try to prevent conflict, usually when violence seems inevitable. There are occasions, particularly in younger groups, when members are afraid of their own behaviour to each other, and need an adult to set limits.

In all these roles, the worker is active, and although he may sometimes feel he is an 'observer' of conflict, he is by his presence a participating member of the group. While he is offering skills and insights to help the members express and handle the conflict they feel, and to help the group accept and use the conflict, he is also offering his spontaneous behaviour as part of the material which the group can use. His feelings towards himself, towards the individuals and towards the group are part of that behaviour.

His aim is to help the group to learn how to reach agreement and how to make decisions. Only rarely and in special circumstances, should he make a decision for a group. It may be easier to make the decision, and sometimes the group will press him to do so (often in order to avoid responsibility itself) but if he complies, he is depriving the group members of deciding for themselves, and of learning how to do it. The decision made is rarely as important as the growth of the group members in learning to make it together. There are several ways of helping groups to make choices and decisions. A vote might be the best way to settle some issues, but this cannot be a regular practice for an adolescent group. If the group members do not stand by the voted decision, the worker's function is not to insist, but to explore with the group why it happened. Sometimes he will help the group come to a decision by asking questions relating to past experience and mistakes. Or he may by reflection, bring into the open factors which could affect the decision. If possible he should pass on some understanding of how group decisions are made, perhaps by describing what happened within the group to make agreement possible.

In all of this, the worker needs to be aware of the effect of his behaviour on both relationships and activities. Sometimes each person in the group may want a different activity. This could be arranged but some activities require several people together. The choice of activity may rest simply on the power of the more aggressive members. If this happened often, the worker may decide to 'stimulate' conflict by encouraging the less aggressive members to stand out for their choice, concerning himself at this point with the individual and his relationships. At other times he may try to help all the members to look at the practical aspects of the activities from which they must choose, being at this point more concerned with the activity. He has to remember that choices and decisions should be based on a consensus of group feeling as well as on verbal statements ("Well yes, we agreed to go to a camp site. We didn't really want to, but we thought we'd better say yes. That's why we got bored when we got there and broke the place up").

The members of some adolescent groups find it extremely difficult to be articulate. As communication is such an important part of decision making (and of other aspects of group life) the worker has to understand the 'language' of the group members and their methods of communication. Slang, hairstyles, dress, gestures, body movements and other symbolic behaviour are some of their means of expression. The worker may encourage self-expression both in creative activities (spontaneous acting and miming) and also by helping them at points at which they can talk (they may produce stories of their exploits imagined or real, in their own language and at their own pace). By encouraging these and other means of self-expression, a worker can help some groups to express their feelings in words as well as in physical behaviour, which can be a starting point in making group decisions.

Using the activities

We have suggested that every group has an activity—that anything which a group is 'doing' is an activity. It is of utmost importance therefore in a friendship group that a worker observes the 'natural' activity of the group, and sees it as a means of helping the social development of the individual and the group. He needs to follow the natural pattern of events in a group, sharing in the activities its members know and understand, and recognising their importance to them. But he also needs to recognise that a group's activities are limited by the members' inexperience. His function is to encourage a friendship group to be more adventurous, providing equipment, funds, facilities, and information about possible activities, to help it discover all that the community (both locally and in a broader sense) has to offer, and then to help it to choose from the available facilities.

The worker must also understand the characteristics of adolescent behaviour, and how these affect their activities. Group members may sometimes enjoy activities which allow them to become children again, but at other times they may want to take responsibility (on their own terms) or to undertake activities which may continue long after the group has disintegrated and the worker has departed. The worker has to recognise this changeability and make all these activities possible as and when they are needed. He then, shares in the activities adopted by the group and helps to widen the area of choice. He uses all these activities as an opportunity to help group members in their relationships and social development.

Sometimes it is misguidedly assumed, on the analogy of individual casework, that group relations are improved mainly by discussing problems. This assumption makes a false distinction between personal relationships and activities; and puts too much importance on the activity of verbal communication. It seems important to re-emphasise that interpersonal relations and activities are part of the same process. Group discussion is only one of the possible ways in which the worker helps group members to deal with some of their problems. The everyday activities of living, working and playing together are also occasions for personal interaction and the resolution of personal problems. Enjoyment is an important word to the young person. Participation in something which is fun, which is adventurous, and which gives a sense of achievement, means that an individual is looking outward beyond himself and often doing things which he did not realise were possible for him. This in itself is often a help towards solving some problems, and if these things can be shared with other people, the individual will learn about relationships by doing rather than by talking. These things happen naturally in any group, but some need the help of a worker.

If the worker looks at all these aspects of 'activities' he will see that money, premises, allocation of tickets, use of a vehicle, arguments, negotiations with other groups, the police or club authorities, are tools as useful to him as carpentry, dressmaking, holidays and expeditions in helping the members to sort out their relationships among themselves, with the worker and with society generally. He uses the material presented by the group, adding to it, and helping the members through their participation to use the programme for their wider social development.

Values and standards

The worker, like every other member, brings to the group his own values, which in turn are modified by the rest of the group. His problems in doing so have already been partly discussed in the problems of field-work. But a worker must be prepared for at least two things. He may overestimate the importance of his own values, and he may underestimate the impact of the group's values on himself. Usually the group's values are modified less by his than he might have hoped, since they are held by a number of people.

The group derives its values from the community—either from the

190

adolescent society or from the total neighbourhood—and also from individual members. All the boys in the group may have a similar attitude towards girls and their roles, but one boy may think it is right to go to work while another thinks it is stupid. It is often difficult for the worker to attempt to change the values of the total group, nor is it necessarily wise for him to attempt to do so. But it is possible to bring value conflicts into the open so that the group recognises the different values and discusses them—why it is wrong to steal money and right to steal things? Is it right to break up our own equipment? Thus instead of an adult moralising, the boys argue out an accepted code of behaviour for their group. At the same time the worker can help some boys to support another in sticking to his job or his apprenticeship, or in not joining in a 'rumble'. If the indigenous leader —the boy who is rated highest—owes his position to his ability to organise fights, the worker will not only try to help the leader, but also try to help other boys to show and/or recognise different kinds of leadership skills.

The values of the group show up when it is with other groups or in public. It is then that it sees its own behaviour reflected by out-siders, and decides the kind of image it wishes to present. The worker helps the boys to move towards a group identity (without endangering individuality) when it is said or accepted "in our group we do this or that, and this or that behaviour is not allowed". The values of the total group have then been translated into rules which are neither made nor enforced by the worker.

Helping the development of a group

We have now considered how the worker becomes accepted by a group, and how he helps it to resolve conflict and to make choices and decisions; how he uses activities and affects the group's values and standards. He recognises that all these things are parts of the same process and that his work is not in separate compartments.

Within this one process, the group moves through stages of develop-ment which vary according to the participants and the circumstances. The worker needs to be aware of these phases or stages. He starts by assessing the needs of the members, and their expectations of the group, and considering ways of helping the group to meet these needs. He helps the members towards a sense of belonging and a group identity. He helps the group to achieve its objectives—be it to plan and go on a holiday, to organise dances, or to drink coffee to-gether or to build its own premises. He does this by helping the members to give and take, to share, to express their feelings towards each other and to learn how to handle their feelings. To this end he uses the activity of the group, and also the conflict and co-operation which emerge, so that eventually the group understands how to meet its own needs, how to make decisions, and how to allocate the work to carry out these decisions.

He does all this by constantly changing his role in the group (as previously described) although basically this is the role of an enabler—a person who makes things possible. The 'things' which are made possible are basically the growth and development of the members, but in practical terms he is offering his contribution through information, equipment, know-how, social skills, leadership, negotiation, getting along with people, and using facilities. His main objective is to help the group to be more and more independent of himself.

We may have given the impression that only the final stages of development are concerned with relating to other groups. This may be true of some groups, but in most adolescent groups it is happening throughout the work. The worker judges when the members will benefit from association with each other and himself, and when they will learn more from using the community resources or facilities and associating with other people. Thus he is constantly moving from being inside a group to becoming a bridge between the group and the community.

The worker's role is complex. He is working with individuals in a group, with sub-groups within one group, and he is acting as a bridge between this group and many others in the community. It is as he is able to separate all these roles and understand them that he is able to weave them together again so that the day to day pattern of his work emerges in spontaneous behaviour.

Variations in groups

The role of the worker has now been considered from many different aspects. Most of these aspects of group life and the worker's role within them are happening at the same time and over a long period. He helps the group to function more effectively by helping its members to get to know one another and to meet more frequently, to agree on objectives and to get things done. But there are many instances in which groups do not need intensive help or need help in only one or two aspects.

A group of young people who have already learned a great deal about relationships within a stable family background, and through helpful experiences at school and in other groups, may be able to reach a point of co-operation very quickly, learning to conduct the group to meet their own needs and achieve their aims. Self-programming comes easily to this type of group, which may need from the worker only information, material help, or advice on a few occasions when difficult problems arise.

Another group may appear to function well and independently and yet may reach a 'block', for instance if its members cannot move on or out into other groups. The drama group which goes on with the same people for ten years is a typical example. This group needs a worker who will draw it into relations with other groups—on negotiations for use of premises or any other practical issue—and will also try to find out why its members need the security and support of this one group, and are unable to participate fully in the social and community life outside.

In such examples, the worker limits his role according to the needs of the group, or takes action at any given stage, frequently to help it over a 'block' in its development. If a worker is therefore involved with a series of groups he may find he is working intensively with one or two over a long period, and carrying out a more limited role with others.

From his understanding of groups and his role as enabler within them, the worker has to go on to adapt himself and his techniques to the pattern demanded by the individuals with whom he sets to work. In detached work, instead of stable, medium-sized groups, he is liable to find a series of smaller groups that change members and interests rapidly. Yet knowledge of groups and their behaviour is still relevant. Even if the form is modified by the situation, other characteristics remain constant as a guide to understanding the behaviour of the small group within the larger network. These small groups sometimes appear to be separate, sometimes parts of larger ill-defined groups overlapping in membership, and sometimes parts of one large group, but are always seen by participants and workers as a large loosely-knit network.

The worker may often feel that his work with sub-groups within the network is similar to his work with individuals in a group. Sometimes he is at the centre of a sub-group with changing fringe members, sometimes he is between sub-groups, helping them to negotiate with each other, and sometimes he is supporting indigenous leaders in order to help one sub-group to contain another. Sometimes he suggests an activity to separate one small group from another, and sometimes in order to bring several small groups together.

On occasions, during a day or evening expedition, he uses his presence in a group, knowing it may never meet as a group again, and it may seem that the group goes through several stages of development in a few hours. At other times the mobility of the friendship pattern may give the worker the impression that he is working only with a large number of individuals. All these impressions may be valid, and the worker has to see his service both as meeting individual and group needs as they emerge from moment to moment, and also in the broader terms of his total clientele over a long period.

Although this might at first seem a strange setting for work with groups, the average youth club often presents the same picture—several well-defined medium friendship groups within a larger, much less well-defined network of smaller groups, coming together occasionally, breaking up, rapidly changing their individual constellations but remaining within a single overall pattern. There are drawbacks in working in such a network. It makes for less intensive relationships between the worker and the individuals and the rapid change-over of members from group to group means that groups often lose some of their identity, solidarity, social skills and know-how when their members leave. But there are advantages as well. The network has more human resources if called upon than does the group on its own. It offers the individual a larger field of choices from within which to 'position himself', and a wider variety of activities and personal relationships.

A permissible analogy might well be the modern school in which the teacher divides her class into groups for projects. She visits first one group and then another. Then all the separate groups come together for a particular subject. During recreation, the class falls apart into a totally different set of constellations. In detached work, the worker is not 'formally' teaching anything, but informally passing on social skills. Yet the analogy might well hold if we remember that the teacher is meeting different needs on different levels within a variety of small groups that are in themselves part of a larger grouping, and that the members of the various 'classes' will pass from one group to another (in relation to academic proficiency) while remaining within the larger grouping of the school. The teacher in this situation sees the small groups within the large as separate and differentiated for some activities but undifferentiated for others. The detached worker might look at the network of small loosely-knit groups with whom he is working in the same way.

ILLUSTRATIONS

Helping individuals in their relationships with others in a group

The group consisted of thirteen girls between twelve and fourteen years, of whom ten were present at the meeting. They were all members of large families, living in overcrowded homes, most of whom were in touch with at least one welfare official. Most of the girls were on probation for non-attendance at school or petty theft. The group which was voluntary, had already been meeting for several months, once weekly in premises and on fortnightly outings. The tensions between the girls themselves, between individual girls and the worker, and between the worker and the group were already both strong and evident, especially by way of the demands of individuals on the worker, and the constant fighting and acting out of aggression between the girls. Articles were 'stolen'. The girls were seriously handicapped in working together as a group and in doing and being what they wanted, and could frequently only get things done on their own 'against the group' or by pairing off into twos and threes and opposing 'all the others'. The group had originally been developed around Jean, a withdrawn child, unable to get on easily with girls of her own age or with adults, who had to be picked up and taken to the club where at first she was unable to participate except by her presence.

Extract from worker's record/Susan

Marie began to peel potatoes in the kitchen with Angela's help. Jacqueline, Sheila, Gillian and Jose were making coffee. Everyone was in the kitchen where it was warmest and there was a pleasant, noisy atmosphere of bustle and activity. Angela began to demand that the cooks be left in the kitchen alone and that everyone else go into the other room and the door be closed. I didn't want to break up the group at that moment and so persuaded Angela to leave the door open, saying that the kitchen was warmest and that everyone wanted to be near the fire. She accepted this grudgingly and gradually gave up whining.

Myra and Jane arrived with the record player and instructions that only these two, plus Sheila and Jose, were allowed to use it in case it got broken. I changed the plug, and they were impatient whilst I did it, and then dancing began in the main room. Jose with Myra, Sheila, Gillian and Jacqueline flitted from one room to the other, and from group to group and often talked to me in the kitchen.

Sheila rushed into the kitchen, her face glowing, shouting, "I feel mad, Miss, I feel mad," flinging her arms in the air, and pirouetting around. I replied, "Well, you can be mad if you like," and she dashed back into the other room, leaping about to the music with Jose, Sheila and Jacqueline. Larks began and a lot of giggling.

The chips began to appear from the kitchen. I received mine first and thanked Angela, saying they were very good—which they were. I could see that although they were able to organise themselves over the cooking, the distribution would be too difficult for them, so I helped them find plates and cutlery and see who wanted what, as if taking orders in a café. There were no serious quarrels, although Angela had tried too hard to organise everybody and get everyone sorted out and she was fed up when it didn't work.

Jose, Gillian, Sheila and Myra got up on the window seat and began to mime "Bobby's Girl", and Marie stood in the doorway longing to join in, butting in and telling them how to do it, so I suggested that perhaps she could be the compere and introduce the "Four Seasons", as they wanted to be called. Then Jane and Rita also wanted to do something, but they were afraid to make the effort, so when the others' song had ended, I casually mentioned that "Bachelor Boy" was a good song to mime to and they straight away said "Yes". It was their turn and Marie joined them. Angela was looking from the kitchen and asked to join in but they said "No", as it was just for the three of them, so I said maybe she could introduce them and she did, but found it hard to withdraw when her bit was over. Jacqueline and I were the audience.

Marie suddenly realised that she had not had any chips and a row was imminent because she had done the cooking all evening and she was "starved". Angela's were in the pan and I could see that Marie would be taking them, so I told her I would cook her chips and I dried them and put them on. She was pleased and quietened down and the quarrel with Angela was avoided.

Angela was in trouble though, because she had cooked herself a large plateful of chips and Myra shouted at her for being greedy—"last week it was the biscuits"—and Jose joined in and kept nicking them off the plate, grinning and acting the fool. Gillian came down heavily on to Angela and told her off.

Sheila went with Jane to fetch milk and together they made coffee. Jane put the table by the door to keep everyone else out of the kitchen, shouting at them when they tried to get in.

Marie and Rita had to go home early and just as they were leaving Jane whispered that Marie had the bottle of shampoo. Now that I knew about it I had to do something, so I called Marie back and when we were alone asked her about it. She produced the bottle from under her coat saying she only had a little. I said that if she wanted it she only had to ask and it would be all right. Apparently, Sheila also had some, and then Jane asked. Myra wanted the bottle of vinegar and Angela asked for the rest of the cooking fat.

With the exodus of the two girls there were only six left and Jacqueline and Sheila began to do ballet dancing. Jane and Jose joined in.

They had asked me to bring a good record and all that I could produce was "Eine kleine Nachtmusik" by Mozart, and they began to dance to it. They were a bit self-conscious so I suggested that we turn the lights out and just have a small amount coming from the kitchen. In the scene they were fairies and Sheila danced around to touch them and they each woke up and danced together. Then Sheila was a statue which came to life and fell in love with Jacqueline, and then there was one dance to "Bachelor Boy" which they had worked out before the meeting to do here, in which Sheila leaned on a broomstick as a boy and all the others were girls and she courted them.

For no apparent reason Gillian who had been watching, started to call Angela names: "You round-toed little bitch", and she was cruel in the things she said—commenting on her stockings and clothes and her size. I thought that it might help if she had something to do, to be included in the proceedings, and as she had mentioned tea earlier on I said I would like a cup and would she like to do it. She did and made it for everyone. I praised it and she seemed a bit happier and left Angela alone. Angela swept up the room. As we had the record player to take back and it was thick fog, we decided to have a taxi. Angela asked me to call for her as I do for Jean and I said that Jean was on my route and she wasn't, so that I was sorry I couldn't.

I brought up the subject of the hotel, hoping that Jane would remember to tell Jean the sleeping arrangements she had proposed, and she did, telling her that she, Rita, Angela and herself hoped to share a room. This pleased Jean very much and when asked if it was all right she replied, "Yes", and wanted to know when it would be. The taxi dropped them each at their homes after a very full evening.

Comments

We see this record as illustrating in a single session the changing role of the worker, as a resource person, in helping towards achievement, praising accomplishment, accepting or rejecting behaviour, encouraging participation. We see it also as illustrating the worker's role in participating in activities and guiding them so as to help individuals in their relations with others. Marie, Jane, Rita and Angela were all helped to participate at times when they or the group needed some encouragement.

The worker also gave special attention to Marie when she was feeling left out, and thus prevented trouble between Marie and Angela. Gillian, too, showed her feelings in no uncertain terms when left out of the group, and the worker singled her out for attention. On both these occasions the worker drew the girl's attention to herself (the worker) to prevent developing conflict, and then withdrew, leaving the girl in the group again.

Two other incidents were concerned with values. Sheila's "I feel mad miss, I feel mad" could have brought disapproval. But it was accepted, "You can be mad if you like". The worker's reaction to the removal of the shampoo was important, not only for Marie, but for Jane who had drawn her attention to it, and for the others. Why had Marie taken the shampoo? Why had Jane mentioned it? They had been told stealing was wrong (i.e. on probation). What would the worker do about it? The problem was obscure and the worker relieved the tension around it by saying, "If you want it, you only have to ask and it will be all right". No longer was only one girl involved. Four others came forward and tested out this possibility. We might ask, "Did the worker believe that if they asked they should always be given?", but this seems to be of less importance than the worker's asking herself, "What do Marie and the others need from me at this moment?"

Angela played a prominent part throughout the record. She tried to organise the group, which refused to accept her leadership. She needed to be the centre of attention and to be important to the worker.

We saw the worker step in to protect the group from Angela, and persuade Angela to accept the situation. On two occasions she allowed the group to deal with Angela, but on two others she prevented conflict or protected Angela. She also found a way of drawing Angela into a group, and towards the end found a practical reason for not giving Angela preferential treatment.

Jean was not mentioned until the end of the record. She may even have been forgotten in the middle; the record reads that "six were left", when there were actually seven. But eventually, recognising Jean's importance, knowing she was wanted as one of a foursome, the worker made sure that it was discussed in front of her.

Why was Angela mentioned so much in the record, and Jean hardly at all? Perhaps because Angela was a 'problem' to the worker, whereas she knew how to help Jean and did not need to mention her, or perhaps Angela was showing the worker how she *could* help her, whereas it was still difficult to know how to help Jean in her relationship with other members.

The record shows that the worker was concerned mainly with the individual and her relationships in the group. The evening was full of activities and although the worker did not suggest them she made them possible by her concentration on individual needs. Some conflict was inevitable and possibly desirable, but by concentrating on individual need, the worker was able to prevent the complete exclusion of anyone or the development of chaos.

The importance of this evening would seem to be first that the girls had a sense of achievement—an enjoyable evening, cooking, eating, dancing—which would mean that they would hope to continue meeting together. Secondly, the tensions and conflict within the group were being contained and a control was emerging which allowed for and encouraged the expression of feelings but provided limits. Thirdly, finding their own needs being understood and responded to by an adult, the girls could respond in the give and take necessary in relationships. Throughout, the worker was acting "naturally", as an interested, accepting adult to what was happening between herself and individual girls, between the several girls, and between herself and the whole group.

We assume that if, with the worker's help, a girl succeeds in relating better to other girls, to the adult worker and later, to boys, and so to herself as well, this can make a contribution to her growth and development at home, at school, and in the neighbourhood.

Helping a group to make a decision

The group of thirteen girls (twelve-fourteen years) met regularly once a week in the premises and planned outings once a fortnight. Usually each girl wanted to do something different, and the worker had to help them make a decision as to where they would go. They had agreed that voting was the fairest way, and on the week preceding this record had decided to vote to go swimming at the White City. Sadie, Sheila and Angela were in opposition.

Worker's record/Susan

Present: Myra, Jane, Rita, Angela, Susan, Sadie, Sheila, Pamela. Myra and Rita arrived at the club, with their bathing costumes. The others followed, but had no costumes and Sadie said it was too cold to swim. The others, except for Myra and Rita agreed.

Sheila said they had arranged to go to the White City, but that the swimming pool was closed so they hadn't brought their costumes. Then followed a long discussion. Sadie said she wanted to go to Battersea Park to see the film stars and had brought her autograph book. Angela said "that's what I want to do". Jane and Susan had come dressed for ice-skating. Everyone argued and then Rita and Angela said they didn't mind where they went, but Angela was torn between Battersea Park and ice-skating.

In desperation they asked me to decide, but I wouldn't. I suggested they should decide whether the White City had been the important part of the agreement or if it had been that we should go swimming. Everyone except Myra and Rita said it had been to go to the White City. Sadie and Rita said, "All right, but we still want to go swimming". I said, "Well let's think about Battersea Park. You said it is 2s to go in." Sadie said, "We're not dressed properly". The others agreed. Jane: "We haven't brought our autograph books." Sheila: "By the time we get there, the stars will be ready to go home." Angela: "Yes, we wouldn't have much time there." There was general agreement about this, so I said, "Well, what about ice-skating, how much will that cost?" Pamela: "It costs more to go in, but the fare is cheaper." Myra: "We haven't got our trousers on." Rita: "Or socks." Sheila: "We'd have much longer there." I said, "All right, now how about swimming?"

The argument started again, until finally Sadie said, "You tell us, Susan". I refused, then Sheila said, "Susan, you don't have to say where we should go, but tell us where *you* would like to go if you had the choice". I said, "Well, I think I'd just like to go to a cinema and watch a film". At this, they all shouted against it, saying, "You can go to a cinema any time". They then discussed the activities again, and this time everyone agreed that they would not have enough time at Battersea Park, and the others persuaded Rita and Myra to leave swimming until they all had costumes. This left ice-skating but Myra said: "I don't want to go, I don't like the ice." Everyone persuaded her and at last she agreed with good grace. As we prepared to go, I pointed this out saying, "Did you notice? Myra doesn't like skating but she has agreed to go. Don't you think that was nice of her?" They all looked in amazement at Myra and then agreed that it was.

Then Sheila said, "If Myra doesn't go on the ice, and Sadie won't skate either, then they could have a drink with you in the canteen if the are bored".

This discussion had lasted three-quarters of an hour so we quickly set out for the skating rink, Jane, Rita and Angela with me, the others behind. Those who had 2s paid their own entrance. Angela and Sheila enjoyed the ice. Rita was nervous and Jane seemed off the ice more than she was on. Sadie, Myra, and I went for a drink for which I paid, and later the others followed. They joined us for drinks, but paid for their own and said we'd all have a drink later when I would pay for them as I usually did. Before going in I had explained that I must leave at 5 p.m. because of an engagement. They voluntarily left the ice and prepared to leave at the same time. I left them walking home arm-in-arm.

Comments

Sadie, Sheila, Angela and Jane had apparently decided to ignore the agreed decision to go swimming and had come prepared for other outings. Being divided among themselves they had little hope of convincing the swimmers to change their minds. The worker had the choice of allowing the group to decide or of making the decision for them. She therefore allowed them to try and work it out, but knew they were incapable of coming to a unanimous decision, and that more voting would probably produce more disagreement. She thereupon helped them to look at the problem. Having produced reasons for and against each activity they again appealed for help in their predicament. When the worker refused to decide they came back to a discussion of the activities as the only way out. Finally they were able to agree, arranging that Sadie and Myra should have extra attention and drinks to make up for not going on the ice. Apparently everyone did enjoy the afternoon. The worker did not dictate, nor was she passive, but she directed the group away from their individual feelings to the practical issues (money, dress, time, etc.) which could be more easily resolved.

Although one girl would accept the leadership of another, no girl was strong enough to lead the whole group, and such was their need for leadership that at one point they seemed prepared to do what the worker told them. The situation could also be seen as a testing out of the worker. It might be interpreted as "Your voting system doesn't work. Now what will you do? Who is going to win? Who do you like best?" Their comments on the cinema might be taken as confirmation of this. If this were a test then it was important that the worker should direct the thinking of the group away from this particular conflict in interpersonal relations and her own part in them, to the discussion of activities and practical issues which were more easily understood by the group.

The worker directed their attention from "what will you do to resolve this conflict?", to a different consideration, "what kind of things might we discuss profitably considering the nature of our disagreements?"

Problems of leadership in negotiation

Representatives of two groups were called together for an informal meeting in a worker's house. Both had shown interest in reopening their 'commercial youth club', and the worker was hoping that they would be able to plan an opening as one group. Group 1 consisted of Dan (leader), Lanky, Tubby, and Ann (and others not present). This group were 'can copes'—able to take responsibility and organise a club. Dan's influence was very strong and he had a large following. Group 2 consisted of Artie, Brian, Tommy, Vic, Shorty, Ricky, and Claire (and one or two others not present). This group was very loosely knit, without leadership, and included boys of varying degrees of disorganisation. The first part of the meeting was a discussion on opening the club, working on the premises, and raising money, then . . .

Worker's record/Peter

I tried to sum up the main points that had been made, and this brought the meeting to order again. I asked if there were anything else anybody wanted to talk about. Dan said, "Yes, we haven't fixed up about a committee". Everybody thought that we should have a committee and agreed to Dan's suggestion that it should consist of four from Dan's group, and four from the other. The names were soon settled— Dan, Tubby, Lanky, and one other from Dan's group, Artie, Shorty, Vic and either Tommy or Brian. Tommy climbed down of his own accord, but was not very happy about it.

Dan and company settled down to watch television, while Artie, Shorty, Tommy, Vic and Ricky left the room. After about ten minutes I joined them in the dining-room, where they were seated round the table in a very formal and businesslike manner. It looked as though I had walked into a lapse in a serious discussion. As soon as I appeared I was drawn in. "Look, Peter, we don't want Tubby on this committee." Peter: "Why not?" Artie: "He's a flash isn't he?" Peter: "It might be an idea to keep him sweet because he can help to keep order in the club." Vic: "Yes, but he hasn't been in the club as long as some of the others." Peter: "What do you think the reason is for people being on a committee—is it always the people who have been in the club longest?" Shorty: "No, it's the people who can get things done." Vic: "But I still don't think that Tubby should be on the committee." (He was supported by the others.) Peter: "Let's forget the things we can't agree about for a minute and see if there is anything we can

agree on. Do you agree to the idea of eight people on the committee?"
Vic: "Yes, that's all right." Peter: "Is it a good idea for four to come
from our lot and four from Dan and his crowd?" (Pause—then general
agreement.) Peter: "Let's see if we can agree who *our* four should be."
They made fairly short work of this, electing Artie, Shorty, Tommy
and Vic, and adding Ricky as an afterthought. I asked them to think
again, as this made five. There was a thought that the number should
be increased to ten. I asked whether it would be fair on Ricky to put
him on the committee of a club which he had never attended. Vic and
Artie supported this thought, and though Ricky looked a bit dis-
consolate at this, we decided that we should review the position later.

The question of Brian arose. He had been nominated by Dan but
as a member of this group. Artie said, "He don't hang about with us.
He's really one of their lot. We don't want him on our committee."
Again I pointed out that Brian was a useful member of the club. Vic
said, "Like what! He's just flash. He won a prize at school three
years running for woodwork."

I recapped the position. We had agreed to a committee of eight,
four of whom they had already elected from their "side". Since they
had done this, they could not deny Dan the right to pick four from
his side, of his own choosing. They took this point, and went on to
agree when I suggested that if Dan wanted to choose Tubby and
Brian for the committee, it was up to him. Brian was brought in and
this was put to him. He didn't seem to mind much either way, and
later Dan agreed that he should represent his boys on the committee.

The discussion closed shortly after this, with Tommy saying, "At
least we've got the committee sorted out", in a very satisfied manner.
Then said that the committee should meet weekly once the club got
going. General opinion seemed to be that the club should be made
ready for opening and then the committee should meet to talk about
the details of running the club.

Comments

At the beginning of this record, Group 1 dominated the meeting
Group 2 apparently accepted the decisions, and only Tommy showed
his doubts, even though he withdrew from being on a committee
voluntarily. When the meeting ended, Group 2 showed its disapproval
by complete withdrawal to another room where they started another
meeting.

Without an acknowledged leader, and in a situation beyond their
understanding, they could only criticise the other side and Peter was
welcomed as the leader they needed. Having tested out the situation,
he guided the discussion, throwing the group back on itself, and
including himself. "Let's decide who *our* four should be." The group
jumped at this, and replanned their representation, expressing their
concern that Brian might prove traitor. Group 2 was in a difficult
position, and expressed its uneasiness in criticism of Tubby as a com-

mittee member. Later developments appeared to demonstrate that their real fear was of being swallowed up by Group 1. They could not see one committee, but two opposing factions, "their side" and "our side". They needed to feel their own group strong enough to make its own decisions before they were ready to negotiate with another group. When, with Peter's help, their solidarity was established, they were no longer concerned about the "other side" and lost interest in Tubby.

Peter placed himself in a difficult position. He had brought together two groups to run one club, without recognising the strong hostility feelings of one group to the other. When he did realise it he came down very strongly on the side of Group 2, accepting their right to a separate meeting, and giving them his support and leadership. so that they felt as strong as Group 1. At this stage he was the kind of leader Group 2 wanted. And the question had become how long would this last?

Peter, however, pointed out the rights of Group 1, and negotiated with Dan as the leader of that Group. Dan was presumably in a strong position, recognising that his own leadership and following were not threatened by Peter's leadership nor by the suggestions. The meeting ended, however, not as one group planning a club, but as two distinct factions, each with its own leader, but prepared to negotiate.

This situation raises a number of questions.

a. Can two groups, each with a leader, run this club jointly?
b. Will the worker continue to be accepted as the leader of group 2?
c. Can the worker be both the leader of Group 2 and still facilitate the development of the whole club?
d. If the worker withdraws his leadership from Group 2, will the group sabotage the plans and activities of the club?

In order to come together and negotiate, each group first needs an identity accepted by each of its members and the group as a whole. Each needs a spokesman through whom to negotiate, who can be accepted as legitimate by all parties concerned. One group's fear of being swallowed up by the other group is a 'feeling' behind the negotiations. The worker therefore tries to handle both the surface events in the situation, the items to be negotiated, the underlying fears of either group swallowing up the other, and the resulting tensions. If in this case Peter withdraws from Group 2, there are four possible results:

a. Group 2 could accept leadership of Group 1;
b. Group 2 could fight for the leadership;
c. Group 2 could sabotage the leadership of Group 1;
d. Group 2 could withdraw.

In these circumstances *a* is unlikely, *b* would seem impossible, as Group 1 is more capable and has a strong accepted leadership, *d* is also unlikely. *c* is the most likely, with two possible results. Group 1 may throw out Group 2, which will still have nuisance value. Or Group 1 will tire of constant sabotaging of their achievements, and will move on to another place where their leadership is generally accepted. The point of this record is that first a worker needs to recognise the inevitable conflict between sub-groups, and secondly to understand the role he intends to play, and the possible results of playing it. Especially in this case he needs to know the limitations and potentials of the indigenous leadership within a sub-group in terms of his ability to represent and achieve what that group needs and wants.

Using community facilities

The group consisted of thirteen boys of sixteen to twenty years some of whom were running a commercial youth club, which provided dancing and refreshments, shared by approximately seventy young people. The group was pressuring the worker, Gerry, to open the club on more evenings. Gerry felt that the success of the club was partially due to its being opened at limited times. In suggesting the outing, covered in the record, he had three aims. First, to provide alternatives to meeting in the premises, second, to induce smaller groups to meet together away from larger numbers, and third, to introduce the group to other ways of enjoying themselves. The group consisted of Dan, Tubby, Ted, Bob, Red, John, Reg, Brian, Mike, Vic, Loftie, Jo, Tommy. Dan was the accepted leader who ruled by force, accepted because he was considered to be a person who would get things done.

Worker's record/Gerry

First session—introducing the group

The purpose of the trip was to follow up a letter received from the Manager of the bowling alley suggesting that some of the organisers or our party should go to see him. I called on Reg at 8.30 to see if he would come. He said that he could not. Brian, who was with him, volunteered to go in his place. I asked Brian to fetch Tubby and Dan. He returned with Vic and Loftie as well. Artie also tried to come but was refused permission to get into the van. He went back in the direction of the café, upset.

The bowling alley proved to be a converted cinema, changed in a most attractive way. It claims to be the largest in Europe, having forty lanes on two floors. Everywhere is very brightly lit. There is a strange 'out of this world' atmosphere about the long lanes and the automatic skittle-replacer machines. Each lane has its own set of

204

benches and tables for the players and the score cards are photograph-
ically enlarged and screened above the lanes for all to see. In the foyer
there is a control desk with flash lights and numbers indicating which
lanes are free and who is next. All around the foyer are Pepsi-Cola,
ice-cream and drink machines. There were people of all ages between
about 16 and 50. Girls wore blouses and slacks and men usually had
white shirts without ties.

The boys were naturally rather overwhelmed by all this and especially
by the complicated looking score cards which were screened. We
had to wait at least half-an-hour for the Manager to be free to see
us and during this time there were signs of doubt arising as to whether
they would be able to cope with the bowling. There were instructors
about but they did not seem to be very active in helping people. Some
of the girls particularly were obviously very skilled.

When the Manager at last came he took us down to the buffet
and ordered coffee for us all. He asked at first which Y.W.C.A. Club
we came from and I explained aside, that we called ourselves 'Jumbo's',
while helping him collect more cups of coffee. He asked about how
many we would like to bring, suggesting a party of twelve. There was
some discussion about when to reserve lanes for us because we would
not be able to come early. Finally it was agreed to reserve two lanes
for 8.30 on the 10th May in the name of 'Jumbo's'. I tried to keep the
conversation going so as to give the boys a chance to speak about their
club and asked the Manager about his other alley. He told us that he
had started that one and had moved to this alley seven weeks ago and
was hoping to move north where he was to start a third. He said there
were already sufficient bookings to take up the first-floor lanes for the
first three days of each week and shortly it would not be possible to
reserve casual bookings on the first floor at all.

The boys were very impressed by the description of the northern
alley which, although it will not have so many lanes as this one,
will also have alongside a swimming pool, dance hall and a hotel with
120 bedrooms. Loftie then told the Manager about our club and this
was taken up by Dan and Tubby, who told him how we had decorated
it and now ran it with profit for eighty or so people. Our last words
to him when we left were that he should come up sometime to see us
when he was in the area.

On the way home it was mentioned, of course, that he was a good
bloke, he had given us free drinks and although obviously very busy
had shown a lot of interest.

Session two—the main visit

We arrived at the bowling alley at 7.50 and pushed our way past the
commissionaire to the first floor where we knew that lanes should
be reserved for us. The boys seemed to expect me to take the lead and
I went in search of the Manager, who was busy with other groups.
The man behind the control desk said that he knew we were to play
at 8.30. The boys filled in the time by watching other players, wandering
around the cafeteria area and sitting in the buffet. Reg was supposed to

start a 'laugh' but did not after receiving severe glances from Dan. As Reg took up a ball from the reserve stand to try its weight, he was told to replace it at once by Dan. We had to wait till well after 8.30 before we were called to change our shoes and Dan and Tubby by this time were becoming quite impatient. They went themselves to ask how long we would have to wait.

There was some embarrassment about changing shoes. John and Red particularly fell to the back of the queue and pretended not to know the size of their shoes. We still had to wait after our shoes had been changed but at about 9.0 we were given two adjacent lanes. An instructor was called for us and two volunteer girl scorers. Dan organised us all to stand around the instructor while he was showing how to hold the ball and to bowl it. Not all paid close attention. We all had a practice bowl and then began to play and to score.

We had divided ourselves into 8 and 6 for the two lanes. The two girls were soon disgusted at the way in which some of us were trying to bowl and asked for shoes for themselves. John and Reg went to get these and the girls gave us a good demonstration. They managed to bowl the heavy balls with the appearance of ease and with good effect. This seemed to spur on some of the boys who were having greatest difficulty. Jo, who could only bowl by using both hands, and had difficulty in stopping himself from going down the lane with the ball, renewed his efforts so that what might have been just a good 'laugh' became a serious intention to play. In my team John had the greatest difficulty in bowling straight but persevered. When he went to collect the shoes for the girls he was laughed at by someone else nearby and I saw him clench his fist, but he managed to refrain from striking out.

I suggested to my team that we divide the game and added up the scores of the first four on the sheet to place against the last four. This idea soon broke down and it turned into a competition between Ted, Bob and myself as to who could get the highest score. At one point we had too many balls at our return rack and a public announcement was made to this effect. Dan and Tubby supervised others to take away some of the balls and we were publicly thanked by the announcer. At another point Reg interfered with the return mechanism so that a line of balls queued down the alley. This meant that one of the girls had to 'wade out' down the alley in full view of all the spectators and manually roll the balls along the return. This brought forth another public announcement as to the state of the weather 'down there'. We thus became the centre of attention on the floor, but it was all with good humour.

After our game had ended (it lasted an hour and a half), we watched some other beginners and had a 'laugh' over one poor man who bowled at the wrong time and jammed the automatic pin-setter. In the buffet we commandeered two tables. There was a little trouble at the counter because cigarettes could not be served after hours but although Dan and Tubby were annoyed they led the others so that they would not cause trouble. The Manager was in the buffet and noticed us and came to ask if we had had a good evening. The boys were polite in their reply.

The trip home was quick. The boys sang as we went along and between the songs talked about the next time that we should go bowling. Ted said that it should be the same twelve who should go the next Thursday. Dan said he thought there should be six boys and six girls. Reg was of the opinion that there should be six who knew how to play and six who did not. Some money was handed in for the trip which cost 4s a head, and the rest was promised over the weekend.

Comments

These records describe the nervousness and embarrassment of a group of young men in strange and, to them, glamorous surroundings. It also shows their acceptance of the authority of this commercial establishment, the strength of Dan's leadership in preventing incidents, and the impression made on the individual boys, who became willing to control their own feelings. In the first visit, and partially in the second, the boys were ill at ease and overwhelmed. This could have resulted in trouble on the spot or in the boys' giving up and leaving with a sense of failure because they could not cope with the situation.

Gerry was aware that the first visit of the small group was important, so that they could get used to the surroundings before attempting to bowl. His first job was to get the boys to the bowling alley and to bring them and the manager together. He was concerned less with the relationships among the boys than with those between the group and the public—the Manager, instructors, players, etc. On the first visit he had to take the initiative. He took the opportunity of putting the manager in the picture. "We call ourselves 'Jumbo's'," and kept the conversation going until the boys were relaxed. This worked, in that eventually the boys were able to describe their own club and invite the manager to visit it. Once the relationship with the Manager was established, the boys' were more likely to return.

On the second visit, Gerry took his cue from the group. He was expected to renew the contact with the Manager, while Dan kept the group in order. Later they became more confident, although each new experience embarrassed them again. They were influenced by everyone's concentration on the activity, and the atmosphere and co-operation helped them to concentrate too. Gerry's role was now that of an ordinary group member, going through the same difficulties in trying to bowl, while remaining aware of what was happening to the boys, knowing that they had to exercise control over their behaviour, and observing that they were able to do so.

Gerry, then, began by being a bridge between the group and the 'public'. Having taken the initiative, he then became one of the group accepting Dan's leadership. The group was able to navigate in these surroundings, so Gerry no longer had to protect or support them,

207

although prepared to do so if necessary. This is the record of a group, venturing outside of the neighbourhood to use facilities in the larger community, which might without preparation, have led to failure and withdrawal. But with preparation, the co-operation of the management, and the worker's ability to switch roles, the boys not only enjoyed themselves and had a sense of achievement, but were willing to try it again later on.

21. Work with the community

We worked with the community because it was a 'natural' and important element in the life of the young people, it had the resources we needed in offering them help, and it was the only context possible for this type of programme. Some of the following background information was developed later in the study and it frequently represents our hindsight. It covers that we would have done, if we had begun earlier to work with the community, or if we had continued longer.

It is difficult to define the word "community". The literature about community is large and complex, covering a wide variety of possible definitions. We need not be too overwhelmed by either the complexity of the problem or the range of solutions, providing we can agree on a way of describing those aspects of community which are relevant to our work with the unattached. We shall not then have a definition of 'community' in any technical sense, but rather an operational statement which could serve our purposes, and still bear some relation to the whole range of thought about this problem.

For our purpose, community is a convenient term to refer to groups of people in a neighbourhood (or several contiguous neighbourhoods) with needs that could be met potentially, by our service. This should allow us to keep in view the social and geographical aspects of the idea of community, while focussing on our main concern 'the actual or potential needs that could be met by our service', those of the unattached young people and of the statutory and voluntary bodies who are attempting to serve them. In order to be aware of the complexities that this statement is intended to imply, we might well consider this whole section—background information in working with communities—as a broader, more detailed exposition of the same statement.

Communities have a function

This is a way of saying that communities can and are expected to do things that other forms of social life are not. The function of the local community is to provide an intermediate form of association for the satisfaction of basic human needs (physical, emotional and social) in a way which is not possible for smaller social units, such as a family, or friendship groups, or the larger ones such as the city or the state. Our special concern is the community's part in providing (or in neglecting to provide) the services and opportunities that the young people need, accept or reject.

Communities have a structure

In order to get things done in a community, a particular pattern of assigning responsibility and affording privileges develops. This regulates the allocation of resources, resulting in a system which defines and locates authority, distributes power (not always the same thing) and often is easily visible from the outside as a series of hier-arches, jobs, positions, titles, and devices for giving and maintaining status. In this sense the community can be said to have a 'structure' which both defines the role of the separate groups and institutions that make it up, and allocates to each its formal function—education, commerce, law enforcement, social welfare and recreation. It also provides a system within which the relationships between the various elements are carried on.

The structural aspect of a community is one of the factors in deciding who will do what, how, for whom and with how much to spend. This affects the established rules and regulations that govern and affect the services offered and affect the opportunities provided for the unattached, and describes for the worker the 'field' within which he can hope to 'beg, borrow or steal', services and opportunities to offer in his programme. It is important because in his work with the social institutions in the community he tries to affect in one way or another the allocation of the available resources to the work with the unattached. He has to keep in mind that what he asks to be given to Paul must in one way or another come from Peter; someone is bound to feel the pinch of any reallocation of resources. Moreover, any change in function (the services and opportunities offered) is liable to result in a change in structure, which however minute, might affect an individual group or the institutional status system. The worker therefore has to understand, accept and work with the 'natural' reactions to his suggestions about the reallocation of resources.

Communities are particular

Although we can generalise about communities, we must always remember that each is different. A rural farming community is different from a seaside port, a holiday town, or a fishing village; urban communities differ just as dramatically and with the same variety of effect on the lives of their residents. Belgravia and Notting Hill are both in London. Both are communities in our sense. Each has a structure and a function and all the paraphernalia for getting things done as a community. But the character and quality of life and the amount of services and opportunities, the shared traditions and 'social habits' representative of each separately, can easily be seen to produce radically different patterns of 'life chances' for their young people.

Function and structure are common to all communities at all times everywhere, but the services and provision for basic human needs, resulting in the interaction of these factors, are in each case particular. The worker must take these particularities into account in his day-to-day and long-range attempts to match the needs of the young people to the services and opportunities available.

Shared social attitudes

We have mentioned shared traditions and agreed 'social habits'. We emphasise that such traditions and habits are based on some degree of agreement on an underlying system of values and standards, and are experienced through social attitudes towards work, education and money, the family, sex and marriage. These social attitudes are reflected in the forms and programmes of the social institutions which offer services and opportunities, and which serve as methods of social control. This is of great importance because the conflict in expectations between those who need the service and those who give it (including ourselves) is the point at which to locate the problem of unattachment, and to work towards a solution.

This reasoning leads to taking as the unit of attention and work the unattached young people in relation to the services and opportunities in a particular community.

How things happen in communities

Even a casual glance at the everyday life of a community will indicate the almost infinite variety of social happenings that make up the day-to-day pattern of its existence. They begin with 'the simple happenings' —people · meeting, talking, exchanging ideas, arguing, fighting, buying, selling, going to work, going to school, doing the washing-up or the gardening, making friends, ticking-off enemies, marrying, dying, playing, doing and being a thousand and one ordinary things that make up their daily life. They continue with the 'more complicated happenings'—planning, organising, operating and managing the complex network of commerce, industry, local government and the community services, education, sanitation, medicine, or housing.

They include the most complex—evolving, creating and using the tools and techniques needed to operate the complex system of allocating resources, prestige and status, and enforcing social control, as well as accepting and rejecting, evolving and deciding upon the moral, philosophical and political standards, which are at once the motives for these actions and the values by which they are judged. A closer observation of that complicated pattern of association and interaction enables the worker the opportunities to relate it to his own problems of field-work.

This complex situation includes people of all ages, and can affect the whole age range of the population.

The actions needed in, through and by the community are so complex that division of labour is essential. This gives rise to specialised social institutions to carry out special functions, schools for education and, of special interest to us, clubs and youth centres for work with young people. Each of these institutions has traditions, functions, structures and as a result, hierarchies and status systems peculiar to its own situation; these both cause and affect their programmes of service. This produces ordinary, everyday conflict, competition and co-operation between the social institutions, including those which are responsible for services to the unattached.

The association and interaction in the community occur in three kinds of settings, person to person, within and between groups, and within and between the larger complex groups we are calling social institutions. This interaction may be spontaneous as in casual meetings between friends, or more or less ordered and systematic, at school, at work or in court. Obviously work with the unattached covers the three kinds of settings.

All of the social events we listed above, from the simple through the more complicated to the most complex, are changes in one sense or another, happening to individuals, groups or social institutions within the community within visible or known limits. Recognition of this is important because the worker suggests and even initiates changes within the community as regards the services and opportunities offered to the unattached. He must therefore be aware that change is possible but happens for the most part within limits agreed by the community itself (and the larger society of which it is a part). It is part of the job of the worker to learn the rules governing change in the community.

Social events happen on several different levels within the same community, two of which are important here. The formal organised level of the major social institutions, private and public industry, finance and commerce, local government, the professions, the statutory

211

and voluntary welfare bodies, form a network which plans, organises and manages large areas of the community's life, determining the power structure, defining the status systems, and allocating the resources, that influence (often to a large extent) the everyday life of members of that community. Another level of community life is that of informal and less organised, sometimes spontaneous activity that makes up perhaps the largest part of the pattern of association between people in any given community.

The first level provides the service and opportunities and the second accepts, uses or rejects, always realising that individuals or groups can and indeed often are engaged on both levels at the same time without necessarily experiencing conflict between their roles as givers or users of services. But in detached work, where a conflict in expectations is apparent, we see the second level of community activity as tending to separate itself from the first, while still remaining within the system, that is the community. This helps us to see the position of the unattached in the community and to think more clearly about the use of indigenous leaders and autonomous groups, both of which are to some degree isolated from the network of formal services and opportunities.

Through, around and between the various formal and informal groupings in the community are interest or activity networks, of individuals or small groups, in various occupational, professional, geographical or social settings, long-lived or short-lived (e.g. the old boys' school tie network, the criminal network). Their loosely-knit associations exist to achieve things that other forms of association do not or cannot offer. Our contacts among the unattached belong to this kind of loose informal association or network. It is freer, balanced between the smaller more intensive groups of family or friendship, and the highly organised large scale forms of association involved in school or work. Even when such a network is part of a formal institutional setting as in a hospital, factory, a prison or university, membership is voluntary, organisation is loose or informal, activities are self-programmed.

All social events and their various ramifications in every kind of setting can be said to involve conflict and opposition on the one hand, and co-operation and accommodation on the other, of varying degrees and intensity. This recognition is important; detached workers are participants in the life of the community and need to know how to behave in conflict/co-operation situations if they are to persuade elements within the community to change their attitude to the unattached, and to alter programmes of service or conditions under which they are offered, entailing the very serious business of re-allocating resources and perhaps affecting status systems.

212

Johnny

We have attempted in the two previous sections to describe Johnny's relationships with others and his participation in groups as factors in his social development. We shall now describe the community as related to the same process by way of the nature and content of the services and opportunities it offers him. Johnny's opportunities for making friends, and participating with others in neighbourhood life, are affected by the following factors: the physical layout of the neighbourhood, distance from shops, work, school or church, by the amount of play space, playgrounds, playfields, open spaces, commons and greens; the occupation and income level of the residents, by the industrial and commercial development of the neighbourhood, by the incidence of social disorganisation, unemployment, broken families, physical and mental ill-health, the crime rate, the number of families on national assistance; the nature and content of education, employment, recreation and social welfare services offered (or withheld) by the community. Johnny also participates in a pattern of social attitudes (about education, work, sex, money or marriage) that will influence, affect and mould his social development, and which are accepted, or rejected, partly or wholly, from parents, friends or neighbours, from school, youth club, church or workmate. These services, opportunities (formal and informal) and social attitudes, based on varying systems of values and standards, are all part of a complicated community context that will, in part, define Johnny's life circumstances—not as separate easily isolated factors but as inter-related and interacting parts of his 'whole life situation'. Therefore working with Johnny as an individual or in a group is not quite enough unless we are aware of the limitations and potential of the community which affect his ability and willingness either to 'take hold and cope' or to assume the role of 'failure'.

All this, even if infinitely amplified does not amount to an 'explanation' of a living community. It can only be a guide to more disciplined thinking about participation in community events. The following hypothetical example, about a situation which did *not* happen in the project, will illustrate the use of these concepts.

Let us suppose that the worker decided after careful consideration that an interest in reading would help most of the young people to communicate more easily, and to acquire social skills. Suppose he has already been able to help several individuals by providing magazines which they read and discuss, and by encouraging them to write short stories about their own lives similar to the ones they have read. He realises that his efforts can bear only limited fruits because he does not have the necessary teaching skills, or know enough about the right kind of reading material, and other necessary resources. He has already tried to persuade these young people to use the library but he has met with no success. They object to the formality, to what they term 'bossiness', resent having to keep silent and appear to be afraid of the whole idea. He sees that his responsibility is for the social development of the young people—in this case the development of reading skills. His need is to find some way of helping them to use the existing community facilities and to get the community institutions to reach out to the young people and help them make better use of the facilities available. He therefore comes to see that his problem is one of working with a library.

He begins by meeting the chief librarian, discussing the fact that a large number of the adolescents whom he knows will not use the library, but need to be helped to do so. He asks if one or two of the library assistants could meet the young people on their own ground, in a coffee bar or on a street corner, in order to get to know them and to find ways and means of developing their interest in reading.

The librarian is sympathetic but points out that the library is already short staffed, and exists to provide a particular service, that the work proposed is the job of other organisations, and that his committee would not allow the staff to adopt so unusual a procedure. He suggests, however, that if the worker puts a scheme on paper, he will present it to the library committee although without much hope of acceptance. The worker prepares a paper in which he outlines the needs of the young people, his own suggestions and the reasons for them. He suggests that:

a. two library assistants and two volunteers should meet once or twice a week with the young people somewhere in the neighbourhood outside the library in order to get to know them;

b. that this would provide an occasion for discussing reading with the young people, of introducing them to particularly chosen books, of arranging activities such as films and visits connected with the books and possibly of arranging a system of awards for reading and participating in the discussion;

c. that this would mean acquiring a variety of books which would have to be considered expendable, a film projector and a fund for outings, expeditions and prizes. Remembering the chief librarian's comment about 'normal procedure' the worker also provides examples of experiments already undertaken by libraries, which include mobile libraries on housing estates, services in hospitals and factories, approved schools and old people's homes, special reading parties arranged for women's groups and TV viewing rooms.

This document is sent to the chief librarian, and a second meeting is arranged. He says that the committee was very sympathetic but did not feel that the staff should be exposed to work on the streets. They were however prepared to help and would allocate a small room in the library where an assistant would meet with the worker and a small group of boys. The worker points out some of the problems which could arise in this kind of situation but thanks the librarian and agrees to try it.

The worker spends some time preparing the assistant for the possible attitudes and behaviour of the boys, after which he brings four boys to the library for the first part of the experiment. The assistant chats with them for ten minutes or so, after which they become restless and rude and undertake a series of jokes and pranks at the expense of the assistant. Eventually they break out of the room, and charge through the library, creating a disturbance as they depart.

The worker meets the assistant again and he attempts to interpret what happened. When asked to explain why he did not discipline the boys, he says that in order to continue the experiment at all he has to encourage and not discipline. The assistant then wonders if he is expected to do the disciplining. The worker suggests that the problem might to some extent be solved by meeting the boys in an environment in which discipline is less necessary. The worker could then go on encouraging and the assistant might be able to get on with the discussion of books and reading. The assistant agrees to try in a café or restaurant, and he succeeds in making contact with the boys on their own terms.

Now that something has begun to happen the worker speaks to one or two of his sympathisers on the library committee describing the needs of the young people and the attempt to meet them. He suggests to the library assistant that if he is interested in continuing to work in this 'detached' way, he might let the chief librarian know.

The worker is still uneasy about the disturbance the boys created in the library and feels now that perhaps he should have seen the chief librarian before talking to the councillors and before trying to interest the assistant librarian in detached work. However, he does not visit him until he is invited to do so some time later. The chief librarian then complains that the worker should have informed him about the assistant's meeting with the boys in the café, and have discussed the disturbance in the library with him as well as the assistant. He adds that the assistant and one of his friends are prepared to give one free evening a week to this work with the consent of the committee members. The library will provide the film projector and an assortment of used books but not the funds for new books and other activities. He repeats that the worker should have taken all these matters up with him before negotiating with staff or councillors. The worker apologises but promises to do better in future.

He now approaches his own committee about the need for new books and a small fund for activities. The members think that they should ask their supporters to send in whatever books they can spare instead of providing new ones, since it is certain they will be destroyed. After some discussion the committee agrees that:

> *a.* a number of new books should be provided when it is felt that the young people will appreciate them;

> *b.* that the borough youth committee and/or a trust should be asked to contribute towards the purchase of these books;

> *c.* that the money for the activities must come from the agency, so the committee will allocate a small sum for these.

It emerges that this will have to be at the expense of the allocation for summer holidays. The committee agrees with the worker that the funds for new books are needed now before the interest wanes, and so it provides the money hoping to recoup it from the borough youth committee or a trust. However, they are doubtful as to whether a reading activity is a function of youth work. Some members suggest it should be done in the schools.

The library assistant now knows several of the boys fairly well and suggests setting up a library in their own clubroom. Attempts to arrange reading in a coffee bar or café had not worked out so it is now decided to use the clubroom. But it is recognised that the boys would never have agreed at all unless the activity had begun in the coffee bar, and although technically the sessions begin in the clubroom, the reading and discussion most often take place in the dormobile during outings, on street corners, at the café or at a dance. At one point the programme runs down but then it revives when two of the boys decide to read up on the possibilities of a holiday abroad, and another begins to read what to do in London "for a giggle". At one point the group discusses setting up its own library to rent out books and make money: at another it decides to write stories and produce its own paper-back; yet again a group plans a display in the library entrance on crime stories, which they claim they know a good deal about first hand. Few of these things come off. Activities are tried and discarded, but in the process the library assistant is able to help individuals to develop an interest in reading and eventually is able to encourage some of them to use the library itself, first because they know him and then because they want what it has to offer.

Some members of the library committee complain, "All this is the job of youth workers and not librarians. It is the responsibility of parents and the schools. It's not our fault if they do not do their jobs properly. It is not part of the work of this department to work with young hooligans."

The complaint of a library user: "Groups of boys are now coming into the library demanding attention, using filthy language, creating

216

disturbances. It's almost impossible to choose or read a book in peace."

A clergyman: "Is it right that boys of fifteen should be helped to read and discuss books which are immoral and liable to encourage their promiscuous and delinquent behaviour."

A borough council official: "Surely the time and money spent on this type of young person could be spent more usefully on providing special library services to the blind, the physically disabled or the aged."

A youth worker: "You said that you were not trying to work as youth clubs do by providing the activities you saw as necessary, but that you would only help with those activities that were suggested by the young people themselves. This does not seem to be true of your reading activity."

The worker's management committee: "This reading activity has continued for four months. You report that the attendance is small and sporadic, that most of the original books have been lost or stolen and that the money for the activities has been spent. In what way has the activity been useful and why should we continue to finance it?"

The worker's job has been many sided. He interpreted the need for the work to the chief librarian and to his committee and helped interpret the need for it to the young people before the assistant librarian became available. He recruited, encouraged and supported the assistant, helped procure the necessary money, and helped by his presence and behaviour in the activity to create a favourable atmosphere. He now accepts the various complaints as valid, and draws some of the relevant persons and groups together to discuss them, all in the hope of helping the library to extend its services to the unattached and thus facilitate one aspect of their social development. He also evaluates the work and passes on the following comments to his committee and the chief librarian.

1. Some of the young people are reading, not the literature he would have chosen but things of their own choice. They are reading with more understanding than they would otherwise have had, and with more attention to detail and more imagination.

2. All the participants now know that the library exists and contains books that interest them, and how it works.

3. Some have already developed such a relationship with the librarian that they feel free to go into the building itself and to 'negotiate from there'.

4. Some boys now know how to find information they require for practical reasons, and find it easier to express themselves to adults as well as in their own groups. Their confidence in themselves shows a slight increase.

5. The worker has also been interpreting the needs of these young people to the chief librarian, the borough library committee, other statutory and voluntary body officials, and the public, and there is hope of other projects being planned jointly.

This example emphasises the complexity of the situation, and the variety of conditions and circumstances that must be considered in what at first glance may seem to be a 'simple straightforward idea'. It is a 'simple model' illustrating how things happen in communities, and the conflict and co-operation involved. It shows that the worker is inevitably involved in different ways on different levels of community life and how his interpretation of the needs of the unattached, and solicitation of services for them, will add new content to the co-operation and the accommodation, the conflict and competition that are everyday ingredients in community life.

Finally, it suggests that the new interplay between individuals, groups and social institutions (occasioned by the worker's presence and work)—which will be visible as new forms of co-operation and conflict—is 'the natural' material for the worker in his work with the community, just as the needs of individuals and their activities in association are the 'natural' materials for his work with individuals and groups.

There is no question in the example of anyone being right or wrong. These fictitious incidents indicate the kinds of things which did happen, and for which a detached worker should be prepared. They indicate the need for him to understand the theoretical considerations about communities outlined above, in order to work effectively.

The role of the worker

The worker learns about those aspects of the community that are related to the needs, interests and problems of the unattached, especially the services and the conditions under which they are offered. He then turns his observation and awareness into usable information. "How does this or that institution or agency define the problem of the unattached? How does this affect what they offer and the conditions on which they do so? What resources in the community could be seconded on what conditions?" In order to do this he must have learned what is needed by contact and work with the unattached young people, and have developed an ordered way of thinking about their needs, his own approach and method, and the potentialities of the community.

The worker makes direct contact with both the formal and informal community services to obtain the information he needs, especially about the social attitudes that govern the disbursement of service and opportunity. In the case of the formal statutory and voluntary bodies, officials and workers, he has to 'pick up' the necessary material for an informed opinion about their usefulness, willingness and ability to offer help. In the case of informal services he has to observe which of the indigenous adult leaders (e.g. the fish and chip shop or café proprietor) offer acceptable help to the young people. He considers the help that he or other agencies can offer indigenous leaders and autonomous groups; whether by passing on information or simple social skills or putting them in contact with statutory and voluntary bodies that can and will do this.

He helps others to see the problems of the unattached by the way he seeks information, asks their advice and guidance, by the kinds of services and opportunities for the young people he enquires about and by the way he discusses the conditions under which they are offered. He offers suggestions, based on his knowledge of the young people and the potentials and limitations of the services, but avoids suggestions which are unlikely to be accepted. He may explain how he and his colleagues get to know the young people, the kind of activities the young people are willing to take part in, how he came to see it all in this way, what problems and failures to expect. He also evaluates his efforts, including his experience in working with other elements in the community, and his thinking about it, and shares with them his developing approach and method.

The worker also supports the agencies, some of which are already working with unattached young people—the probation service constantly and welfare workers occasionally. Others may want to contribute to the programme. They all begin at different points with different ideas, abilities, programmes of service and different kinds of difficulties. The worker may have to help by supporting in discussion and at times even participating in planning and operating attempts by the agencies to co-ordinate their work in reaching the unattached. The worker is participating in two halves of the same process; he allows himself to be worked with by the community agencies he has contacted just as he tries to work with them. The only difference between him and his colleagues in other agencies is the knowledge he has gained through his role with the unattached, and the freedom from tradition which was implicit in his appointment. If he does not recognise, understand and appreciate this he may involve himself in a foolish attempt to totally recreate the pattern of service, a task which is impossible and beyond his mandate.

He must always seek the usable in what already exists, how he can interpret this to the young people and help them to use it. Only by seeing the work with the community as a two-way process in which he receives information, skills, and insights as well as gives them, can he begin to reconcile the expectations of those who need the service and those who offer it.

Five primary processes run through the worker's activity in the community:

Observation of the relevant community events and activities.

Awareness of how these are seen and interpreted by the youth-serving agencies, in the context of the needs of the unattached as defined by the worker.

Formulation On the basis of observation and awareness the worker formulates the problem and suggests possible solutions in terms that the agencies can understand and accept.

Interpretation Each step along the way he interprets what he is doing and why, how he came to think about it and do it in this way, in terms of the needs of the young people and the potentials and limitations of the agency.

Controlled participation He always remembers that in his relationship with the agencies he is a participant in community events and therefore affects them. He has to observe his participation and its effect on these events in terms of the possibilities of enlarged and more varied service to the unattached, remembering that he himself is part of the process.

This work might be seen as a communication triangle, with the needs and interests of the young people at the lower right-hand corner, the services and opportunities within the community at the apex, and the methods, techniques, processes and procedures at the lower left-hand corner of its base. The worker and his statutory and voluntary body colleagues establish at various points and on various levels a running dialogue concerned with more adequate, efficient and effective communication between the three points on the triangle.

Limitations of the worker's role

It might be well to re-emphasise three limitations of this work with the community. It is limited to the needs and interests of the unattached, to interpreting these only to those who are or might conceivably be concerned, and to the attempt to find and use the necessary resources.

The focus has to be on work with the unattached, because the mandate from the larger community, and from the young people already contacted, is restricted to work with the unattached. Consequently this is the only area in which the worker may enter the conflict concerning reallocation of resources in that community. Concentration on the task assigned and accepted will obviate the temptation to try to do too much—'and butt into other people's business'. This is more important than might appear since the approach outlined above is not intended as a full-blown social philosophy, with a total range of ends and means, that will allow 'a worker' to go about changing 'whole communities', but is simply one approach and method available for engendering particular kinds of social change in relation to the needs of particular individuals and groups for whom the worker is recognised as a legitimate spokesman.

In focussing our attention on the local community and attempting to explore the relevant elements in community life, we may have exaggerated the autonomy of the local community. Although it is of prime importance to us as the 'location of our enterprise', it is but part of a larger social system, a city, a county, and a nation. Many of the decisions that condition its life are made partly on wholly elsewhere—aspects of housing policy, the provision of educational facilities, the bank rate, tax policy, originate to a large extent outside the local community. The allocation of nation-wide resources affects employment. Many of the social attitudes about the problems of adolescence, about crime and punishment, about the role of education are partly or wholly reflections of the opinions of groups and social institutions in the whole society. A prime example in our case is that the grant for this project came from a central body outside the local community.

ILLUSTRATIONS

Interpretation as a process in community work

Although this illustration deals with our project committee, it is included because we worked with that committee (the representative of a voluntary agency, the Y.W.C.A.), on the problems of interpretation in much the same way as we worked with other statutory and voluntary bodies, it is, we believe, representative of this aspect of our work with the community. In the course of several project committee meetings, the committee revealed pronounced reservations about the use of money as a 'direct aid' in field-work practice. The committee agreed to set aside a full committee meeting to discuss the matter.

Committee meeting discussion

The chairman asked the administrator to make a statement to start a discussion about the use of money in field-work practice. The administrator said that in the early days of the field-work we had used money solely in the 'traditional terms'—for the worker's travel and expenses, for equipment and for subsidising activities. We had been very cautious indeed about lending or advancing even the smallest sum to the

221

young people. On the whole we had come to the work with very definite ideas about the limitations in using money As the field-work progressed, it had become apparent that for any number of reasons the young people (supported by the value and standard system of the neighbourhood) thought, felt and behaved differently about money; they saw it as part of relationship, a way of testing the other party out, a sign of acceptance, support and approval. As we came to recognise this we came also to see the usefulness of money as a positive element in our work with them. We did 'give money away' in at least two kinds of situations, when it was needed and expected as part of the process of helping a boy or a girl, and when we saw it as part of the process of helping a group. We were aware that using money in this way might arouse misgivings in the committee, since we ourselves had had to deal with our own reservations before we were able to work in this way.

First phase of committee discussion

In the discussion that followed, committee members voiced a number of their reservations about this use of money including:

1. It's wrong to give money. It has all the appearance of charity and might well be seen as such by the young people and their parents and quite rightly resented.

2. It's against youth work principles to give money unless it's done by the proper agency, or the national assistance board, and then it's probably better to give it to the parents and not to the young people.

3. If you do give it away you will confuse the nature of your service both in the minds of the young people and the neighbourhood.

4. It's dangerous and should be avoided because it's an easy way out for both the young person and the worker and doesn't really solve the problem.

5. It's bad for the character of the young person who will surely develop wrong attitudes. What is needed is that he should be helped to see that he must earn what he needs to spend.

6. It gives the wrong idea of the relationship if the worker does what parents or older brothers and sisters do. It might make the relationship in the eyes of the young person more like that of a member of his family than would be good for the work.

A committee member then made another point: "in starting this project we realised that we should have to approach problems in a new way, and this would appear to be one of them." The administrator then produced examples from field-work records showing how money had been used.

1.   On one occasion five shillings a week pocket money was given for two weeks to a schoolboy prior to his court hearing, during which period he was extremely anxious about the possible outcome of the hearing. He had twice broken into a public phone box for pocket money and it was feared that in his overwrought state he might very well do worse. At the staff discussion it was decided to subsidise him to the sum of five shillings, to allow him some leeway on the 'slate' at the stall, and to encourage his friends, if the occasion arose, to share with him. This was done partly to prove to him that not everyone was against him, but also because we feared that if he did do something silly while awaiting his hearing, he might involve others in the coffee stall grouping. It seemed inadvisable to arrange this subsidy through his family, friends or probation officer, so the money was given to him direct.

2.   Another subsidy was paid to a boy who after more than three months of unemployment, had got a job that did not begin for one week and for which he would not be paid until the end of two weeks work. This meant a gap of three weeks before his first pay packet. He was in a 'working state of mind', looking forward to getting started, and we felt that the strain of waiting might revive the old 'work-shy syndrome'. His girl friend was as concerned as we were. We talked it over with both of them and it was decided that we would provide £2 a week for three weeks until he got his first pay packet.

3.   The third illustration was concerned with subsidising a group whom the worker had taken into town, paying all the cost in an attempt to draw the group together and to include two of the boys that the worker felt needed to be part of the group. The group was now repeating the trip on its own, the worker wanted the trip to go well and so he subsidised it. After some discussion with the group, the worker agreed to put in one pound to bring the amount up to what was thought necessary for a successful outing. This allowed the two boys who could not afford to contribute, to feel free to join in.

Second phase of committee discussion

During the second phase, the administrator and the consultant attempted to answer the questions that arose from these examples. From this discussion it was found that although the committee could not entirely agree about what had been done, it was beginning to understand why the field staff had acted in this way. The committee felt that in work with *individuals* this approach might sometimes be

223

justified, but still had reservations about the use of money in working with *groups* and wanted to devote another meeting to exploring this more fully. The administrator agreed to prepare examples of field-work records showing how money was used to help a group to learn to negotiate through the worker with the authorities (the Y.W.C.A.), to take responsibility when it was given a lump sum, and to negotiate within the group about provision and use of money.

The most important result of the discussion was that the committee came to realise that its most pressing concern was not really about the method but about what was termed the "practical aspects of the problem": "What shall we tell our executive committee? (the project committee was a sub-committee of the agency executive). How shall we interpret this aspect of our work to them? What are we to do if another agency with the same reservations as our own asks us to explain your behaviour in this matter? What would those allocating grants say if they knew what was happening? How can this be explained in the budget? How can we reconcile it with the policy of the agency with which it appears to conflict?"

Third phase of the discussion

In the third phase of the discussion the staff helped the committee with the 'practical problems'. It was agreed that:

1. Examples from field-work records and comments by the staff about workers' behaviour could be available for interpretation by committee members.

2. That the staff would always be available to help with this interpretation.

3. That the final report would put the use of money on record to make the grant-aiding agencies aware of what had been done.

4. That arrangements should be made in the accounts department to list these expenditures and budget for them.

5. That the matter of money as a direct aid in field-work practice could not be settled once and for all and would have to be kept under periodic review.

Evaluation

When evaluating the meeting later the staff realised that three value-systems were in operation about money, that of the young people in the neighbourhood, that of the committee and that of the field-workers in relation to the job. As the discussion progressed, there was a movement away from the personal opinion of the committee members towards the needs of the worker on the job, and finally the meeting moved towards the problem of the committee's responsibility. The committee's reservations were modified by their appreciation of the practical problems entailed in this aspect of the work. Most important of all it was noted that the objective of the staff in interpreting the work was to help both parties, the staff and the committee, to agree on ways of meeting the committee's responsibility in this matter.

The committee, the staff,
and the meeting

The elements in the situation were the committee, the staff and the meeting. The role of the committee was to voice its own reservations, as the personal reservations of the individual committee members who were collectively taking responsibility for the work. They also voiced the reservations of the agency and of the larger society from which it derived its mandate. The committee also had to help in allocating responsibility for the different aspects of the work. It was agreed that the field-work staff should continue to work in this way, and that the committee would interpret to its agency as the occasion arose. The committee also required that the final report should include discussion of this matter.

The role of the staff was to respect the reservations of the committee, and of the wider community they represented, and at the same time attempt to meet them. They had to use the field-work records in a way that would be helpful to the committee. They had to explore with the committee the implications of the material offered and to mention honestly any reservations of their own. They also had to prepare and present the material and to frame their contribution in such a way as to help the committee keep its thinking and action centred on the work at hand, and to provide the committee with information, guidance and support to enable it to carry on the interpretation at other levels in the community. The meeting itself had to provide a situation in which the staff and the committee representing the different values and standards in operation, could each state their case, explore the limitations and potentials in each presentation, resolve what could be resolved and leave the door open for further discussion.

Comments on interpretation

Staff members anticipating a need to interpret their policy would do well to ask themselves questions such as these before a meeting:
"What is it I am trying to interpret?" Too often a worker is

tempted to try and interpret staff needs which are not directly related to the needs of the programme, but rather to a theoretical preoccupation or an ideological commitment, or he may interpret the problem solely in terms of generalised conceptual statements. It is necessary to be quite specific about what one attempts to interpret, and to try to stick to the point.

"To whom am I trying to interpret?" The worker must remember that different publics have different terms of reference for judgement and evaluation, and that each public requires a different point of departure, a different organisation of his material, a different line of reasoning. He must always try to assess the values and standards of the group to whom he is trying to interpret, and then try to begin the discussion on their ground not his.

"For what reasons am I interpreting?" It is important for the worker to consider why the group he is attempting to contact wants to know more about his work, and why he wants to explain his work to them. Does he want simply to answer their reservations? Does he want to solicit their guidance, help, advice? Does he want them to give him money? Is he hoping to arrive at a common agreement about the nature and content of his work? What does he hope to achieve in his interpretation?

"How do I interpret?" This will depend on answers to the previous questions. He may present field-work records and comment on them specifically or attempt to draw generalisations from them. He may ask an outside expert to join a discussion. He may take some of the people to whom he is interpreting, into the field to see the work for themselves or to participate in it. He may refer to examples in literature or to other people's work.

Perhaps the most important aspect of interpretation is that one should not set out to change other people's attitudes, but try to provide the situation in which they could change their own. A worker tries to help people to understand the needs of the young people and the programme, only so far as this is necessary to get the job done. But when interpreting to a policy-making group, it has to be recognised that the field-work often moves too speedily for adequate interpretation at a monthly meeting. Apart from using casual meetings, the committee has to accept a division of responsibility; they must rely on the staff to make decisions, and to decide on priorities for interpretation to the committee.

Reciprocity in community work

This illustration is an example of what happened when a community agency made suggestions that affected our programme and conditions of service. The notes on which this illustration is based were taken from a series of summaries on work with a girls' probation group made by the worker and the project administrator as an aid to interpreting the work.

In the early days of the project, girls presented a particular problem because they did not come to the stall, were difficult to find in the neighbourhood, and to keep in touch with once we had found them. On two occasions the probation service was approached with the hope that probation officers could help us to contact girls. The first time, while we were still uncertain as to our own function as a service (and therefore unable to interpret this adequately), the probation officer could make no suggestions. The second time, a few months later, the probation officer mentioned a number of schoolgirls on probation who were too young for youth clubs and seemed unable to join more informal groups, but who needed help in their relationships and with their own problems.

We had expected advice on how to contact girls but we now realised that we were being asked to provide a new service for girls on probation, and to help the probation officer herself in her work with them. Our worker suggested that we might be able to start a small group for these younger girls, but pointed out that this would have to be discussed in detail with the rest of the staff and the project committee before anything definite could be done.

Staff conference

The matter was discussed in staff conference, during which these reservations arose:

1. The girls (of twelve and thirteen years) were under the youth service age, that is, under the age with which we intended to work.

2. If we did this kind of work, the group of younger girls on probation would probably have to be completely separated from the rest of the project and one worker would have to give most of her time to it. This would mean fewer staff available for work with the larger coffee stall grouping.

3. We had not anticipated having young people referred to us, but rather making contact and then referring the young people elsewhere if the need arose.

On the other hand it was noted:

a. That this would be our first opportunity to meet girls apart from boys, to learn what was necessary in this kind of work, and to work with girls before their interest in boys was fully developed which we reasoned might make the task somewhat easier.

b. That the girls in question needed the kind of help we could offer, an intensive group experience, and that one of the agencies in our community, the probation service, had recognised the girls' needs and our usefulness and had asked us to take the job on. This was also important because we were sometimes engaged in making the same kinds of requests (as regards the needs of the unattached) to other agencies and it was reasonable that we should find ourselves in a converse situation.

c. That as we had a responsibility both to the enquiry and to the needs of the young people, this would provide us with our first experience in 'reciprocity', in inter-agency planning and in offering a joint service.

d. That in working in this way, we could find out whether a service of this kind was needed, how it could be provided, and who should take responsibility for it.

After weighing these different factors, the staff decided that a group for the younger girls on probation should be started, that one of our field-workers should be responsible and that part of her job would be to work closely with the probation officer in planning and developing a programme for this group.

Probation officer and worker

While the group was getting started, the worker and the probation officer met several times and agreed on the following points:

1. That the probation officer should refer girls to the group, but should decide jointly with the worker when and how members should be introduced.

2. That the probation officer should provide the worker with the background information she thought necessary about each girl.

3. That although the worker would be prepared to discuss progress with the probation officer she would not pass on information which she considered confidential.

4. That the worker could not become an 'authority' to the girls. She was not to be expected to be a detached probation officer nor a caseworker, but would provide the group facilities they needed.

Although the group was intended as a support to the probation officer in her work with individuals, its function would be to help the girls in a completely different way through a voluntary group experience.

We quickly became aware that in working with such a group we had to be concerned not only with the needs of the individual girl and of the group itself, but also with those of the probation service as a social agency. This meant a departure from our own approach and method, and would therefore have to be seen as an entirely different aspect of the enterprise, with a role for the worker different from that of the detached worker or the stall, in the café, or in our own premises. We had to provide different criteria for evaluation, taking into consideration our relations with the probation officer, as well as the service we were offering the girls.

As the work with this group developed, the field-worker and the probation officer were able increasingly to co-operate in serving the girls, as in the following instances:

1. Through her informal contact the worker was able to visit regularly a mother who was 'anti-authority', and without discussing the subject directly, was able to help both mother and daughter to understand that the probation officer could be helpful, so that eventually the daughter started to keep her appointments with the probation officer. The latter, knowing that the girl was attending group meetings regularly and seeing the worker, did not insist on interviews.

2. On another occasion, the probation officer prevented a girl from being sent away from home for persistent truancy, as she felt that the girl's growing relationships with the other girls and the worker and her participation in the group might help her more effectively.

3. In another instance, a girl who had been attending group meetings regularly for a year began to show indications of readiness to go back to school. The worker discussed this with the probation officer, who provided a new school uniform and other encouragements.

4. On several occasions, the probation officer and the worker were able to discuss the differences between a girl's behaviour in interviews with the probation officer, informal interviews with the field-worker, and in relationships with other girls in the group, thus providing a more complete picture of her problems and potentials, for each worker to use in the respective areas of their work.

A developing service

As the work continued (over two years) the worker not only provided a service in support of the probation officer, but also served as a means of communication between several agencies concerned with the same girl, and between each girl and her parents, her neighbours and her friends. The service was always based on the needs of the girl and indeed, in the early days a large number of these needs were met by the worker herself. This caused her to realise the danger of becoming involved with each individual as a caseworker. In order to avoid this, she had to find other ways of getting specialist help for the girl and her family. At this point she began to extend her role to include working with the Family Service Unit, Child Care workers, teachers and school officials, youth leaders, the moral welfare officer, part-time employers, and the warden of a childrens' home, as well as with the probation officers and our own project committee. Of course the content of this work varied with the needs of the girl and the family Some examples are as follows:

Work with a single agency

a. At Christmas the worker realised that certain families would not only be unable to supply 'extras for the holidays' but were already having difficulty in providing adequate winter clothes. She collected money, clothes and toys from various sources, but in order not to confuse her own role in the eyes of the group and families, she contacted the Family Service Unit. They were already supplying families with Christmas parcels, and arranged to add to their list the families in her group which she wanted to help. She discussed with the Unit how the various items might be allocated to the families. They then gave the parcels as part of their normal procedure and the worker's participation was not revealed.

b. When a girl was in a seriously depressed state due to problems at home, the worker instead of making a home visit on her own notified the Family Service Unit, which was already working with the family, explained the situation to them, and left them to deal with the situation.

c. The worker, realising that a girl's problems were increasing due to her mother's complete inability to cope with her family's situation, referred the family to the Family Service Unit and prepared the mother to accept help from the Unit.

d. A mother became worried about her daughter's contact with another girl in the group who had been stealing, and mentioned this to the Family Service Unit worker who contacted the field-worker. Together they were able to work out ways of reassuring the mother and assuring the girl's continuance in the group.

Work with several agencies

a. At one stage Doris met serious hostility from the rest of the group and the worker had to advise and arrange her withdrawal. They continued to meet outside the group, and as Doris was no longer on probation, this was her only contact with an accepting adult. The worker learned that a Child Care officer had visited Doris at home because of her truancy. She then contacted that officer. Together they worked out ways of helping Doris, the project worker explaining her approach and possibilities, and the Child Care officer explaining her statutory responsibilities and limitations. Eventually the two workers agreed that Doris could not cope with her problems in her present environment, and the Child Care officer recommended that she should be sent to a children's home from which she could attend a different school, returning home for weekends. The Child Care officer took Doris to the Home where the field-worker continued to visit her. The two workers shared the interpretation of Doris's needs to the warden and to the teacher at the new school. It eventually became apparent that the girl was not adjusting to the new school and was unhappy. The field-worker suggested a second change of school, and this was arranged after discussions between the warden, the teacher, the headmaster and the two workers. During and after the transfer to the new school, the field-worker continued to visit and support Doris, always reporting back to the Child Care officer and to the parents. Eventually as Doris settled into the new school and became more friendly with the warden, and more attached to the Child Care officer, the field-worker was able to withdraw gradually until only an occasional telephone call was needed for the contact.

b. Lily (fifteen years old and no longer on probation) was turned out of her home by her mother and became unhappy with the family with whom she was temporarily staying, but feared to offend them by leaving. The project worker was able with Lily's agreement, to discuss the situation with the Child Care officer who arranged for Lily to move to a hostel and found means of supporting her until she was ready to work.

c. When a group of girls were going on a holiday which had to be more heavily subsidised than was usual, the worker involved the local youth officer, who visited the group and recommended to the youth committee that the holiday should be grant-aided.

These are only a few of many examples of the worker's involvement with agencies. It became clear that a service which had set out to meet the needs of a few girls, and to support the probation service had now developed in such a way that the worker had become a bridge between several agencies. As the work developed however, approval was offset by criticism, and time had to be given to interpreting the work to many agencies.

Criticisms and interpretation

a. Youth leader: "The girls say we ought to pay for their holiday as you did. We can't cope financially." The worker sometimes helped the club leader to recognise individual need or else to see where resources could be found within the community.

b. School teacher: "You have brought a group of the most difficult girls together. They encourage one another in their bad behaviour." The worker had to interpret that the girls were in need of the group experience just because 'normal groups' would not have them and so they tended to become isolated.

c. Project committee member: "Surely it's not a full-time job to work with fourteen girls." The worker described the girls and their problems, the work she was trying to do, and the time each aspect of the work was liable to take.

d. Probation officer: "You should not have allowed this girl to go away on holiday when she should have been in court." The worker met the probation officer in order to arrange more adequate communication, so that each would know in good time the arrangements of the other.

e. A father: "A club like that ought to teach a girl to be good, but our girl just learns to 'make-up'. There's no discipline." The worker explained the purpose of the group and helped the father to accept his daughter's growing up and changing needs.

f. A neighbour: "The noise in that club is terrible, there's no discipline." The worker found herself having to sympathise with the neighbours and to explain some of the things that were happening in the club.

All of this involved the worker in several kinds of interpretation on several levels, which became the occasion for further involvement and co-operation.

The point of this illustration

In summary, the point of this illustration might be outlined as follows:

1. Community work is a two-way process. The detached worker may expect other agencies to change the nature and conditions of their service, but there are also occasions when the agencies see detached workers offering something which if modified, or adapted is relevant to their own service. The detached worker has to decide whether his her work can be modified to meet the requests of the agencies.

2. It is from the actual day-to-day give and take in the field that reciprocity evolves, and material arises which, when rightly interpreted, suggests the nature and content of the service, and the role of the worker. This in turn will require modifications in the programme and possibly in the criteria for evaluation.

3. As the other agencies concerned with the work become more actively involved in its planning and operation, the work progresses from being a single agency effort towards 'two agency co-operation',

and may even become a service provided jointly by a number of agencies.

Recognition of a conflict

In the early stages of the project, criticisms were levelled against the idea of working outside the traditional club setting, against the minimal conditions on which we gave help, and against some aspects aspects of the behaviour of the field-workers.

We had already contacted individual youth leaders and other officials, explaining our plans and that we were open to ideas, as we were prepared to try out various methods of work. We discussed some of the problems of working with the unattached in the neighbourhood, but neither we nor the youth leaders were clear about the kinds of work that ought to be done, and we agreed that our assignment was to try to find out some of these things. Even so, as we realised much later, we should have tried to discuss the project and problems more thoroughly at this stage.

Notes from staff conference

For the third time, the difficulty of meeting criticisms was introduced. The staff felt that some of these might get back to the young people, who were liable to 'defend' the coffee stall and use this situation to reinforce their prejudices about clubs. After some discussion we realised that we were not only worried about the young people, but that we resented not being appreciated and understood, and we might also tend to 'defend' our work and thus precipitate more criticisms. We recognised that we were now part of a conflict within the community, and had to find some way of using and trying to resolve it. The following comments that had been made to us and/or about us were noted:

1. We gave things away to the young people, which made them expect the same from clubs—this was not good for the young people, and even if it had been, the clubs did not have the same resources as the project.

2. We were not working with the 'unattached'. Many of the young people with whom we worked were known to several leaders, but they came to us because we were 'soft' with them.

3. It would have been better to put the project money into the clubs so that they could do a better job. It is always easier to get money for fancy research than for the ordinary work of established clubs.

4. Recording everything that people say and do is not ethical. In

any case the youth leaders wouldn't have time to do it, and this 'social group work' was not new. Everyone had been doing it for years in the youth service.

5. The lack of discipline in the project made it more difficult for the youth clubs, and would not help the young people to face life realistically.

6. The club leaders would like to work with the young people we knew but if they did the clubs would be in a shambles.

After discussion the staff agreed that we should invite six key people to a meeting to discuss the project and the problems arising from it. These included youth leaders, a police officer, youth officer, youth employment officer and probation officer.

The meeting with community colleagues

Only three visitors attended the meeting, but after a brief report of the project, several of the criticisms were aired. They were not answered directly, but we discussed the values of offering different types of clubs and opportunities for young people. The suggestions made, but never followed up were:

a. That leaders and officials should come to meetings occasionally to see the kind of problems we were facing and how we tried to deal with them.

b. That they come to one of our project committee meetings and talk over their reservations with our committee. We explained that some of their doubts would be shared by the committee.

c. If they wished, one of us would go to their staff or management committee meetings and try to explain what we were doing.

d. That if they agreed, it might be well to hold other meetings with some of the youth workers in the community.

Follow-up.

Although the suggestions were not taken up, all the project staff made a point of meeting individual youth leaders and other workers, in order to discuss the problems and difficulties of both sides. It was as these were freely discussed and accepted, that at least some of the criticisms merged into mutual exploration.

The relevance of this illustration

Conflict and co-operation are natural elements in all of community life. Co-operation is usually thought to be a 'good thing', and conflict a 'bad thing'. The presence of conflict is often denied, 'swept under the carpet', or disguised or hidden in some way. Conflict, its recognition, use and possible resolution, is part of the material of community life, and is one of the factors out of which a programme of this type emerges. In working with a community one should expect conflict and not react to it personally as we did at more than one point. One must attempt to see the conflict objectively, and recognise as we did later that criticism often produces a series of legitimate questions about the implications of the work for the function and structure of other services. At first we tended to see any reservations simply as 'criticisms'. It was only after a prolonged series of discussions and meetings between ourselves and the agencies that we saw them in their proper context, as part of a job.

In accounting for the conflict, a worker must always try to see the particular circumstances which have occasioned it. Our 'critics' were not only voicing legitimate personal opinions but they were speaking for established social institutions that saw our work as implying criticism of theirs. They felt criticised by the very fact that it was felt necessary to attempt this work in this place, at this time. They thought the criticism was widespread and well backed, and saw evidence for this in the support given by a government department.

In discussion the worker should not aim to change the attitude of others through a conversion operation, but should show his recognition of the legitimacy of reservations, and try to create circumstances for mutual discussion and evaluation of the work, in the hope that the conflict can be resolved in so far as it affects the provision for young people.

Evaluation and community work

In the early phases of the field-work our criteria for evaluation were almost wholly concerned with our ability to contact and work with individual young people. As the programme developed we had to add to this items specially concerned with our service to groups and to the larger coffee stall network. As the community work aspects of the programme developed (especially during termination) it became apparent that none of these criteria would serve as guides to its evaluation so that new ones would have to be found. We offer the following series of entries from the consultant's diary covering some of our thinking in this respect as a basis for a discussion of criteria in evaluating community work.

Excerpts from consultant's diary

ENTRY 1.

At the staff meeting yesterday there was a good deal of discouragement about not being able to pass individuals and groups to youth clubs as

235

easily as we at first thought would be possible. The difficulties arose from the resistance of the young people and because several of the clubs recognised that the changes in service and in conditions of service involved in accepting referrals, would probably entail changes in the structure of their programme and perhaps even their agency. What I found most interesting in the field-workers' reports of their discussions with the leaders was that the leaders had used the interview with the worker to explore the problems of this type of work and to ask serious and well thought out questions about its implications for their service, their programme and the structure of their organisation. I doubt whether the staff was right to feel so despondent. I think we had been using too limited a criterion in this instance, that is in assessing the termination procedure. I feel we might consider as criteria how much of our thinking about this problem we are able to pass on to the agencies concerned. I noted that in some cases, the leaders were beginning to ask poignant and relevant questions which indicated that although they were still not ready to accept individuals or groups, they were in fact beginning to think more realistically about the unattached and their concern and responsibility for them.

It might be that a training session should be set aside to help the staff make better use of their contacts with the agencies. If this works out it may be possible to show the project committee that an added criteria for judging this aspect of the work, is how well agencies who do not accept referrals respond to our request in terms of rethinking their own position. In short instead of only evaluating whether an agency will take individuals or groups, shouldn't we be thinking of ways of judging the effectiveness of 'community education' aspects of the work?

ENTRY 2.

I feel that several agencies who have decided to accept referrals from us, as well as those who feel they cannot, might be approached with a view to coming together to discuss the whole matter of the unattached. If we can manage this, it might be possible not only to see the termination as involved in passing on contacts, but to see it as another aspect of community education, which would mean not only evaluating how many young people were passed on, but assessing what part we played in helping the community to think about the unattached.

ENTRY 3. Passing on social skills

In several supervision sessions recently, it appeared that workers were judging their performance solely in terms of how successful they had been in helping their opposite number (the worker of an agency) to make contact with young people. Although this is of paramount importance, I think we should be thinking of helping the opposite number to learn how to make contacts on his own. If we don't do this we may find that after the referrals he has now accepted from us 'grow through' their need for his service, he might find it difficult to develop a 'following of his own'. He might not have the time for this kind of

236

work, but one of the criteria for assessing this aspect of the termination should perhaps be, can we pass on to our colleagues our know-how on some of the social skills in the same way that we attempted to pass them on to the young people as members of the network. This would mean having to include opposite numbers in staff conferences, case conferences and in training sessions.

ENTRY 4.

Just as we taught the young people to negotiate with us for money, space and equipment, we should be helping them to see how to use and where necessary modify those techniques when dealing with the other agencies, and above all to help the other agencies to know what to expect and how to play their part in the other side of the negotiation. More and more it becomes obvious that the criteria for judging the community work in the programme will have to be separate and different from those used in evaluating the individual and group aspects.

ENTRY 5.

The project committee must be helped to see that the final report will have to include an evaluation of our work with the community, and that some of the findings will have to be related to the need in this kind of work to assess how successfully the project was able to include passing on information, know-how and social skills to other agencies in the community. This will mean helping them to see that only one set of criteria, and not necessarily the most important, will deal with direct service to individuals and groups. Another set will have to consider the direct contribution of the programme to the community.

ENTRY 6.

As termination progresses it becomes more apparent, not only that we started our work with the community much too late in the enterprise, but that if the evaluation of the community work aspects of the project is to be of any value to others doing this kind of work, the agencies themselves should be involved with us in evaluating the project. Only in some kind of joint evaluation can we hope to be able to see the full implications of all this, since however well intended we may be we can only experience this work from our own side of the fence and from within our own frame of reference. Its probably too late to do much about this but we shall certainly have to include a comment of this kind in our findings.

Points emerging

Emerging from these extracts are several factors.

1.   The change in the content of the field-work process brought about by our more intensive participation in the existing network of provision for youth, necessitated new criteria for evaluation related to the community aspects of the work.

2.   As in other areas of the work, these should not be single factor criteria, but should take account of all relevant aspects of the situation.

3.   Evaluation is not completed once and for all, at one point in the programme, it is a process. As the content of field-work practice changes, new criteria have to be developed from the new experience.

4.   The proper approach to evaluation in community work of this kind is probably for the several agencies to make a joint evaluation, not only because a single agency usually see only one side of the process, but also because this co-operation may well lead to other types of joint effort.

In developing criteria for evaluating community work we must recognise that whereas in work with individuals and groups one is evaluating one's ability to offer information, advice and guidance and pass on social skills, in working with the community one is evaluating ability to interpret, communicate and pass on social skills in a different situation, namely to colleagues and to other statutory and voluntary bodies.

22.   Work with ourselves

It may seem strange to say that our most important work throughout the project was the work with ourselves. We have already pointed out that our primary concern was the individual young person, and that we came to see the community aspect of our work as an important part of the field-work enterprise. But this is not so contradictory as it might seem, since the work with individual young people depended upon making relationships that could further their social development. This in turn depended on our own skill in using ourselves to that end. Similarly our work with the community depended on our knowledge of it, our insight into how it worked, and the part we could play in the reallocation of resources in respect of the unattached. Both these factors depended in the last analysis on our own ability as individuals and as a team to use ourselves, our knowledge, insight and skills as the primary resource for the accomplishment of the programme.

In order to 'make sense' of all the various field-work events, our participation in them and the context in which they occurred, and in order to offer a service and operate a programme, it was necessary to keep much of the focus of attention on ourselves. It was what we did, and how and why we did it that was the primary factor in the situation.

Introduction to training

At first the work with ourselves was fairly general; discussions

238

covered a wide assortment of problems: "Why do I want to do this kind of work? (motivation); what do I have to know to lead a group discussion? (knowledge and skills); how will I know when I have said or done the wrong think in talking to or working with a young person? (awareness and insight); so many things are always happening, how can we know what is important, where to begin, what to do next?" (the need for a frame of reference). These questions were discussed 'piecemeal,' usually at some length, and often came up in several different guises. Sometimes 'answers' could not be unanimously agreed because each of us had begun from a different premise or held a different point of view. Often we found ourselves discussing a different type of question from that which had been asked. The discussions tended to be abstract and theoretical and rather unrelated to the work in the field. At a very early stage we saw the need for a more systematic way of working with ourselves. We arranged regular weekly meetings of three kinds; first training, to build up a frame of reference within which to think about and discuss the field-work events and problems, develop new skills, and examine and agree upon basic assumptions; second supervision, to offer each worker regular individual discussion and practical help with his field-work problems; third staff conferences, to work together as a team in allocating resources and staff time, in scheduling field-work, planning and implementing the programme, budgeting expenditures, and in sharing the responsibility of the whole endeavour. We also agreed upon a system of recording and to produce from it the necessary information for training, supervision and staff conference sessions, and for this report. The 'divisions'; recording, training, supervision and staff conference were agreed simply for administrative convenience, and should not be mistaken for separate isolated aspects of the work. They should be seen as ways of describing from different points of view the same process, that of working together as a team in the particular circumstances in which we found ourselves.

All this training was in-service training, in that it was specific to the needs of the individuals to whom it was offered and to their job in the field. It took place concurrently with the field-work and was seen as part of it. In this sense it can be said to have been 'problem centred', since its content was governed by the needs of the field-workers to function more effectively and efficiently in the circumstances and under the condition of their work in the field.

The training situation

At an early stage we had to confront the differences between the seven staff members. There were five field-workers, one administrator/supervisor, and one research and training consultant. The differences related to social background, training experience, job experience, age and sex. These in turn presented differences of an intellectual, emotional and physical nature, and in attitudes based on class, religion and differing standards of values. These differences were just as much the 'natural events' of the training programme as were the needs, problems and behaviour of the young people. They had to be recognised and used as material for training, and were therefore part of the content of training and its starting place. Consequently different means of communication were necessary in order that the training process should be helpful to each staff member.

The differences were recognised or verbalised by individual staff members at different times, but their importance was not understood by everyone in the early stages. Feelings of inferiority, superiority, and rivalry came into play, together with other difficulties which arise naturally in a group learning to work together. The early training therefore had to aim to help each staff member to discover what the others brought to the work, the legitimacy of differences and personal reactions, what everyone together could contribute and what each individual needed to improve his field-work. This resulted in an increasing awareness that part of the training necessary for 'helping other people' would have to be about 'ourselves'.

The second consideration in training was the 'common factor': our willingness to try as individuals (and as a team) to do this kind of work with this kind of young person and in these circumstances. In short, the field-work was the common factor, attempting to work with the 'unattached' was the reason for our being together, and for a training programme. Only in relation to the work did the individual differences have any significance. This was important, as workers sometimes felt at first that training would help them personally, or 'straighten them out', or that it would show them as 'maladjusted' or 'abnormal'. Naturally the field-work and the necessary training did have side effects on the 'personality' of the worker, but this was not the purpose of training. As the name suggested, in-service training is simply intended to help the worker offer a better service to those being served.

The third element in the training situation was closely related to the first two (the differences and the common factor) and its recognition in the early stages was partly the result of the interplay between them. This was the need to draw out underlying basic concepts and assumptions, to consider them in more detail, and to talk about them, in order to develop a consensus of opinion not only in general terms, but in the consideration of several aspects of the work.

We came to recognise that each of us carried within us as part of our intellectual equipment, a store of concepts (and their underlying assumptions) which came into play as soon as we set about thinking or discussing. Usually these were unannounced. Sometimes indeed we were unaware of their presence or the premises on which they rested. They were often 'hidden', not only from the listener but from the speaker. This was natural in our everyday behaviour, but it tended to create difficulty when common agreement was necessary. It was also complicated by the fact that often the concepts were not only part of our intellectual equipment but had also gathered around themselves strong feelings; our thinking about things was often heavily charged with our feelings about them. Strictly speaking, we should have to admit that thinking and feeling are often aspects of the same process. The presence of these emotions, (regardless of their origin) were an added factor to contend with in reaching an agreement. Not only did hidden assumptions often impede communication and agreement, but the feelings aroused by having our underlying assumptions examined, challenged or laid bare (by ourselves or our colleagues) added to this difficulty.

The necessity for clarifying concepts (and understanding the underlying assumptions) was indicated not only by our own experience, but by the dialogue in the field of youth work which gave rise to the project. We had to develop the necessary conceptual tools to carry on the discussion, and to agree on their exact composition and on the way in which we would use them.

Our object was to create a setting which would facilitate the interplay between the individual differences (between staff members), and the field-work events, and to build a common language that would allow us to define the problem, work out solutions and learn what we needed to know (information and skills) in order to provide a better service for the unattached.

The content of training

The content of training is more fully set out in the background information items of the three previous sections (work with individuals, groups and the community). In this section we shall summarise the training sequence under headings indicating its several phases, the content of which was based on some of the questions that arose from the field-work. The phases of training therefore, naturally follow the stages of field-work as outlined in the sequence of events, since it is of the essence of this type of training that it should be carried out in response to the needs of those in the field, rather than from any prearranged schedule. Even so, many of the topics under each heading, were themes running through the whole project.

Phase One Getting to know one another—Who are we?—How did the group come together? Why? To what purpose? What can we do to grow towards being a team? Why important? Because in asking,

241

"where did I get my particular values and standards, and why do I keep them?" we can perhaps learn something about why and how they arise in the lives of the young people. In discussing our own potentials and limitations we can perhaps also find a way of seeing, how they came about—what could have gone 'right', what could have gone 'wrong'. All of this might have relevance to our work with the young people.

Words and concepts—What kinds of words and concepts are we using? Are they relevant to a discussion of the young people? What is a 'personality'? Where did each of us acquire one if we were not born with it? How did it happen? Who and what influenced the way it developed? Is it something static, unchanging? If not, how and why does it change? Can you say a person "has a personality" or should you say he "is one"?

Phase Two Much of the success of the project was dependent on how we defined the problem, what to do and how to do it. These questions could be only partly answered by reference to already known 'facts', 'opinion', or by reference to commonly accepted theories. They could only be answered by using observations brought in from the field.

Who is observing—It is important to be aware of who is doing the observing. I am 'the worker', not the young person, the constable on the beat, an amateur sociologist or psychologist, attempting to validate his pet theory. I, the field-worker am observing. What am I observing? I am observing what is happening in the field—events, circumstances, conditions and the thoughts and feelings and other behaviour that go into making them up, in relation to a situation that includes my own participation.

How do I observe? By noting the specifics (Johnny did, Johnny said). By noting the context (the rain, his shortage of money and my questions to him). In short, what is happening, how and if possible why, but the why is carefully labelled as my opinion since I can never know most of these things with absolute certainty.

Why am I observing? I am observing in order to be better able to participate with the view to contributing to the social development of the young people and this will condition what I observe, why and how.

What can go wrong? Any number of things, but primarily that I will introduce unwarranted and hidden bias in my observation. Some bias is unavoidable but often some of my observations is distorted by unwarranted assumptions which are often hidden, for instance that an observation about differences in standards and values is necessarily a difference between right and wrong. A second thing that can go wrong is that emotional distortion can colour the observation sometimes out of all recognition.

Phase Three Contact with individuals. This phase followed, the purely observational phase of the opening months and the field-work staff were already in contact with a sizeable number of young people, at the stall, in public houses, coffee bars or on street corners. They brought to the training sessions, questions about the uses to be made of these contacts.

Who is contacting whom? I must remember who I am in these particular circumstances, what I have to offer, and that the contact is mutual. What does the young person need? Why has he accepted the contact? What is he offering? Who is he? Isn't 'encounter' a better word than 'contact'.

How does the contact happen? Its informal nature helps to define my part in it (I am not an official) as well as to define the young person's need to seek help outside 'the official network'. Why does he need this sort of help? How do we have to see the situation in order to give it?

Why is the contact happening in this way, or failing to happen? Why are we reaching out beyond the 'formal setting'? Why has the larger community encouraged us to do this and given us the mandate to work in this way?

To what end? What are we trying to do in this encounter? What are the young people trying to do in the same encounter? What can we hope to achieve together?

Concepts and assumptions—All these questions are about relationships. What is a relationship? How does it come about and why? What can go wrong? Why do the young people need relationships with us, with other young people, and with some of the other statutory and voluntary officials? Is relationship a useful concept in this context? What are its limitations?

Phase Four About groups. At this stage, we recognised the need for us to facilitate relationships within groups. We felt that individuals would gain more, and we should work more effectively if small groups were helped to form into moderate-sized groups. This turned out to be less appropriate than we expected but it occasioned a series of training sessions about work with groups. What are groups? How do they come about? Why are they universal in human society? What kinds are there and why do people join them? Does everybody belong to groups? Why are they important? What do members get from participation? How would it help us in our task to help them form? What do they offer that two-person relationships cannot?

How do we work with groups?—What is the role of the worker? How do I help the individual? How do I help the group? What about relations between the group and the community and between groups. Concepts and assumptions—We have already agreed on our definition of personality, and we have said that it develops partly through relationships with other people, parents, relatives, friends, school and workmates. In discussing groups, why people join them and what they get out of them, we are adding to this concept by suggesting that personality, growth and development is also affected by way of the individual's participation in groups. Is this a valid way of thinking about the matter? What does it suggest about the problem of 'unattachment', and the kind of solution that might be relevant?

Phase Five The appearance of the network. The exploration of groups and their behaviour may not have been directly useful in terms of forming 'artificial' groups, but it provided a jumping-off point for more adequate observation of field-work events, and for the formulation of more pertinent questions. How do I function within a large network that is highly mobile? Why is mobility important? How can I use knowledge of group behaviour when working with constantly changing groups? What is the relation between work with individuals in groups, and work with a series of groups in one network?

Phase Six The full programme. The emergence of the network brought with it renewed recognition of the problems of experimental work. Whereas the earlier attempts had been related to work with individuals and groups, making it possible to use material from our own experience and that of others, the later demands from the field meant a departure from most of the known methods and procedures. All this came at a time when the field-workers, through relationships with individual young people, were beginning to exert some influence on the situation. It was during this phase that some of the content of earlier discussions were reconsidered in the light of new experience. How far should I try to organise, to help groups to plan ahead and to keep to arrangements? How far can I accept and work within this pattern of mobility and still give effective service? What is an activity? What kinds of activities are important? How far must I identify with the young person in order to help him? Is our service providing further problems of 'unattachment'?

Phase Seven The community. In the termination phase of the field-work, training tended to be centred on the community.

Why is the community as it is? How did it come to be that way? How does it affect the young people, their needs and behaviour? Which factors within the community and which from without condition its response to their need? How is this related to our aim? Are we trying to service the community in the same sense we are the young people? In what sense is the community part of the programme? Should we be trying to affect that section of it concerned with serving the young people. In what sense does our contact with the community change us? Is all this within our mandate?

What should we be doing? Should we be passing on our know-how to other youth-serving agencies? If so, how is this done? What about the conflict that might ensue? Is the 'social education' of the other agencies any concern of ours? How does it happen? How do we facilitate it? How do they facilitate our social education? Concepts— Should most of the concepts we have been using be broadened to include the community work aspect of the programme and the service? Should we begin by recognising the part the community plays in 'making the problem in the first place', and the part it must play in offering a solution?

The methods used in training

Although the training sessions were informal, we soon came to see the advantage of 'structure', however loose. The basic form for the sessions was discussion, guided by the consultant, who helped the group to explore the material presented, to question it, and to relate it to field-work experience and needs.

The material was presented in a variety of ways. It could be a question about a concept, a skill, or one arising from a previous staff conference. There was sometimes discussion before the training session in order to reach agreement as to how the material should be presented. Often the consultant stimulated discussion with a question about a concept or skill. Or he gave a brief lecture on the subject to be discussed, exploring it from several points of view, posing questions, suggesting how to find answers, and attempting to relate the material to the field-work. At other times a field-worker would use his record, previously distributed, so that the group could ask questions and discuss different aspects of the work. The discussions normally ended with a summary of the points made, agreements reached, and the relevance to previous sessions, followed by consideration of material for the following week if not already agreed.

Sometimes 'topics' continued through several sessions, as with discussion of relationships, work with individuals, information about groups and the community or when recurring field-work problems suggested the content of several consecutive sessions. In the early days discussion of the 'identity' of a worker lasted for several weeks, as did 'interpretation' during the termination period. Sometimes a crisis in the field caused us to interrupt the development of a theme in order to take up a special topic (e.g. a sudden growth of members in the network or persistent destruction of the premises). During the worst months of the winter, colds, influenza and general debility made the work in these sessions too heavy a burden. At these times training was suspended for a while to give the staff a rest or one of the field staff would report on some relevant reading.

Perhaps the most serious weakness of the training programme was that it did not allow for a prolonged discussion of each topic. It was

R

sometimes too easily stampeded by events in the field, too little concerned with a detailed analysis of the social factors involved, either because the work was developing so quickly that there was difficulty in keeping up with it or because so much needed to be done that an attitude developed which suggested that,—"just thinking seems criminal". If we had stopped long enough in the early days, to work out better the implications of our definition of the problem, we might have understood earlier the need to emphasise community work, and this might have allowed us to give more time to this most important factor in the situation. But a comparatively rigorous attempt was made to follow the pattern outlined, not because it was significant in itself, but because it was the easiest way to cover most ground, to engender the widest participation and keep the session work centred. It had another advantage in that the staff conference, the case conference and the supervision session were so loosely set up (in order to respond to field-work needs) that the 'slightly structured' training situation was often seen as a relief after so much apparently "random response' to events in the field. This allayed a little of the anxiety as to whether we were "in control".

Methods used in the discussion

The methods used might best be described as "open but pointed". They were "open" in order to encourage participation, but "pointed" in that the consultant, as discussion leader, was responsible for keeping the discussion to the point without inhibiting participation. Each session was 'task centred'.

It should be emphasised that while different methods were used in leading the discussion, at no time was there a pretence that these were free and undirected discussions. It was agreed at the beginning that whatever method the discussion leader used, he would explain his reason for using it. Part of the training was for the participants to understand the different discussion methods used. The consultant sometimes introduced his own concepts and assumptions from relevant literature. The 'ploys' were explained and the role of the discussion leader explored so that the participants did not get the 'eerie feeling' that they were supposed to pretend that the discussion just happened in this way. Nothing is more disconcerting than participating in a group in which the discussion leader uses techniques but attempts to give the impression that the discussion is spontaneous. It put the discussion leader in the position of being a 'know-all', 'too clever by half', and the group in the embarrassing position of acting out a charade. Where this happens, more time is usually spent in working out the discussion leader's next move and attempting to avoid or block it than in getting on with the discussion.

246

It was only in the final states of training that the group, by agreement, decided to discuss a subject without direction, and asking simply for the discussion leader's comments. This was then explored as another technique with its own particular values and difficulties.

The use of different techniques

The following is a brief outline of some of the techniques used by the discussion leader in the course of leading the discussions.

a. Repeating what had already been said: Gerry said we "shouldn't use discipline at all in our work, as the young people already had too much of it from elsewhere" and we all seemed to agree. A bit later Peter said that there definitely were occasions when discipline was necessary and he gave us several good examples and we all seemed to feel that this was in fact the case.—How can we go about squaring those two statements?

b. Challenging an assumption: When you say that it is obvious that we do need discipline, you must have somewhere in the back of your mind some idea of why it is needed, and if it could be "enforced", what it would do for the young people, what it would do for us—perhaps we should explore this for a bit. Could we begin with "what do we mean by discipline".

c. Stating it in another way: Instead of saying, or more often implying, that discipline is a "natural need", couldn't we say that it's often a social need, in that the individual may have to experience it in order to accomplish something else, such as understanding what people expect of them. This is perhaps what Jumbo meant about needing work discipline, implying that 'society' may need to discipline in order to make the person aware of norms. This is what Marian was implying, I think, when she asked, "Isn't discipline necessary to get a child started going to school regularly". Perhaps we should explore why we need to discipline before we try to discover why others need it.

d. Questioning an agreement: I doubt we have a genuine agreement here since some of us seem to have added the idea of "punishment' to that of discipline and others have especially excluded it. Lets go back to Jumbo's first comment and see if we can start from there again and clear this up a bit.

e. Clarifying concepts: I think we ought to take up Susan's comment that we need to find some way of distinguishing between self discipline, voluntary discipline, discipline willingly accepted as part of a situation, and discipline enforced from outside or above, always remembering we have already agreed that 'punishment' is not part of the concept.

f. The large context: Peter is right, this is a thorny problem and discussions of this type about discipline run all through religions, educational and political history. We are always attempting to make rules and regulations (the law) and enforce them with social pressures, sanctions, rewards and punishments, violence and threats of violence. On the other hand, there is also often an attempt to create the conditions within an individual, a group, or a society that will facilitate 'control from within', religious disciplines—especially prayer and meditation, education—especially as they concern self knowledge, democratic and co-operative forms of government—especially as they emphasise the community's proposing and adhering to standards of discipline that grow up from within the community itself.

We have already touched on some of these; young people and the law (punishment or rehabilitation); young people and school (personality, growth and development as well as academic or vocational training).

g. Setting a problem: What do we mean by disciplining ourselves to be more objective in our field-work observations? What is involved in this kind of discipline? How do you do it? Why do you do it? When is it necessary? Peter, you introduced the discussion of the self disciplining of the field-worker. Can you get us started on this point?

h. Questioning an observation: I don't think we should allow ourselves to say that the girls "like being disciplined by the boys". I think there are two things that might be ill advised about that kind of observation. It adds another connotation to the word 'discipline' which would have to be made clear before the observation could stand. I rather think there's something behind the behaviour of the girls that the statement doesn't tell us about, namely the possibility that what the girls are after is attention, participation together with the boys in an activity, and that this is a "price the boys make them pay". If this is so, and from previous discussion it looks as if it might be, the word 'like' to mean 'enjoy' and the word 'discipline' to mean 'manipulation' should be examined very carefully.

i. Keeping to the point: (Perhaps the most often used). It is true that the kind of discipline used in the homes, schools, or youth clubs is relevant and we agreed we would take this up later. But we must first have some agreement as to how we are going to use this word, the concept it refers to, and the assumptions that underlie it in terms of our own behaviour in the field. If we straighten that out first, we can then develop discipline from several points of view, the home, the school, the adolescent peer group, the work, etc. If we don't get to all of these today we can pick them up next week.

j. Clarifying an agreement: We must be clear in accepting Gerry's statement, "that we are not policemen or probation officers, that is we have no statutory discipline requirements to meet except those of an ordinary citizen, and that in our work we must attempt to create a setting in which the young people develop and accept whatever discipline they choose in order to achieve what they want". Perhaps what he is suggesting is that instead of emphasising the negative aspects of discipline, we should emphasise the aims and achievements aspect of it. This would rest on the assumption that if a boy (or a group) is clear about what he wants to do, and that what he wants to do is reasonable of fulfilment (without endangering himself and others), the discipline will take care of itself, as one of the factors in the process of achievement. This is perhaps another way of stating the case for 'control from within' and suggesting that, if we help individuals and groups in their choices and decisions in such a way that they are reasonable (and legal), the necessary discipline will evolve without our needing to enforce it from outside and above. This is an important point since it could differentiate the role of the detached worker from that of other workers who are quite rightly bound by statutory limitations. How shall we go about trying to find out if we really agree about this statement? Not only because it implies agreement about discipline which we have been discussing this morning but because it relates to the role of the worker which we discussed a few sessions back and which we shall be discussing again shortly.

The above illustration was not intended as our 'stand' on discipline, but simply as an example of how we tried to carry on the 'open and pointed discussion' in the training sessions. Nor was it of course a full recorded session, but simply selected examples of the discussion leader's method of attempting to keep the discussion going, illicit participation, and get the task accomplished.

Discussion of a field-work record

As soon as we were reasonably sure that our field-work recording could be relied upon to give an adequate picture of events, we began to use the records as the basis for discussion, and as an indication of the kind of skills we needed to develop. The following illustration presents the full field-work record; we then indicate from the notes of a training session, the use we made of it.

NAME OF GROUP   Younger Group
WORKER   Peter
PLACE   B——— Club

Narrative recording:

Jim, Fred, Ludy and Jacko arrived at B——— at about ten to eight. Straight away Fred was asking about the photos, but I had to disappoint them on that score. I asked whether they had been to the heath today, to which Fred replied that they hadn't, but that they wanted to go. I said I would go along with them tomorrow afternoon.

There was a lot of ferreting around and Jim discovered another sex

249

magazine which was handed round then discarded. I tried to get a card game going, but only Ludy was interested. Jim had the idea of sawing up a ladder to make a couple of sleds for tomorrow, and as an old, stout ladder was available we set to with the tools which were stored in the room.

This activity lasted for about twenty minutes, with considerable energy being expended. Jim and Jacko set to work on one end, and Ludy and Fred on the other. There was constant dispute over who should use the small number of tools, and I vacillated between the two groups trying to keep peace and at the same time get some sort of concerted effort going. They were determined to work individually, however, with Jim proving the most awkward. He worked himself up into a foul temper when things did not go right, and when I came to help him made me the butt of his temper and accused me of hiding the tools and impeding the work. His attitude was really aggressive, and began to get on my nerves. The others were constantly investigating the lumber and demanding my attention, and this dual attack set me on edge and I found myself becoming involved in futile bickerings over the tools with Jim. This came to a head when he lifted the seat from one of the wooden chairs, intending to nail it on to the sled. I pointed out that we couldn't misuse the club furniture in that way, at which he looked extremely frustrated and argued that he wanted the seat. Eventually he lost his temper, shouted "Take your f—— seat, then", and flung it violently across the room. I picked it up and put it back.

At about this point, Stan came in. He immediately picked a quarrel with Fred, which came to nothing, then did his share of poking around. This resulted in the discovery of a paraffin lamp, which Jacko immediately pumped so as to produce a fountain of paraffin to which Stan applied a match. I put it out, but Jim by now thoroughly anti-me, lit a fire on the billiard table. The polished surface of this table was now a real mess, with scratching, burns and nails, as well as a daubing of blue paint which had been upset in the corner long ago.

An uneasy peace followed this, during which we investigated the heap of old clothing in the corner. There was a little dressing up, and a few laughs, but Jim broke it up by demanding that I should go to the workshop for some more nails. I told him to go himself, but he said they wouldn't let him in. I explained that I couldn't go and leave them alone in the room. Jim agreed that he supposed I couldn't trust them. I reminded him of the two fires that had been started that night. Fred commented that I couldn't hope to get on with them if I wasn't prepared to trust them. I still refused to go. Jim waved the hammer he was holding and said he would throw it through the window if I didn't go. I now had a definite 'me against them' feeling. I couldn't give in to Jim's blackmail, so suggested that we should all go. Fred seconded this, and eventually we all went with the exception of Ludy, who looked busy, and who let most of them back in again once they had let me get well ahead.

After a further ten minutes, most of the activity on the sleds stopped, and in spite of my efforts to get some card games going, foraging was far too enticing. Stan was the only card enthusiast, but when it became obvious that nobody else would play he became troublesome, and walked round shouting and looking for things to break. Jim joined him in this, from anger, I think, though Stan had now sensed a good 'laugh' at my expense and was watching acutely for my reaction to his misbehaviour. The mood spread. Stan picked up a distemper brush and began to daub the walls, Jacko found a box of crockery and started juggling with the pieces. Jim started throwing saucers at the wall. I told them they were getting rather silly, and we had better close before they do any real damage. There was a protest at this, Stan declaring he wouldn't go and at the same time putting on his coat. I told them it would take me at least till closing time to clear up the mess they had made, and this was a good enough reason for them.

Jim hung back, and as a parting request asked for a small tent on which he had set his heart. We had had lengthy discussion about this earlier, when he had challenged me to give my reasons for his not taking it. I had explained that the loss would be discovered, and that it would mean trouble for me and the loss of the room for the boys. He had taken that with misgivings, but still looked most hurt when I reiterated my refusal as he left. A few minutes later there was a knock on the door, plus much shuffling and shouting, and as I opened it— forewarned but not forearmed—I got two ears full of ice, one from Jim and one from Stan.

The meeting lasted an hour.

Summary recording/Peter

Summary statement My activity suggestions were rejected, and the boys busied themselves with making sleds. All went tolerably well (with the exception of my getting on the wrong side of Jim) for half an hour, then Stan arrived. From that time things became more difficult, the activity was abandoned and the group set out to cause mischief— lighting fires, stealing, breaking things up. This caused the termination of the meeting after only one hour.

Comment An interesting evening which started well and gradually deteriorated. The really encouraging sign was the purposefulness of the activity, though they did not have enough patience to finish it. I explained to them why they had to leave early, and got rid of them because I could see no other alternative.

Questions An alternative course of action at the close would have been to close the club and leave with them, disregarding the state the room was in. Would this have been a preferable line of action?

At one stage I refused to leave them alone in the room. Any ideas about the possible results of this action, and alternatively, the results of leaving them?

Analysis of narrative/Peter

a. There was little doubt that Fred at least wanted me along with them at the heath. There seemed to be a general agreement that we should go, and the affair was very speedily settled. This led the way to

b. when the group almost entirely rejected my suggestion for activity, and let me know what they wanted to do; namely, prepare for tomorrow's outing. This movement was led by Jim, and was conducted in such a manner as to emphasise the fact that they didn't want to do what I suggested rather than that they had found a more useful method of spending the time. Because of this misleading attitude, I misinterpreted what they were about and thought they were simply getting up to mischief while in fact Jim at least was thinking in extremely constructive lines. His attitude remained aggressive throughout, however, and at no time did they declare their intention: "We would prefer to spend our time preparing for tomorrow rather than play cards".

c. The activity was extremely productive, and had all the added zest of their having thought of it themselves. Unfortunately, their enthusiasm caused them to disregard items such as the billiards table, the polished surface of which was ruined, and various other items of furniture and equipment which they wanted to break up to improve their sleds. I had to attempt to limit this breakage of club property, and perhaps made a poor job of it. However, it certainly roused Jim's rather volatile temper, and from there, I feel, came the seeds of the later lack of control.

d. We were unfortunate at this juncture in the arrival of Stan on whom the following observations can be made:

i. He is not a very firm member of the group. Because of this he cannot co-operate with the group as the group members themselves are slowly learning to do.

ii. He is part member of both the older and the younger groups. When he comes into the younger group he brings with him the views and attitudes of the older group. This gives him a sense of superiority and the other generally admit this in their behaviour towards him.

iii. I do not have such relationship with him as I have with the other boys. Consequently there is a lack of sympathy between us, though superficially we get on together.

I belief that his entry at this point contributed towards the loss of control and the animosity which grew up between myself and the group. I believe he had been disappointed in not being able to contact the older group that night, and came into the group looking for a 'laugh'. He was not in the group enough to want to join them in their activity, and went so far as to suggest to them that they didn't really want to go to the heath tomorrow. Later, he joined with Jim—though I believe from a different motive—in causing the nuisance which led to the termination of the meeting. At one point he summed up the feeling of the group, and incited them to further heights, by shouting: "Peter tells us to stop doing something and nobody takes a blind bit of notice!"

Programme planning/Peter

Short range Hampstead Heath tomorrow. Immediate action taken in the construction of two sleds at the expense of one of B——'s ladders. Meeting place, etc. arranged. Sleds to be finished off before I meet them.

Long range Nil.

Summarised staff discussion of the record

Peter gave a résumé of the record. He said that the initial momentum of the meeting was generated by the snow outside and an expressed wish for the group to go sledding on the heath. This started the activity, and then squabbling and bickering started because of quarrels over tools, who should do what, when and how, etc. The late arrival of Stan fanned the flame and Peter's relationship with the group steadily deteriorated during the evening. A feeling of hostility between the boys and Peter developed and eventually degenerated to the point where if he had not closed the club, the boy would have broken the place up completely.

Discussion 1. Observation of the presence of conflict:

It was an evening which started well with lots of activity and enthusiasm and which degenerated sharply within an hour into something very difficult to cope with because the relationship was by then too bad. Once the boys started to break up the room, Peter could not accept this as genuine activity and consequently the relationship worsened. The boys' reaction to the evening was different from Peter's. For them the evening probably started off boringly and developed into something exciting. It would seem that the boys did not want the kind of relationship with Peter that he wanted with them.

Discussion 2. Observation—cause of conflict:

Peter had to take a responsibility for the things around him which prevented the boys doing the activity which they wanted to do (i.e. breaking the place up) and consequently the boys let out their aggression against Peter because he represented certain norms which they were unwilling or unable to accept. The leader in this case symbolised attitudes and norms which were unacceptable and his sense of responsibility infringed on their activity. Here was the root cause of the conflict.

Discussion 3. Some of the boys' needs:

They must have liked Peter and looked upon him as someone who could take their aggression without aggressing back. They needed sympathy with an adult. They wanted a 'laugh'. They needed individual recognition. They wanted a group identity.

What was Peter doing?

Initially he hoped to present them with an evening which would occupy them pleasantly and given them things which he thought they would like to do and hoped that they would plan a meeting for the following day. But once they started the campaign against Peter he was reduced to trying to preserve the relationship with them for as long as he could, and ultimately he reached the point where all he wanted to do was to get rid of them. The boys thought at first that Peter was playing the Club Leader role and they thus viewed his suggestions of activity with grave suspicion. They didn't believe that the situation at the B——— Club was permanent.

Discussion 4. The role of the Worker:

It seemed to have been moulded together by the situation in which the group found itself and by the surroundings. It appears that the whole meeting of the group turned, not so much on the newcomer who came in and changed the meeting and made it more difficult, but on the fact that Peter was obliged to take on the responsibility of the building. Either he had to become authoritarian and stop them right at the beginning and ruin the relationship with the group or go through this particular sequence and help to keep the relationship which he had established. He had ultimately to remain as an adult working with boys. They would not have expected him to join them in wrecking the place. There is a point at which the boys know you are an adult and and only acting out with them. The group must always know what the role of the leader is and it must be acceptable and consistent.

In this record of Peter's it appears he had to switch his role in the middle of the evening to one which the group did not understand and consequently could not accept.

Discussion 5. Was this typical?

This was typical of the smaller friendship groups, but not on the whole for any length of time, because they either came out of it and accepted one of their own members as a leader and settled down for a bit, or they found they couldn't get things done, broke up or fell apart and their members moved on into other small friendship groups. On the other hand, it wasn't typical in that none of us had worked inside someone else's premises and that this particular group appeared to have more than the usual proportion of disorganised boys.

Discussion 6.

What might Peter think about doing next?

It seemed that Peter had to think seriously about the effects of working in someone else's building, on his relationship with the boys in the group. Either he had to find some way of interpreting the group to the club leader of the building, so that he did not feel obliged to become authoritarian because of his situation, or he needed to think seriously about meeting the boys elsewhere.

The second half of the discussion was concerned with these questions:

a. What were the elements in the 'total situation' (the boys' needs

and behaviour, being in someone else's premises, the worker's attempt
to define the situation for himself and to the young people, etc.).
b. Which of these was most important to the worker having to act
in these circumstances?
c. What can we add to our generalisations about the role of the worker
from this discussion?
d. Was it a 'good recording', useful to the worker himself in his
thinking and planning, useful to us in helping us to see the field-work
events more clearly and in perspective? What were its shortcomings?

This illustration suggests how a field-work record can be used to
help the worker himself to be more objective about what he is doing
and perhaps to get some suggestions of alternative action, and to
relate the material of the discussion to other aspects of the training
programme, in this case to the previous discussions on the value of
recording and the role of the worker.

Developing a skill (consultant)

In several recent sessions we have come a bit unstuck about 'interpretation', about what it is, why it needs to be done, and how it's done.
We have seen that we ourselves are constantly doing it by our very
presence and behaviour in the field, yet we still find that there are
occasions on which it has to be done deliberately, that is, planned and
thought out with a specific objective in mind. Peter brought up the
matter as regards his talking with the club leader whose premises the
group was using. Marion mentioned it in her discussion of how the
boys reacted to the girls wanting to have a meeting now and then on
their own. Gerry mentioned it when he told us of trying to get across
to Bob's mother that he could not tell Bob what to do, and Jumbo
brought it up when he spoke of the difficulty of explaining to court
officials that 'he had to stand up for the boy' in court, regardless of
how it might effect the work of the court officials. Although each of
these illustrations can be seen to have had other aspects, we shall
concern ourselves this morning only with that part of the process in
each case that we shall call interpretation. During this short presentation I shall outline how I think this concept (interpretation) might be
used and then we might try to set up some interpretation sessions, that
is, try a bit of role playing, in order to see what are the ingredients of
interpretation, why we call it a skill and how this skill could be
developed.

(Susan asked if we shouldn't be more definite about the kind of
interpretation we were going to discuss. When asked to develop this
point, she said she meant were we going to interpret the way in which
we worked, the need for this kind of work, or the needs of the young
people? It was agreed that this might be left to be clarified in the open
discussion if it were not made clear in the short presentation to
follow.)

Consultant's presentation

What exactly do we mean by interpretation. I think we can safely begin by saying that by interpretation we mean an attempt to get over to somebody else information, facts, attitudes or opinions to help them understand how we see the matter under discussion. We do this in the hope that there can emerge some agreement leading to common action, or leading to the other person's seeing our reason for doing something in a particular way.

There are several elements in this statement that we need to see separately:

It might at first seem that information and facts are easy matters to get across to someone else, but if we remember for a moment what we said about the kinds of bias that enter into our own observations and the difficulties that arise when we try to avoid them, and then consider that the other person will more than likely have terms of reference that give these facts and this information a different weight, or a different value, you can appreciate that we are navigating in a more complex situation.

It is important to note as well that the beginning of any attempt at interpretation might best be an attempt to help the other person understand why you see things the way you do, why the matter in hand is important to you, how you think and feel about it. This means explaining the situation that gave rise to the discussion and being definite about this being only one side of the case, namely yours.

Your aim is common action based in part on the validity, as seen by the other party, of what you are doing, saying or proposing.

The process is mutual; the other party will be 'trying to get something over to you', attempting to help you see and appreciate 'her side of the story', her reasons for thinking and feeling and behaving in a particular way. In this sense it's important to see interpretation as an exchange, a kind of dialectic in which you should not expect 'complete acceptance' from the other party; this would more than likely be feigned or complete defeat for yourself. What you should hope for is a third level of discourse arising out of the interpretation occasioned by both of you attempting to 'get over', or 'defend' your thinking and feeling. For this reason interpretation requires empathy which we discussed when we were discussing relationships between individuals. In this sense it might be well to see interpretation as a kind of relationship in which both.thinking and feeling are part of the situation that, it is hoped, will end in common action.

It can easily be seen that this is a skill since it depends on knowing what is happening in a situation in which you are trying both to give and receive in order to achieve a particular purpose. It is a skill because it can only be gained from the experience of doing it, from participation in it, and from 'having it done to you'.

It might help if I sketched out a short lift of the techniques of interpretation in the kind of work we are doing. We can try them out when we get to the role planning to see if they are relevant to the kinds of problems we face.

1. Be sure of your facts, of your own thoughts and feelings on the matter under discussion.

2. Be sure you accept them well enough to explain or defend them.

3. Be sure you are clear in your own mind about what you want to accomplish, and your suggestions about how it can be accomplished.

4. Think of the other person, what is the frame of reference for his thinking and feeling?

5. Think of the situation, the outside pressures contributing to or distorting the conversation. How can they be used or avoided?

6. Realising all this, that the process is mutual and that if it is not you cannot 'succeed', you must respect the legitimate reservations of the other party, and accept the responsibility that this kind of 'relationship' confers.

7. Don't plead, don't wrangle, don't over-state or under-state for emphasis.

8. Remember you are doing all this to get something done, not to make a private or personal point—to have a 'victory' or 'conversion' of the other parties.

9. Remember that what you started out to achieve will necessarily be modified by what the other person can give or accept; learn to expect that the objective of your interpretation in the first place will usually be modified by this process.

Now obviously these techniques are not separate bits of 'discipline' that can be gone through before or during the event like checking the laundry list. They are aspects of the same thing, an attempt to communicate for a particular purpose in particular circumstances. Even listing them in this way, although perhaps necessary and helpful, is dangerous because it gives the impression that the process is 'mechanical', and that knowing the 'rules' will achieve the required results. This is of course not so: that is why we refer to it as a skill and not a 'formula'. You will need to experience this type of thing in a number of ways on a number of occasions, fail, succeed and fail again before you have developed the necessary skill. Of course, once you feel fairly confident about it you will be able to do it without any reference to 'techinque', but in the early stages of developing this skill, talking about techniques and learning to use them is the only recourse open to us if we don't already possess the necessary skill.

Open discussion

The discussion fell into several parts, firstly questions and answers about the presentation, agreement and disagreement as to whether or not this way of thinking about the matter was helpful, and how it might be more helpfully stated. This part of the discussion ended with an agreement that it was only partially helpful to state 'interpretation' as had been done, since it made it appear separate from 'awareness' and might better have been approached by discussing 'awareness' in trying to communicate.

The second half of the discussion was taken up with role playing. Marian played a moral welfare worker and Peter an 'illegitimate father'. In these roles they discussed 'the girl in trouble'. Then Peter played himself, the field-worker, discussing the problem with the moral welfare worker. In the second situation Peter played a court official, and Jumbo tried to 'explain' why, although the boy had committed the crime and could be said to have 'a bad character', he was still bound to speak up for him in court, because of the kind of relationship he had with him at the coffee stall. And then the roles were reversed: Jumbo played the court official and Peter, the worker.

The third part of the discussion was an analysis of what each person had said and done, and why, and how they each felt about it, with an emphasis on what had gone wrong, why it had gone wrong, what techniques each person had used and what it felt like to interpret and be interpreted to.

Short summary (consultant

What appears to have emerged from today's session is that when we came to the role playing we tended to emphasise our relationship with the other agencies rather than with the young people in the field. This could have been because we felt the need to consider this aspect of interpretation, because latterly it had arise so frequently in the field, or it could have been because the opening statement of this session used these kinds of illustration or because the presentation was slanted in the direction of interpretation in formal situations (statutory and voluntary bodies). We might take this up again next week and see if we can cover the same ground another way.

It seemed to emerge that the techniques within this presentation were valuable at least as points of departure for analysing the role playing, but that we may have been wrong in discussing interpretation in this way. We might take up as suggested the discussion of 'awareness' as we covered it in earlier sessions and try to see what the workers 'self-awareness' might be in situations where he is trying to get across facts, information, opinions and attitudes. This would be an alternative to using a new category for discussion, i.e. interpretation. The staff discussed this idea and agreed to try it.

Several things in this illustration are relevant to in-service training:

1. The opening statement set the task and the bounds for the morning's work and tried to get agreement as to how it would be accomplished.

2. The presentation covered only enough of the relevant material to start the discussion.

3. The role playing was an attempt to give the participants an opportunity to 'experience' what they were talking about.

4. Once the participants had experience in a contrived situation, they could compare that experience to what we had said and to their pre-

vious experience. The value of this is evidenced by the fact that after having experience in role playing, they tended to want to discard talk about interpretation and to continue their discussion of it as a problem of awareness in communication.

5. One result of the session was to point up that more sessions of this type were needed, in reference to individuals and groups of young people.

6. In this illustration it should not be assumed that we were trying to teach a skill in a single session. Obviously such a skill could be developed only by working in different situations, and seeing its different aspects over a long period. We were simply marshalling past experience, and using discussion and role playing in an attempt to interpret and examine it in several dimensions. By focussing on it in this way we hoped to modify our future behaviour in similar circumstances, and that new experiences could be added material for re-examination and discussion.

Recording

The five fundamentals on which we believe field-work practice should be based are:

1. Awareness of field-work events and problems, based on accurate regular observation.

2. Objectivity in observation.

3. Ability to see the separate parts of the problem so as to be able to think, discuss and act in relation to 'the particular'.

4. Ability to see the 'whole' that is, the problems, in the relevant larger contexts of which they are a part.

5. Ability to use the above four factors in making choices and decisions in establishing priorities for action in the field.

Recording based on an agreed system is one of the skills and techniques which field-workers can use to put these five fundamentals into practice. We see the possibility of improvement in every aspect of the work (planning programmes, offering a service, developing a method, interpreting the work) if recorded material is used.

Much depends on being able to state the problem so that something can be done about it with the resources at hand, and on readiness to change the statement as developments in the field falsify it. Much depends on having the necessary material ready to hand in a suitable form for consideration and action. So much depends on interpretation to the young people, committees, and the statutory and voluntary authorities, that recording seems to be an essential.

It is important to note however that recording can only tell the worker about what he has asked in the first place. His preconceptions affect the material he observes and records, and his interpretation of it. All he can do is describe the reality of a situation as he understands it, and then try to understand his own preconceptions which have led to his describing it in that way. The preconceptions on which most of the project recording was based are included in *Background* in each of the Approach and Method sections.

This difficulty need not be too big an obstacle to getting started if a worker is willing to do random observational recording in which he does not set, describe, or state any problem too firmly beforehand, and to use the resulting material to suggest more relevant question to be fed into the next round of recording. Thus although the recording is systematic, it is also open to modification by the results of regular random observation.

The reasons for recording

There are as many potential reasons for field-work recording as there are field-work events, but in general the reasons for recording are the following:

1. To help the worker understand his job. The most important reason for recording is that it is the easiest and most effective way for the worker to learn to understand the nature and content of the field-work and his part in it. It can, when well designed and regularly carried out, provide him with most of the information he needs to be effective.

2. To provide the basis for supervision. Both the individual supervision session (described in the next section) and the weekly staff conference require a focus for discussion about the day to day and long range problems of field-work. Persons, groups, social institutions, processes and procedures, a worker's own behaviour all need to be discussed in the light of detailed and accurate information.

3. To provide a basis for evaluation. As the field-work programme develops, the worker and the team will want to consider alternative activities or services, to know how a particular service has worked out in practice, what to change and how, what to develop more fully or abandon altogether. Evaluation of the work with an individual or group, the other agencies, or the staff, is needed constantly. This requires detailed accurate information that can only be found in field-work records.

4. To provide a basis for programme planning. At every point of the development of the programme and the service, information is necessary about activity preferences, equipment and services in order to assign staff responsibilities, and allocate the resources (including finance).

5. For the use of others. The worker is a member of a team; other field-workers, volunteers, the administrator, supervisor, colleagues and officials want to know what is happening in order to co-operate with the worker on the programme or make a direct contribution to the service.

6. For public interpretation. The agencies sponsoring or interested in the work will want to know why the work is needed, what it is about, how it can be done and how they can support it. It is especially important in any attempt to meet new needs in a relatively new way to have the information from which to interpret what is happening and why.

7. To contribute to a reservoir of information. If the problems arising in field-work are present in other communities the worker will want to exchange information with others who are attempting to solve them, to 'compare notes', discuss possibilities, and exchange techniques and information about findings. To do this he needs the material made available by field-work recording.

8. To provide material for training purposes. Training material based on the worker's experience in the field and on his own interpretation of that experience will be valuable to him and to his colleagues as a basis for in-service training. It will also be of some interest to those training or being trained who are concerned with similar problems.

9. To relate to the literature in the field. Many of the problems in the field-work have been discussed in the specialised literatures (individual psychology, social psychology, sociology, social anthropology). By keeping field-work records that state the nature and content of the problems encountered, a worker might be able to see the relevance of some of the literature to his own predicament and thus be aided in his practice.

The most basic of all reasons for recording is that it offers the worker opportunity for self development in direct relation to the service he is offering to the young people.

Angles of observation

In observing and recording, the worker asks himself a number of questions about the same events from several different angles. These include:

1. Particular behaviour—of individuals, groups, social institutions and himself. What is happening? "This is the third time this group has asked to go on a trip and each time I have agreed that it would be a good idea, they have let the matter drop. Why does this happen? Are they testing me out? Do they expect me to do all the planning and

organising? Have I been less enthusiastic than they feel I should be? What do I do about it? Get the tickets, get the dormobile, present them with an accomplished fact? Bring the matter up myself and ask why they have not followed through?"

2. Social attitudes—of individuals, groups, sections of the community and himself. What is happening? "My attempts to discuss employment, getting to work, what you get out of settled jobs, are meeting with no response. Why is it happening? Is it because I'm not sufficiently accepted to have the right to broach the subject at all, in which case would they consider it an interference? Is it that I'm not talking their language or using examples that can be seen and appreciated in their experience? Is it that they get so much support in their way of thinking about jobs and work from attitudes in the community and that my approach seems so different as to be irrelevant? What are my attitudes towards work? Do they have any relevance to their circumstances? Where did I get these attitudes? What do I do? Should I keep trying until I find out how best to carry on this type of dialogue? Should I try and learn more about their attitudes in an attempt to work out the possible content of such a discussion. Should I leave it to the experts?" (e.g. the youth employment officer).

3. Processes and procedures—as they affect individuals, groups and the community and his own attempt to offer a service. What is happening? "The club to which I am taking the group insists on entrance fees which the boys refuse to pay. But I think I could keep three of them interested long enough for them to get to know the place and perhaps continue going on their own. I feel they could get a good deal from it. Why is it happening? Apparently because the boys feel it is an unjust demand and enjoy trying to 'beat the authorities', because the club feels it cannot make an exception without being unfair to its regular members, and because I haven't found a way of helping the boys to see that paying the subs is one of the rules of this particular game and that it is taken quite seriously by those who operate the club. What do I do? Should I pay the group's subscriptions ahead in block in order to make sure that this opportunity is kept open for them? Should I suggest to the club leader that someone from the project would be glad to speak to his committee if he thought it would help?"

Limitations and potentials—of individuals, groups, the community and himself. What is happening? "Tom is at home again and working at last, yet his relationship with his father has not improved, and there is every sign that he will shortly be involved in another bust-up at home. This would start the same chain reaction, leave job, leave home, petty theft, in trouble with the police. Why is it happening? It might be that Tommy's parents who do not get on, use Tommy in their conflict, and/or that Tommy tries to play off his parents against each other. It might be that Tommy's father is too strict with him. What can be done? Should I use this apparently peaceful interlude to help Tommy find digs which he asks me to do every time there is a bust-up? Should I find an occasion to speak to Tommy's parents, with his permission, offering to introduce them to a family caseworker who might help? Should I pass the whole thing on to the probation officer, saying I have definitely now come to a belief that Tommy should not be at home?"

Facts and figures about individuals, groups and the community. What is happening? "There is another drastic decrease in the numbers who attended the dances. In the first month there were between 50 and 70 each time. Now in the sixth month there are 25 or less. Why does this happen? i.e. Are the boys running the dance losing interest? Have the customers found a new place? Is it simply the 'natural pattern of mobility?' What to do about it? Should we just let it slowly fade out and begin thinking of other ways of offering the committee group something to do or should we attempt to help them revive it in the hopes of giving them a longer term experience of success?"

There is no hard and fast rule for finding answers to these questions. Only the worker's own use of the recorded material in thinking about and planning his field-work, and in relating it to supervision, training and staff conferences will, after some practice, help him to see what is relevant. Even then he will often find himself at the end of three or four weeks of recording a particular development in his work, with too much recorded material about one aspect and too little about another. But this in itself will teach him more about how to get relevant information.

Techniques of recording

There is no hard and fast rule about how to record. Written records are in many forms, among which are:

a. Narrative recording: an objective story of the situation including the worker's participation, together with his comments and suggestions, and notes for programme planning, supervision, staff conference and training.

b. Episodic recording; a description of a single event or incident.

c. Anecdotal recording: the addition to a record of an anecdote that explains a particular point or poses a problem.

d. Notation: the addition of a note to act as a reminder for the worker to expand or use later.

e. Check sheet: a prepared list of headings to suggest information to be filled in, checked off or listed. This can either be added to the narrative record or used as a guide.

Timing. Obviously the worker does not record during a session in the field, not only because of the effect it would have on those with whom he is working, but because it would prevent his full participation in what is happening. He may choose to write full records immediately after the session, or to make notes then to be developed later. He will read back through the records at regular intervals, and when he wants to see a particular problem in perspective.

Neither the form nor the time factors can be decided unless a worker has some definite idea of the use to which he will put a particular record. The proposed function of the record decides its form and content, and the amount of time and attention given to writing it up.

Project recording system

After several attempts to prepare a record keeping system which was both economical (in that it did not take too much time or attention) and efficient (in that it provided the necessary information for different aspects of field-work), we agreed upon three basic records to cover the various aspects of the work. These were observational recordings, sessional recordings and administrative recordings.

The most important factor and the one most easily overlooked was that names, dates, times and places were essential to each recording.

1. Observational Records: The neighbourhood—mobility patterns of young people in street, coffee bars, playground, youth clubs, dance halls, and other facilities.

The community: location of social services, schools, ethnic groups; specific aspects of social life seen as relevant to the problems of the unattached and/or the possibilities of service; the patterns of autonomous group life, the "street life" of adults and young people in the neighbourhood, housing, etc.

Special problems relevant to work with the unattached: employment, education, vocational training, presence or absence of opportunities in the neighbourhood or community social attitudes of those who offer opportunities, of those who accept or reject them. Similar circumstances: work with the unattached in other neighbourhoods; similar or different approaches and methods, or their absence.

The main purpose of this observational recording was to give background material for discussion and thinking that might help to avoid preconceptions about the circumstances of our work, help us to 'isolate specifics', (i.e. the natural mobility patterns of the unattached) and to see them as part of a larger pattern (natural patterns of association in the neighbourhood and community) and provide the material for tentative generalisations. Another purpose was to help workers learn how to observe social life in the community more objectively.

Observational recording provided some of the material for the constant rethinking of programme aims and objectives. It was the most difficult kind of recording to do since it took time away from direct service. It was easier in the early stages, when we were still working out an approach and developing a programme both because it seemed more necessary then and because there was more time for it. Observational recording became less frequent as contacts in the field increased and the programme developed. This was a pity since without it we were apt to repeat our apparent successes in a routine way rather than continue to adapt the programme to immediate need.

2. Sessional Recording covered all aspects of the work with individuals, groups and the community. It was mostly in narrative form, describing what happened in a session. If the session was a meeting with an individual, the record described what took place between the worker and the individual. If it was a meeting with an agency official, the same applied. If the session involved work with a group, the record was a description of what individuals said and did, what the group did, and what the worker said and did.

The narrative was normally followed by a summary of the session (pointing up the main incidents, and whether or not it achieved its purpose), and a simple analysis in which the worker suggested why things had happened as they did, and why he had behaved as he did. Often he suggested what should be done next, and prepared questions and comments for use in supervision and staff conference.

On the whole the sessional records covered most of the project sessions, except in times of crisis, (when they were of great importance but almost impossible to write) in holiday periods, and sometimes when cold, damp and fatigue made a break advisable.

We tried to make regular three-monthly summaries but rarely succeeded except when a group was a particular problem, or in the early days of the work when we needed to boost our own confidence in our work. Few of the records needed to be full, process recordings. We soon learned that one or two full sessional recordings a week and others covering only the essential factors were adequate.

Once narrative recording was regular, it was less irksome than observational recording because it was more obviously useful. (In programme, evaluation, supervision, training and staff conference.) It also offered a sense of accomplishment (sometimes illusory) that allowed workers to feel that something had been happening over a period of weeks when the records were read again.

3. Administrative records: This part of the recording system did not consist of single records but was a series of files designed and organised for use as resource material and as an ongoing record of the growth and development of the programme. The contents of the files covered:

Policy: as laid down by the agency and the project committee and as modified and applied to the programme by the staff. Records of contacts with agencies and officials.

Work schedules: covering individual field-work responsibilities, special assignments, holiday and emergency coverage of stall, premises, groups, activities. Schedules of supervision and training sessions.

Finance: statements, budgets, expense sheets, and correspondence with grant-aiding bodies.

Premises and equipment: all relevant data covering the use of premises, rent, heat, light, fire precautions, repairs, decoration, etc. undertaken, by whom, for what reason, at what cost; lists of equipment, costs, destruction, disappearance.

Programme records: notes on outings, activities, costs, successes and failures, suggestions.

Related material: reports, pamphlets, articles from newspapers, magazines, other agencies, journals, related to the problem of unattachment or the programme and service.

Much of the material in this file consisted of correspondence, statements, and plans for and notes of meetings and sessions within the sponsoring agency and with other agencies. This file was kept reasonably up to date mostly because clerical help was available.

It is obvious that even a relatively simple recording system can get out of hand, become an end in itself, a race to fill up filing cabinets with closely typed foolscap, or even on occasion, a device for avoiding work in the field—the excuse being "I have to spend this session on my records as I am so far behind".

It can also be the occasion for fancy theorising, reading into the records ideas and concepts that distort rather than clarify, that complicate rather than simplify the events they are meant to describe and interpret.

We found ourselves on occasion doing all these things, either because we had hit upon a problem which we could not for the moment understand, because we seemed to be getting 'nowhere at all', or because we became momentarily enthusiastic about some abstract theory of why or how something was happening, and what we could do about it. But the variety of field-work events and the challenge they presented were usually enough to help us get through these digressions fairly speedily.

Another point about record keeping might seem to be negative. In working with the unattached there is bound to be a great deal of 'apparent chaos' that neither should nor could be 'controlled'—adequately planned activities that do not come off, spontaneous activities that get out of hand, long periods in which 'nothing happens'. These aspects of the day-to-day job are bound to cause anxious feelings in the worker that he isn't in control, that nothing is really happening, that he is a failure and taking his salary for nothing. Recording, aside from its other advantages, can help alleviate these feelings by helping the worker to feel that he is doing something, even if it's only recording, and because a chaotic situation appears more ordered and reasonable once it is on paper. Moreover, once the record is re-read in relation to previous records about the same group or person, the event or situation tends to fall into a less anxious perspective.

Most difficulties in recording can be solved by reference to the cardinal principle, namely, that the only valid reason for recording is to help the worker locate, develop and discipline the inner resources he needs to do the job. Over elaborate recording systems which demand too much detail, the fetish of a particular record form, the fear of not doing them properly, the use of records to show off, prove oneself or disguise one's mistakes can all eventually be modified, if attention is focussed on "how does this help in field-work practice?" Even the most pretentious system will crumble, the most awkward deviation right itself, if it is tested against this essential question.

The only 'absolute imperative' about record keeping is confidentiality. The records are about other people, individuals, groups, agencies in the community. A worker has no authority whatsoever to reveal their contents to anyone except to a colleague who is bound by the same imperative (i.e. the supervisor). Records must be kept in a locked private place. Files must be marked as confidential, and destroyed when they are no longer required for the programme. These records are the worker's own property and for his use only. They are about people and situations that are fraught with enough hardship, difficulty and indignity as it is, without their burden being increased by irresponsible use of observations, which, it must always be remembered, might be erroneous or irrelevant.

Supervision

Supervision as discussed in this presentation, is a face to face conference between the field-worker and the supervisor. In the project neither of the two supervisors was in direct contact with the young people. The consultant supervised the men and the administrator the women workers.

We saw supervision as an important part of the work with ourselves firstly as a way of sharing responsibility. The detached worker had to make many decisions, often of far reaching consequence, at short notice in an unstructured situation. This was too much responsibility to bear alone. Programme responsibilities could be, and often were, worked out in staff conferences, but relationship responsibilities, (worker/young person, worker/official, worker/worker) which were most often at the heart of the problem, needed the individual consultation that supervision provided.

A worker's own preconceptions, not only affected his observations and his interpretations of them, but even more decisively affected his own understanding of the part he should play. Generalisations about observing and interpreting could be worked out in training sessions, but the methods which an individual worker could use for effective participation in field-work events needed the kind of guidance, help and support that only supervision could provide.

We also saw supervision as an 'experimental relationship' between colleagues. This provided a situation in which both parties could explore the nature and content of a relationship as objectively as possible so as to help the worker learn by that experience how better to offer himself in his relationship with the young people.

The word supervision has unfortunate and perhaps misleading connotations. On the one hand it suggests the authoritarian imposition of standards and values as well as conditions of work, derived from its association as an administrative device. On the other hand it is used to describe a much more intensive process in some forms of case work. In this context supervision is not the imposition from above in the administrative sense, nor is it concerned with the intensive psychological interpretation of field-work events. It is simply an opportunity to work out with another person the implications of field-work events or the field-worker's participation in them. The only justification for using the word here is the probability of its becoming accepted in general youth work practice, and because we could not find a better term.

We do not suggest that supervision is the only way of offering guidance, support and practical help, nor that it should be expected to achieve all these objectives at the same time. It may not be equally necessary for every worker.

The roles of the worker and the supervisor

The worker is responsible for providing records for the session, and for producing from these the information that he wants to discuss with the supervisor in the light of his knowledge of the situation. He might wish to discuss a specific incident, attitude, theory, or generalisation. His presentation might include his difficulties with an individual, a group, colleagues, agencies, in developing skills, or in using an agreed approach.

The presentation of 'difficulties' as material for discussion is only one aspect. The worker might also bring information, incidents and attitudes to his work, which he sees as successful. This is the other half of the process. Success in work performance is a relevant for supervision as the nature and content of difficulties.

The supervisor is responsible for reading the records and listening to the information presented. He brings his experience, knowledge and skill and the lack of direct involvement in the field, which he uses to help the worker to distinguish the various elements in the situation (e.g. the individuals, the sub-groups, the activities, the feelings), to see them in relation to each other (e.g. the behaviour of A and B to C and the effect it has on the activity), and to see his participation as it affects the work as a whole (the individuals and groups, the worker, the policy-making committee, the particular community).

Incidents

1. Difficulties in working with an individual. The worker said he did not like Kevin. He thought Kevin had sensed this and asked what he thought should be done about it.

The supervisor might
a. ask the worker to elaborate on the evidence of Kevin's 'sensing the dislike';
b. explore with the worker the context of his dislike of Kevin—as a person? his behaviour? his appearance? his attitude to other boys?
c. explore the necessity of continuing relationship with Kevin;
d. examine the possibility of someone else working with Kevin.

2. Difficulties in working with a group—The worker said the group appeared to be trying him out, acting up in public on buses and on the underground in order to get him to try and stop them, but he felt that if he did attempt to interfere they would resent this and interpret it as trying to push them around. This would not be so serious if he knew the group better but might hamper his relationship with the group at this point. Since he felt he would not be in a position to intervene in this way for some time he wondered if it wouldn't be better to avoid going out with them for a time so as to avoid creating the circumstances in which all this happened.

The supervisor might
a. accept the worker's suggestion;
b. explore with worker the reasons for the testing out;
c. discuss the group members to find out if the group is as strongly united as it appears or if there is a way of working with individuals;
d. discuss the possibilities and implications of allowing the group to be dealt with by the public officials concerned.

3. The worker said he was feeling discouraged because now that the premises were open and the boys were coming regularly three nights a week they talked a good deal about decorating it but wouldn't start work. They sat around and talked and larked about. The worker added that the boys were doing "absolutely nothing".

The supervisor might

a. explore the phrase "doing nothing";

b. discuss recorded incidents and help worker to describe his own participation in them, how this had been helpful or otherwise and to what ends;

c. enquire why the premises must be decorated and find out whether the worker sees this as his own need or the boys';

d. discuss why the boys are coming three nights a week.

4. Difficulties in working with a team—The worker said he tended to say, "yes" at staff meetings to things he knew were not right for him in his field-work. He was not able to stand up for what he believed at staff conference because he felt he was unable to explain himself.

The supervisor might

a. find out the points at which the worker said, "yes" and discuss the difficulties in 'explaining';

b. discuss the procedure at staff conference to consider whether more time should be given for discussion or more opportunities for comment;

c. discuss the purpose of staff conferences and explore the reasons why the worker can not use it as it is meant to be used.

5. His difficulties in working with colleagues from other agencies. The worker said he felt Mr. Goodwin did not understand the intent of the boys' visit to his club premises last weekend but was afraid to discuss the matter with him, for fear of appearing too clever or of butting in on someone else's business. He asked how he could pass on the information and his interpretation of it without getting into that kind of difficulty.

The supervisor might

a. ask for evidence of Mr. Goodwin's lack of understanding,

b. discuss the worker's understanding of the "intent",

c. explore possible reasons for the fears,

d. consider reasons for Mr. Goodwin's having to understand the other point of view;

e. discuss the skills needed in interpreting to an agency.

6. Difficulty in developing or using the appropriate skills. The worker said he found it very difficult to help a group make a decision or a choice since he usually felt he already knew the answer and consequently felt tempted to "just tell them what to do", which often prevented him from leading a useful discussion.

The supervisor might

a. refer to records for incidents illustrating the comment and base discussion on the incidents separately;

b. discuss the reasons for helping the group to make its own choice;

c. explore the various methods and skills possible in helping a group to make its own decision—based on actual incidents.

7. His difficulties in accepting an agreed upon approach. The worker said he realised that 'moralising' about petty thieving didn't help and that it might even weaken his relationship with the young person, yet he found himself doing so.

The supervisor might

a. discuss the apparent results of the moralising (based on incidents);

b. explore with the worker other methods of discussing the subject with the boy;

c. explore the attitudes of the boy and of the worker to petty thieving.

Helping to explore alternative roles of the worker

The worker's group had for the third time begun to tidy up and to plan for an opening. The worker felt that after two previous attempts, this might not come off. Just as things seemed to be going smoothly a bust-up would take place that set the group back again, so that the boys lost interest in opening and wanted to give the whole idea up. Then they became more disorganised and thought they just weren't capable.

In the previous sessions the supervisor had suggested that the worker should read the last two months of his narrative recording, make a list of the possible reasons for this recurring behaviour and bring it to the supervision session.

Discussion in session. (From supervisor's notes)

Worker said he thought there were four possible reasons why the group always had a bust-up before they were ready to open the premises for a dance:

1. They didn't want to run the dance even though they told themselves and him (the worker) that they did.

2. They had not patience to wait for the time it took to get ready.

3. He (the worker) was doing something 'wrong' that caused the recurring bust-ups.

4. The natural composition of the group was wrong in that it did not contain enough of the necessary elements to persist with the event and to 'pull it off'.

We discussed each of these in turn. We decided that even if the boys did not want to 'accomplish' the opening for the dance for reasons of which neither they nor we were aware, there was nothing we could do since we had to begin where they were or where they thought they were. The worker had already on several occasions suggested, "We don't really have to open if you don't want to. We could go to somebody else's dance, taking our own girls with us or meeting others there or anything else you think you'd like to do". This kind of suggestion was always turned down and any attempt to get behind their reasoning deeply resented. "Like we said, we want our own dance."

We agreed that we had to accept the situation as they stated it, so we passed on to the suggestion that it took too long for the group to get ready for the opening since their span of interest was so short. The worker felt this was a probable explanation since the boys often began by saying, "We'll be done tonight and we can open tomorrow". The worker had tried two types of responses to this "If we work hard enough it's just possible", which didn't work since it increased disappointment when they failed, or "I doubt we will make it considering all that needs to be done", which didn't work because it discouraged them before they began. The worker thought if they could somehow shorten the tidying-up time (cleaning, decorating, repairs to the toilet, kitchen, bar, etc.) the chances were that once open, the dance would prove a success and they would be willing and able to carry on for a while. We discussed ways of shortening the time required for tidying up, agreed that this might be a good point at which to take some action, and decided to discuss it again after considering other possibilities.

The third possibility, that the worker was doing something wrong, centred on the worker's feeling that he should perhaps 'push' the tidying-up process by taking over himself, assigning tasks, enforcing work discipline. But he felt very dubious since he knew from experience that if he did they would at first say, "Yes, you take over". Then they would complain that he was pushing them about, and probably end up by saying, "Well, you wanted to do it—it's not our idea so leave us out". This would confuse the whole issue and probably divert them from doing something that they really wanted to do, and needed to do in order to obtain the satisfaction of success. After some discussion it was agreed that the worker had already established a relationship with the group, which at least for the present precluded his taking this kind of a lead. We passed on to the last suggestion, that the group did not contain the kinds of elements necessary to get the job done in the time required, and that by implication the bust-ups were inevitable, unless they decided to give up and try something else. We explored this by discussing the group as a whole (7 to 9 boys) and then several of the boys individually. It emerged that Bernie, the indigenous leader, was a hard worker, but only on a short-time basis, that his leadership was effective only when there was rapid visible progress in a task, that he tended to lose control when the opening night was put off. Jack, the opposition leader, often complained that "things weren't getting done" and by implication that it was Bernie's fault. Controversy usually ensued, which was not very heated or much of a problem unless Bill, a 'seriously disorganised' member of the group used it to provoke a bust-up. On the day after the bust-up all the boys except Bill were usually genuinely disappointed at their own behaviour and their inability to get on with the work.

The worker said that if the dance did get under way, there would be plenty to occupy both Bernie and Jack, and that the leadership conflict was only serious while the group wasn't doing anything. He also thought that once the dances started the outsiders, friends and acquaintances and a number of girls could create a situation in which Bill could be contained or retrained and his near hysteria played out without the danger of a bust-up.

Two factors emerged as important. First, the cleaning up had to be done as quickly as possible so as to open the dance without delay. Secondly, in order to do that, Jack must be occupied so that he wasn't nagging Bernie, and Bill must be prevented from acting up so that some progress could be made.

The worker suggested that Bill and his current girl friend might be taken out by one of the staff and that another field-worker might help for one or two nights to get the work done. He would take special care to arrange that Jack had to work with the others on a special task that he accepted and to see that he got the credit for this so as to reduce his need to jibe and hamper Bernie.—Agreed.

A behaviour problem (*Prepared from supervisor's notes*)

The worker referred to the question of stealing which had been discussed in the training session. She had been worried about the stealing in her group for some time. She could understand as we had discussed in training, that there were many ways of looking at stealing. It might be the only way a girl thought she could get things. She might want to identify herself in some way with the worker. It might be the result of some disturbance which the worker could not understand. But she felt strongly about stealing herself and therefore was not sure how to deal with the situation.

I suggested that we should look at the different circumstances in which the group members stole articles. From the records, it became clear that several stole from each other, from the group, from the premises, from the worker, and from the public when they were out. I asked if there was any indication that they were worried about the stealing, as nothing in the records suggested this. The worker said that some seemed to take a great deal of it for granted, but two or three girls seemed worried about stealing from the group and from herself. She said she usually commented when things had disappeared, but that even when she thought she knew who had taken things she did not say so.

I asked if the worker knew how the girls felt about 'possessions' and 'owning things'. She said most of the girls didn't have much chance of having 'possessions'. She had noticed in several homes that they had to share clothes, and even places to put them. Nothing lasted more than a few days, and they were unable to take care of anything. We agreed that this could account for one of the girls' 'attitudes'. The worker said she was already trying to help them take some pride in their club equipment—even in little things like keeping a towel for

273

the washing up instead of using it for cleaning other things. We agreed that 'our club' might be a useful point to start dealing with the problem. We discussed the possibilities of using the next 'incident' as a basis for discussion with the girls, but the worker was doubtful about it.

Subsequent sessions

The question of stealing was brought up by the workers at intervals throughout the year, each time in relation to action which she had taken when something had been stolen. This was explored in terms of the incident, of the girls' attitudes to it, and of the worker's action. The emphasis in the supervision moved from the worker's attitude to stealing to her action and its helpfulness to the girls in each incident.

supervising the supervisor

In the three previous sessions the worker had been discussing the progress of a film making group. This included the planned private showing of specially selected films at the homes of two of the volunteers and at the National Film Theatre. The worker was also beginning to explore the movement of the group towards some sort of agreement on what kind of film to make. The worker was dissatisfied with the help he had got from the supervision sessions, had read back his notes and prepared 'a case' to show where he felt the supervision had gone wrong.

The following is a reconstruction of the supervisor's notes—The worker said he felt I was riding a hobby horse and pressing a private preconception about the need for the young people to verbalise their problems and to develop some kind of terms of reference in which to see themselves, their circumstances and to discuss them. He didn't doubt that this was a real need. He thought it was an important point, but he felt that I had imposed that idea on the film making activity, and in the last four or five supervision sessions had made it look attractive to him and suggested it as one of the aims of the activity. This had put him in the position (perhaps unknowingly) of trying to bring it about, by constantly suggesting or implying that after each film showing the boys should discuss the characters and situations in the film. He felt that he should take this opportunity to help them explore the similarities and differences in their own predicaments in the hope of reaching some sort of self awareness.

Although he felt this was a good idea in principle, it was not working. He felt that I had complicated matters considerably by pressing him to make it happen, or to pretend that it was happening instead of helping him to see how he could use what really was occurring.

He ended by saying he felt much better now that he had "got it all

274

off his chest", but that he wasn't sure where all this had taken us. I said I thought it had taken us a good way in that it certainly would make me take a serious second look at the whole matter, and that since supervision was a two-way affair he had offered me something I hadn't recognised on my own—the awareness that I was imposing on the events, a distorting preconception. I said I thought we might leave the matter for today and I would read through his last 3 or 4 week's records again and try to get back on the right track. We discussed the need for him to show up at the premises as well as the dances with his whole group and discussed how this might affect the other group.

Supervisor's comment

This type of thing happens in supervision of group work either because the supervisor does not have the right information in the right form and proper guidance from the worker in using it (which was not the problem in this case) or because the supervisor lets his own need— to theorise to prove a point, or be one up on the field-worker— distort his proper role. My failing in this situation was caused by my need to bring in a theory which the situation at this point did not warrant. I think the origin of the problem can be found in my being both a consultant to the project and a supervisor to this worker, a conflict in roles. As the consultant I am anxious to propose and test hypotheses but I should not do this in a supervisory situation.

It is important to note that in each illustration the particular action of the supervisor was not specified. This was intentional because the factor which to some extent affected the direction of the discussion was the context in which it took place. An incident in supervision can only be seen in relation to regular supervisory sessions over a period of time. During this time the relationship between the two people develops, and the particular needs of the worker, together with the stage reached in the relationship, are factors which guide the supervisor in his exploration of the problems. Only in looking back at supervisory sessions over a period might it be possible to see how the supervisor uses his experience, knowledge and skills to the ends previously described.

The supervisory session provides the opportunity for a discussion between two people who have the same objective in terms of the work. It allows the minimum involvement in anything not directly concerned with the work (the personal problems of either party). It is job-centred and focussed on the needs of the worker as he sees and presents them. It also allows for the process to be mutually informative and stimulating and therefore builds up the work in all its aspects.

The practice of supervision presents dangers and difficulties. It may provide an opportunity for mutual exploitation and become too intensive and 'soul searching', or an end in itself. Other difficulties are the events in the field, and keeping the session job-centred.

On the other hand the supervisory process at its best can offer an opportunity for both parties to develop as persons in relation to the job. It is an opportunity to learn more about oneself and others, and about the knowledge and skills necessary to do a better job with all the satisfaction that this can provide. It can offer intellectual tools with which to think more clearly about the work, to develop more adequate criteria, to see the whole job in perspective and to see the enterprise in terms of the larger social issues of which it is a part.

Of course, not all of this happened every time for every worker, (nor for the whole team during the project) but supervision offered much of this on a number of occasions and offered all of this as a potential. Supervision then was one of the aspects of training that we used to help make better use of ourselves in relationships with the young people.

Staff conferences

Training, recording and supervision could be called efforts to achieve the self knowledge and self discipline necessary to doing the task. The practical focus of the work was the staff conference, the situation in which we and our resources were developed, and allocated. It was the point at which the decisions and choices that shaped the nature and content of our work were made.

At first the staff conference tended to handle too much. It became overweighted, ill-defined, and drawn out (at one point a whole day from 9 a.m. to 5 p.m. was necessary). But as we slowly came to a better understanding of training and supervision, how case conferences about a particular boy or girl could be used to take some of the burden, and how some matters could easily be settled by smaller informal meetings which reported back, we made the staff conference the principal business meeting of the week, concerned solely with the planning and administration of the programme. Staff conferences were held weekly throughout the three years of field-work. Occasionally a project committee member was present, and sometimes officials directly related to the work in the field, or youth work colleagues interested in similar problems joined the meeting. It was held mid-week. Our working week was from Wednesday to Wednesday with the weekend, the most eventful period, occurring mid-week.

A staff conference

The following notes are from a staff meeting concerned mainly with holiday plans.

276

Staff conference notes

Present Jumbo, Peter, Susan, Marian, Gerry, John (student), George (Consultant), Joan (Administrator).

We recalled that we had decided to devote some of the time to a discussion of holidays before receiving reports.

Discussion One Peter said he was feeling more and more pressed by preparing a holiday for his group. He thought the detail of tickets, car transport across the channel, accommodation at Jersey, was completed, but this was nothing compared with the problem of helping the boys find the rest of the money. He wanted two things, first to know exactly how much money the Y.W.C.A. would give towards the holiday, and secondly more time to work out how to get the boys to participate in the plans. He felt recording, supervision, and training should all be suspended for the time being in order to catch up, since other programmes had to be kept going meanwhile, and there just wasn't enough time. After a good deal of discussion it was agreed that each worker would judge for himself what had to be dropped so long as a note was filed listing the date for which the records were missing, and that supervision was cancelled in advance. Training should be spontaneous discussion for anyone who wished to attend for the rest of May and all of June. Susan said that the holiday work might require added clerical work and thought that if recording, supervision and training were slowed up a bit, it should be possible to make clerical help available for the letter-writing and arrangements.

Joan referred to the earlier comment about finance and suggested that complete budgets should be provided as quickly as possible. We were obviously going to need more money than we had anticipated, and it was now a question of workers reporting their needs rather than being told how much they could have. Peter said that he had estimated the basic needs, but he knew that one or two boys could not provide all they had promised for their own keep, and there might be pocket-money problems and emergencies. Marian said the girls had saved up most of their contribution, and she hoped a large donation would be forthcoming for the rest. If so her allocation from the Y.W.C.A. could be transferred to another group. Susan said she thought that everyone should be allowed an extra £10 for emergencies. Joan said she thought money might be available from the magistrate's court or from a trust for those with particular needs. After discussion it was agreed that each worker should prepare a complete holiday budget before the next meeting, giving reasons for any extra demands, and that the money would be found from one source or another.

Discussion Two Gerry said he felt that although the holidays were important and most of the young people were very interested in them, we could be thinking about holidays in the wrong way. We seemed to be working up an almost artificial atmosphere about them. Instead of offering to help the young people to use the existing facilities including the commercial travel agencies, we were making contacts for them on

T

our own, which the young people might not be willing or able to use when we left. He added that he was planning in the same way as every one else but he still thought we might be using the wrong approach. After a good deal of discussion it was agreed that although we were doing some pushing, the young people really wanted to go on holiday. The various groups had after all chosen holiday locations and were doing quite a lot of the preparation with passports, clothes, tickets etc. It might be best to give them this experience and then worry about how much they had learned for future use and later on we could encourage smaller parties and shorter trips purely on a 'do it yourself' basis. George suggested we take this up again at a training session and work out how the holidays might be used as a basis for passing on social skills.

Discussion Three Marian said she felt we needed to give special attention to our policy about mixed groups on holiday. Joan said that we had agreed after previous camping experiences that it would be unwise to have mixed holiday groups. At this point Gerry said the whole thing should be seen in the light of what he had been saying. Because we had involved ourselves so deeply in the holiday idea, we had now made ourselves responsible for 'enforcing' a no mixed groups decree, whereas if we had just let things happen and simply offered ourselves as resource persons about holiday arrangements, they would have worked the whole thing out on their own, including what they would do about mixed groups. We agreed that this might be so, and also that nothing might have been worked out at all. Even so we were setting up standards that we knew were not those of the young people. George agreed but pointed out that we still had to consider our mandate from the larger society; we could see that this might be the wrong way of handling the matter, but the parents, project committee, and other agencies might not. We had to balance our own view against the fact that we were to all intents and purposes a social agency in that community. All we could hope to do at this point was to offer the opportunity for separate holidays for boys and girls and hope that the young people enjoyed them, wanted to arrange more, learned how to do so, and then planned holidays themselves when and how they wished.

Marian said she wasn't interested in all this. She wanted to know what to do if boys turned up (in France) where she was taking her girls to a work camp. She and the girls had agreed that they wanted to go on their own but the boys objected. Some of them might be planning to go to France "just to keep an eye on things over there". Peter said he thought it would be very good if the boys did manage to get to France. He was certain they would never have tried it on their own but now they would have a definite objective and people whom they knew at the other end, and they would reason that if the girls could do it, they could. Marian said this was very interesting but she was unimpressed, since it was very important that the girls should have this time out of the neighbourhood without having to cope with the boys, especially since the two or three boys likely to go would be those most likely to cause difficulties. We suggested that Marian should explain all this to the camp authorities when she arrived and leave it all to them, being prepared to 'stay neutral' if the boys arrived, and working with boys and girls together if the boys were allowed to stay. We considered writing ahead to the French camp authorities but agreed not to do so and decided to give special attention later to the two or three boys who were most likely to go to France and to try to create diversions.

Discussion Four Gerry said that two of the boys who needed most to go with the group were being 'disciplined' by the boys themselves who were saying "you can't come with us, you're sure to muck things up". Gerry didn't think this was strictly true, since one boy in question, Mac, although a hell raiser in the neighbourhood, tended to quieten down considerably in strange circumstances and behaved reasonably well in the West End. He said he didn't know how long it would take Mac to settle in on holiday and feel he could risk a bust-up, but he thought the group should be encouraged to accept the boy and take him along. The second case was more serious since the boy, Red, was almost certain to be difficult, but Gerry felt he too should go and not be rejected once more. Gerry felt the group was being very tough on both of them. After some discussion it was agreed that Gerry should take the problem to supervision, but he felt that although the case of Mac could be explored in supervision, that of Red was certain to be more difficult and required a case conference. Several of the workers were in frequent contact with Red, but it was more than ten weeks since the probation officer had been contacted about him. It was agreed that there should be a case conference on the following Wednesday and that all the workers who knew Red would bring their records. The probation officer would be invited. Jumbo said that the probation officer was most important in this case and that if he couldn't come someone should visit him and report back to the case conference. Agreed.

The next item was concerned with the need to provide adequate coverage in the neighbourhood and on the coffee stall during the holidays, in order to provide programme for those who stayed at home. Jumbo undertook to man the stall throughout this period. The rest of the staff said that at the next meeting, details would be given of the particular individuals and groups who would require help.

Reports

John described his evenings in the coffee bar and the outing to the West End with a small group in the dormobile. They had all brought friends and were squashed in the vehicle. Joan said that surely the numbers would have to be limited for the safety of everyone. John and Marian both said there was no argument which would convince the boys. George suggested having a second van and driver available in case of a recurrence. Everyone agreed to think of alternatives and to

279

be prepared for all eventualities as plans for a trip were started.

Jumbo reported on coffee stall contacts for the weeks and the grapevine news. He had heard comments on Gerry and the premises, on Marian and the girls and about various changes of girlfriends. He had heard that Frank had left his job again and suggested a separate conference to discuss Frank's future. Jimmy had been put on probation. Mac was going to court on Wednesday. Kim had asked for a guarantee for his new suit. Alan had at last left for the Merchant Navy. A small group had arrived for dinner on Sunday, and Tommy and Shorty had asked for a bed as they said they had been turned out. They had said that would stay in the premises if they couldn't find accommodation. After discussion and decisions for action on some of these problems, the week ahead was planned.

Plans for the week

Susan required the dormobile for the Saturday afternoon to take her group swimming. She planned several home visits and would take Jean to school for several mornings. She would meet the girls at the premises on Wednesday, and hoped to see the probation officer to discuss Angela. Marian would drive Peter and the younger boys the following night. She would spend Sunday, Monday and Wednesday in the premises with Gerry, would meet the girls on Tuesday, and hoped to take three couples to the theatre on Friday evening. Gerry would be in the premises on Friday, Sunday, Monday and Wednesday. He would suggest a trip on Sunday afternoon. They had mentioned the airport several times. John agreed to go along if needed. Peter would meet the boys to discuss holidays whenever possible. He would help on the stall on Wednesday and Thursday. He hoped to spend an evening on the stall on Wednesday and Thursday. He hoped to spend an evening in the pub with Arthur and Kevin. John would help Gerry on Friday and Sunday, help on the stall on Tuesday, and spend Monday and Wednesday in the coffee bar the younger boys were using. Jumbo would spend his evenings on the stall and sort out some of the problems of individual boys with employers, probation officers and court.

It was agreed that budgets should be discussed individually before the next meeting which would include discussions on:

1. Holiday expenditure.

2. Details of coverage during holiday period.

3. A more extended report on Susan's work with the probation group.

4. The policy on using the dormobile as our rules were unrealistic to the boys, and it was necessary to find some way of meeting the unpredictable demands.

5. The post-holiday period.

As the conference closed, charts showing the whereabouts of staff were filled in, records and expense slips handed in, and supervision and conference times checked.

The use of staff conferences

This account is fairly typical of staff conferences, except that they usually included details and discussion of field-work events from the previous week.

The uses of the staff conference included:

1. Sharing information—keeping each other informed about individuals, groups, and events within and without the project.

2. Co-ordination—arranging work schedules, clarifying individual field-work responsibilities, ensuring adequate coverage for people, places and activities.

3. Allocation of resources—deciding on the use of money, and equipment, etc., balancing different needs, considering how to get more.

4. Programme planning—deciding what activities to sponsor, initiate, or participate in, and how to do so.

5. Decision making—exploring the choices and decisions to be made, so as to arrive at a team agreement and still leave the responsibility to the individual worker.

6. Evaluation—discussing all aspects of work, bringing into the open reservations about what was happening, so that the whole team could consider changing the approach and method and come to an agreement about some of the essentials.

In all these ways, the staff conference helped workers to be responsible for their individual tasks, and at the same time helped us to operate as a team.

The staff were more of a co-operative than an 'administered or managed' group. The roles were well defined although they had to be rethought out on several occasions. The administrator and consultant were not there to plan the programme or impose rules, but to help in the evaluation of field-work events, to suggest possible solutions, to help carry out agreed decisions, and interpret to and negotiate with the management committee. All this of course took a good deal more give and take than most of us were at first prepared for. But as the parallel became clear between the method of work of the staff and the nature of the work in the field, our ability and willingness to cope became more evident.

Perhaps the biggest drawback to this way of working was that it asked too much of the field staff in terms of time and responsibility.

But it was generally accepted by the staff and project committee that the opportunities it gave for the field staff to work out problems that might otherwise have been the sole prerogative or responsibility of administrator, consultant and/or project committee, produced a type of training directly related to field-work practice which more than compensated for its drawbacks.

23. Social education

We thought it necessary to divide the discussion of approach and method into work areas (individuals, groups, ourselves, the community) to indicate the different levels at which the programme needed to operate, and the particular processes and procedures we saw as appropriate to each level. But the apparent segmentation that results tends to obscure the common elements that underline the approach.

Common elements

The work was based on the following prerequisites:

1. That the provision of opportunities for the social development of the young people was the purpose of the work.

2. That the social development of individuals could be facilitated in a variety of settings, and involved the interplay of individuals, groups and the community.

3. That the natural events in the field were indicative of the kind and conditions of help required, (in respect both of the young people and the community), and could be used as material for the programme.

4. That the programme was a means of encounter between the young people, ourselves and the statutory and voluntary bodies, and should aim at a reconciliation of conflicting expectations.

5. That the community was a factor in the definition of the problem, the focus of solution, the location of the effort, and the provider of the necessary resources. It was responsible in that its problems with the unattached were the concern of the youth-serving agencies on the one hand, and the origin of their mandate on the other.

6. That the workers were primarily resource persons in their relationships with individuals, with groups and agencies, in helping to provide opportunity for social development and for encounter between the several parties. There were certain factors common to all areas of their work—objectively, non-judgmental attitudes, the offering of practical information, guidance, support and social skills and the reciprocal influence between worker/individual, worker/group, and worker/community.

An educational process

Taken together these common elements indicate our approach and method of contacting and working with the unattached. It is a variation on the 'accepted' school-centred use of the educational process as described in Ottoway's discussion of "the scope of education" on pages 3-7 in *Education and Society*. (See selected bibiliography). This covers what have perhaps become the essential elements in any 'definition' of the educational process:

1. Education is providing opportunities for personal growth and development (personality) and as preparation for membership in society.

2. Education as an 'activity' facilitating the above, either formally by the subject matter taught, or informally by 'out-of-class' activities.

3. The role of a teacher in teaching the subject matter and in offering informal opportunities for out-of-class activities, as well as in facilitating relationships between himself and the students and between students, individually and in groups.

4. The educational tools and techniques used in attempting to fulfil these objectives.

5. The setting—the classroom, the school, the neighbourhood, the community and the larger society as 'conditioning' the whole process.

It can perhaps be appreciated that the educational process as here described, when adapted to needs of field-work with the unattached, is the basis of our discussion. Its adaptation includes the following variations:

a. Its objective is wholly concerned with the social development of the young person.

b. Its content is more immediate and directly taken from the life experience of the recipients (fights and arguments on school, family, friendship and boy/girl problems, etc.). In this way it attempts to recognise and use what the recipient brings to the situation.

c. It differs in form, that is the conditions under which it is offered, the place and the circumstances under which it occurs. All these are more directly related to the needs of the recipients than can naturally be the case in more formal kinds of educational setting.

d. Consequently the role of the person offering the service is modified and he becomes a kind of resource-cum-guidance person, offering a service informally where and when it is necessary, to those who are willing and able to accept it.

e. Similarly, the training required for this person and the administrative set up that supports and helps him, are modified to meet his needs in working in this way. This form of education modifies those aspects of the educational process which are concerned with formal, academic, professional or vocational training, although its basic orientation has much in common with all three. Especially where they are concerned with the personal growth and development of the participants. It appears to us that this adaptation of the accepted educational process, to meet the needs of our particular clients might best be designated as social education. This might be defined as 'that aspect of the educational process that aims at passing on knowledge, understanding or skills to facilitate the social development of individuals by means, in circumstances, and under conditions appropriate to the needs of the recipients'.

Seen in this way Social Education at once suggests (as regards youth work and especially work with the unattached) the objectives of the work, the role of the worker and agency, the most appropriate tools and techniques, and a known and accepted point of reference (the educational process) which together offer an approach and a method.

Chapter Six

IMPLICATIONS

When we started the project we saw the unattached as young people who did not belong to clubs and youth organisations. This was due to traditional ways of thought in the youth service, to our need to see the problem in 'manageable terms', and to other limitations in our earlier thinking.

We supposed the cause of unattachment lay in the background of the young people, in the lack of helpful relationships with parents, relatives and neighbours, which could offer guidance and support and be used as models for relationships with other adults (the teacher, the employer, the youth employment officer). We thought this need could in part be compensated by a relationship with a detached worker. We imagined the unattached to be a single grouping of young people, with approximately the same needs and problems, only a few of whom needed special service. So the primary need seemed to be to develop relationships with them and to help them in the area of recreational opportunities and activities. We aimed to bring the young people and the youth organisations together, although we already recognised that this would mean changes in the services offered. We saw this as requiring primarily know-how and skill in making relationships with individuals and with groups, and hence we saw our in-service training programme as restricted to training in this field.

We saw the probable solution as an extension of the traditional club work programme to enable youth organisations to reach out and accomodate the unattached. We saw the coffee stall, theoretically at least, as a temporary measure that would be needed only pending agreement between the parties concerned. In short we began by seeing a complex situation as a simple two-party relationship (young people and youth organisations) with ourselves attempting to bridge the gap.

As the work developed, we saw the problem of contacting and work-ing with the unattached in much broader terms. We saw unattachment as referring not only to youth clubs or organisations, but to other aspects of the young people's lives (to work, to school, to the youth employment office).

Although we continued to see the breakdown in relationships in the personal background of the unattached as one factor in their un-attachment, we saw the solution as requiring much more than simply 'contact and relationship' with a detached worker. We saw a complex of groupings, each changing and interrelated, the 'can copes', the 'temporary disorganised', the 'simply disorganised', and the 'seriously disorganised'. Each had different needs, different problems, requiring different kinds of help, offered in different settings. We realised that the whole range of young people needed, and could use, various types of youth work service, and would accept them if the conditions and setting were appropriate.

We saw recreational needs as only part of a much more complicated set of needs, and consequently broadened our idea of the kinds of agencies that needed to be brought together. Not only should the youth organisations be involved, but also the statutory and voluntary bodies in other spheres of work with youth. We saw that to work with the unattached required not only skills in working with individuals and groups but also skills in working with the community, both in a network of statutory and voluntary bodies and in a network of autonomous groups and indigenous leaders.

Instead of seeing the probable solutions simply as an extension of the youth service pattern, and in specialised training in detached work for the club leader, we came to see the need for community wide programming, with a variety of specialised training available in the field of youth work. We saw the coffee stall as one of a wide variety of settings, commercial, formal and informal, which were needed in the youth service. In short, we moved from the young person/organisation description of the problem to a more complex young person/community description.

24. If we had continued

We shall therefore begin by describing what the implications might have been for us if we had continued the project indefinitely. The following is a list of items which we would probably have included in the future development of the programme. We present them here to indicate the direction we feel the whole programme might have taken. Some items had already been started when the project ended, others were later developed by local groups. Some might well have been abandoned if events in the field indicated their irrelevance.

ITEM 1. *Continued co-operation with the local youth club.* (See termination in Sequence of Events.)

ITEM 2. *An informal youth centre* with facilities for a wide range of activities and an informed atmosphere, to which detached workers could bring small groups, or which groups and individuals could visit casually without commitment.

ITEM 3. *A youth information centre*, designed especially to meet the needs of young people. This could be a department of the Citizens' Advice Bureau, but its approach and location would need to be different. It might be in a disused shop, or in the open youth centre. It could open on some evenings in the neighbourhood hostel (see item 2) and on others in coffee bars. The worker would have to be able to make contact with young people, and be familiar with the other facilities which he could use. He would have to be prepared to give information without receiving any at first, and if necessary to go with a young person to other agencies and support him until contact could be made.

ITEM 4. *Youth work in a commercial setting.* It might be advisable to work out with the managers of dance halls (or other commercial enterprises) a programme of work with young people in that setting. Fashion shows, holiday planning, employment and educational opportunities could easily be offered within such establishments without interfering with the spontaneity and enjoyment. Small booths might well be set up in the entrance or in the corner of the lounge, or hall, and a separate room provided by the management for private consultations. Detached workers might be regulars at the dance hall, meeting young people inside and outside. The dance hall would be within the youth-serving network, and the manager and his staff would need to be helped to see how they could offer this added service, by allowing workers to join in and by occasional conferences to plan special events. Doormen and other staff might be offered the opportunity to join local youth training courses. The statutory and voluntary bodies might also need help in understanding that on occasion money might be more usefully spent in the commercial setting, than in trying to create new formal youth clubs.

ITEM 5. *More Adventures Unlimited.* We ought to find ways of helping organisations such as Adventures Unlimited to extend their work in offering weekend and holiday opportunities for adventurous expeditions.

ITEM 6. *Special Clubs.* Numerous special clubs might well be started, examples of which are:

a. A club to help boys who are apprentices to 'stick it out'.

b. Special interest clubs for the older boy and girl who no longer wish to be with their younger associates but who would prefer more 'adult' pursuits.

c. Remedial Reading. We might find out if groups would use facilities for remedial reading if these were provided. These clubs might be the responsibility of volunteers, and might meet anywhere by pre-arrangement with the group.

ITEM 7. *A Detached Arts programme.* A detached arts programme might be offered in a form acceptable to the young people. Participation in one of the arts might help to balance comparatively low verbal ability, most often environmental rather than innate, by offering non-verbal means of expression. The serious lack in this community of contact with the arts, the partial success of our National Film Theatre programme, the indication of interest in our film making venture, the idea that the arts, especially cinema, theatre and the dance can be a link with life outside the community, also indicate a need for this kind of programme.

Questions: Could approval and support be found for this aspect of the work? Could the singing in local public houses, the talent contest in the local dance halls and the popularity of cinema going, be seen as 'natural events' that could provide opportunities for this type of work? What is happening in the local schools, in respect of art, that could be followed up outside the school setting?

ITEM 8. *A guidance counsellor in a local school.* A guidance counsellor in a local school could pick up the boy (or girl) who was having difficulty, and attempt to work with him in the school setting, using the resources of the school, and also those of the formal and informal agencies in the community. This seems necessary because many boys fail to take advantage of the various schools services. Although they often resent school and school authorities, they sometimes find after leaving that the advice they got at school is relevant, and with encouragement would return for more if someone were available to take them on informally. In other instances it would be helpful to have someone from the school who would meet boys informally outside and continue the guidance and support that he started before they left. It would help the project if someone from inside the school setting were taking part in youth work outside, as this would provide a closer tie between the school and the other youth-serving agencies.

Questions: How would the local headmaster react to this suggestion and how would his teachers react? Do the teachers and headmasters feel that this is part of their job, or do they see it as requiring a specialist, full-time and trained, who would work with difficult boys inside the school and 'follow' them out into the community? Who in the community would join us in getting together with the local school authorities to think this out, parent/teachers' associations? mental health workers? probation officers? youth clubs? Could we suggest a five year experiment of this kind in a local school? What kind of person would be needed, what would he do, how would he do it?

How would the experiment be financed?—Could the school guidance counsellor be related to the open youth centre, the neighbourhood hostel, the youth service unit? (see following items).

ITEM 9. *Appointment of a special youth employment officer.* A special youth employment officer might work with the socially handicapped, that is, the hard core of difficult employment cases. He could cover several youth employment offices and also work in formal and informal youth work settings.

This is necessary because the socially handicapped boy often needs prolonged guidance and support which the local officers cannot be expected to offer, since it takes time and attention away from the demands of the regular service. It also requires additional skills and therefore specialised training. It would need to be recognised that part of the officer's job would be to 'make contact with the young person where he is', that is, outside the formal youth work setting.

Questions: Would the youth employment officers who made this suggestion be prepared to think it out more completely? How exactly do they see the problems of these boys? What kind of training would be necessary and where could it be found? What kind of person would be required with what background and experience? How could this idea best be introduced to those within the youth employment service who could do something about it? Could an experiment be designed to explore this idea for a few years, highlight its potentials and limitations, and demonstrate whether or not it could be effective in helping the socially handicapped with job placement and work adjustment? Would a small committee of experts be helpful to discuss the terms of reference, and set the criteria for evaluation? What kinds of experts should be consulted? Who should be approached first? Could the employment officer for the socially handicapped be related to the hostel, the open youth centre, the sheltered workshop, why, how? (see following items).

ITEM 10. *A sheltered workshop for 'seriously disorganised' boys.* This would enable boys to develop work-tolerance, learn something about work routine and especially about getting on with workmates, the foreman and the manager in a specially designed work setting. It could be run by a manager with some industrial skills and some youth work experience and have available the services of a special youth employment officer. It would offer jobs, perhaps farmed out from local firms, and possibly training in some simple work skills, but this would be incidental to its main objective of offering the socially handicapped an opportunity in a 'sheltered' work setting, to make an adjustment to work.

Something of this kind is necessary for boys who have been 'job hopping' for so long that they cannot adjust to work and often resent their inability to do so, becoming aggressive or despondent and discouraged. It would also provide the special employment officer with a practical base from which to work out some of the hard core employment problems.

Questions: How are other sheltered workshops set up (for the physically and mentally handicapped?) What are their problems? How are they administered? How did they get started? Who would be interested in sponsoring this effort? Who should be contacted first, the local education authority, the ministry of labour? What kind of manager is needed? What experience and training should he have had? What exactly would his job be? What kinds of work could we offer the young people? Could a study group be started to discuss this suggestion? Who should be included?

ITEM 11. *A community employment council.* Some of the local commercial associations, or business men's clubs might be encouraged to form a community employment council that could see the need for offering jobs to 'problem boys'. Some of these would be known to the special employment officer, and some to the sheltered workshop manager. The council could be used as a way of interesting local small industry in the needs of these boys. Employers might be found who would take a special interest in a boy and in his work adjustment. The manager of the sheltered workshop and the special employment officer would be available to help the employer to help the boy.

The local youth employment officer cannot be expected to give the best jobs to the 'worst boys'. Obviously this would endanger his contact with employers, and might reduce his chance of placing with that employer again. He therefore needs employers who are interested in providing opportunities for 'problem' boys. A council of this type would also help the manager of the sheltered workshop who would want for his boys, placements where he could keep up his contact and help.

ITEM 12. *A neighbourhood hostel.* (See termination in Sequence of Events.)

ITEM 13. *A Youth Service Unit.* A Youth Service Unit might be set up as part of a Family Service Unit, modelled on it or connected with it. Its sole concern would be the hardcore of the unattached, that is, the 'seriously disorganised'. It would have to be locally based and casework oriented, although it might also run group activities for its clients. It would be a multi-purpose service (as is F.S.U.) in that school, employment, family, boy/girl and probation problems would be within its purview. Its job would be to contribute to the rehabilitation of hardcore cases in any way it could. It would be a part of the community wide programme in that some or all of its staff would be available to the programme in the field. It might have at least one worker whose full responsibility lay in working in the community. It might have a front lounge always open for young people.

This is necessary for the same reasons that the special youth employment officer is thought to be necessary, namely that the school, the youth employment office, the local hospital or the family casework agencies, cannot offer the intensive kind of help that is necessary, at the time and place or on the conditions that are required. Prolonged guidance and support perhaps of a casework nature, perhaps including psychiatric help should be especially designed to meet the needs of these young people.

The unit might use a special employment officer, the sheltered workshop and the neighbourhood hostel. Its workers, by circulating within the network might become known and accepted as 'people who would help', by the young people in the open youth centre, the youth clubs and the rest of the programme.

ITEM 14. *Supportive work with groups on probation.* The work with a group of girls on probation has indicated that this might be extended to include more groups of girls and of boys. It might be possible to test further the value of such group work by appointing several workers for a period of two to three years, or alternatively by appointing several part-time workers or volunteers to lead groups with the supervision of one highly skilled worker. Could we together with the probation officers persuade the Home Office to support an experiment on a larger scale? Would the youth service or the local council of social service see this as within their terms of reference?

ITEM 15. *A committee for girls' work* (already started). This is important because traditionally the main concern in youth work has been for boys and provision for them is still much better than for girls. Although most of the items listed are intended for both boys and girls, as we would advocate mixed ventures as far as possible. Such a committee would need to consider the possibilities of a 'neighbourhood hostel' for girls, and also the points at which girls needed more specialised help.

ITEM 16. *Detached psychiatric help.* Discussion should be opened with psychiatrists and psychiatric social workers to find out under what conditions some help, even of the most rudimentary kind, could be offered informally, that is outside the usual office and institutional setting. This would be for young people who had just begun to see that they might need this help but who were unwilling or unable to take it in the traditional setting. Perhaps the psychiatric social worker could, like the general practitioner, the visiting nurse, and the peripatetic teacher offer help where and when needed. This would require finding the point of contact within the network convenient to the worker offering the service, and as unthreatening as possible to the young person receiving it.

ITEM 17. *Contact and work with indigenous leaders and autonomous groups.* One area of contact between the young people and the community exists within the 'unofficial network', for example within the commercial services—the café, the public house, fish and chip shop, and dance-halls. It might include autonomous groups such as housing estate tenants' associations. Some way should be found of including the unofficial network or parts of it in the programme. This would be a difficult task and would take a good deal of time and effort. Contacting and working with indigenous leaders and autonomous groups is like contacting unattached young people. It requires a similar approach and has a similar objective, that is, to pass on to the indigenous leaders the know-how and skills to be more effective in what they are already doing, and to offer them resources from the network.

ITEM 18. *Introducing neighbours.* Even though communities like our own provide indigenous leadership, whose contribution to this kind of work is invaluable, they cannot always offer the necessary link with the world outside the neighbourhood. Young professional families might offer this if they lived in the community and were willing to help. We might try to find a few flats in one corner of the neighbourhood, and acquire money to offer them, rent free for five years, to young families who would be willing to enter into the informal youth work network, and simply be 'good neighbours'. The Society of Friends might be asked to take part. Four or five of these families could meet regularly to decide what contributions they could make. They would be neighbours whose values and standards, ideas, ideals and ways of behaviour were a link with the world outside the community. They would perhaps be especially valuable in work with the girls. Their homes might be available for small meetings and serve as natural points of contact within the informal network. These families would need advice and guidance in how to be most useful and would have to be helped to avoid certain 'good neighbour' attitudes.

ITEM 19. *A model flat for the 'just marrieds'.* Something might be done to help those 'going steady' and the newly married. A model flat, well planned, well decorated, might be made available in the community. A male and female worker might spend an evening a week with a special group, offering advice, guidance and help about things relevant to this stage in their lives. Volunteers could be there on other evenings, offering some opportunities for entertainment. Sometimes a boy is 'abandoned' by his mates when he is going steady, intending to marry or just married. Often he and his girl friend want to be separate from the 'old gang'. This sometimes results in their being isolated for a time just when they are facing new problems with which they need help. If the girl's mother or older sister is not helpful, this is a difficult period for her. The boy might want to change jobs now that he is getting married and could use advice. The girl might now be ready to talk about 'homemaking' in which she was not interested before. In such a setting, she would probably be more ready to seek advice and help and to participate. Above all human relations would need the most attention, since both the boy and girl would now be learning to get on together in an entirely different way. Small groups of young people meeting in the flat might be helped to work out relationship problems. This could easily involve the young professional families mentioned above (item 18).

ITEM 20. *A committee of concern* might be established as a formal link between the various aspects of the work. Its main job would be to keep the whole network of youth work provision interacting, and help it to adapt to the changing patterns of adolescent need and the availability of community resources. It would keep the channels of communication open between the various groups and would keep the whole programme in contact with the other community services (education, health etc.).

The very essence of the developments suggested here demand a broadly based co-operate effort among a large section of the youth-serving elements in the community (formal and informal). Certainly we could never have accomplished this programme on our own, even if the community had allowed us to attempt it. The problem is too largely concerned with the operation of other agencies to be the prerogative of a single one of them. In these circumstances we should have hoped to interest the local youth committee or the council of social service in taking over the programme and eventually running it as a community-wide effort.

Many of the twenty items listed above as possible for the development of our programme had we continued in the field, might well be both appropriate and practicable in other circumstances. The point here is that when taken together, no single agency could have attempted, much less accomplished them.

If we had not been able to interest the local youth committee or council of social service in taking over such a programme, we should probably have tried to form a committee of concern to whom we could eventually have transferred the work.

The situation where the local Youth Committee would be the proper body for such an enterprise is discussed later in Chapter Six.

25. *The first perspective—the local community*

We have emphasised the importance of the local community as the origin of the problem and of its solution and as part of the content of the programme as well as the provider of resources and the origin of the mandate. This line of thought makes the local community the focus of the enterprise. We have attempted to outline below the implication of this for others in the field. We asked ourselves what we would have done if, instead of continuing in the field as assumed in the 'projected programme' above, we had been beginning again, with the experience and findings of our previous field-work already as it were in 'our pockets'.

If a community-wide programme of youth work provision is required, it follows that no single agency could provide the programme on its own. Even if (which is very unlikely) it had the necessary resources it would scarcely be able to engender the community-wide co-operation necessary to its accomplishment. For these reasons it seems to us that an attempt should be made in the local community setting, to induce the widest variety of agencies concerned to come together for discussion and joint planning and to create the administrative machinery to carry out these joint decisions.

The most obvious group of people for this purpose would seem to be the local youth committee. The question as we see it, is how could the local youth committee become the point of origin for wider concern, and the setting for planning, organising and providing the programme and service?

Perhaps the central question becomes: How can an extension of the local youth committee be undertaken? How can the committee be reorganised to enable it to take on this task? What changes in form and function are necessary? How can they be brought about and by whom? How should it be done? Surely the original enabling circular (1486, 27 November, 1939) is open to the interpretation necessary to this task. We suggest that an enquiry into the working of several local youth committees in several different areas be undertaken to collect the background information necessary to test the relevance of this suggestion. What are the youth serving problems of these communities? What do the young people think them to be? What do the agencies think them to be? How are other elements in the community concerned? What is the function of the local youth committee? What could the function be? Why?

A five-phased programme

1. The recognition of unattachment.
2. The need for experimental contact.
3. The clarification of unattachment.
4. The need for community-wide planning.
5. Evaluation and continuing change.

In suggesting five phases for developing a programme to meet the needs of the unattached, we assume that the local youth committee has already considered the matter and agreed to attempt to provide a community-wide programme for them. We also assume that the local youth officer will be the key figure in 'getting the ball off the ground'.

Phase 1: the recognition of unattachment

It is basic to the work to help the community to formulate its concern in terms that are understandable and acceptable, and to make clear the necessity for action. We assume that there is already some feeling, however vague, in the community that the unattached 'are a problem', or 'need help'. It is of great importance at this stage that the youth officer should begin to collect information from those who have noted the presence of the unattached in the community (neighbours, shopkeepers, the police, the local press, the formal youth work agencies, the other social services, the schools, etc.). What are the estimated numbers of unattached? Why is unattachment a problem? What is its cause? What 'type' of young person is reported as being unattached? How do the unattached behave individually and in groups? What are the needs of the unattached? Where did the information come from? On what evidence are the facts, figures and opinions based? This information (gathered by way of interviews, group discussions, questionnaires, correspondence, etc.) will need to be included in a preliminary report for the youth committee, and used as the basis for the second step, that of gathering information from and about other areas of the community where the problem has not been noticed or is thought definitely not to exist. Finally, information should be gathered about the same problem in other communities. This last need not be too detailed or difficult. Other local youth committees or professional associations, national or regional voluntary bodies will doubtless be helpful. This first phase should produce some idea of the problem as seen by adults in the community, together with their reasons for concern. It is important to know who is most deeply concerned with the problem in a community. Obviously, if it is the police on one hand, or the youth clubs on the other, this will very much affect how the problem is defined, what solutions are suggested and expected and what resources are available. The numbers considered to be unattached will also affect the cost of any possible programme and the size and scope of the operation. This phase can be used to help people and agencies to get to know one another and to begin the process of inter-action, which it is hoped will result in co-operation, if and when a definite programme is agreed upon and its implementation begins.

Phase 2: the need for experimental contact

The opening of phase 2 will be for the most part concerned with helping the adults to appreciate that the information collected in phase 1 above does not include the ideas, opinions and needs of the young people, and also in deciding how best these can be obtained by youth workers in direct contact with the unattached.

In our opinion it would be inadvisable to begin field-work with less than two workers, perhaps a man and a woman worker. We strongly recommend that no conditions be laid down as to what they are to do for the first six months, except to try to make contact, to observe the conditions in the field and to record their experiences. A small committee might also be provided, of people willing and able to advise and support the workers, not to give preconceived ideas and plans but simply to help work out the problems of the field-workers as and when they (the field-workers) need help. It might be remembered that those most concerned with the problem in a particular community are not always the right people for the committee of support. They should of course be part of the wider setting in which the work takes place and will be more directly involved once solutions are suggested and the planning of the service begins.

The first six months or so of field-work will most probably be concerned with learning about the unattached from direct contact with them. Where do they congregate? What do they do? What do they say are their needs? Which community agencies do they use? Which do they avoid and why? What do they expect of the worker? It is more than probable that, after some weeks or months of contact, the workers will be 'asked for something'—advice, guidance, jobs, money, or to join in on a trip or an outing. Two things are important at this point. Firstly, that the worker should have resources to use as the occasion arises (a day late might mean that the contact is broken). And secondly, that the worker, the committee of support, the youth committee, and especially the young people themselves, should be helped to appreciate that the service offered at this point, is temporary. It is always a temptation to see the first crop of needs that arise in the field as the 'real needs' and to begin to organise a full scale service around them before the more complete picture is available. The first series of job requests, of recreational needs, sports, holidays, etc., and of school problems, can all too easily be a convenient peg on which to hang the whole enterprise. It is important to keep going, broadening the base of contact, widening the kind of services offered, and deepening the individual and group contacts, before attempting to define the problem and propose the solution.

By the end of the second phase, perhaps a year's 'reconnaisance' in the field, it should be possible to compare the information that emerged from the first phase with the information from the young people and the workers in the field.

Phase 3: the clarification of unattachment

It should now be possible to formulate some kind of working hypothesis about unattachment in the community, that will at once suggest the nature and content of the problem, the kind of solution required, and the resources available. In attempting this it is important to involve commercial interest, autonomous groups and any other concerned adults who have not previously been approached. If they, and the resources they represent are not involved at this stage, they might well not be available later, as part of the programme. A difficulty in formulating the problem and its solution might well be that the power and status systems operative within and between the various agencies, community groups, and professional orientations, as well as the traditions of service and the established categories of financial allocation, will all tend to influence the definition of the problem and the kind of solution suggested, often inordinately. Yet it is the task of the committee to explore these pressures, many of which are legitimate, and to work out their implications as far as possible in terms of its own information about the needs of the unattached. It is in the process of doing this (conflict, compromise, accommodation, etc.) that the roots of community-wide programming are based.

The working definition necessary of the task will have to suggest the kind of service necessary, which of the related parties will be involved, and what it will cost; it also needs to be tentative so as to allow events in the field as they emerge from daily contacts with the unattached, to suggest the content of the programme, the time, the place, and the conditions of service as well as the methods of work.

Phase 4: planning and implementing

The fourth phase of the work will no doubt be planning and implementing a programme of service. After a year's work in the field, it will probably have been realised that a variety of things need to be done in order to broaden the contacts of the unattached and provide the necessary services. Something may need to be done about clubs and club work. Something about providing an open youth centre, something about employment, advice, personal counselling, recreational opportunities, or holidays abroad. It is essential to be definite about specific needs, to design specific programmes to meet them, and to encourage the relevant parties to take well-defined action and responsibility for each of the new services. They also need to understand their action in relation to the overall agreed upon plan for provision.

All the planning and action requires joint consultation and co-ordination. Each step in the provision of service can be used to create and strengthen the appropriate administrative machinery and to enhance the atmosphere of co-operation. Information about the work, its successes and failures, should be flowing back into the committee to be shared and used as further material for joint thinking and action. This work will require a new approach to the allocation of resources (e.g. grants) which should allow the committee to 'put teeth' into its effort to implement co-ordination and set standards of service. The joint budgeting of community resources in respect of youth work is the ultimate test of the success of this way of working, for on it depends the nature, content and availability of services to the young people.

Care must also be taken to work towards breaking down the barrier between the 'attached' and the 'unattached' services. However successful a programme of this type may be in contacting and working with the unattached, if it simply creates by providing special services, a second category of youth work—work with the unattached—it is in part at least a failure. It is true that the initial stages are geared towards work with the unattached, but the overall objective should be a community-wide pattern of youth work provision that does not need to discriminate between attached and unattached, simply because the services that will be provided will be acceptable to different types of young people and available to all young people who need them.

Phase 5: evaluation and continuing change

The last phase in the operation should be the evaluation of work. This has been a part of each phase, but now it becomes a kind of 'overall' stocktaking at the end of several years. The evaluation should include some of the following questions. What has been the impact of the whole enterprise on the original problem (contacting and working with the unattached)? How many have been contacted? How many have participated? What was done, by whom? For whom? For what reasons? At what cost? With what results? What changes have taken place in the pattern of relationships between the unattached young people and the various youth work services—within and between the services themselves—between the formal services and informal community groups—between all of these and the larger community? What strengthening is there of community consensus about youth problems and youth work? What evidence of improvement in community-wide co-operation?

All of this is important because after five or more years of work with the unattached, the problem will probably no longer be a pressing one in the community, but something else will have arisen that needs attention—work with the under twelves or work with the newly-weds. If the attempts to contact and work with the unattached have been successful the community will already have the necessary administrative machinery, the channels of communication, and most important of all, the experience of thinking and working together that will facilitate work on any new concern suggested by the evaluation. This is only the barest outline, yet we believe that together with the material in *The Problems of Field Work*, and the description of our experience as developed in *The Sequence of Events* it should be possible for the youth committee and officer to appreciate the implications of our experience, for others attempting to work in this way.

The role of the youth committee and the youth officer

The role of the local youth committee depicted here is clearly different from the usual role, although we see nothing in what we have suggested that goes beyond that body's statutory power (see discussion of the enabling circular 1486 in Conclusions). The role is more nearly that of a planning and implementing body in respect of community-wide youth work provision, and less that of a forum and advisory service for a group of separate youth work agencies. It thus expresses concern for a wider variety of young people and takes responsibility for providing a wider variety of services, some of which might not previously have been seen as within the province of youth work (see 'A Wider Concern' in this section.) The committee has become more widely representative and has included perhaps commercial clubs, café and dance-hall proprietors and representatives of autonomous community groups. It has thus become responsible for providing the setting for the co-ordination and co-operation necessary to community wide programme.

The role of the local youth organiser or officer has changed in that he has become more a community worker attempting community education than an adviser to a collection of separate youth work agencies. He has helped to create the atmosphere for a more broadly based consensus about what is needed and how it can be provided. He is working with informal community groups as well as established statutory and voluntary bodies, and in consequence, he needs fresh kinds of knowledge and skill. A wider variety of skills in the field of youth work will therefore have to be available.

26. The second perspective—the youth service

The second perspective to be considered is that of the state or condition of contemporary youth work. There appears to be little or no consensus whether or not the various groups of young people referred to as 'the unattached' are the responsibility of the youth service, whether or not they should be contacted in the first place, and what they should be offered once contacted. This is not surprising since concern for the unattached is comparatively new. Nonetheless, this lack of agreement must be recognised and we must realise that un-attachment refers to a far wider social phenomenon than simply unattachment to clubs.

Even if there were some common agreement within the field as to the necessity for widening the area of those to be served, the skills, know-how, tools and techniques, are not yet available in the field for this kind of work. An added factor then becomes, the kind and variety of training necessary.

There is no certainty in the field as to what the work of the local youth committee should be, how it should be done and to what end, except in the most general terms. There are no agreed terms of refer-ence for discussion between the various elements in the field, the youth worker, the detached worker, the management committee, the borough youth committee, the training centres and the national youth organisations based on accepted social work or educational theory and practice. This is evidenced by the lack of (or the comparatively un-developed nature of) appropriate literature in the field.

A wider concern

Perhaps the most profitable point of departure for further discussion and enquiry, is the recognised need for concern and responsibility for a wider variety of young people, and for a wider variety of services and settings. The focus on youth work has been too narrow; even for the young people served, the conception of service has been mainly in terms of clubwork, uniformed work, and, if out of doors, adventurous pursuits. In keeping the emphasis on life inside the club as a main focus of activities and in concentrating on those who can accept this, youth work has been defined in such a way that those who are not willing or able to use this service become the 'unattached' and hence the occasion for this project.

Further thinking might well go into the categories to be served and the variety of services and settings necessary. Those too young for formal club membership, could benefit by increased opportunities for recreational and other services, as could groups that have passed 'youth service' age and continue to need facilities. The 'can copes' who on the whole get on without clubs perhaps need other kinds of opportunity that might broadly speaking be referred to as 'cultural activities'. The 'temporarily disorganised' are often in need of advice, support and guidance, without which some of them might 'become worse', or continue to 'flounder'. They too need, among other services, increased cultural activities. The 'simply disorganised' perhaps the largest category after the 'can copes', need a much wider variety of recreational and other opportunities for social development. The 'seriously disorganised' are often left almost unaided until they 'come up against the police'.

The club and recreation ground idea of provision is often inadequate to the scope and variety of needs as suggested above. Should we not include the commercial clubs, dance halls, autonomous neighbourhood groups and indigenous leaders in theory and in practice in the overall provision? Should not the programme be considered as 'taking place' in a much wider variety of settings in the community, and in fact be helped to do so? A wider variety of services also seem necessary—services that relate to employment, further education, boy/girl relationships, special interests and to a more detailed and developed use of existing community resources for the social development of individuals and groups. Instead of being seen as different and often unrelated efforts, and enterprises, youth work needs to be seen as a community-wide programme of provision of service to youth.

This enquiry should in no way be construed as implying that the traditional club setting is ineffectual in offering to the main body of its members, opportunities they need and want which are of lasting value to them.

The traditional youth club can offer to the 'can copes' a number of things that no other setting can offer.

1. A well structured situation within which to learn to get on with himself, his age-mates and the adults in charge.

2. The opportunity to participate in well-planned and well-run activities (sports, arts and crafts, organised games, music, drama, etc.) that will develop physical and social skills and offer opportunities for leadership.

3. An opportunity to relate to an adult in a situation where the rules are known, the adult is a club leader, the boy a club member, and to use the known and accepted 'rules of the game' as a training ground in which to learn to related to other similar adults outside the club (the teacher, the foreman, the employer).

4. The opportunity to be part of something larger than himself—the club—and to learn what this means in terms of (a) 'getting something', the feeling of belongingness, his identity as a club member, acceptance from club-mates and staff, privileges and rewards within the club, and (b) giving something—loyalty to the club, subscriptions, and the modification of behaviour necessary to being an accepted part

of the whole, taking responsibility when necessary, respecting others 'rights' and learning how to 'behave'.

5. Probably most important to a certain kind of young person is the opportunity to escape from the conflict that plagues his 'unattached' brethren since what to do, how to behave, the rules, the schedule of rewards and punishments for this or that behaviour are clear and understood by all concerned. Within this 'congregation', or small community, the rules of the game are a settled matter (even though members may have no say in making the rules or applying them). This affords a sense of security that is important to young people who have to make so many choices for themselves at this particular time of their life. It affords a kind of guide book to what is expected, and the opportunity to learn how to meet these expectations and to try and act out various ways of meeting them. This is a very real gift to a certain type of boy or girl, especially if the rules he learns also apply in the world of work into which he will soon be passing. (Honest, team spirit, respect for the constituted authorities, for others' property, a sense of loyalty to the employer or the company, a sense of who he is within a given hierarchy, how to achieve the rewards and how to avoid the punishments.)

Few of these things can be offered to the 'clubbable' boy or girl as effectively or as efficiently in any other setting. But this does not in our opinion imply that the club member could not or should not also be offered the opportunity of other types of youth work settings of a more informal nature, or that he will need the club experience for any preconceived length of time. One boy might outgrow it in six months, another might keep up his membership for three or four years, while a third will need to stay for six months, leave for three months, return again to participate at a different level and stay on for a year. Nor do we mean to suggest that all the 'can copes' in any given community necessarily need a youth club experience. Obviously many of them get similar things elsewhere. What we are suggesting here is that the traditional club setting should be seen as one type of youth work wherein boys and girls whom it suits, are given the opportunity of an intensive experience which they could not get elsewhere.

The traditional club, considering its programme of activities, the role of its leaders, the 'demands' it must make on its members for loyalty, subscriptions, and modification of behaviour as a condition of participation, does not appear to be a setting which offers much to the unattached. This may at first seem disappointing since many people hoped that by contacting and working with the unattached, a detached worker could introduce many of the unattached into club life. We had ourselves entertained this idea but in our experience it is not practicable. The traditional club has a function for those who want and use it, and might be seriously hampered by attempts to reform the programme. It has a responsibility to the 'can copes' to provide the best possible opportunities for meeting their needs.

Much of the talk about the unattached tends to imply that somehow the clubs are at fault, that in the distant past every young person belonged to a club but that now clubs have somehow become unable to attract them. This is mostly untrue. The unattached were always there, but were not considered important. Newly developed acceptance of community responsibility together with higher levels of anticipation on the part of the young people, and increased ability to make their needs known, often to the annoyance of the authorities, has occasioned a new awareness of the unattached and their problems which has focussed attention on the place of the youth club in attracting the 'unclubbable'. To some extent youth clubs have accepted this focus of attention, firstly because they feel it should be their concern, and secondly because money is available to expand programmes if ways can be found of doing the work.

There is in our opinion one dominating reason why the emphasis in any discussion on the unattached should in part be shifted from the youth club to a community-wide network of services. This is because the community itself sees the club as being for 'clubbables'. The school, the employer, the other voluntary and statutory agencies and even of more importance, the club members and their parents have ready-made expectations of a club. Any attempt to change this might well increase anxiety and hostility at the very point in the community (the youth serving sector), where reassurance is needed and at the very time when a new network of services would require the understanding and co-operation of the same individuals, groups and institutions that were being threatened.

The only time that the traditional club should be called upon to adapt its work to the needs of the unattached should be if a management committee, the leader, and the other statutory and voluntary bodies, agree that it could not function as a traditional youth club because of the nature of its membership, and if in a community-wide programme several youth clubs decided together that one of them might well adapt to the needs of the unattached.

We have not discussed the changes that might enable the existing youth club to provide more effective and efficient service for its members: e.g. the usefulness of group work, the changing role of the traditional club leader, the possibility of self programming, etc. The work of the clubs was not within the purview of our enquiry.

We may have drawn the lines a good deal more sharply than can be done in real life. An abstract category, 'the traditional youth club', covers an almost endless variety of forms of club life, ranging from the closed, highly structured boys' club, through the mixed club with a less highly organised programme, to clubs that have a wide variety of loosely organised activities to suit the needs of many kinds of young people, including the 'temporarily disorganised' and the upper reaches of the 'simply disorganised'. But on the whole the traditional youth club is seen by all concerned as offering membership in an already established institution, with established activities, ways of doing things that are there when you join and in which you participate. It is this complex of attitudes, structure and programme that we refer to as the traditional youth club.

The open youth centre is much nearer the mark in offering something the unattached will be able and willing to take—a comparatively informal setting, with emphasis on the coffee bar, on records and just getting together for a chat, with 'activities' in the background to be joined or avoided "when we feel like it"—with few demands for loyalty or formal participation. This less-structured arrangement can more easily act as a point of contact for many types of the unattached, but has the advantage of being a non-segregated situation in which the 'can copes' are just as likely to want to take part as are the other categories we have been discussing.

Nonetheless, the open youth centre alone cannot build and maintain an adequate community-wide network for the unattached. Firstly, because it could not work on its own with the 'seriously disorganised', because it could not 'protect' its programme from their raids, aggressive and destructive behaviour, nor could it offer the variety or intensity of help necessary. Nor could it wholly satisfy the needs of the 'simply disorganised' who need both as individuals and groups, a good deal more intensive work than the open youth centre can be expected to offer. It is a more useful setting for this type of work than a closed club because it does offer opportunities for contact but it cannot be expected to offer a full programme.

We have argued so far that neither the closed youth club nor the open youth centre can be expected to offer a full programme, but that each should be seen as a point of contact, service and opportunity within a community-wide network. But this does not imply that either the traditional club or the open youth club could or should not be the initiating agency in any attempt to build the wider network in a given community. A traditional club that saw the needs of the unattached and the implications of a community-wide programme, could employ a detached worker who would not aim to bring the unattached into the club, but would try to find out what they needed, and to help the community, through the club, to see how it could be provided. This would mean taking a decision not to keep the programme attached to the club, and not to water down services to the 'can copes' in the traditional programme. If this is done, the community must know that the club will continue to fulfil its responsibility to its regular members. Much the same can be said of the open youth centre which could begin by contacting, as individuals and in small groups, the unattached who frequented the centre, and could use this contact not only to help the young people in the centre but to discover their need for service outside the centre, to help the community see what those needs were and to suggest ways of providing for them with a community-wide network of services.

In either case this would require a good deal of preparation for the staff member, management committee and perhaps even a sacrifice of status prerogative and traditional ways of doing things. It would also require a community worker in addition to the specially trained club or youth worker.

A wider variety of skills

We also suggest a greater emphasis on providing a wider variety of specialised skills. If a community-wide programme of youth work is to become a practical possibility, there must be a much wider variety of skilled youth work specialists, including not only trained youth leaders, but detached workers, and youth workers skilled in supervision, in-service training and community work. This implies a need for training in several areas of youth work specialisation.

The youth leader in the formal setting

The youth leader attempting to work in a club or an open youth centre might well be prepared not only for work inside the club (with individuals, with groups, with the members committee and the management committee) but to see the club as one of a network of formal and informal youth work settings. Current youth work training seems to prepare leaders for work inside clubs, but not so much for the wider programme. Some youth leaders get little help from their training to interpret to the management committee and to the regional or national organisations, the limitations of the traditional club work setting. In reinterpreting traditional club work patterns, the youth leader is often unable to state the case, to suggest the next move, or to find people who can help him to do these things. He therefore often seems to be locked in heated discussions (with his management committee and the elements in the community they represent) about activities, numbers, discipline and finances, and unable on the whole to help his club to relate effectively to a larger neighbourhood and community pattern. By adding an introduction to community work and a special sequence on interpretation in his training curriculum he could be better equipped for these aspects of his work. Training in youth work might also help him to recognise

305

and use a much wider variety of settings in his service. All too often the average youth worker functions best in the club setting, feels more at ease, more confident, competent and effective inside the club building. Ways and means should be explored of showing the trainee how to recognise and use the natural events outside the club as an opportunity and setting in which to offer his service. Of course not every worker will want to or be able to operate outside the club, but those who do should be offered opportunities to learn how to do so. Those who do not should learn how to recognise and help the community to recognise how they and their agencies can co-operate with detached youth workers. The curriculum might above all include a philosophy of education that would help such workers to relate in an ordered and systematic way the bits and pieces of youth work to the larger pattern of overall community educational provision.

The detached youth worker

Training in detached youth work could probably follow the basic youth work training and offer further specialised training to those who feel they have something to offer in a non-club work setting.

If the basic training has included the suggestions directly above, and given some experience in the club work setting, further training might centre on:

a. The comparative study of values and standards, beginning with: Why do I want to do this work? What do I think I can bring to it? What are my limitations and potentialities? (Not as a psychological examination but as an occasion for discussing the differences in values and standards between the various sections of the community and the various groups of young people.) What are the differences in values and standards? How have they arisen? How are they expressed? What is my role in recognising and using these differences?

b. A study of social education and its objectives, approach and method, skills and techniques in working with individuals and groups outside the formal youth work setting.

c. Working with the formal youth work agencies; what to expect; how to 'use them'; how to be 'used by them'; how to work towards co-ordinating the various services needed by the young people; how to interpret their needs as well as his own to the agencies concerned and to the community.

d. Working with the informal autonomous groups and indigenous leaders in the community; why this is of vital importance; how it differs from working with the formal agencies; what to expect; how to do this kind of work; how to 'use' these groups and persons; how to have them 'use' him in respect of work with young people.

e. A detailed extension of the philosophy of social work or education that was part of the basic course in youth work, extended to cover process, procedures and principles of social work or education as they apply particularly to the work of a detached youth worker.

The youth officer

Central to the whole conception of this kind of work is the need for specialised training for the local youth officer. Current practice, is seems, barely recognises this need, or its great potential. This is partly due to the tendency to play down the very real differences between the job of 'the good club leader' and that of the trained community worker. Needless to say we see him as the latter with club work as only one of his points of concern. Following our comments on his function, we hazard the suggestion that apart from youth work training and experience the youth officer might well require specialised training covering:

a. The nature of community and community behaviour. How do communities grow and develop? How do they behave? What problems do they have? What can be done about them? What is being done about them in relation to youth work?
b. Youth work administration. 'Institutional behaviour', that is the behaviour of the various statutory and voluntary bodies, including the youth committee. How institutions 'come to be that way'. How and why they change. Conflicts in objectives, values and standards, in the allocation and use of resources in traditional processes and procedures. The function of the local youth committee. How to assess its limitations and potentials. The tools and techniques necessary to committee work. The policies and procedures of community-wide youth work programming. How committees 'behave'. Why and how conflict can be recognised and 'used'. How co-operation can be engendered.
c. A detailed and developed reference to social work or educational theory and practice that includes social education, community work and administrative behaviour in terms relevant to his work as the local youth officer.

In-service training officers

Following the same line of reasoning, some provision should be made for specialised training for in-service training officers, whose services would be available to the local youth committee and to the local youth officer. These in-service training officers might well work on a circuit covering several local areas. They should offer in-service training, including supervision, to youth workers doing club work and detached work; intensive youth work training to part-time youth workers and volunteers; youth work seminars, conferences, discussion groups and short courses to members of the local youth committee, management committee, autonomous groups and indigenous leaders, and people in commercial settings; orientation courses to workers in adjacent fields, probation officers, teachers, social workers in order to help them use the servives provided by the programme and to help the programme use their services. The further specialised training of the in-service training officer could be similar to that of the local youth officer with the addition of special training in:

a. educational processes and procedures necessary to informal, adult education;

b. supervision;

c. learning how to contact and work with indigenous adult groups and autonomous leaders, and in passing on to them social skills;

d. community interpretation. How to help the various elements in a community-wide programme to get their case across to the public (as well as to each other and the young people). This might include how to carry on a community self-survey for youth work provision, to interpret the results, and to pass the information to the relevant authorities and the public.

Youth work research specialist

Some provision might also be made for the return of a small number of workers who have had basic and specialised training in community work, together with several years of experience as local youth officers, to a special course in youth work research, to prepare them to carry on research and enquiry in the field, and to help them to help local youth committees to do so.

Part-time workers

Absolutely vital and integral to this work must be the determination to find, train and keep a wider variety of part-time workers including volunteers, ranging from programme specialists (dance, sport, drama, arts and crafts, etc.) to assistant leaders, which as the Bessey report indicates has already been seriously considered. We envisage that much of the detached work can be adequately done by the right kind of part-time worker, providing he has in-service training, is part of a team that offers guidance, support and an identity, and that the team itself, being part of the community-wide programme, has the resources with which to support and help him. This is a vital point because no local community can financially support the kind of enterprise we are suggesting, without a well developed and organised volunteer training and recruitment programme, which has rigorously explored and 'exploited' she natural resources available. In our experience this aspect of the work most often fails for lack of the know-how and skills necessary to attract the right people, train them and create an environment which can hold them. For this reason, the specialised training of the youth officer and the in-service training officer should be especially concerned with volunteer recruitment and training.

With the implementation of the Robbins report, with the study of human relations in colleges of technology and with the diffusion through the adjacent professions of knowledge about human relations, it should be possible in the near future to recruit 'a new kind of volunteer', who has already had a basic grounding in this subject. Another factor is the hope that as leisure increases due to technological changes such as automation, more people of the 'right kind' will be available for this kind of work. One might even anticipate a resurgence of Victorian middle-class enthusiasm for philanthropic and charity work, but in this case, with contemporary outlook. These suggestions might lead to a generic course for youth leaders that would provide a basic training for the whole field, followed by specialised training in the various aspects of youth work which would provide the field with the necessary specialised skills for a community-wide programme of youth work on a local basis. Communities wishing to broaden their concern and responsibility could then assemble a youth work team able to carry out the programme envisaged here. Such a team might well have a youth work community worker as a local youth officer, with a paid secretary to do the clerical work; a youth work supervisor to work with youth club and detached youth workers, a training officer, perhaps on a circuit covering several communities, and the advice and guidance of a youth work research specialist, when and if he were needed. Such a team would implement the community-wide programme of youth work provision, planned, organised and administered jointly by the members of a local youth work committee, representing the statutory and voluntary youth-serving agencies, and the autonomous groups and commercial interests involved in youth work provision in that community. Of course a good deal of detailed thinking and enquiry would have to go into drawing up such a training programme before it could be seriously considered for implementation. Yet we believe that we have outlined a possible and perhaps profitable direction for that thinking and enquiry to take (see appendix for suggested courses).

Advantages of the scheme

A scheme such as this, once in operation, would have several advantages; it would offer the trainees a common agreement about ends and means in youth work, and terms of reference within which to discuss, develop, disagree, etc. It would be especially appropriate if the basic generic course could be designed along the same lines as the human relations orientation offered to the probation officer, the child welfare officer, school guidance counsellor, etc. This we feel would be of immense value to those attempting the community centred approach in youth work provision.

Opportunities for different kinds of specialised training following the generic course (and after appropriate field-work experience) would broaden the career structure in the field of youth work and perhaps attract a wider variety of entrants. The field is now perhaps too narrowly occupied by 'doers' and could usefully include here and there a small number of 'thinkers' who might help to balance things out more evenly.

A young person could begin as a volunteer, an assistant leader, or a part-time leader, take the generic training, return to the field for a while, and later go back for specialised training in detached work, community work, in-service training or youth work research. Indeed, if the basic course and the specialised training were related to other fields besides youth work, valuable interchange between the professions could be a practical possibility. The common basis of agreement and the career structure together would provide the rudiments of a profession within the general field of social work or education, which by the nature of its concern, responsibility and discourse, would clarify issues, examine needs, evaluate successes and failures, and propose new solutions.

We believe also that well-trained youth workers, capable of working as a team, attempting a community-wide programme of youth work provision, supported by youth work specialists (especially in community work and in-service training) would be an economic proposition. They would use community resources, especially volunteers, indigenous leaders and autonomous groups and help the local community to mobilise other human and financial resources and make more effective and efficient use of those already in operation. Taking the long view, youth work experts who could help local communities might well be an economic asset.

A more definite and developed reference to education or social work

In order to discuss adequately a wider concern or responsibility, a community-centred programme of youth work, or a wider variety of skills in the field, together with the necessary training, all these questions need to be related to social work or educational theory and practice in order to offer a secure and acceptable base to the whole enterprise. Unless the whole endeavour can be seen as part of the general educational and social work provision made by the larger community for all its members from nursery school to college and university (including further education for adults), youth work is in danger of becoming a stop-gap provision for the 'between school and work population'. It could become a tiny minority service, or a fancy extra (intensive social group work with a fortunate few) or a straw in some fashionable wind, now a preventative device, now a mental health measure, or an attempt at group therapy, which would lead to its being concerned only with the 'seriously disorganised'. In one way or another, youth work is all of these things, but the winds of fashion are unreliable guides to the size or scope of the provision required, or to the most appropriate approach or method. Only a detailed reference to accepted theory and practice in social work and education can provide the necessary framework for an adequate development of youth work provision.

We hope it is clear from this discussion of the Youth Service that we are not suggesting the unattached as the only focus for a wider youth work programme nor the detached worker as the 'king-pin' of the local service. We do suggest that work with the unattached using detached workers as an integral part of a community-wide programme of youth work should attempt to meet the needs of a much wider variety of young people through a much broader programme of service.

Summary

The basic assumptions of this scheme are (a) that the generic course should lead to certification; (b) that the scheme should operate on three levels, the basic generic course, the further training of specialists, and adequate provision for in-service training; (c) that a central youth work training council be set up in the Department of Science and Education, which together with the Youth Service Development Council would be responsible for the co-ordination of existing training and the planning of further training schemes; (d) that the whole enterprise should be seen as an extension to educational provision, and as such be based on a more detailed reference to social work or educational theory and practice.

27. *The third perspective—the related services and the general public*

The third perspective that has to be considered in relation to the unattached is that of the relations between the related services and those members of the general public who are interested or concerned with youth work.

311

The teacher, the probation officer, the youth employment officer, and the social worker, are often concerned to know what youth work is doing, for whom, how and why. What groups does it serve? What service does it offer? What can each of the adjacent professions, working with the same young people offer the youth worker and the youth work setting or vice versa? Local and national government ask, "What is the money for? Who are they contacting? What kind of training is necessary? What kind of priorities can be set for expenditure? Is it an educational or recreational enterprise? Will it prevent juvenile delinquency?" Taxpayers and ratepayers want to know if all this expenditure is necessary. Wouldn't the young people (except for the odd criminal) grow out of it on their own any way? Other sections of the general public see it as an opportunity to discipline the young people, or 'adjust them to society'. Still others maintain that that clubs are provided and if "they don't use them that's their affair".

The related social services

This approach to youth work, and efforts to sponsor community-wide youth work provision suggest that the relationships between the youth service and the social services are of the utmost importance. Many of the suggestions we made in the projected programme could only be brought into being by the closest thinking and working together of the statutory and voluntary bodies concerned. In fact, the success of this kind of work depends more on the pattern of community co-operation than on any other factor.

Too exclusive a preoccupation with the needs of youth work could defeat its own ends. We tend to see the other 'related social services' as grouped around youth work, related to our definition of the problem, its needs, methods, approach and objectives. This can lead to a kind of professional imperialism that regards youth work as the paramount concern of the whole community, ignoring the many other social needs which are the concern of the other services. However the other services might also view it simply as an extension of their own work, of the youth employment service, probation, or family case-work, any or all of which it can only be in part.

We must be careful not to regard 'youth' as a special category of person with a special class of problem and so separate from society. It is, of course, true that different societies at different times emphasise different stages of human development. (The Victorians 'the middle-aged', the Americans until recently 'infancy', the Chinese until recently 'old age'.) For various reasons we are moving at present in the direction of an emphasis on youth as 'adolescence'. In the long run these valuations of special periods in the life cycle tend to level out as do the ideologies of 'economic' or 'psychological' man that support them. All we need note is that in the local setting youth and its problems should not be seen as entirely separate from what went before (infancy and childhood) and what is to come (adulthood and maturity).

Another difficulty in relations with the adjacent professions is a tendency to underestimate the legitimate social conflict that must almost inevitably ensue. Thinking and working in this way will almost certainly lead to matters of finance (allocation of budgetary resources) systems of status (job, title, established channels of authority). Older traditional processes and procedures will be called into question, both on the worker/officer level and on the agency/management committee level (as well as on that of the national or regional professional organisation). All this need not be bad or 'an unpleasant affair' but it does require recognition, care, consideration, and a mind of mutuality. And most difficult of all, it requires the acceptance by all parties of some inevitable change, however slight, in function, structure and identity. We therefore suggest that serious and prolonged consideration be given to both the theoretical and practical problems arising from the encounter between the various services. On the training and professional level one might begin conversations between the various certification councils concerned (child care, social work, youth work, etc.) in the hope of getting agreement about 'common factors' to be emphasised in the several training programmes (perhaps human growth and behaviour) as outlined in the generic course. One might also develop inter-professional conversations to explore the theoretical and practical aspects of co-operation and co-ordination, and to provide literature, papers, articles, and books that would emphasise the common factors in social welfare training on a community level.

On the local level, in-service training schemes could be created that included the various related services in a discussion of common assumptions, methods, and problems, to prepare a more developed and definite relationship between youth work and the related services in terms of specific local problems. We suspect this situation (relations between youth work and the related services) will improve when professional status based on advanced training comes into force.

None of these problems are amenable to simple solution, yet we believe that when emphasis on the local community as a 'therapeutic agent' (as in the case of care of the aged, juvenile delinquency, and the mentally ill) becomes more widely accepted in the several areas of social administration, some at least of the problems of inter-agency relations will be resolved. This of course will be especially true as jointly planned administered and financed community service begins to take the place of isolated single agency efforts. The very process of thinking things out and working together will tend to resolve differences, often based more on traditions of service, and the varying states of professional development, than on the needs of the local community.

An analogy here might well be the ecumenical movement, both in its work at the top (between the various governing bodies of the churches) and the 'work at the bottom' in experimental co-operation at the parish level.

The conditions of consent

We have seen that the various areas of conflict in this presentation reflect a lack of common agreement, both in local communities in the field of youth work itself, and within the larger community. This kind of agreement could provide the basis for the common action suggested here. The problem therefore, is to decide how best to arrive at a common mind, but this is a circular process. The larger community has to be aware of the need and be willing to support the enterprise; a trained and articulate profession has to be able to help the community translate this awareness into action. Local communities have to want to do the job and to be willing to evolve the co-operative attitudes and machinery necessary, and to feed back the resulting information into the youth work training process and into the larger community, in order to keep the latter informed and thus to take the interpretation a step further.

Both in the local community and in the larger community, priorities have to be set (housing, education, hospitals, modernising the industrial plant and rationalising the productive process versus expenditure on youth work provision) which requires informed guidance and support from those in youth work. Each of these factors depends on the rate of progress of the other. The only feasible solution as we see it is a trained and responsible profession that will ask for the mandate and do the job; that will take responsibility for helping both the local and the larger community to recognise the needs and set about meeting them.

It is always possible that ultimately the larger community might choose other priorities, decide the work is not necessary, or that it can be better done by someone else or in a totally different way. But as with other social problems in an open society (punishment versus rehabilitation in law enforcement, the implications of the Newsom and Robbins reports, etc.) the primary essential is the availability to all concerned of the relevant information with which to make the decision.

Chapter Seven

SOME CONCLUSIONS

28. The fact of social change

The discussion in the field of youth work is not 'a thing in itself', isolated from the pressures, trends, ideas and attitudes of the larger society, but is one kind of response to them. It is engendered by the social changes that have affected (and will continue to affect) the needs of the young people, the mode or style of their expression, and the role of the youth worker, the programme and the service.

It is sometimes claimed that social change is more rapid, extensive and disturbing of the established order, and presents a greater challenge or opportunity today than at any time since David entered Jerusalem, or the invention of the spinning jenny; the fact may be welcomed or bewailed. Be that as it may, all we need to note here is the fact of social change, in so far as it has occasioned the discourse in the field of youth work of which this presentations is a part.

There can be little doubt that a combination of economic, political and technological pressures, trends, and innovations, have effected changes in the social life of a wide variety of persons, groups, and social institutions in this society to a marked degree in the last twenty-five years. These changes have brought opportunities for increased social, educational and vocational mobility, which in themselves have become occasions for new economic, political, and technological changes. That these changes have brought problems—increased juvenile delinquency, loss of roots in the neighbourhood—as well as 'blessings' is not at issue here. All we need note is that these changes have in turn affected the nature and content of the educational, recreational and work life of the young people with whom we are concerned and are therefore relevant in a discussion of youth work. The following statements, while far from comprehensive indicate the trend of our thinking.

1. Whatever else has resulted from these changes, one thing is apparent, that they have engendered changed patterns of expectation,

especially in young people. These new expectations and aspirations may not always be approved by the adult world and established social institutions, but their existence is recognised. The amount 'they' earn, the number of 'their' motor bikes or even cars, the amount 'they' spend are matters of constant concern to whole sections of the population. It is no longer found surprising that at one end of the social scale, almost every boy and girl wants an opportunity to go to college, and at the other end many want, and often get, a holiday abroad.

2. These changes have occasioned various explanations of social phenomena. The murderer on television does not murder out of a generalised hatred for all mankind, as he often did in the early thrillers of the 'romantic' period. He now has 'motives' which can be discerned both by himself and us; psychological motives, such as fear and anxiety with their origin in early childhood; social motives, such as status, role in family or group, or membership in a minority group, which are often seen to originate from deficiencies in society rather than in the individual criminal.

'Social scientists' have been at work for many years, but were usually experts working in universities, government or industry. The rapid and widespread change of the last twenty-five years calls for a much wider public discussion on "why" people are that way, "how they get to be that way", "what can be done about it". This is not restricted to the teacher, the social worker, or the local magistrate, but it now includes large sections of the general public. Dr. Spock's Baby Book is said to be only second to the Bible as a best seller in the western world. It is worth reflecting why the young mothers who read and use this book no longer rely wholly on mother, grandma, or the accepted mores of the neighbourhood and community as guides in baby care and mothercraft.

Traditional *mores* are now devalued. The 'answers' in contemporary society have to be rethought to fit the circumstances. We are not concerned with whether or not this is 'bad' or 'good', nor with the fact that in the field of human relations (teaching, social work, personnel management and youth work) these explanations are seen by some to be shallow, 'pseudo or semi-scientific', or as propaganda for a particular school of psychology or a particular ideology of social change. We simply note that changed social conditions tend to require and produce different explantions of social phenomena. This is evidenced by the press and television programmes which on the whole tend to give sociological and psychological explanations and to discuss in those terms, illegitimate births, the purpose of education, the changing patterns of family and marriage, teenage behaviour, and a host of other social concerns.

3. This transition from traditional to a more deliberately worked out explanation of social phenomena has naturally resulted in changed concepts of how to achieve the desired ends. Questions of discipline, of personality growth and development, and of the kind of curricula that might best achieve these ends, are discussed quite differently now, in regard to the content of what is done, the way in which it is done, and the structure of the social institution doing it. If law enforcement is to be rehabilitation instead of punishment, if education is to have other ends than academic vocational or professional proficiency; if religion is more concerned with relationships between people than with doctrine or dogma, social institutions like the school or university, the law court, the prison, and the church, need new structural forms related to their newly formulated tasks. Thus both the traditions and the institutions which were their custodians are seen to be changing. We must also consider the social and economic complexity referred to as the 'modernisation of Britain'. Recent technological changes have caused social changes, which in turn create increased expectations requiring increased national productivity for their fulfilment. This means that the human resources available must be used to the best advantage. This in turn raises questions about what needs should be met, by whom and in what way, in order to speed 'modernisation', and about the criteria for the allocation of resources (profits, wages, education, housing, the social services). This directly affects what is available for youth work and the part youth work will be expected to play, by the various parties concerned, in the movement towards greater national productivity.

4. This process changes concepts of what the community should offer its members and how and why it should do so. Criteria for income adequacy, housing standards and the provision of amenities are changed. Taken together these represent a changed concept of social responsibility and changing criteria for the allocation of local and national resources. These changes in the larger society have naturally occasioned changes in the theory and practice of youth work, and in almost every other aspect of human relations work. New explanations are now being offered of 'adolescence' and adolescent behaviour, and new knowledge and insight into its physical, emotional and social aspects have made adolescence almost synonymous with youth. It is naturally the young people who bear the brunt of living through these social changes, who are most closely involved in the resulting patterns of social life, and whose reaction to these changes require new explanations. In order to see and feel the impact of social change on discussion of youth and youth work, we need only compare one of the opening speeches of a conference on youth before the First World War, with its heavy overtones of moralistic thinking, class

consciousness and even chauvinism, with the orientation and content of the series of articles published in *New Society* last year. (See Bibliography, No. 111.) The increased mobility, the changed patterns of adolescent behaviour, the new expectations and aspirations of young people, have all created in youth work the task of meeting new needs, of doing old things in different ways and of reassessing the theory and practice of youth work in relation to the new problems and modes of explanation mentioned above. Current discussions about the role of the 'youth worker', *vis à vis* that of the club leader, the nature, content and usefulness of social group work, the meaning and usefulness of self programming, are indications that this reassessment has already begun.

Before 1939

Before 1939 youth work was mainly concerned with the provision of recreational opportunity and 'character training', for those young people who, due to social deprivation, left school early to supplement the family income. It was therefore mainly situated in socially deprived neighbourhoods. On the whole, it was assumed, that the more fortunate young people, whether in school or not, received these things at home, in school, church and friendship groups. The club movement was mostly voluntary, and often reflected the concern and dedication of the middle-class charity and reform movements, and also passed on middle-class values and standards in the shape of 'character training'. We do not imply that any of this was unnecessary, improper, or ill advised. Its fruits are well known, its efforts are rightly celebrated in the social history of the early part of this century.

The social changes mentioned above have altered the social conditions the early club movement sought to ameliorate, and consequently, much of the traditional club work programme is no longer relevant to the social circumstances of many young people today. This point is well appreciated by most sections of the club work movement which is engaged in extensive rethinking. A good example was the willingness of the Y.W.C.A. to undertake sponsorship of this project.

29. The enabling circular

This change in the idea underlying youth work provision, transcending the traditional bounds of the clubwork movement can be seen in the enabling circular of the Board of Education of 27 November 1939 (circular 1486, see appendix). The contents relevant to this discussion are:

1. That at that time more than 50 per cent of the young people were uncontacted by a youth serving agency.

2.   That the social development of young people was seen to be one of the objectives of the enterprise.

3.   That youth welfare was seen in terms of an educational concern larger than simply that of the school setting.

4.   That the whole discussion was one of social responsibility in the broader sense of the phrase.

5.   That all young people from 14-20 were considered eligible for the service.

6.   That the effort was seen as having its origin and focus in the local community.

7.   That the local youth committee was to be the setting for its planning, operation, etc.

8.   That the effort was to be a joint one between statutory and voluntary bodies, within the historical pattern of development and the 'educational' services in the community.

All the elements we have suggested as necessary to youth work provision are present in that circular. But it did not come to fruition in terms of community-wide provision for youth work because of the circumstances discussed and inferred above. Perhaps the most important reason is that it did not attempt to provide a trained and articulate body of youth workers who could take up its implications, test and restate its contents in the field, and interpret to the general public the problems, (as well as their possible solution) and the cost of the enterprise in human and financial resources.

30.   The Albemarle Report

In November 1958 the Albemarle committee was appointed by the Minister of Education with these terms of reference.

To review the contribution which the Youth Service of England and Wales can make in assisting young people to play their part in the life of the community, in the light of changing social and industrial conditions and of current trends in other branches of the education services, and to advise according to what priorities best value can be obtained for money spent.

In paragraph 2, page 1, the report says:

We were appointed at a most crucial time. First because several aspects of national life, to which the Youth Service is particularly relevant, are today causing widespread and acute concern. These include serious short term problems such as that of the 'bulge' in the adolescent population. They include also much more complex and continuous elements of social change, elements to which adolescents

319

are responding sharply and often in ways which adults find puzzling or shocking. . . .

With these terms of reference and the recognition of the situation in the field quoted above as background to its investigation, the committee, after ranging wide over the field of youth work, gathering evidence from a variety of statutory and voluntary bodies, as well as knowledgeable individuals concerned or interested in youth work, reported its findings in 1960.

As was well appreciated at the time, the Albemarle report was a momentous event for the field of youth work. Our interpretation of its importance (for the purposes of this discussion) is three-fold, in that it emphasised:

1.   The youth service as an educational service that should be of value to all young people of 14-20, and which needed to respond more keenly to changed social conditions by working in new ways (see for instance self programming, paragraphs 173-6).

2.   That the provision of training opportunities, both in order to increase the number of full-time youth workers available, and to provide new skills to the field, was an immediate priority.

3.   That the number of young people uncontacted by the youth service was indeed considerable and that there was a need for further enquiry into the ways and means of contacting them.

The aftermath of the Albemarle report can perhaps best be judged by the kinds of training opportunities offered by the local and national youth work bodies, the presence and programme of the Leicester college for training youth leaders, and the work of the Bessey committee, its report and the resulting training programmes for part-time youth workers.

The relevance to this
presentation

Yet even the changes in youth work theory and practice, as outlined above, have not been adequate to the task. Even with new awareness, knowledge and skills, old problems have remained intractable, especially those of contacting the large numbers of young people not yet 'touched by the youth service'. This has not only caused disappointment and frustration but given what can only be described as an aura of continuing crisis (paragraph 2, Albemarle report) to youth work generally. Considering the size of the task, the numbers contacted (even though "numbers are not everything") and the money spent, the questions naturally arise "are we on the right track; are we thinking in the right way; what should be the next step in our thinking; where do we begin?" It was in such an atmosphere, with questions such as these in mind that we began work. We undertook this study in the hope of contributing to this dialogue of crisis in youth work, we formulated the questions of how to contact and work with the unattached, and organised our report to the same end.

Why was it necessary?

There is no quick answer to this question. We can only indicate the following considerations as relevant:

Possible changes in the role of the family in terms of the guidance and support it could offer young people facing adolescent problems of school, work, boy/girl relationships and the 'future'.

Possible changes in the neighbourhood and community that might influence what the family can offer and how it offers it, including the changes in what young people think they need and the conditions on which they will accept help.

Changes in the levels of awareness and the opportunities available which might influence the young person's idea of who he is, what he wants to be, and how he could go about trying to achieve it. Our discussion might well begin with life in an English village before the industrial revolution resulted in the growth of the great cities, exploring the kinds of support, guidance, etc., that were available to the young people as an intrinsic part of village life, tracing the effects of rapid industrialisation and urbanisation on young people in the Victorian middle and working classes, and following the same threads of enquiry into contemporary society.

Was our work and its description necessary in this form? In one way, yes, since the solution of a social problem must be related to the conditions that have given rise to it, the conceptual tools available and the state of awareness of the parties concerned. A solution to the problem of contacting and working with the unattached that suggested the need for more corporal punishment, would have to seek the same kind of agreement in the same three perspectives that we have discussed here. It would have to refer to educational sociological and psychological theory, develop an approach and method in the same way, work out a training programme for its "disciplinarians" and in the end do the things we have suggested but for different reasons and to different ends.

In another way the answer to the question, "Is this necessary in this form?" could be, "No," if we mean, "are the particulars such as the concept of relationship, group process, etc. always necessary in exactly the form we have used them here?" Yet, even if these were abandoned, other conceptual tools would have to be developed to fulfil the same needs, and they would have to evolve from a process of

321

reasoning similar to that used and elaborated here, since the field of possible explanations open to youth work is limited by the nature of the accepted conventions, and social analysis prevailing in the larger society. The chances that, let us say astrology, or moral philosophy could provide a basis for discourse in this field, are highly unlikely. The terms of reference must clearly be derived from sociology and psychology and related to educational theory and practice. Is any of this really new? So far as we can see, not one of the more important items we have mentioned can be said to be new. But to some extent they are an innovation in relation to youth work. This is easily substantiated by a glance at the following:

1.   The residential settlements in the socially deprived neighbourhoods of the great industrial cities recognised from their earliest days that one of their functions was passing on simple acceptable social skills to individuals and groups, in a local community setting.

2.   The health visitor, the district nurse (and recent suggestions for an educational visitor), all recognise the need to offer their service in informal rather than formal institutional settings, in order to make it acceptable.

3.   The community centre movement has long recognised that only local effort can find the resources, sustain the effort and engender the necessary co-operation to carry on the programme of community improvement.

4.   Adult education has from the start recognised that informality in method and in setting is the best way of offering information, guidance, and know-how, whether in homecraft, the industrial or fine arts. Perhaps the most outstanding example of this has been the Workers Educational Association and the Educational Settlements.

5.   Youth work itself, expecially since the Albermarle report, has offered a galaxy of ideas and suggestions from commercial coffee bars, and the barge project to adventure weekends and other informal opportunities. Even the idea of a team of youth work experts, each contributing his different skill to a community-wide programme of youth work provision, has been in the air for some time.

Why hasn't it been done before?

If these ideas are not new, and are in one form or another already in circulation, why have they not been implemented? In fact they have, but not for young people and youth work. Even a cursory glance at provision for old people jointly planned, organised and administered by the old people's welfare committee of any borough doing a 'good job', will discern almost all of the characteristics we have been discussing here.

1. A local community consensus as to the needs of the old people, the available resources and the priorities.

2. A local old people's welfare committee with a joint planning orientation.

3. Trained, professional welfare workers, with specialised training in working with old people.

4. A wide variety of volunteer help as well as the use of autonomous groups, indigenous local leaders and the involvement of 'good neighbours'.

5. A wide variety of settings in clubs, church halls, hostels and special premises, as well as in old people's homes.

6. A wide variety of services available from recreational to special medical care and appropriate housing—home help and meals on wheels, as well as an organised system of regular 'friendly visiting' and provision for emergency service.

7. Emphasis on self programming and self help that tends to keep the system of contact and provision broad, flexible and informal.

8. A consensus in the larger community that does not seem to resent either the content of the programme, the methods used to achieve it, or the cost.

This type of programme is possible because a wider area of common agreement, attitude, opinion and concern has established itself over the last twenty-five years in respect of provision for old people, than has grown up in respect of provision for youth.

Such a change of attitudes seemed to be less threatening to those who serve the aged, than to those who serve youth; less of a 'threat' to their established ways of thinking and feeling, and thus arouses less anxiety and opposition. There is also a comparative absence of any widespread traditional method of working with older people, that would need to be modified in order to think and work in this way, and hence little or no institutional resistance to this approach. The idea that the old people are 'deserving' can easily be stretched (rationalised in the psychological sense) to meet all the necessary changes in established approach or provision. The necessary machinery, community committees for work with the aged, staff trained as old people's welfare workers, are not (for the reasons given above) seen as a threat by the existing programme of service. We do not mean to imply that this description of old people's welfare work is necessarily typical, nor that even at its best is always meets the needs of old people, but we suggest that old people's welfare services are beginning to apply successfully the concept of community care.

This has not happened in youth work on account of several factors.

The behaviour of young people is seen by some sections of the community, including elements within the field of youth work itself, as a challenge to the established order. Educational and professional expectations of young people are often seen as unrealistic, too demanding. In contrast to old people, young people are seen as healthy and capable. They should not need special consideration. All they need do is take advantage of the opportunities provided on the conditions laid down. It is often assumed that the answers to moral and ethical questions are clearly provided within the protestant middle-class ethic. How young people are to know the traditional answers remains somewhat a mystery as they are often without contact with the churches, or the middle classes. It is often assumed that "their problems are of their own making", that their behaviour is "wilful misbehaviour", and that any other explanation is an attempt to be "soft" with them. The vested interests of the youth serving-agencies in established traditional programmes of service, moral allegiancies and institutional structure make it difficult for them to alter their pattern of service, without at the same time changing the nature of their service, the conditions on which it is offered, and their administrative structure.

Youth work is not a vote getting issue like provision for the aged. It impinges on organised politics only as an element in the discourse about "shouldn't they be disciplined more severely", and about punishment versus rehabilitation. Some groupings within the general public are convinced that young people already get enough. They emphasise the spending money, availability of consumer goods slanted to the adolescent market, of educational opportunities "if only they would take them" as evidence that youth is already well provided for and that further public expenditure should go elsewhere. It is not traditionally acceptable to "give things" to youth, except in formal education, but there is a long "charity" tradition in relation to the needs of the aged. Moreover the middle-class aged are not on the whole seen as being in need of the same range of provision, which allows the charity concept continued play (one can see some of this in the controversy that centred on the use of the word "donation", *vis à vis* old age pensions during the election of 1964).

A study of how the borough old people's welfare committees work and how they go about interpreting and implementing the idea of community programming might be useful. The objection that we have not yet enough knowledge to work in this way with the unattached, is a red herring. Little or nothing is known about the ageing process, but enough is known about the social aspects of ageing to make community care possible. We believe the same is true of community-wide provision for youth. In short, the question is not about the needs of young people, but about the values, standards and social attitudes of the community. Because of the impact in many parts of contemporary

324

society of the social changes referred to above, our discussion has much in common with those concerning other areas of our society. In law enforcement and crime there is a tendency to use the court, the approved school, borstal and prison, as rehabilitation units rather than as 'punishment inflicting agencies'. In education, 'privileged' (class or I.Q.) provision is giving way to a much broader basis of educational opportunity, including education for social development and the use of leisure as well as for academic, vocational and professional efficiency together with continuing provision of counselling and guidance.

In industry a similar discussion is in progress about 'human relations' on the shop floor, interpersonal relations between workmates as individuals and in groups, and between shop floor staff and the management. The work of the personnel officer is moving away from a concern with only 'the tangible aspects of production' towards an interest, understanding and offer of service in the area of human relations in the enterprise. There is also a movement toward workers' participation in the management process itself. These kinds of discussion when taken together tend to give new content to several traditional concepts important to youth work.

Authority tends to be seen as less rigid, less vertical, less hierarchial, in need of justification before it can gain acceptance. It is seen as emerging from the consent of those over whom it is exercised, rather than from the superiority of its possessor, as something that should be open, shared, and invested in the bearer only in relation to the task at hand.

Mobility is seen as something desirable, useful, and on occasion necessary, an advantage to the possessor and to society, something to be achieved, often with overtones of adventure and self satisfaction rather than as a threat to order, authority and traditional procedure. On the whole mobility is felt to be a good thing, so that social institutions should be reformed not merely to allow but to encourage it.

The concept of 'an activity' is gradually changing to a much broader category of individual and social action. It is less concerned with the socially approved schedule of events, and has fewer moralistic overtones, although not without a moral basis of its own. It gives more recognition and weight to the spontaneous, and does not demand any set schedule of specific goals. It can be 'good in itself'.

Discipline tends to be something which can grow from within the individual or the group; to be thought of as non-punitive, seen for the most part as an educational process rather than as punishment from and by superiors. It is something that should grow from a recognition of the needs of the task and the value of personal relationship, rather than from imposition from outside or above.

Counselling and guidance are used to help the individual or the group to learn how to make choices and decisions, solve problems, decide on priorities, how to ask the right kind of questions and where to look for an answer. In short, counselling and guidance tend to be non-judgmental instead of an imposition by an external authority (personal or institutional) who "knows better" and who has the "rule book handy".

Relationship tends to emphasise the mutuality of the human encounter, its inner meaning and value to the parties concerned. A relationship tends to be seen as a situation holding possibilities and limitations, an arena where anything may happen, as opposed to relationship as strictly defined by the social or legal position of the individuals involved, i.e. the husband/wife relationship, the father/son relationship, the teacher/pupil relationship. How long this new interpretation of the concept will be seen to be adequate to its task, is another matter.

The concept of process which ordinarily referred to a set of related actions within a limited frame of reference (i.e. the process of boiling an egg, of passing an examination), tends now to be seen more in terms of experience at one point on a *continuum* that includes what has gone before and what is yet to come. It tends to shift the emphasis from seeing things as having 'happened', that is, as static situations. It emphasises that aspect of experience that points to 'all things becoming' and includes a reference to interrelatedness and interaction, as an aspect of all events. Both relationship and process as concepts, as we have described them, are related to the recognition and experience of the pace and continuity of social change as well as its complexity. 'Relationship' and 'process' may have been used too often in this presentation, owing to the lack of other adequate terms of reference in the field of youth work discourse.

The changing content of concepts and the new vocabulary are not restricted to education, youth work, social work and related fields. As we have seen, in industry, management, town and country planning, local and national government (indeed all areas of society where the impact of social change has been recognised and experienced, and where appropriate action to meet the new needs has been undertaken), a rationalisation (in the ordinary use of the word not the psychological) in the terms used, and a reconstruction of the content of the relevant concepts has taken place. The result has been a series of new professional vocabularies which provide the terms within which to discuss particular concerns. That every social problem is at once a 'technical' complexity and almost automatically leads into other problems is now a truism. The town that simply wants to do something about its traffic congestion is soon involved not only with parking meters, one-way streets, special zones, but almost inevitably in land cost, traffic engineering, town and country planning, origin and destination studies and transport patterns, a wide variety of 'aspects of the situation', a wide variety of experts and expertise.

The complexity of modern society requires a wider range of participation in the solution of social problems. It has not only brought changes in the content of traditional concepts and the appearance of new technical vocabularies, but also a host of new 'professions', a variety of new technologies, each with its own speciality, that presume not only to document the change in this or that social pattern, but to aid and abet it, to use it, and relate it to other changes. All this means specialised training for workers on the factory floor, for the different jobs within management, for different types of teachers, social workers, for the magistrate, and even the priest, specialised training that will further differentiate the new professions. To what extent this is a bad or good thing is not our concern. That a combination of all these things is now affecting the theory and practice of youth work, should not be surprising. Regardless of the exaggerated form that some of this specialisation has taken or of the excessive formalisation of ordinary routine tasks that might here or there have occurred, the conclusion is well nigh inescapable that the technological innovations (and the social changes that have resulted from them) have occasioned the same need for specialisation in the field of youth work, as they have in other fields of human relations. Youth work too needs trained and specialised practitioners as do other fields of human relations; youth workers who would be available to help communities to deal with the impact of these changes on themselves and the young people, in the same way that town and country planning experts and traffic specialists are necessary to deal with different aspects of the same social change. As Shaw said, "every profession is in part a conspiracy against the public". Yet there is no reason to expect that the worst aspects of this cannot be avoided in a situation such as youth work with a long and well developed tradition of part-time and volunteer helpers. As the recommendations of the Robbins report are implemented and the results begin to affect the outlook of the young adult population, there will be reason to hope that the numbers of interested and capable volunteers available in youth work will markedly increase.

One might argue that youth work should be someone else's responsibility, a part of secondary education or social work, but one cannot expect, considering the complexities of contemporary society, that it will 'happen on its own'. It does not follow from this that youth work need take on 'scientific airs'—it is after all a value based service. Nor need it attempt to become a specialised 'psychology or sociology'. Indeed we have argued that it should relate itself more definitely and in more detail to general education and generic social work. But we believe that a series of specialisations of some sort will be necessary

327

when the larger community recognises the implication of its concern and responsibility to its young people. Just as the problem of the unattached is related to that of social change, its solution is a part of the same social process, in that the complexities of offering this kind of service in contemporary society requires specialised training and 'professional know-how'.

We cannot deny that some practitioners desire the status that is believed to come from 'new fangled théories and fancy jargon' but this can best be seen as a by-product of an early stage of any attempt to arrive at an organised, systematic and agreed upon basis for practice. This problem of hankering after 'fancy dress' is not only a failing of youth work but can be seen in the talk and behaviour of most of the newer adjacent professions.

As regards the Christian commitment in work of this type, we must point out that the changes we have described in the content of traditional concepts has not left the church itself unaffected. The content of the *Honest to God* debate is surely one indication of the change in emphasis in what Christians mean by 'authority' and 'discipline'. This is especially true of the concept of 'relationship' which is now seen as fundamental to the nature and content of Christian witness. The move with Bonhoeffer, Bultmann, and Tillich, away from purely traditional forms, and the implications of this for institutional change, is surely evidence of the churches' recognition of some of the kinds of change we have been discussing. We must also remember that much of the youth work in the past was based on traditional concepts of character-training with heavy moralistic overtones, which are even now in process of change within the Christian church itself.

These comments have a special relevance since the majority of those who undertook to work in the project were Christians (not all in a formal sense). We found the opportunity offered by the *Honest to God* debate of participating in the re-evaluation of the traditional Christian values and standards, an important, indeed a primary aid in making the necessary changes in our own attitudes and approaches. We feel that without this background much of what we believe we were able to offer the young people would have been impossible.

In conclusion it is very much apparent that usually, for whatever reasons, there are not enough adults available to young people, adults who care, who are sufficiently objective to be useful, and who have the necessary personal resources to be helpful. Our observations, the approach, method and solutions suggested, are ways of stating that fact. Whatever is done, how it is done, and by whom, must in the end be tested against its ability to remedy that lack. Whatever is necessary by way of money, skill, organisation and administrative machinery, whatever motive will provide the desired result, whatever terms of reference are chosen for studying and stating the problem, the aim must always be to provide a greater number of interested, under-standing and capable adults to offer themselves in relationships to young people emerging to adulthood.

APPENDIX I

About the Enquiry

Several points in the report were not as clear as we had intended, and rather than complicate the text itself we have attempted in the following a more detailed discussion of them.

A   *An Institutional Study*

We have tried to make it clear that we were doing a youth work enquiry, by which we mean an attempt to:

1. establish and identify the needs of the unattached for service;
2. assess the nature and content of the services needed as well as those already offered in the light of 1 above;
3. attempt to meet the needs not now being met, by inaugurating new services when necessary;
4. develop a possible approach and method in offering the necessary services as well as in meeting the needs of our own particular contacts;
5. document the whole enterprise in order to prepare a report which would contribute to the discussion in the field of youth work about work with the unattached.

With these circumstances in mind we see this report as the result of a youth work enquiry that took the form of an institutional study— a study of certain aspects of youth work (with the unattached) from the point of view of the youth service (statutory and voluntary bodies) as a social institution, whose recognised and accepted function is service to young people—a study designed, implemented and evaluated with a special emphasis on the role of the detached worker in the local community.

B   *'Approach' as used in this report*

The approach we are suggesting can perhaps be most accurately designated as a 'situational approach' in that it sees a particular problem (in this case contacting and working with the unattached), not in terms of a single cause (e.g. emotional deprivation, psychological inadequacy, social deprivation), but in relation to its history, nature and content within the wider context of which it is a part. Essentially the situational approach suggests that (*a*) the problem, (*b*) the needs it represents, (*c*) the possible solution, (*d*) the most appropriate methods of implementing the solution, as well as (*e*) the resources with which to do the job These are all aspects of the same situation. We therefore suggest that an appropriate guide to thinking about the problem might be:

Detached observation of the particular circumstances of which the problem under consideration is seen to be a part. The needs, behaviour and social attitudes of the participants as seen by themselves as well as the observer including the ways in which the various parties define

330

the problem and the reasons they give for doing so. All of these observed from the point of view of defining, not an 'isolated problem' but the 'problem situation'.

Formulating the problem—abstracting from above the observations that are seen to be relevant elements in the problem situation for further consideration, with the aim in mind of defining the problem so as to suggest what can be done about it and how it can best be done in relation to the needs of the participants, the resources available and the nature of the mandate.

A suggested programme of remedial action—based on the previous formulation of the problem situation that offers specific guidance as to the points at which the worker might best intervene, the things that can and should be done, how, why and to what purpose, as well as in what sequence. And in this manner suggesting as well the information, know-how and skills necessary to work in this way. This should include criteria for evaluation of the different aspects of the work.

Objective participation in the situation—which by way of implementing the suggested programme seeks to influence, affect and change the situation.

Reformulation of the problem—from the information and experience gathered in organising and participating in the programme. In response to the changes in the situation occasioned either by 'natural social changes from without' or by changes from within 'caused' by the programme.

C *The elements of the problem situation*

After a number of different angles of observation were brought together, discussed, taken apart and reassembled, we came to see the elements in our situation as:

1.   The attitudes, opinions and beliefs of the young people and their behaviour seen both as the 'cause' and 'result' of these.
2.   The attitudes, opinions and beliefs of their parents, relatives and neighbours and the social and cultural setting of which these are a part (family, class, neighbourhood traditions), as these affect either giving to or withholding support from the young people.
3.   The attitudes, opinions, beliefs and behaviour of the statutory and voluntary bodies in the neighbourhood and local community, who offer the services (school, club, employment office, etc.) as well as the programmes of service they offer and the conditions on which they offer them.
4.   The attitudes, opinions, beliefs of the larger community as to what unattachment is, what help should be given—by whom, why and how. Its attitudes towards adolescence, work, education, the law and personal relations as they affect either the young people, the neighbourhood or the statutory and voluntary bodies (including ourselves).
5.   The current situation in the field of youth work, attitudes, opinions, beliefs of the various groupings in the field towards work of this kind

331

as well as the availability of skill, know-how, conceptual tools and trained personnel with which to do the job.

6. Ourselves, both as individual youth workers and as a team, representing a voluntary body, our skills, our know-how, our attitudes, opinions and beliefs, our own physical and social resources.

Each of these elements is seen separately and together in relation to:

1. The pattern of needs—the needs of the young people for information, guidance and support, and for a wide variety of opportunities and services, both as individuals and in groups; the needs of the community including the willingness of the youth work bodies to accept or reject the needs of the young people and to offer their services accordingly; the needs of the staff and the sponsoring agency who contact and work with the unattached in these circumstances.

2. The available resources, physical and social in kind and amount ranging from opportunities for work, education, housing and recreation through social institutions. Conditions of co-operation, the specialised procedures developed to allocate these opportunities and the conceptual tools available for working in these circumstances (philosophies of social welfare, theories of education and youth work, etc.), including as well physical facilities, buildings, equipment, playspace, layout of neighbourhood, money and personnel (indigenous leaders as well as professional workers and volunteers).

3. The process of social change—as it was the occasion of any and all of these and as it would continue to affect the problem situation. Increased opportunity for social, educational, vocational mobility, new levels of aspiration, new concerns in the larger community for the unattached, new emphasis in the larger community on the 'problems of adolescence' and the ways in which they are explained and discussed.

It was with these elements in mind that we came to define the problem situation in this way.

1. The definition of the problem: as a conflict in expectations between the young people on the one hand, and the statutory and voluntary bodies on the other, about the nature, content and conditions of service for the unattached.

2. The most probable solution: as an attempt to provide an opportunity for the several parties to come to terms with each other by way of contact in the field, either directly or through us in the programme.

3. The method (designated as social education): as the provision of necessary services at the time, place and on conditions acceptable to the young people, in a setting related both to their needs as individuals and groups, and to the resources available in the community.

4. The resources (the natural pattern of events in the field): as the material for the programme and as an opportunity of engendering modification in an extension of the already available services.

Thinking in this way requires that the information from one phase or aspect of the endeavour be fed into the work in other areas, or used in preparation for the next phase of the work, that is to provide a 'dynamic' within the situation for its continuing development, as well as to suggest a 'logic of the situation' as a guide in thinking about it.

With this description in mind it can be easily appreciated that we saw the 'approach' as being concerned with our basic thinking about the various elements of field-work and used the word 'method' to designate what we did and how we did it (our work with individuals, groups, the community and ourselves). Obviously this is not an important differentiation yet it was a useful one to us, especially in the early phases of our thinking, and in the field-work when so much depended on our interpretation of our work to other agencies. In short, we thought of approach as answering questions of why and what, and method as answering questions of how. This differentiation is more a discursive technique than a reflection on the social reality with which we worked, since the approach conditioned the method used which in turn (hopefully) changed the situation and so modified the approach. Yet approach is a more basic matter than method because it determines what will be observed, how it will be observed, and the interpretation that will be put upon it.

D *Limits imposed by nature of contact*

We should perhaps note that at several points in the presentation more detailed information would doubtless have been useful to the reader (family, school, work and other background information) which was not available to us. This was because our relationship with our 'clients' (the young people), and later in the field-work with statutory and voluntary bodies, placed definite limitations on the kind of information that was available to us, the use we could legitimately make of it and the help that we could expect in interpreting it.

By the very nature of our circumstances (as detached workers giving a direct service to young people) we were prevented from asking questions for purely research reasons, and had to gather what was offered by way of information about family, school, work life, probation, housing problems and similar matters within this limitation. Some of this was either partial, inaccurate, or distorted. Yet we were morally bound in these circumstances to agree to the young person being the primary source of information about himself. Other persons and agencies could be consulted only with the consent of the young person and within the limits of that consent.

The same limitation obtained in our relationships with the statutory and voluntary bodies, who quite rightly saw us as a youth work agency providing a service to the young people (and occasionally to the agencies themselves) which required that we observe the same restrictions about information sought, used and interpreted in our relations with the agencies as we did in respect of our relations with the young people.

E *The interpretation of field-work experience*

For the following reasons it is quite likely that some unavoidable discrepancy exists between 'actual events as they happened' and the interpretation put upon them in this report:

1. Often the events themselves were clear enough, but the context in which they occurred was not.
2. Often the participants themselves (young people, field-work staff, statutory and voluntary bodies, etc.) differed as to the content and significance of an event.
3. Often, a possible interpretation was chosen which 'fixed the event' well enough on a short-term basis, but which was unhelpful in trying to see the event in perspective in the sequence of events or on a long-term basis. In each case, two kinds of compromise had to be made; one which took place at the time (or shortly thereafter) which was aimed at helping those doing the work (the field-work staff and the sponsoring agency) better to understand and to act, and the second of which took place during the writing-up, where it was necessary to make some kind of ordered and related whole of the wide variety of incidents, events and situations that made up the 'total' field-work experience, and to do so in such a way as to use that experience as a basis for this discussion.

It is important to note that we see any bias in the report as due to the angle of observation from which we chose to develop the presentation—namely that of the field-workers and the programme as seen by the sponsoring agency and the interpreted by the consultant.

In an attempt to balance out this bias we have, whenever it was possible, tied to share with the reader some of our underlying thinking, and basic assumptions, in the hope that he will be able to spot and, perhaps, rectify whatever distortion his own experience leads him to discover or suspect.

With the wisdom of hindsight we now see how many, if not most of these difficulties could have been overcome. The report could have been given over for detailed and prolonged discussion to several groups in the field of youth work, who could by their involvement have given a more realistic interpretation of some field-work events and a more practical turn to the various suggestions concerning possible modes of field-work practice, so underlining the sense of urgency which should lead to the implementation of the findings of the report.

APPENDIX II

Facts and figures

COFFEE STALL ATTENDANCES IN PRELIMINARY PERIOD
JULY 1959–SEPTEMBER 1960

62 weeks—231 nights. 7.45 p.m.–11 p.m.

Total number of attendances around stall		3743
Of these, the attendances of customers		3239
(14 per night average)	*Boys*	1585
	Girls	214
	Men	1205
	Women	435
Of these, the attendances of new customers		980
and the attendances of regular customers		2259
20 regular customers (19 boys and 1 girl) accounted for		1115 attendances
Approximately 12 regular men and women customers accounted for		155 attendances
Leaving 948 customers to account for		1969 attendances
		3239

All 20 regular customers continued into the expanded project and 15 of these continued with workers throughout the project. Of the more casual customers, an unspecified number became part of the expanded project.

MAIN PROJECT STATISTICS

(Ages 12–20) over 3 years

At least 450 boys and girls knew one or more workers.

Of these at least 326 boys and girls were known to the workers, (including meeting in coffee bars, public houses, etc.).

Of these at least 257 participated in programme—either casual personal help or on trips on occasions.

Of these at least 236 participated in programme for periods up to six months plus erratic participation.

Of these at least	159	were well known to workers and received
Boys	88	help over periods of up to 3 years, either
Girls	71	individually and/or in groups.

Of these at least	99	received concentrated help from workers over
Boys	60	periods of up to 3 years (mostly 2 years);
Girls	39	that is, workers gave concentrated personal
		service, and also worked with a large
		proportion in groups.

Tentative categories

Of the 159 well known to workers and receiving help from 1–3 years, individually and/or in groups, of these

seriously disorganised	11
simply disorganised	93
temporarily disorganised	35
can copes	20

Spot checks on numbers

July 1961   Core group of 45 receiving help regularly plus 27 known to workers, plus 60 appearing, disappearing and reappearing, plus many observed and contacted in bars, etc.

July 1962
- 57 regulars in club premises and outings (plus 50 coming and going)
- 6 regulars in boys' clubroom (plus 6 coming and going)
- 13 regulars in girls' clubroom
- 22 receiving regular personal service outside groups.

TOTAL   98 plus 56 coming and going, plus 40 being met casually.

July 1963
- 9 boys on holiday and meeting regularly
- 9 girls on holiday and meeting regularly
- 13 younger girls on holiday and meeting regularly
- 18 receiving concentrated personal help
- 50 being met regularly in groups

TOTAL   99 plus at least 100 being met casually.

Staff sessions

The statistics of the staff sessions have been based on a four-week period in which there were no emergencies, full day or week-end outings. The hours cover those of the five field-workers. Although each one varied in the amount of time given to different parts of the work, the totals and averages are as follows:

	Total for four weeks	Weekly average	Weekly average for each staff member
Field-Work	*hours*	*hours*	*hours*
Programme (groups, trips individuals, activities)	240	60	12
Home Visits	34	$8\frac{1}{2}$	$1\frac{3}{4}$
Other Personal Service	112	28	$5\frac{1}{2}$
	386	$96\frac{1}{2}$	$19\frac{1}{4}$
Related to field-work			
Preparation	44	11	$2\frac{1}{5}$
Odd Jobs	96	24	$4\frac{4}{5}$
Phoning	28	7	$1\frac{2}{5}$
	168	42	$8\frac{2}{5}$
Training and conferences			
Staff Conferences	54	$13\frac{1}{2}$	$2\frac{3}{4}$
Training Sessions	40	10	2
Supervisory Sessions	21	$5\frac{1}{4}$	1
Recording	120	30	6
	235	$58\frac{3}{4}$	$11\frac{3}{4}$
TOTALS	789	$197\frac{1}{4}$	$39\frac{2}{5}$

This means that the field-work covered $19\frac{1}{4}$ hours—approximately half the time of a staff member. Preparation and related work $8\frac{2}{5}$ hours —approximately one fifth of the time. Training, conferences and recording $11\frac{3}{4}$ hours, that is three tenths of the time.

Although accurate figures are not available, it is estimated that one half of the Personal Service, Odd Jobs, and Telephoning involved work with adults and agencies in the community, on behalf of the young people. This means that $5\frac{3}{4}$ hours, almost one seventh of staff time was used in this way.

These figures do not take into consideration the hours of the administrator/supervisor, nor of the consultant, who divided their time between administration, training, planning, and work in the community, nor of the project committee which met at least monthly. They do not include the crises and extra work which sometimes seemed to be the 'normal' work. But the total picture is an indication of the amount of time and money that is necessary, apart from direct work with young people.

Summary Statement of accounts

EXPENDITURE

	1961 (7 mths.)			1962			1963			1964 (5 mths.)			Total		
Salaries and expenses	2158	11	0	4654	0	11	6018	0	7	2687	5	9	15517	18	3
Premises, stall and equipment	164	19	4	612	17	6	880	4	1	293	17	8	1951	18	7
Office expenses	47	2	4	36	1	3	74	14	0	46	14	6	204	12	1
Programme	19	15	0	380	18	11	578	11	4	141	16	1	1121	1	4
	2390	7	8	5683	18	7	7551	10	0	3169	14	0	£18795	10	3

INCOME

	1961 (7 mths.)			1962			1963			1964 (5 mths.)			Total		
Ministry of Education	2100	0	0	4320	0	0	5460	0	0	2360	0	0	14240	0	0
Carnegie Trust	437	10	0	751	16	10	949	0	5	411	12	9	2550	0	0
Y.W.C.A., L.C.C. and Donations	292	10	0	930	18	11	1157	1	4	373	3	3	2753	13	6
	2830	0	0	6002	15	9	7566	1	9	3144	16	0	19543	13	6
Less: Refunds	428	5	6	319	17	9							748	3	3
	2401	14	6	5682	18	0	7566	1	9	3144	16	0	£18795	10	3

APPENDIX III

A *The administrative origin of the Service*

Circular to the local educational authorities for higher education.
Circular 1486, Board of Education, November 27, 1939.

THE SERVICE OF YOUTH

1. The social and physical development of boys and girls between
the ages of 14 and 20, who have ceased full-time education, has for
long been neglected in this country. In spite of the efforts of local
education authorities and voluntary organisations, provision has
always fallen short of the need and to-day considerably less than half
of these boys and girls belong to any organisation. In some parts of
the country, clubs and other facilities for social and physical recreation
are almost non-existent. War emphasises this defect in our social
services; to-day the black-out, the strain of war and the disorganisation
of family life have created conditions which constitute a serious menace
to youth. The Government are determined to prevent the recurrence
during this war of the social problem which arose during the last.
2. They have accordingly decided that the Board of Education shall
undertake a direct responsibility for youth welfare. A National
Youth Committee has been appointed to advise the President of the
Board and a special branch of the Board has been organised to
administer grants for the maintenance and development of facilities.
The Committee includes members of local education authorities and
voluntary organisations and also others competent to speak on
behalf of industry, medicine and physical training. The purpose of
this Committee will be to provide central guidance and leadership to
the movement throughout the country.
3. The Committee has already taken practical steps to deal with the
immediate difficulties arising out of the present abnormal conditions.
They have facilitated the re-opening of clubs and pressed for the release
of premises requisitioned for war purposes, and they have recommended the provision of financial assistance, through voluntary
organisations, to help clubs and centres to hire premises where necessary, to provide equipment and to secure competent leaders and
instructors. This financial assistance is being provided and will
include grant-aid to the Central Council of Recreative Physical
Training for carrying on the Council's valuable work in maintaining
and developing the supply of trained leadership in all forms of recreational activity. The Council will be happy to co-operate with any local
authority, voluntary body, industrial or other organisation that
requests them to do so.
4. But the problem goes deeper; it challenges our whole sense of
social responsibility. Now, as never before, there is a call for the close
association of local education authorities and voluntary bodies in full
partnership in a common enterprise; nor need this entail any loss of

prestige or individuality on either side. The Board have made clear their intentions by setting up a National Youth Committee representing all interests, with the Parliamentary Secretary as Chairman. The National Youth Committee will have as its counterpart local Youth Committees representative of both the local education authority and the voluntary organisations. For administrative purposes the local education authority will communicate direct with the Board, but the National Youth Committee will welcome suggestions from both them and the voluntary organisations on matters affecting youth.

5. The Board, therefore, urge that all local education authorities for Higher Education should now take steps to see that properly constituted Youth Committees exist in their areas. Suggestions are made in the Appendix to this Circular as to the steps which might be taken to this end. In some areas excellent Committees already exist and there is no need for any change except in name. Elsewhere it may be necessary to reorganise an existing Committee or to set up a new Committee. In some places it may be thought best to form a sub-committee of the Education Committee under Section 4 (5) of the Education Act, 1921, with adequate representation of the local voluntary bodies; in other places it will be found preferable to establish an Advisory Committee in close association with the local education authority. Special arrangements will be necessary in County areas to associate Youth Committees in the Boroughs and Urban Districts with the County Education Committee to whom such matters stand referred; but this should present no difficulty where, as is frequently the case, there is already machinery for delegating the work of Higher Education. It is important that from the outset the constitution and functions of the Committees should be clearly defined. In all cases it is essential that the Secretary should be a person fully acceptable both to the statutory and voluntary bodies, and the local education authority should generally make themselves responsible for seeing that the Committee is properly staffed and equipped with office accommodation and clerical assistance.

The Board will be glad if local authorities for Higher Education will give this matter their early consideration and will inform them, not later than 1st March 1940, of the arrangements for constituting Youth Committees in their areas.

6. The first duty of the Local Youth Committee is to formulate an ordered policy, which shall provide for meeting the most immediate needs and which shall indicate the lines on which a real advance can be made under more favourable conditions. For this purpose the Committee should ascertain the local needs and decide where assistance can best be given. In doing so, it should bear in mind that the better use of leisure on which the welfare of youth largely depends, cannot be considered without reference to social and economic questions. For example, when young people are living under unsatisfactory conditions and are employed for unduly long hours, often on work of a dull and arduous character, they cannot be expected to take full advantage of any facilities offered for the use of such leisure as is left

to them. The Committee will also plan the lines of future development showing clearly how the field should be covered and where the responsibility for any new facilities will lie. In this way, the foundations of an ordered scheme of local provision will be laid without imposing an undue strain on public and voluntary finance.

It is not the task of the Local Youth Committee directly to conduct youth activities, but to strengthen the hands of local authorities and voluntary organisation. But co-ordination is not enough, a new initiative is needed. Young people themselves must be encouraged to find through the Local Youth Committee new constructive outlets for their leisure hours and for voluntary national service.

7. The principle directions in which local education authorities can assist financially are: first, in the provision of staff, office accommodation and clerical assistance, to which reference is made above in paragraph 5; secondly, in making grants where necessary, towards the rent of buildings and salaries of full-time leaders and towards the upkeep and maintenance of premises, including the provision of equipment; and lastly, in providing competent instructors in such subjects as physical recreation and craft work for classes in clubs and other centres. Approved expenditure by local education authorities under Section 86 of the Education Act, 1921, will rank for grant at the rate of 50%. There are many other practical ways in which the work of youth welfare can be fostered by local education authorities. They can, for example, grant the use of their school premises free or at reduced charges, they can offer the use of playing-fields on favourable terms, they can make special concessions in their evening institutes to local voluntary organisations and they can give facilities for the purchase of equipment.

8. The association of voluntary effort with the public system is typical of the history of the growth of the educational services in this country and will give the service of youth an equal status with the other educational services conducted by the local authority. In the Youth Committee the individual traditions and special experience of youth possessed by the voluntary organisations will be joined with the prestige and resources of the local education authority. The Board realise that the requirements of the civil defence services and the disorganisation of the public system of education under the present abnormal conditions make heavy claims upon the attention and the resources of local authorities. But the service of youth, too long a neglected part of the educational field, to-day assumes a new significance in the national life and the Board are confident that the local education authorities will do all in their power to meet this challenge.

M. S. HOLMES

B *Youth Services*[1]

The object of the youth services in Britain is to provide for the leisure-time activities of young people under 21 years of age, and to offer

[1] For fuller information see C.O.I. reference paper R.5506, "Youth Services in Britain".

them opportunities—complementary to those of home, formal education and work—for discovering and developing their personal resources, so that they may be better equipped to be responsible members of the community. Membership of youth organisations is voluntary and the facilities they offer are sufficiently varied to appeal to every type of boy and girl.

STATE AND VOLUNTARY PARTNERSHIP

Responsibility for youth service in the United Kingdom is shared by the education departments, local education authorities, voluntary organisations and the Churches. There is no attempt to impose uniformity or to create any national youth organisation. A number of young organisations have spontaneously developed over the last century, mainly by voluntary effort. In 1939 what is now called the Youth Service came into being as a partnership of voluntary organisations, local authorities and central Government.

The status of youth services as an essential part of the educational system of Great Britain was confirmed by the Education Act of 1944 and the Education(Scotland) Act of 1945; in Northern Ireland, youth welfare work is promoted under the Physical Training and Recreation Act of 1938, and the Youth Welfare, Physical Training and Recreation Act of 1962.

The education departments provide grants in aid of the administrative and training work of national voluntary youth organisations, towards the expense of training full-time youth leaders and towards the cost of premises and equipment of youth clubs provided by voluntary bodies.

Local education authorities co-operate with voluntary organisations in their areas; most give some financial help and lend premises and equipment; most also employ youth organisers to help in the promotion and encouragement of youth work. Where voluntary services are considered inadequate, local authorities themselves organise youth centres and clubs. Most local authorities have appointed youth committees on which official and voluntary bodies are represented.

In addition to grants received from the State and local authorities, voluntary organisations may receive help for special projects from charitable trusts, notably from the King George's Jubilee Trust.[2] The greater part of the funds of the voluntary organisations is, however, raised by their own efforts.

Since 1960 developments in the youth service have been greatly influenced by the recommendations of a committee set up to examine the service, under the chairmanship of the Countess of Albemarle. On the advice of the newly formed Youth Service Development Council, the Ministry of Education has made larger grants towards the headquarters expenses of national voluntary youth organisations and special grants for voluntary projects, some of which are experimental; has authorised a building programme for the period 1960–63

[2] During the years 1953–60 the King George VI Foundation distributed nearly £1.2 million for projects from the memorial fund in remembrance of the King.

at an estimated cost of £7 million; and, to supplement existing facilities, has established a national training college at Leicester for youth leaders.

A Standing Consultative Council on Youth Service in Scotland, with functions similar to those of the Youth Service Development Council for England and Wales, was set up by the Secretary of State for Scotland in 1959. In 1963 permanent arrangements for training in youth leadership for full-time youth leaders and organisers were made. Two types of course are available; a two-year basic training course and a two-term course for those already having certain prescribed qualifications for the work. More money is being made available from central funds to national voluntary organisations in Scotland. A White Paper on the development of the Youth Service was presented to the Northern Ireland Parliament in 1961. This did not propose any change in the general pattern of the Youth Service but local education authorities were urged to take a more active part in youth work than they had previously done. Such changes as required statutory authority were given effect in the Youth Welfare, Physical Training and Recreation Act (Northern Ireland), 1962. In Northern Ireland the existing Youth Committee was replaced by the Youth and Sports Council as part of moves to expand the part played in youth welfare by the local education authorities and sports organisations.

THE VOLUNTARY ORGANISATIONS

The voluntary organisations vary greatly in character, since nearly all of them were formed to serve specific groups of young people, but most of them provide educational and religious activities as well as social and recreational pursuits for their members, and all of them seek to inculcate high ideals of personal conduct and service to the community.

Twenty-seven national voluntary youth organisations with memberships of at least 10,000 are constituent members of the Standing Conference of National Voluntary Youth Organisations, a consultative body which takes action only in the name of its member bodies and with their consent. A further 22 bodies are associate or observer members, for example, the Church of England Youth Council, which represents some 200,000 young people who are members of clubs sponsored by the Church of England. The corresponding body in Scotland is the Scottish Standing Conference of Voluntary Youth Organisations, in Northern Ireland the Standing Conference of Youth Organisations, and in Wales the Standing Conference for Wales of Voluntary Youth Organisations.

These major organisations have a total United Kingdom membership of nearly 3 million young people under 21.

Among the youth organisations with a mainly religious origin and purpose are the Young Men's Christian Association (YMCA) and Young Women's Christian Association (YWCA), the Boys' Brigade, the Church Lads' Brigade, the Girls' Life Brigade, the Girls' Friendly Society, Girls' Guildry, the Methodist Association of Youth Clubs, the Salvation Army Youth Organisations, the Catholic Young Men's Society of Great Britain, the National Federation of Catholic Youth Clubs, the Young Christian Workers, the Grail, and the Association of Jewish Youth.

The Boy Scouts Association and Girl Guides Association have world-wide affiliations; they are undenominational and non-political, and were founded by Lord Baden-Powell in 1908 and 1910 to develop character and good citizenship in boys and girls.

The National Association of Boys' Clubs, and the National Association of Youth Clubs, are concerned mainly with the 14 to 20 age-group. Each affiliated club has its own rules, but all try to give their members opportunities to take part in physical, mental and social activities, to develop their capacities and grow to maturity as individuals and members of society.

The National Association of Training Corps for Girls comprises the Girls' Training Corps, the Women's Junior Air Corps and the Girls' Nautical Training Corps; all wear uniforms and formal discipline is encouraged. The pre-Service organisations for boys (the Combined Cadet Force, Sea Cadet Corps, Army Cadet Force and Air Training Corps), combine social, educational and physical development with training for possible entry into the armed forces.

The National Federation of Young Farmers' Clubs in England and Wales, the Scottish Association of Young Farmers' Clubs, Northern Ireland Young Farmer Clubs, in addition to encouraging interest in agriculture and appreciation of country life, provide training in the arts of citizenship and develop ability to serve the community.

The Welsh League of Youth (Urdd Gobaith Cymru) aims to 'develop Christian citizenship among the youth of Wales', and its work takes full account of the Welsh background of its members.

The Youth Hostels Association in England and Wales, Scotland and Northern Ireland have a network of hostels for walkers and cyclists, particularly intended for young people of limited means. They seek to promote knowledge and love of the countryside, and are closely linked with each other and with similar organisations in other countries.

Adult organisations with youth sections include the British Red Cross Society, St. John Ambulance Brigade and the political parties.

OTHER ORGANISATIONS CONCERNED WITH YOUTH WORK

King George's Jubilee Trust was established in 1935 by King George V, to promote the welfare of the younger generation. The trust fund originally consisted of the nation's gift of about £1 million, subscribed to mark the King's silver jubilee; the income has since been augmented by gifts, legacies and the trust's own appeal in 1960–61 (marking 25 years of its work). The fund, which now stands at £1·4 million, has disbursed £1·3 million to the headquarters of the principal voluntary youth organisations and to many local projects, particularly those of an experimental nature.

The Duke of Edinburgh's Award is a scheme for young people which is operated by local authorities, schools, youth organisations, industrial firms and other bodies, and is designed as a challenge to boys and girls to reach certain standards of achievement in three progressive stages in leisure-time activities. The scheme for boys between the ages of 14 and 19 covers sections on public service, expeditions and pursuits and physical fitness. The scheme for girls between the ages of 14 and 20 is divided into sections on design for living, interests, and adventure and service.

The Outward Bound Trust maintains five schools for boys which offer 26-day character-building courses, based on adventure and testing experience. A similar school for girls, with modified courses, opened in the summer of 1963. About 4,500 boys and 850 girls take part each year.

The aims of the Central Council of Physical Recreation, the Scottish Council of Physical Recreation and the National Playing Fields Association bring them into touch with many youth organisations.

In addition to organisations on a nation-wide basis, there are a large number of town, district or village social clubs run by voluntary groups for general or particular purposes; photographic societies, folk dance, table tennis or jazz clubs, for instance. In small communities social clubs may not be specifically for young people but those with the more strenuous activities (for example, tennis clubs) usually have a high proportion of young people as members.

---

[1] The above is an excerpt in full from a C.O.I. booklet *The Social Services in Britain*.

APPENDIX IV

Suggested questions for local youth committees

These are questions a local youth committee might well ask while working in the way we have described in the report.

1. What factors influenced the committee to attempt to work in this way? Its own traditions? A small group on the committee? Elements in the community? Outside pressure?

2. What were the major problems in the pre-planning stages, and how were they resolved or bypassed? Problems of committee structure or function? Problems of agency prerogative? Problems of absence of consensus?

3. What were the major problems in the planning stages? Anxiety about having to change established patterns? Of entitlement and service? Allocating responsibility for parts of a proposed programme?

4. What were the major problems in the implementation stages? Unexpected reactions in the field from young people or the community? Difficulty in involving the autonomous groups and indigenous adult leaders? Need to change agreed upon plans?

5. What were the major problems in the evaluation stages? How were criteria evolved? Who did the evaluating and how?

6. What were the problems in each stage of the development programme? Who needed interpretation and why? Who did the interpreting, how and why?

7. What was the nature and content of the more important instances of conflict and of co-operation? How did these situations arise? Why? What was done about them? (or not done). Why, by whom, with what effect, positive or negative?

8. What was the role of the local youth officer at each stage? What did he do? Why? How? What did he need to know in order to do it? Information? Knowledge? Skills?

9. What was the role of the committee at each stage? What did they have to do separately and in committee?

10. In the process of working in this way, what new elements were introduced into the situation either on a short term basis or permanently? Other youth work agencies? Related social welfare agencies? Experts? Volunteers from outside the community? Autonomous groups and indigenous adults from within the community? Why? How? To what affect?

11. What new approaches and methods were introduced? Why? How? By whom? To what effect in each of the particular areas of work?

12. What side effects on the community, positive or negative?

Working in this way would require collecting information about:

1. The community, its physical layout, its social traditions (es-

pecially the patterns of co-operation and conflict between the statutory and voluntary bodies). Its views on youth and youth problems, its resources in respect of youth work.

2. The committee, its history, tradition, structure, previous functioning, its day-to-day operation.

3. Processes and procedures—in each area of the work—direct contact with the young people—within the youth committee—between the youth committee and the representative agencies—(their membership, staff and management committee), between the committee and the related social services in the community.

4. Attitudes and opinions—relevant to the provision of service—of the young people, the neighbourhood, and community groups as well as the related agencies on the committee.

5. Who took leadership? Who opposed? Why, how, to what effect?

Suggestions

The person carrying on the study would need to be attached to the committee. His task needs to be known, agreed upon and accepted by the whole committee, and he must be free to collect and interpret the necessary information. This would mean he should have access to the files, correspondence, committee minutes, reports, and that he should be free to attend the various committee meetings (local youth committee as well as the committee meetings of the member agencies and related bodies) and that he should be free to interview and record in any part of the enterprise.

It should be agreed from the start that the enquiry would have three aims.

1. To feed back relevant information into the planning and implementation of the programme through the committee.

2. That the findings and recommendations of the study be part of the overall evaluation of the enterprise.

3. That the enquiry be so written up as to be useful to others attempting the same work, as a guide to the approach and problems for other local youth committees—as possible training material for the further training of local youth officers in community work, and as material for the further training of detached workers—as well as interpretative material to be used in interpreting the work and its problems to the related social services and to the community.

This work would require a trained social administrator with experience in community work and in youth work. It would take from three to five years and be a full-time job. The person chosen to do the job might well be chosen with the idea in mind of his continuing in youth work after the study ended as a consultant to other local committees attempting to work in this way.

APPENDIX V

Training opportunities

One of the ways of looking at youth work training to provide the necessary variety of skills to the whole field is by way of a two-year basic and generic course leading to certification with further youth work training available after appropriate field-work experience. Such further training might include training for community work, in-service training and supervision and youth work research.

The generic course

The two-year generic course might be organised around themes or training sequences such as these:

1. Human growth and behaviour.
2. The social environment.
3. Educational theory and practice, or social work theory and practice.
4. Youth work theory and practice.
5. Youth work skills including and running concurrently with appropriate field-work placement.

Theme one—Human growth and behaviour. Basic human needs (physical, social, emotional, etc.) human growth and development (infancy, childhood, adolescence, young adulthood with the emphasis on adolescence).

Problems in human development—the physically, socially or emotionally handicapped individual. Theories of human behaviour, sociological, psychological.

Theme two—The social environment. (Social institutions and basic human needs, the family, the neighbourhood, school, church, etc.) Values, standards and norms, their embodiment and expression in social institutions and social behaviour. Social change and social conflict (how they happen and their effects on values, standards, social institutions and individual behaviour). The social environment and adolescent behaviour. Group behaviour (why people join groups, what groups offer their members, the roles of members, internal conflict and co-operation and external relations).

Theme three—Educational theory and practice. Educational aims, theory and philosophy (values and standards) in different settings, the nursery, the primary school, secondary school, youth work, etc. The tools and techniques of education. Working with individuals, groups and the community. The role of the school as an institution. The role of the teacher and the programme. Education and social change. Technological innovation and changing social needs as evidenced in the role of education in a changing society. (Or social work theory and practice covering the same material from that point of view.)

Theme four—The theory and practice of youth work. Adolescent needs and youth work opportunities and services (friendship, adventure, sport, recreation, boy/girl relationships, work and jobs, relations with adults). Social education as a method of youth work. The social development of individuals. The nature and content of education as an extension of educational processes and procedures. The role of the community, the agency and the youth worker in community programming for social education.

Theme five—Youth work skills in working with individuals. The recognition and use of relationship. The limitation and potentialities of relationships. Information, guidance, support and referral. Skills in working with groups. The recognition or the use of the group in network to help the individual. Helping groups resolve conflict. Helping them how to make decisions, choices. Youth work skills in administration. Working with task centred groups. The management committee. The membership committee. The local youth committee. Finance. Facilities—office management. Recording, supervision and interpretation in youth work. Working with assistants and volunteers. Youth work skills in several settings. The role of the worker in the club or local youth centre. The role of the youth worker in detached work. The role of the youth worker as a specialist (community work, supervision and in-service training, research). The role of the youth worker, planning and operating the programme jointly with other youth work agencies as part of a community-wide provision.

Further training opportunities

After certification and appropriate field-work experience, a second level of training might be made available to youth workers for training in specialised fields.

1. Community work in a youth work setting especially for local youth officers.
2. In-service training and supervision as a combined specialisation.
3. Youth work research for the further development of youth work theory and practice.
4. Training in detached youth work.

Suggestions for further training in community work

The objective for the course of training that follows is seen to be the provision of trained youth work specialists who can help local communities to plan, organise and offer a community-wide programme of youth work provision. We see the need for training for this type of worker to be in the nature of an emergency, and feel that a course of this type might well need to be offered before generic training opportunities become more widely available.

It is suggested that this course be one year in length with the equivalent of six months of "practical" field-work running concurrently with the theoretical part of the training. It is suggested that the youth workers who have already had some basic training and experience in the field and especially local youth officers be offered the opportunity for further training in community work. It is further suggested that when the course is first given, one or more of the following be offered, the chance to participate:

1. Local government officials.
2. Further education officials.
3. Training officers of the national voluntary youth bodies.
4. Graduate students who might be interested in making youth work their field of special interest, especially sociologists and social psychologists.
5. Voluntary youth work management committee members. But it is felt that the basic intent of the course should be to provide possible applicants for jobs as local youth officers. The course content could be organised around ten areas of theory and practice, several of which it can be assumed were covered in basic training. They are included here not only as refresher items but in order to help the participants see the material in direct relation to community work.

Area one Basic human needs. This area should be concerned with the physical and social needs of individuals, emphasising how the group, the school, industry, government, etc. are engaged in attempting to meet them, within the various systems of recognition and responsibility, with special emphasis on the willingness and ability of the local community to help meet the needs of the young people.

Area two Why and how things happen in communities. Picking up on the special emphasis in area one about the local community meeting basic human needs, area two should be an introduction to the structure of local community life, social institutions, power, status and the various value and standard systems. It might lead on to discussion of how and why communities change with special reference to youth work services. The participants might be introduced to the problems of social conflict in the local community, as preparation for a discussion of the need for its recognition and used as a social process in relation to community work and youth work provision.

Area three The related social services, government, national and local; the school, the church, national and voluntary bodies concerned with youth work; social work and social workers as they are involved in providing these services; the concerns and function of the secretary of the council for social service, the family caseworker, the probation worker, the youth employment officer and career master, etc.

The participants should be helped to see each service from the point of view of its usefulness, its limitations and potentiality in a community-wide programme of youth work provision. This should include a consideration of common basic assumptions, aims, objectives, values and methods which underlie the apparent diversity in function of the different services. The emphasis should be on their relevance to the problems of a community centred co-operative effort.

Area four What is community work? A detailed exposition of community work in a youth work setting. What it attempts to contribute, why it is necessary, what the worker needs to know and do. The aims, methods and materials of social education. The concept of community-wide planning for youth work provision.

Area five The problems of community work. Developing the above (area four) in detail from case material drawn from the experience of the participant, covering the different aspects of the work from the point of view of the worker doing the job (especially the local youth officer).

1. How to observe community behaviour in respect of services to youth. How to record it. How to interpret the records and how to use them.

2. How to help communities define their needs in relation to youth work.

3. How to help those concerned to work out appropriate services to meet these needs.

4. How to develop functional relationships between the various youth-serving bodies in respect of co-operative programme planning.

5. How to help the community mobilise the necessary resources—money, facilities, attitudes, and to find, train and use, the appropriate personnel including volunteers and part-time youth workers.

6. How to interpret the needs of "special groups" (i.e. unattached, girls, the newly married) to the statutory and voluntary bodies and to the community as a whole.

7. How to help in the interpretation of the work of the statutory and voluntary bodies in the community.

8. How to help communities formulate their experiences, so as to make it available in the development of social policy.

9. How to help in engendering co-operation, and co-ordination of services between statutory and voluntary bodies in respect of youth services on a community-wide basis.

Area six Tools and techniques. Community work as both an aspect of the work of each youth service agency and as the special job of the local youth committee.

1. Working with committees. The committee as a task centred group. Knowledge about committee behaviour. The role and job of the committee worker in working with committees. The limitations and potentials of that role.

2. Helping committees to identify their needs. How to design, use and carry out community self survey.

3. Helping committees write reports and interpretive material.

4. The problems of communication in a committee setting. Methods of helping to achieve practice and participation.

5. Evaluation of committee work. How it is done and why, by whom.

Area seven Beginning a new service. The community worker is

351

often faced with the problem of helping a statutory or voluntary body to start a new service.
1. Assessing when a new service is needed.
2. Ensuring the broadest possible understanding and participation as well as avoiding conflict between the various statutory and voluntary bodies.
3. Timing. The different phases of development.
4. The place of the local youth committee in starting new services.

Area eight Working with autonomous groups and indigenous leaders.
1. What is an autonomous group in a local community? Why could it be important to youth work? How to contact? How to help? How to use in programme?
2. What are indigenous leaders? How can they be found? Why look? How to train? What can they contribute? How to use in programme?
3. How to interpret the need for this type of work to formal youth work bodies.

Area nine Working with new communities. The differences in working with new communities, where instead of having to help modify traditional patterns of service and co-operation, the worker may have to help in the creation of new patterns of community behaviour (new housing estates, urban renewal programmes, new towns).

Area ten Influencing social policy. What part does a community worker play in helping the community to influence the development of social policy as it affects the provision of services and opportunities to young people, employment, allocation of resources for youth work, educational policy generally?

Area eleven Administration. The community worker in working in this way is faced with a good number of everyday administrative problems that may get out of hand and interfere with the proper allocation of his time and resources.
1. Economy and efficiency in procedure. The use of full-time, part-time, volunteer clerical help. Sharing administrative tasks with member agencies.

Area twelve The literature in the field. The sociology of education and of community. United Nations material on community organisation and community development, as methods of social work.

Practical field-work

Each participant should probably have at least three placements during the year in a combination of any of the following:
1. On the board or management committee of a youth-serving agency.
2. In the programme of a related service—probation, family casework, youth guidance and counselling, etc.
3. In the schools (classroom or administration) secondary or evening institutes.

4. On a local council for social service, a further education committee or any other statutory or voluntary body with a community-wide concern.

5. In the office of a personnel officer, or public relations office of an efficient commercial company.

The methods used in this training might well be lecture cum group discussion and should include discussion of problem case material prepared by the participants from their own past experience and from observation in their field-work placement.

If a scheme of this kind were to develop and a number of participants were to take up jobs as local youth officers, the next stage might be to run a course some years later, to which several of them could return to be offered further training in youth work research.

An *emergency* training course
for detached workers

One of the most difficult problems when writing up this report was that of considering the emergency training of detached workers. Two factors were obvious in the report—that we believe detached work to be highly demanding, and that some of the knowledge, information and skills necessary can be offered in basic and further training. But considering the pressing needs of some of the unattached, their numbers, the willingness of many youth work agencies to attempt to serve them, and the lack of trained youth workers to do this kind of job—our previous suggestions for training are surely inadequate as a short term solution. We therefore propose a six month intensive emergency training course for detached youth workers.

Organisation of course

As there is need for some common agreement about the nature of the work, some recognition of its demands on the worker, and of its limitations and potentials for the agency, we suggest:

1. That the training should be localised so that a small group of detached workers can be trained together with the idea of their dividing into teams of not less than two when their emergency training is completed.

2. That the agencies which are going to attempt detached work should share in the selection of the participants in the course, who will be selected for work with a particular agency at the same time.

3. That agency representatives should agree to participate in the training programme.

Much of the difficulty about detached work, about what the worker does, why and how, is difficult between the worker and the agency. This might in part be overcome if both participate in the training, as the understanding of the agency representative would develop during the training, and it would also be possible to relate the particularities of the neighbourhood and the agency to the training.

The agency representatives could attend different phases of the training, which might include a weekend seminar and workshop for several members of the management committee. It might also be possible to involve in the same way several workers from the related services (youth employment officers, probation officers, family case-workers, etc.).

The theoretical training might equip the worker to think about the relationships between himself and the young people in terms of the services he could offer and the particularities of the community in which he would work. The subjects which might be studied have already been described in the report under *Implications*. The object here would not be to offer full-time training in any of these broad subject areas, but simply to offer the participant enough to enable him to develop some of the understanding and awareness necessary to the task, with emphasis on offering him conceptual material that he could use in "talking to himself" (and others) about the problems he encounters in the field.

The aim of the practical training would be to equip the participant to cope more effectively with the problems he would meet in the field. It should include short term placements in clubs or youth centres, and a series of two-week placements chosen to match the situations in which the young people with whom he will be working, are involved, e.g. Approved school, Borstal, police and court, appropriate secondary school, appropriate factory, shop, office, appropriate coffee bar or public house, appropriate social services. As many of the placements as possible should be in the community in which the participant will work. Practical work might run concurrently with lectures and discussions, and the material arising from the placements might be used in the discussions.

Selection of trainees

This is perhaps the most important element in this scheme. If in the 'regular' training scheme (see *Implications*), some of the participants choose after basic training and field-work experience to take up further training in detached work, the variety of placements have already given some indication of the possible result of future training. But in emergency training, selectors will have to depend on one type of experience only. We therefore suggest:

1. That the sending agency, together with the emergency training panel, make the choice with the emphasis on considerations that have to do with the local situation (the kind of young person, the agency setting, the related services).
2. That the selection also consider how well the two people to be chosen complement one another and would get on together as a team.
3. That the net for prospective candidates be widely cast without regard for previous training and experience, e.g. students dropping out of academic professional training, who want more interesting or adventurous work, "naturals" already in the neighbourhood or community, interested in this kind of work.

4. Since at best the worker's "stint" can only be temporary (perhaps five years in the field at most) due to excessive demands on time and personality, candidates already in "good jobs" might be seconded with the right to return to those jobs if they wished, or be given a definite undertaking that further training in suitable alternative lines of work would be provided at the end of their detached field-work period.

When the number of detached workers likely to be available even in the best of circumstances, is compared with the extent of the need and the willingness of youth work agencies to do this kind of work, it becomes apparent that a second emergency exists, that is, emergency of training for suitable part-time workers to work as members of detached worker teams. Therefore we suggest that part-time youth workers and volunteers be included in the emergency training course on the same basis as the other participants (with adequate subsidy for salary lost during training).

The training course and the experiences of the participants might be documented and evaluated for guidance in planning further training. Help might be required in starting the course, but there would be individuals within the educational and social services within any town, city, or district, who could help with different aspects of the training.

APPENDIX VI

The relevance to some other work in this field

There are a number of youth work projects now in progress or being planned throughout the country. We have chosen eight examples either because we know enough about the circumstances in which the work took place to form our own opinion as to their relevance, or because a detailed document is available. In each case we comment only on the aspect of the project which appears to be relevant. The various threads are drawn together in a general comment at the end of the section. The examples are:

1. The Bristol Social Project.
2. The Dolphin Club experiment (Liverpool).
3. The Report of the National Association of Youth Clubs.
4. The work of the London Standing Conference of Housing Estate Community Groups.
5. The North Kensington Social Council.
6. The Barge Project.
7. The Woolwich Y.M.C.A. street work project.
8. The Avondale Project.

ITEM 1. *The Bristol Social Project.*

(*Stress and Release in an Urban Estate—a study in action research*, John Spencer, Tuxford and Denis, Tavistock Publications.)

Whereas the concern of the Bristol Social Project was about the rising tide of juvenile delinquency, and the objective 'to find ways of encouraging local initiative and getting local residents to take a greater degree of responsibility for their community'—the Coffee Stall project was concerned with learning how to contact and work with unattached young people, without special reference to juvenile delinquency, its presence or prevention—a very much smaller area of concern, and with special reference to providing training material. This difference in concern and objective is matched by a difference in the approach to the work undertaken. The Bristol Social Project was a full scale research project covering several areas of community life, a variety of social problems and using social science methods and techniques, that is, action research and the multi-discipline approach (see Chapters 1, 2 and 3 of the Bristol Social Project), whereas the Coffee Stall Project was a youth work enquiry in a local community, with special reference to the problems of contacting and working with the unattached. Yet none of this seriously affects the points at which we agree or differ with the findings or recommendations of the Bristol Social Project concerned with youth work. In the notes that follow we are concerned only with chapters 7, 8, 9, 10, 13, 14, 15 and 16 as they cover the ground related to the discussion in this report.

Chapters 7 and 8

The Upfield Teachers 'group' (7, pages 107 to 122) and Upfield Social Workers group (8, pages 123–31). The material in both these chapters seems to be especially relevant and to offer suggestions of vital importance. We feel that community-wide youth service provision should include just such in-service discussion and study groups, and we see the work outlined as a useful indication of how it might be done in terms of youth workers, and workers in the adjacent services. As we pointed out in *Implications*, if we were to begin work again, we should probably attempt to work in this way.

Chapters 9 and 10

Toughs, Bums and Expressos (9, pages 135–66). The Expressos in sociological perspective (10, pages 167–215). Overall and as well as in detail the material presented in these chapters exactly parallels our own experience on three fronts.

1.   The behaviour of the young people towards one another, towards other adults, the worker, the neighbourhood and the community, and the social attitudes on which that behaviour was based.
2.   The behaviour of the community (the more formal types of neighbourhood association, and some of the statutory and voluntary bodies) and the social attitudes on which this behaviour was based.
3.   Because of these factors, the need mentioned on pages 214 and 215 to contact and work with the informal associations in the community.

The only difference of importance was that in our situation we saw the location of the conflict in expectations as between the young people and the agencies to a much greater extent than between the neighbourhood and the young people. This is not of great importance if as we suggest the local youth committee is seen as the appropriate body for this kind of work. It would have to include contacting and working with the informal as well as the formal neighbourhood associations in its attempt to build a wider community consensus about "youth problems and their solution".

Chapter 12

Children, neighbourhood and committee. (12, pages 234–61) is relevant to this discussion not because we had similar experience in terms of co-operating in the operation of an adventure playground, but because this chapter describes the factors that go into any attempt to use as programme material, the neighbourhood setting and the natural events arising from its particular pattern of association.

Part 5. *Conclusions and recommendations for social policy* (pages 279–322, especially chapter 17, pages 312–22). The recommendations of the Bristol Social Project we see as relevant to this discussion are:
1.   That a central youth leaders training council be set up by the

z

Department of Education (page 294) to which we fully concur for the reasons given in *Implications*.

2. Page 295. The need for professional training. Our experience in the field leads us to give full agreement to this.

3. Page 299. Further enquiry be undertaken to continue to gather relevant information on how to contact and work with the unattached. We see this presentation as in part fulfilling that suggestion.

4. Page 310. That special consideration be given to training for community work. We include this as a specialisation to be offered in further training after certification. (See *Implications* and Appendix.)

5. Page 320. Where to begin? Our Bristol Experience has led us to emphasise the principal *of starting at the top rather than the bottom of the power structure, and of working most closely at the start of the project with those who are in positions of authority in the society*. Social policy is influenced more effectively by those at the top than by those at the bottom of the ladder and conversely opposition to change from those at the top may lead to stronger resistance. It follows from this that the understanding of top policy makers constitutes the initial phase and that failure to secure a measure of consensus at this level will give rise to obstacles at a later stage. (Italics in original text.)

We see the basic problem of both these projects, our own and the Bristol Social Project (in so far as it is concerned with youth work), as a problem of finding ways to engender the community consensus necessary to enable those concerned and interested to state the problem, work out possible solutions and find the necessary resources with which to do the job.

That the Bristol Social Project chose the language of social group work, in their case with psychoanalytic underpinnings (chapter 4, page 73, paragraph 1) as the most appropriate language in which to attempt to engender the necessary consensus—whilst we in a much smaller area of the same concern see the most appropriate language as that of social education using social group work as one among several techniques as in the end of little importance (except in training), compared with the fact that both reports from their experience in the field agree on the emphasis that needs to be placed on the local community as the 'problem situation' on the need for special training for workers doing the job as well as on the importance of the community itself being willing to participate in any effort directed at amelioration.

ITEM 2. *The Liverpool Experiment.*

(The Dolphin Club Experiment as reported in *On the Threshold of Delinquency*, J. B. Mayes, Liverpool University Press.)

The Dolphin Club Experiment is relevant to this discussion at several points, the most important of which are:

1. Its intensive work with individuals and groups.

2. The importance of the social patterns prevalent in the particular community.

3. The role of the worker, the agency and other community agencies in the 'treatment' programme.

The Dolphin experiment is relevant in these ways, only to part of the work discussed in this report, namely the work with the girls' probation group, and the work with the younger boys' group. At these two points it has much to recommend it to those who want to attempt to offer more intensive individual and group experience to special groups within a larger contact group. Whereas we were able to proceed along much the same lines as did the Dolphin Club in the girls' probation group, we were unable to work in this way with the younger boys' group even when we attempted it (in the premises of a boys' club in the neighbourhood). On the whole our experience in the girls' probation group parallels that of the Dolphin Club in several important respects.

1. The young people. For the most part the group was made up of younger girls on probation referred to us by the probation officers 'in trouble', at home, school, or with the law (petty theft, truancy, etc.). Behaviour in the club towards one another, ambivalence towards the workers and the setting, as well as towards 'discipline' and 'authority'.

2. The family and school setting. For the most part problem families, each facing a variety of difficulties, budgeting, housing, husband/wife and parent/child relations, often difficulty between siblings. Some young people, overprotected by one or other parent or ignored, alternately pampered or severely disciplined without reason, in family settings which were hostile to the 'outside world', mistrusted it, or 'just didn't care'.

3. Other agencies. Most often several other social agencies were involved with each family and often with each girl (school attendance, probation, national assistance, family casework).

4. The role of the worker, not only with individual girls, but the group as a whole and each of the smaller friendship groups within it, as well as with parents, and statutory and voluntary bodies.

5. Method. Because of the nature and variety of the needs of the girls, the kinds of families they come from and the interests of other agencies, a combination of individual help, intensive group work with the smaller groups in the larger grouping and constant interpretive work with parents and the agencies concerned.

Our overall comment on the Dolphin experiment in relation to the approach we are suggesting here, is that there will always be need within the larger grouping of young people in any community, for intensive work of this kind, but we would see such work as only one part of the community-wide provision, with other kinds of youth service available when required.

ITEM 3. *The report of the National Association of Youth Clubs.*

It is possible to see the work discussed in the report of the N.A.Y.C. as another aspect of the same attempt to find ways and means of working with the unattached. Indeed, had it been possible (which in the circumstances it was not) it might even have been advisable for the work of both projects to have been related during their field-work phases, and written up and published jointly so as to emphasise their interdependence and their joint relevance to the problems of working with the unattached. That this may have made for a more adequate presentation can perhaps be appreciated when it is realised that the N.A.Y.C. report offers information about a variety of work settings in different parts of the country, while we have been able to explore more fully the problems of this type of work in a single community. Taken together then, the separate reports complement each other. The only decisive point of difference being that we were required by our terms of reference to provide detailed training material and to elaborate our method of work, aiming at professional interpretation (youth workers and the youth service), whereas the emphasis of the N.A.Y.C. report is on a wider interpretation to the general public of the need for this kind of work.

Because of the agreement between both projects on basic problems, the overall characteristics of the young people (as unattached) and the method (detached work), and because it can be assumed that those interested in this aspect of the work, will be familiar with the N.A.Y.C. report, we limit our discussion here to several general statements. There is overall agreement about 'basic problems'; the problem of identity in terms of the need of the young people, the committee, and the workers to be reassured on this point; the problem of the loneliness and isolation of the worker (especially in the early months of the work) perhaps more a factor in the N.A.Y.C. work than in our own situation, yet an important point of agreement nonetheless; the importance of the problem of values and standards, both insofar as they are the occasions for conflict between the young people and the community, and between the young people and their parents, and specially insofar as it is an ever present factor in the relationship between the worker and the young people; the importance of the community in attempting this kind of work; and lastly the need for the work, the willingness of the young people to accept and use contact, and the importance and usefulness of the detached worker approach. There was also a similarity in the observations about the young people in that they were for the most part unable or unwilling to use the 'traditional youth services'; many had 'needs or problems' above and beyond the concern of these services even if the young people would use them (the definition of unattachment, page 47); the antipathy to authority was a factor as were mobility and estrangement between parents and young people; and employment problems and work were factors of importance in the overall picture.

The method of work was also similar. The detached worker was seen as 'unattached' to any traditional setting that might preclude the young person accepting contact: the young person/worker relationship was of central importance; there was need to work on three levels concurrently—with individuals, groups and the community;

and the worker needed support throughout the enterprise (staff meetings and supervision).

There are three points at which the N.A.Y.C. report provides information which this report cannot offer.

1. The use of the school setting to contact and work with girls, which should be carefully considered as an alternative to some of the suggestions this report makes and compared with the Avondale Project (see item 8 below).

2. The use of the factory setting in work with young people (which should be seen as an addition to the *If we had Continued* in *Implications*).

3. The valuable material on work in Midford, a country town with problems decidedly different from those of the urban inner ring neighbourhood. This should be seen as adding perspective to the overall picture offered by both reports together.

ITEM 4. *The London Standing Conference of Housing Estate Community Groups, now the Association of London Housing Estates.*

The following are extracts from information prepared by the Community Development Department of the London Council of Social Service or The Association of London Housing Estates which has some seventy affiliated groups. At the end of 1962 the latter started a three year experiment in attempting to offer help to volunteer youth leaders (indigenous adult leaders) running youth clubs on housing estates in London. We feel it is relevant here because it suggests the kind of work needed in order to bring into the provision of youth work elements in the community which are usually outside the terms of reference of the formal youth work bodies.

YOUTH WORK ON LONDON HOUSING ESTATES

The Community Development Department of the London Council of Social Service has been concerned for some years with provision for social needs on housing estates in the County of London. It has worked in co-operation with tenants' organisations, many of which have developed spontaneously. These community groups are independent bodies with a family membership and subscription of 6d or 1/- a week which enables all members of the family to take part in activities organised by the tenants' association in their own clubrooms.

All affiliated groups feel the need to provide in some way for the young people among their members and most groups reserve one night a week in the clubroom for their youth section. These youth sections are helped by adults living on the estate who are often the parents of the young people themselves working voluntarily in their spare time to help the youth section. Volunteers often have a very good relationship with the members but have little experience or training.

It is clear from experience that the greatest general need is felt to be for leaders. This is not necessarily met by introducing a trained leader from outside, even if such people could be found, unless he is

361

familiar with community development methods and prepared to work with the community as a whole. Some volunteers are willing to learn and improve their skills, providing that training courses are tailor-made to their needs.

Many of the groups provide facilities for young people reluctantly because they lack experience in running such groups; they are afraid of large groups of youngsters and suspicious that outsiders will be attracted and this will lead to trouble. Some groups have experienced trouble with visiting "gangs" and without the necessary skills to meet the situation, have closed the club. On the other hand, other groups have flourished, attracting difficult youngsters, some on probation and others from homes where there is no place for them.

The work being done for young people in the blocks of flats is of an experimental nature with special needs which cannot be met by the existing provision. It is primarily a community project and any worker in this field should have some basic understanding of the needs of the whole community of which the young people are a part, and an ability to work with adults. What is wanted is an experienced person with an intimate working knowledge of a small area, its facilities, committees, and personalities, who is acceptable to the tenants' groups, sympathetic to their needs and able to give help when called for; a readiness to help at whatever stage of development the groups may have reached is most important.

The findings of the experiment in employing detached workers to help adult leaders are not yet available but it can be appreciated that one of the areas of work (with adult indigenous leaders and autonomous groups in contact with young people) which we came to see the need for, but about which we could do nothing, is now being explored. It can be anticipated that the findings of this study helping housing estate community groups in their work with youth, will offer information and material directly relevant to the community-wide provision of youth services (as outlined in this report) by way of suggesting how autonomous groups and indigenous leaders working with young people can be contacted and helped.

ITEM 5. *The North Kensington Social Council Project.*

The following are extracts from a report written by Paddy Macarthy, who was appointed as detached worker for the Portobello Project.

During the summer I became aware that we were dealing with four groups in the club (coffee bar).

1. There were the youngsters who could very easily fit into normal club structure, and in fact, did, in many cases, also belong to other clubs, although some had settled down as 'regulars' of our coffee bar. These kids seemed to find our atmosphere pleasant and undemanding, when probably they would have been better served in clubs which would have stretched them further.

2. There were those who were going through a phase of behaviour problems related to their adolescent state, and who found our setting, with its minimal level of adult intervention and presence, to be most

acceptable (and accepting) in working out their problems of identification and personal status. We were a haven in which they could act out their needs for regression and aggression with relative impunity. I think this is the real value of the normal coffee bar set-up under very permissive leadership. These kids are completely normal; their family and social relationships are adequate. They are just facing adult life for the first time, in job situations which are frequently boring, and for too long hours. They only need somewhere where they can raise hell, live a little, and dive back for a little time into the glorious irresponsibility of childhood without the censorious adult world automatically depriving them of their new-found claim to adulthood.

> Although the coffee bar is not intended as a normal coffee bar set-up, I think there is no real reason for attempting to exclude these two categories, even if this were possible. The following two categories, however, do demand from us a real decision which will sooner or later have to be made.

3. Our third category consists of those who, through bad social and family conditions, have not developed adequately. Sometimes the families themselves are criminal, almost always they are inadequate. These are the ones who have benefited hardly at all from the post-war social advances. The kids themselves have poor school attendance and work records, and their delinquency (usually petty larceny or shop- and house-breaking) is so regular, that the interval between their appearance in court is almost predictable.

4. There is the group which we classify as the 'Rhythm and Blues' group, because of their current addiction to this musical form. None of the characteristics of the third group are *common* to this group, although some do share its background. What is common to this group is their almost complete separation from their families, and absence from home during waking hours. These kids are normally, although not always, in regular employment, and so larceny is not a feature of their conduct. Their delinquency, which is neither as prevalent nor regular as with group three, takes the form of violent attacks on rival groups, or, on 'Rockers'. Their current favourite weapon is a girl's back-combing comb, with the comb held in the hand, so that the spike-handle projects. This group has money and is highly mobile. Apart from the West End-South Soho area, which is their weekend caravanserai, they make frequent trips to Hayes, Slough, Basildon New Town, and anywhere where there is an R and B club or where they have acquaintances from their weekend jaunts. Amphetamine pills are used by most of the youngsters in this group to keep them going throughout the night during their weekends, and some are on them throughout the week. I am no authority on drugs, but my impression is that a few are almost, if not quite, at the point of addiction. Behaviour of this minority is occasionally completely frenzied, but whether this is due to overdosage, poor resistance or fatigue, I could not say.

This class of youngster is growing. A year ago, if one visited their haunts in the West End, between 10 p.m. on Saturday nights and

6 a.m. on Sunday mornings, the age-range was generally 18–20. Now there is a fair proportion of 16–18-year-olds, and the majority are in the 17–18 age range, with quite a few 15-year-olds.

Three weeks ago, we had a small survey. We selected this particular week because it was completely 'normal'. It was not in the holiday period, there were no stars appearing at any of the usual clubs, and there were no big parties planned that we were aware of. Of 32 youngsters from whom we got useful answers, 15 boys and 15 girls had not spent an evening at home in the week; two girls had spent one evening at home, and one of these only because she had got her hair lacquer wet in the rain and spoilt her hair-do.

I took the greatest care not to give the impression of fishing when getting this information, and I am convinced that it is almost, if not quite, correct. Indeed, the strongest reaction from two of the girls was surprise that anyone should stay home in the evenings.

The custom of the weekend long party is also growing. Something like 25% of our girls are away from home for the whole weekend, and few are where their parents imagine them to be, if, indeed, their parents have been favoured with any explanation at all.

My real concern with this group stems not from their very occasional delinquent violence, nor even from their use of pep pills (I do not possess sufficient hard information about the long-term effects of these, nor about their real addictive potential, although I cannot believe that any young and growing organism can benefit from being over-driven and under-rested in the way that these pills make possible), but from the very real breakdown of communication between these kids and adult society. Theirs is a complete one-generation society, which receives nothing from the outer society except what is introduced by commercial interests, whose sole aim is exploitation.

Perhaps I should explain at this point that this withdrawal into a teenage ghetto society has, in my view, nothing in common with normal adolescent rebellion and rejection of adult standards and codes, which ia a healthy stage in maturation. This is a social breakdown in that it represents the failure of organs of social concern to adjust to the fact that the nuclear family is incapable of coping with the stage that the contemporary working and lower middle-class family with teenage youngsters has reached. The upper- and middle-class family with teenage sons and daughters can normally rely on whole hordes of teachers and tutors who will have charge of their children throughout this period. But with the working-class and lower middle-class the relatively greater degree of affluence has enabled parents and children to go their separate ways. Even where clashes do arise over questions of staying out late, or overnight, these are short-lived, since no real sanctions can be applied, and in my experience parents soon give up the attempt to enforce the unenforcible. One only has to postulate the theory that the working-class kid rebels against the cultural secondary modern school to reject the idea as ludicrous. They never absorb enough to make rejection necessary. They are not critical, just indifferent.

I do not believe that the forms of work, that is, with both groups three and four, are compatible, either within the club or in the detached situation. To work with the first group we should be working within a restricted locality, with small, not very mobile groups, with an increasing amount of what would virtually be social casework on a residue of 'hard cases', setting up and working through the same sort of self-programming projects as Bill Richardson is doing with the Adventure Playground group, or as we did with the initial group.

With group four, we have to adopt a much more highly mobile form (the acquisition of a Utilibrake type of vehicle might well be called for), and the main body of the work will probably be done right outside the area, wherever the kids are. How long such a structure as ours could function adequately in this schizophrenic condition is problematical.

As to our base itself, we are already in some difficulty over the lack of clarity of our target. If we aim for the group three youngsters, tailoring it to their needs and desires, we are unable to develop it along the lines which will strengthen our hold on the R and B group and their kind. They remain a peripheral group, and since work with group three implies a permissive approach, the R and B group have every opportunity to react in destructive terms with an impunity they would not find in commercial set-ups. If we turn the facility over to work with the R and B group, we at once create an atmosphere too sophisticated and too restrictive for the group three youngsters, and effectively exclude them. So far as I can see, we have the ultimate alternative of positively excluding the R and B groups to leave the way clear for working with group three type youngsters, or of creating a venue for the R and B types which will be unattractive to group three, and will in any case be too inflexible in structure to give their presence any value.

Several points should be noted about this work as reported here.

1. It has been successful in contacting the unattached, using the detached worker approach.

2. It has been forced into premises (as we were) at one point, by the young people.

3. It points to the problems of working with several categories of young people, each with different needs and so for different types of service.

4. The work with the young people is seen as a community problem, and is based within the social council which could be the beginning of community-wide provision as described in the report.

ITEM 6. *The Barge Project*

The Barge Project was a youth work experiment carried on for five years, 1948–53. The following are extracts from the 5th annual report of the project, 1953, taken from the material under the heading 'general conclusions'.

THE NATURE OF A GANG

The purpose and activities of an adolescent group can be constructive or destructive according to the personal make-up of the individuals who form the groups and the company, circumstances and surroundings in which they find themselves. As these fluctuate from time to time, so too does the activity of the group: and in its turn the activity has its effect on the members.

THE CAUSES OF GANG FORMATION

Conditions such as economic deprivation, inadequate housing or recreational facilities, lack of a feeling of status in the community, adult hostility, parental rejection, family breakdown and personal and spiritual maladjustment among the members of the gang—and particularly the leading members—can lead to anti-social activities and delinquency which in turn evoke repressive measures from the community to put them down. Thus the trouble can become self-perpetuating.

THE POSITIVE ASPECT OF THE GANG

Even anti-social groups are capable of responding to opportunities for acceptable outlets, provided they were given a chance to develop status and prestige in a constructive way, and to understand some of the implications of responsibility.

UNCLUBBABLES DO NOT EXIST

Thus, apart from the occasional psychopath, there are no such phenomena as 'unclubbable' boys in the sense that they cannot be brought together to take part as a group in socially acceptable forms of recreation.

THE LACK OF ADEQUATE PROVISION

It may well be that in most cases the standard form of youth club or other unit is unsuited to attract and hold the gang members. A first essential is that of a smaller group than is normally considered to justify the provision of separate premises or the employment of a full-time youth leader.

BOYS

Response to stimulus
Boys for whom such special measures need to be taken do not fall into any clear categories or types. It appears however that many of them respond to a challenge of a physically dangerous or adventurous nature: but this is certainly not true of some who seem to have become 'difficult' as a result of some actual or imagined physical weakness.

Behaviour characteristics
The behaviour of these boys is characterised by an extreme volatility: thus moods of great gaiety and enthusiasm may alternate with phases of sullen and even hostile obstructiveness: similarly, between acts of apparently senseless destruction and violence there may be interspersed episodes which reveal great tenderness and a real sensitivity to human feelings.

Home and family influence

The influence on such boys of home and family, however, bad, broken or otherwise adjudged by contemporary social standards cannot be exaggerated. In some cases it will still have a direct claim upon their time and loyalties, in others where circumstances have caused an estrangement, this denial of a fundamental feeling is one of the sources of the tension leading to delinquent and anti-social behaviour.

LEADERSHIP

Personal relationships and the leader

The crux of the whole problem lies in the formation of a relationship and confidence between the adult 'leader' and the boys. In the first instance this calls for a worker with a combination of the natural gifts of sympathy and an intuitive understanding of adolescents with considerable skills of casework and group-work.

The need for time

It also calls for patience on the part of all responsible and interested. The length of time required to forge such new bonds of friendship is usually underestimated: even when formed, they will have to undergo weeks and months of being put to the test from both sides, before the worker can with any likelihood of success attempt to exert any form of direct influence or leadership on the boys.

The character of the leader

Since this means that in order to become accepted the worker has to become a member of the group and be weighed up as such, it will be appreciated that he will in large measure come even to identify himself with the group. He will need to have a sound basis of personal ethics and cultural values.

The need for a full-time worker

One of the essential features, especially in the early stages, of building up a stable relationship is the 'availability' of the adult. It is not enough that he should be sufficiently regular in attendance at club evenings for him to become accepted, he should also be there to lend a hand and give advice in the many crises, family, personal, employment, financial and so on, which occur in the life of the insecure adolescent. Willing help, readily available on such occasions, often goes a long way toward establishing confidence and friendship. In particular, since casual work habits are often one of the symptoms of such boys, it is necessary for the leader to be available during the day-time. This means that, quite apart from the necessary qualifications, full-time service is needed from the adult worker.

The need for supervised leadership

It will also be essential for his work to be supervised by a group of people, who must expect to give much more than the ordinary duties of a normal management committee or governing council. For them to provide advice and make plans of any real value, it is essential for the worker to provide at regular intervals detailed reports on both behaviour of individuals and the general atmosphere of the group.

367

In addition they should themselves be prepared to attend meetings of the club, at the discretion of the leader, so that they may be seen to exist as real and fallible human beings by the club members.

THE CLUB

The need to attract

In order to provide a practical and realistic opportunity for such a boy to 'belong' the unit offered should be sufficiently attractive (not necessarily in terms of luxurious equipment or fittings, but rather in terms of being in some ways 'unique' and 'different') to overcome the often sophisticated hostility which is felt against youth organisations.

The means to hold members

For boys feeling suspicion, insecurity and 'agin the world', a place of one's own, just for oneself and one's mates is highly attractive. This means that the unit must be small and shaped round the members and their apparent wishes rather than that they should, at any rate at first, be required to conform to any pre-ordained pattern of activity and behaviour.

Activities

It is not possible to put on a 'programme of activities' in the accepted Youth Service sense of the phrase. Consistent application even to pastimes which at first appear highly attractive and enjoyable is rarely found. Activities which are clearly seen to contribute towards the material improvement of the club, oneself or one's family are most likely to succeed, e.g. interior and exterior decoration, erecting shelves, making Christmas presents. Ultimately this is a question of leadership. If he has a genuine interest and some competence, the leader, by his example, can make almost any activity 'go'.

The danger of permanence

With the advent of a Youth Service officially recognised as part of the educational system of the country it is clear that an element of formal institutionalisation must be present in youth organisations. As a result, one of the conditions of success is inevitably taken to be durability and permanence. Bearing in mind the need for 'uniqueness' in order to attract, and for a high degree of flexibility in order gradually to create a social organisation suited to the peculiar needs of the group participating, youth units of the Barge type should not be expected necessarily to last longer than is required to meet on the one hand the obvious needs of the group and on the other the demands of society with a view to effecting a change in the members' behaviour.

Need for experiment

Since an important point of economics is raised in this proposal for short-duration units, there is need for further experiment to see whether uniqueness and flexibility can be achieved for a comparatively low capital outlay. There must not however be any attempt to be 'skimpy' so far as the salary of a full-time worker is concerned.

There are several elements in the general conclusions of the Barge Club Report that are particularly relevant here.

1. The 'antisocial' groups (the 'seriously disorganised') need service beyond that offered by the usual club programme, are amenable to contact and will respond. In this sense they are neither 'unclubbable nor unattachable'.

2. "The crux of the whole problem lies in the formation of a relationship of friendship and confidence between the adult leader and the boys." There is a problem of values and standards, which is part of the leader's work, and the leader must be full-time and have adequate support 'supervision' from the sponsoring committee or others. All of this parallels our experience.

3. The 'activities' must be seen in relation to the needs of individuals and not preconceived "as a programme of activities", and the setting in which this can best be done must be experimental, that is, detached from the network of established youth work agencies.

On the whole, the findings of the Barge Club were similar to those of this report in respect of the 'seriously disorganised'. We would see a variety of this kind of informal setting offering intensive individual and group help for this kind of young person as necessary, beginning at different points in a community-wide programme, being followed through until the young people concerned no longer needed it, abandoned, begun again elsewhere with other young people as the need arose, accepted as part of the ongoing community-wide provision, closely related to the other kinds of work in other settings with other kinds of young people.

ITEM 7. *The Woolwich Y.M.C.A. project*

The Gang Club experiment, sponsored by· the metropolitan division of Y.M.C.A, was started in Woolwich in 1962 and continued for eighteen months. The worker who supplied the report was George Reynolds, General Secretary of the Woolwich Y.M.C.A. The idea behind the work was the belief that unattached groups (gangs) were in need of service which would have to be given outside the club building. The project began by contacting 36 gangs, intending to require that each 'gang' find itself a 'gang counsellor', an understanding adult in the community. Of the 16 groups with whom work was possible only 2 were able to do this. We see this work as relevant at two points to this discussion.

1. In that the young people were in fact contactable and did use the service.

2. That the work depended upon the relationship made, and for the most part sustained outside the established club setting.

Although we might differ about the use of the word gangs in this instance to describe the groups, we would suggest that further efforts might be made to interest local adults (indigenous leaders) in taking responsibility in this way, together with the kind of trained worker that Mr. Reynold's suggests. We see this kind of work (as the Barge and Liverpool Projects) as one aspect of an overall community-wide provision for youth work, rather than an isolated attempt to work with the unattached.

369

ITEM 8. *The Avondale Park project.*

The Avondale Park project was started by a group of voluntary care committee workers (L.C.C.) who were concerned that the Child Care Committee was not in close touch with young people after they had left school. They were worried by the increase in juvenile delinquency, and the lack of 'good home' influence at the critical period of adjustment between school and employment. They acquired funds from a foundation, and with the willing co-operation of the Child Care Committee and the headmistress of the school, appointed a worker, Mrs. Blackler, to maintain contact with girls during their last term at school and after leaving, by holding weekly discussion groups as part of the school's timetable; visiting the girls in their homes while still at school, having private talks with girls or parents who requested them, and continuing visits and weekly meetings outside school. The value of this project was described in a report in December 1960, after which the work was extended to other L.C.C. schools.

ITEM 9. *Summary statement.*

We see several points emerging that might well suggest some of the common factors in the different efforts of contacting and working with the unattached. All the work discussed here should be seen as appropriate to one or another of the youth groups in any given community-wide provision for youth service. The points at which we see these different projects as having common elements are:

1. That the unattached in most of the work we have been discussing are seen to be in need of more than just recreational opportunity, although this is important both in itself and as a way of offering other kinds of help.

2. That the unattached in large part are willing to accept contact providing it is outside what they see to be the established setting. It should be noticed that this may not always be as true of girls as it is of boys. The success of the National Association of Youth Clubs in contacting and working with girls in a school setting, the work of the Avondale in the same setting, suggested that girls may well be more amenable to contact in 'traditional settings', providing other factors especially relationship with an accepting adult, are provided. This may well require further study.

3. That the characteristics of what we have referred to as the 'seriously disorganised' are in most cases similar, and that they require a more intensive type of service as in the Dolphin and Barge Projects.

4. That the characteristics of the other groups within the larger grouping of the unattached (which we have called 'temporarily' and 'simply disorganised') although they vary from community to community, have at least three characteristics in common.

a. A degree of antipathy to what they see to be authority and to the statutory and voluntary bodies, especially the youth service agencies.

b. A degree of social distance from parents and the parental social milieu—whether or not this is more pronounced than in the case of 'ordinary adolescence' is an open question.

370

c. Attitudes and behaviour in respect of work and careers, and including further education.

These three factors seem to be present regardless of class and family background or geographical area in most of the work being discussed here.

5. That in almost all cases the worker/young person relationship is the most important factor in making contact and working with unattached individuals and groups.

6. That in most cases 'activity' in this kind of work is best seen as arising from the needs of the young people, rather than the needs of (structure or function) of the agency.

7. That it is of great importance in this kind of work that the detached worker gets support from colleagues, especially selected to be helpful to them in facing the problems of field-work.

8. That terms like 'unclubbability' or 'unattached' might best refer to the problems of the youth work agencies offering the services, rather than to the young people since when the service offered meets their needs, they are amenable to contact.

9. That the overriding need in most cases seems to be for accepting, knowledgeable and understanding adults who will offer themselves and their skills on terms understandable and acceptable to the young people at times, in places, in a manner, as well as on conditions that makes sense to them.

10. The job of the detached worker is difficult and a demanding one which requires as well as support, appropriate and adequate training.

Taking into account the considerable areas of agreement between these various attempts to contact and work with the unattached, it seems to us that the next step might well be an enquiry, perhaps by the information unit at the National Training College for Youth Leaders that would do a comparative study of these projects and others like them to ascertain in more detail those common factors, in order to offer guidance to those attempting work with the unattached.

For our part, and from our particular angle of participation in this kind of work, it would seem that our findings further substantiate those of other projects, not always in detail, yet on enough basic points to allow those who follow in this work to have relatively well based points of departure for further thinking and discussion.

APPENDIX VII

The Christian Commitment.

(A paper prepared for the World Christian Youth Commission in May 1964 by Rev. H. A. Hamilton, Associate General Secretary, World Council of Christian Education, and published by his permission.)

The conscious formulation 'the unattached' is itself evidence of the immense gap that is increasingly revealed in the structure of modern society. 'Youth' and, especially 'unattached Youth', have now become a 'problem' to be investigated. This is a measure of the distance between 'insiders' and 'outsiders'.

A conscious use of the phrase 'the unattached' by those who are older implies a disappointed expectation which, from the beginning, distorts their view of the need. To try to correct this may well be one of the most helpful ways in which we can work.

For the most part, the phrase is used and the questions are posed in countries where established institutions are meeting with diminishing returns, try as they will. There is, however, increasing evidence that 'non-attachment' tends to be a feature of the behaviour of young people, whenever and wherever they are drawn into urban society and, especially where they become involved, at whatever level, in mechanised industrialisation. There may, indeed, be a variety of reasons behind the phenomenon of non-attachment in each particular instance. Some of these will come from the disintegrating of those social patterns which were, among other things, the training for personal responsibility of man to man. Sometimes, this will be more obviously due to the debunking of traditional gods and the consequent loss of the standards of behaviour which they 'approved'. Elsewhere the dominant reason may well be the loss of personal stature and dignity which come from the humiliating experience of being treated as a means to an industrial end. We shall, perhaps, be wise to compare the evidence which comes to us from traditional societies with that that comes from new societies, as well as to compare that which comes from countries where youth activities are free with that which comes from countries where youth activities are controlled by the State. The consequence of these complex factors is the emergence of a state of mind which is unwilling to be attached and, often, incapable of an 'attachment'. It is not simply to be seen in their attitude to the Church or any other institution, it can be seen also in their own transient personal relations. We need, I think, very much to learn how far it is likely to be both a chronic condition and one liable to repeat itself. Certainly, these areas of present need must be seen as having a far deeper claim on Christian concern than any anxiety about unattachment to the Church or to any Youth Institution.

There is, of course, a great range of reasons why so many young

people today are unattached; just as, it must be as fully recognised
there are a great many reasons of all kinds why other young people
are attached. There are 'unattached', at one end of the range, so to
speak, who are so for the very good reason that they are self-contained
and mature enough to form spontaneously the relationships and share
interests and concerns through which they grow. At the other end of
the range, there are those whose condition of unattachment is more
pathological and exhibits itself in delinquency and aggressive social
defiance. In between these extremes is an increasingly large company
who should be the basis of any enquiry and experiment we may be
led to do. It is most important for us to recognise that these are to be
found among all income groups in society and through the whole
gamut of educational opportunity (not that this is an even distribution). Sample studies of those elements in education which tend to
make young people capable of attachment and of those even in 'good'
schools which do the reverse could therefore be very valuable. Is
our immediate concern, throughout this whole range, with those of
whom these two things are true?

1. They are not openly rejecting either Christian Institutions or
organised youth work. They are simply not even accepting them as
having any possible claim on them or anything to offer to them which
they need. Experience suggests these as some of the prevalent causes
of this attitude:

a. such organisations do not offer any purpose beyond themselves
that is anything to do with LIFE;

b. because they seem to be forms of retreat from reality and ways of
'substitute living';

c. because they are in the control of adults who do not offer a mutual
relation but either an authoritarian or a patronising one;

d. more subtly because youth organisations are for youth. Segregation
is as unsatisfying as it is unnatural.

Though these causes are out in a more or less rational form, they
represent attitudes which only here and there are articulated but
which deeply influence action.

2. Those who, with this tacit rejection of adult-directed institutions,
more aggressively, but not more confidently reject the standards, both
of behaviour and of belief which are directly or indirectly associated
with the institution. Once again, this may be less the result of a
positive conflict than an expression of the failure to find anything to
which to respond, either by loyalty or by rebellion. The present
characteristics of the social behaviour of this group are definitely not
the evidence of healthy encounter with traditional standards which
is the age old process of growing up. Indeed, this generation may well
feel, at this very point, deprived of its proper birthright. There has
been no obvious authority in belief or behaviour against which to
test their mettle. Dimly they feel aware of needing to fashion for
themselves in a world which seems to be so entirely different from
their fathers' world, some certainties in love and life. Even if much of
their behaviour and, in particular, their sex relations are certainly

subject to little direction or control, there is evidence enough that some are seeking their own new 'mores'. Both these characteristics involve us in thinking of the condition of unattachment as being possibly no more of a problem of youth than it is of middle age, and indeed, of old age too! (The loss of the three-tier family as a social unit in the West and of the powers of 'elders' in tribal families in new countries is one of the social phenomena with a close relation to the question before us.) One thing else is clear, both from our evidence and from experience; the most incapable of stable attachment and certainly the most obstinately difficult to reach are those who have grown in a domestic environment of emotional tension or confusion; and, alas, these are not a few. This fact gives further ground for saying that the action required by the situation must happen on the total social front.

To a consideration then of possible ways of approach, in these two directions at least, we must now turn.

The essential work of social and personal rehabilitation calls, like all bridge building, for simultaneous action on both sides of the divide. An experience of renewal, change of mind, has to happen in different ways on both sides before each can be open even to see each other still less to receive each other. If we are asking ourselves what positive part we may be allowed to play in this process, we shall find it surely as we are willing to discover the need as it is on both sides. We can, of course, only do this at the point of imaginative and, as far as may be, actual identification.

Before we try to think what this process would ask of us there are, perhaps, some proper attitudes in which we must make our approach even to the consideration of the question. The first is that, whenever Christians openly expose themselves to the Word of God, they must expect to hear it spoken to them in unfamiliar ways. One of the most obstinate of these, historically, has been the difficulty for God's people to recognise when He was speaking to them through the mouths of those who rejected Him and despised them. The contemporary situation we have described is nothing surely, if it is not an inescapable confrontation of the Church by its Lord. When Martin Buber says, "I have hid my word for you in their deafness", he is asking men to try to possess the living word which must be heard in the very fact of men's rejecting of what is now being spoken. To recognise this is to be willing to be searched by the current symptom of 'non-attachment' and gladly to allow radical questions to be asked and to stay with them until some answer is given.

These questions surely are directed against the very structure of the Church's life as an institution and against the dominant mentality which shapes its activities. Particularly must the bogus character of the separation of sacred and secular, spiritual and material be exposed to view. The shallowness of moral judgement and the confusing of bourgeois standards with a true Christian ethic must be disentangled; but to begin to say what should and what should not be questioned is already to be imposing a prejudgement on a situation which must be allowed to speak for itself as relentlessly as it will. It should be raised, too, by people who are anxious not to defend any theory or institution but only to learn what God is saying.

What is true of structure is as true of the formulations of faith. Whatever the Christian Gospel is, one thing is certain, it is to be found at work in the actual world of human need to which it was given. This means that, in the end, only those can interpret what it essentially is who have possessed it afresh, and perhaps for the first time, in the encounter with human need. This is how the great doctrines of the Church should be understood and how, possibly, they can be renewed to a generation which needs them. *We need to give much time to the study of this.* The same kind of questioning is directed against the character of the relationships within the Christian institutions, introverted as they so often are and persisting as they do so often merely at the level of social bonhomie. The situation in which the community of the Church is set, asks questions of it about the age structure, the class structure, the openness to go out into the world and the readiness to receive the world. How best to point these questions, so that they come to the Churches acceptably and yet as needing to be answered, *is again one of the preliminary tasks which we* may need to attempt. This total exposure to the situation is the most necessary thing to happen in the thought and life of the Church; and, first of all, to happen in the thought and life of any group like our own which may possibly act in the role of interpreter. The needed prerequisite quality of mind is the willingness to stand on either side of the gap called 'nonattachment' and to be there with as imaginative an understanding as possible. If W.C.Y.C. is willing to enter this field, it must be willing, in other words, to enter it on both sides. For the need is for 'translators' who are as at home in one language as another and can really think as Christians in other than their own familiar terms.

The preparation for this pre-evangelistic task is a severe theological discipline. It reminds us to ask what are the emotional and experiential conditions for the understanding by the whole person of what the gift of the Gospel really is. We have to be sure we know what the essential structure is and what we have to give. It is something more than the rationalisation of it; it has to do with the dimension of personal relations into which the distinctive Christian Word must always be spoken. This compels us to face the cost of any significant action. All the accounts of the individual experience of men or women who have exposed themselves wholly to the questioning and to the need of the 'unattached' and have gone on suffering them in love, speak of what it is going to ask of any of us to begin to try to cross the divide ourselves in the hope of making any rudimentary bridge, even on which others may walk more confidently. There will be little value in our adding one more study of the problem of the distance. Have we readiness to act and the time to act and the vision to inspire others to this action of costly self emptying. I do not see that anything else can be of very much avail.

The other direction in which it may be proper for us to initiate action is in an attempt to move inside the defensive, and the rather frightened mind of the middle-aged; or to gather groups of young parents with growing children, who can already see coming events casting their shadows before. Even this might not be as difficult a kind of understanding as to attempt to move inside the minds of those older and more conservative 'defenders of the faith' who have so definite a picture of the Church as a Divine Institution and of the necessary practices of beliefs and behaviour that they are prisoners of their own past. This is not to say that this should not be attempted but that, perhaps, the shape of some experimental group life which each of the five organisations separately are in a position to undertake; so that, slowly, there might grow a body of Christian laymen who are as resolute to see the place where they themselves live and work as the arena in which their faith can be realised and the means of communicating it refashioned. For their own children's sake they must learn this; for the service of that generation in the world for which they bear the closest responsibility they must learn it; and such laymen can help the churches to learn and act.

Such a purpose might well be the dominant theme of the 1967 W.C.C.E. World Institute, which is to be a confrontation of Christian laymen with educators. It may well be the character of work that we are, jointly with the D.E.A.,* pursuing and the line which the Department of Laity is already following. The other world bodies have so many ready-made situations where such a policy would become practicable that, indeed, they are already pursuing it or could well do so.

The crucial thing at this stage is that all of us who have this concern deeply in our hearts should recognise that any remedial Christian action will emerge only out of painful, searing, physical and mental acceptance, in love, of a generation which is painfully 'different'. What we need to know about the strategy of action must be learned at the point of personal involvement, whether this is something we ourselves do or something we inspire other groups to do. Possibly, in the two directions quoted in this paper, some beginning might be made.

* D.E.A. Division of Ecumenical Action.

ANNOTATED BIBLIOGRAPHY

We have used as basic texts, seven books and three reports, reference to which we feel will make for better understanding of the background and much of the content of this report.

The texts are:
1. *The Social Purposes of Education*, Collier.
2. *Adolescence—its Social Psychology*, Fleming.
3. *The Social Psychology of Education*, Fleming.
4. *Teaching—a Psychological analysis*, Fleming.
5. *Comparative Education*, Hans.
6. *Total Education*, Jacks.
7. *Education and Society*, Ottoway.

The reports are:
1. *15–18* (Crowther)
2. *The Youth Service in England and Wales* (Albemarle)
3. *Half our Future* (Newsom)

Each of these texts and reports are listed with publication title, date and cost in the selected bibliography.

When taken together we feel these seven books and three reports provide possible terms of reference for further examination of this kind of work in terms of it being an extension of accepted educational theory and practice in Britain. Of course other books could have been used to the same purpose but we feel that these specific books, in this particular combination, referring as they all do to education, each including different aspects of that process, are most easily related to this presentation and to read them is therefore the simplest way of filling in the necessary background.

As we pointed out above (Appendix I), our work was in the nature of an institutional enquiry, and since youth work and the youth service is considered a part of the educational provision and is located within the network of educational institutions, we have attempted to relate the discussion to accepted educational theory and practice. Yet it is obvious from our discussion that we see youth work as extending over into both social work and the social services as well as employment and labour services. Therefore, as further work with the unattached is undertaken, it will be necessary to work out in some detail (perhaps as we have done in respect of education), the relation of youth work to accepted theory and practice in both of these fields.

VALUES AND STANDARDS

Basic to any discussion of education in contemporary society is the question of values and standards. What are the aims of education? What are its objectives (academic, vocational, professional proficiency)? What particular set of cultural suppositions do or should underly this (religious, philosophical, political, etc.)?

It is in answering questions like these that the material for practical considerations is gathered by the educational establishment. What is the content of the curriculum to be? What are the numbers, groups or classes to be served? What level of proficiency is to be expected? What is the role of the teacher—the school setting, the neighbourhood, the community? What local and national resources are to be set aside in order to do these things? These and a host of other decisions are made in the light of answers to questions about values. This is as true of the work with the unattached as it is of the work in the school, and more formal clubs.

The questions of values and standards then must be a point of departure for any discussion of work with the unattached. Several aspects of the discussion in the texts listed on the following chart deal with the problem of values and standards; the standards and values of the larger community that lay down the nature and content of the service; the standards and values of the young people (changing and in a state of transition); the standards and values of the teacher (youth worker) and of the school, as a social institution (the youth work setting).

BACKGROUND REFERENCE CHART

Topic: Values and Standards.
Text: The Social Purposes of Education—Collier.

	Whole Book	Chapters	Pages
General Discussion	X		
1. Changing attitudes towards authority and tradition		III	22–36
2. The creation of a tradition—the place of individual conscience		V	53-60
3. Educational objectives		VI	61–85
4. The development of values and attitudes in the growing personality		VII	89–111
5. Self and conscience		VIII	112–28
6. Science and ethical decision		X	146–58

Topic: Values and Standards.
Text: Comparative Education—Hans.

	Whole Book	Chapters	Pages
General Discussion	X		
1. Religious Traditions of Europe		V	85–105
2. The Anglican Tradition		VII	129–50
3. The Puritan Tradition		VIII	151–73
4. Humanism		IX	174–94
5. Socialism		X	195–214
6. Nationalism		XI	215–34
7. Democracy and Education		XII	235–53
8. The Educational System of England		XIII	254–72

Topic: Values and Standards
Text: Adolescence—its Social Psychology—Fleming.

	Whole Book	Chapters	Pages
General Discussion	X		
1. Theories about adolescence		IV	34–44
2. Psychological needs and adolescent attitudes		V	45–51
3. Personal and Social Development		XI	141–63
4. Learning to Live		XVI	209–29
5. Adolescents with problems		XVII	230–8

Topic: Values and Standards.
Text: Education and Society—Ottoway.

	Whole Book	Chapters	Pages
General Discussion	X		
1. The Cultural concept		II	21–40
2. Social forces and cultural change		III	41–59
3. The Social determinance of education in England		IV	60–77
4. The educational needs of our future society		V	78–102
5. Education and the social structure		VI	103–24
6. Beyond Sociology		XI	208–15

Topic: Values and Standards.
Text: Crowther Report.

	Whole Report	Chapters	Pages
1. Changing social needs		IV	36–44
2. The pressures of economic change		V	45–53
3. Burdens and Benefits		VI	54–62
4. Neglected educational territory		XXVIII	313–18
5. Characteristics of Further Education		XXX	332–45
6. Conclusions		XXXVIII	447–75

Topic: Values and Standards.
Text: Newsom Report.

	Whole Report	Chapters	Pages
1. Education for all		I	3
2. The public, the schools, the problems		II	
3. Education in the slums		III	
4. Objectives		IV	

	Whole Report	Chapters	Pages
5. Finding approaches		V	
6. The school and extra curricula activities		VI	
7. Spiritual and moral development		VII	
8. Going out into the world		VIII	

Topic: *Values and Standards.*
Text: *Albemarle Report.*

	Whole Report	Chapters	Pages
General Discussion	X		
1. Young people today		II	13–34
2. The changing scene		Chapter II Part 1	13–28
3. The world of young people		Chapter II Part II	29–34
4. Youth service and society— —a new focus		IX	102–7

VALUES AND STANDARDS
(*References in the selected bibliography*)

Acland 1	Macquirie 63	Morris (P) 77
Acland 2	Mackenzie 64	Robinson 102
French 32	Mackinnon 65	Robinson 103
Groombridge 39	Madge 66	Sprott 113
Grunfeld 42	Morris (M) 76	Wirth 129

INDIVIDUAL GROWTH AND DEVELOPMENT

Basic to this discussion is the assumption that school, and youth work are aspects of the same educational process, sharing the same concerns, objectives and methods, differing only in the setting in which they take place and in the material used. Youth work tends to use the more 'natural' events in everyday life, with an emphasis on recreation, whereas the school setting must emphasise academic, vocational and professional proficiency. But both are concerned with different aspects of the same process, the growth and development of the individual young person. Thinking in this way we assume that the natural growth and development of personality takes place naturally in the family, the neighbourhood, the local community, aided and supported by parents, relatives, neighbours, friends, school, church and work settings.

Two factors may combine in some cases to make this 'natural development' less 'easygoing' than is most often the case. The first factor is that the home, neighbourhood, school or church, etc., for whatever reasons do not or cannot play their part fully or 'properly'. The second is that 'adolescence' as a period of rapid physical, psychological and social change either 'upsets or disturbs' the even balance of personal development, or less seriously and more naturally takes the shape of a need to break away from family and neighbourhood ties. Either of these factors could contribute.

The reasoning of this presentation supposes that some of the support, which for any number of reasons has been absent or unacceptable could be offered by way of detached youth work which should be part of community-wide youth work and educational provision. The discussion on the texts listed on the accompanying chart, together with this presentation might, we feel, suggest the kind of background material necessary for a further consideration of adolescent needs and behaviour as regards youth work generally with special reference to work with the unattached.

Topic: The Individual (growth and development).
Text: Adolescence—its Social Psychology—Fleming.

	Whole Book	Chapters	Pages
General Discussion	X		
1. Bodily changes		II	5–20
2. Reaction towards adolescence		III	21–33
3. Theories about adolescence		IV	34–44
4. Psychological needs of adolescence		V	45–52
5. Personal and social developments		XI	141–63
6. Learning to live		XVI	209–29
7. Adolescents with problems		XVII	230–8

Topic: The Individual.
Text: The Social Psychology of Education—Fleming.

	Whole Book	Chapters	Pages
General Discussion	X		
1. A digression on instincts and related topics		III	9–15
2. Needs and their satisfaction		IV	16–21
3. The changing of behaviour		V & VI	22–9
4. Family influences		VIII	39–48
5. Community influences		IX	49–54
6. School influences		X	55–9
7. Individuals within groups		XI	60–5

Topic: The Individual.
Text: Teaching—a Psychological Analysis—Fleming.

	Whole Book	Chapters	Pages
General Discussion	X		
1. Understanding human nature		II, III,	19–26
		IV	61–6
2. Growth and development		VIII	38–43

Topic: The Individual.
Text: Total Education—Jacks.

	Whole Book	Chapters	Pages
1. The Child		IV	50–67

Topic: The Individual.
Text: Education and Society—Ottoway.

	Whole Book	Chapters	Pages
1. Social interraction		VIII	145–66
2. Understanding human behaviour		X	190–207

INDIVIDUALS
(References to selected bibliography)

'Adolescent 3
Baker 6
'Children' 13
'Faults' 25
Freegard 31
Gibbens 35
Ginsberg 36
Ginsberg 37

Herford 46
Laufer 60
Marshall 67
Mays 71
Miller 74
Morris 78
Oeser 86

Parkinson 93
Pear 94
Philp 95
Pilkington 96
Spicer 111
Steward 116
Turner 123

GROUPS

It is part of the argument of this presentation that help must be offered to unattached individuals in groups, because the group is a natural, necessary and important form of association for adolescents, a form which offers them opportunities for growth and development unobtainable in any other way, and because it affords the worker an additional environment in which to offer help, as well as additional resources in that it offers opportunities to the group to help the individual. For these reasons it is necessary for those attempting this kind of work to know something about groups, what they offer their members, why and how they behave as they do, and how they can be used to help individuals. The texts in the following chart will point up the importance of working with groups as one aspect of the proposed programme, and will also suggest something of how this can be done.

Topic: Group Behaviour.
Text: The Social Purposes of Education—Collier.

	Whole Book	Chapters	Pages
General Discussion	X		
1. Authority and Participation		XII	171–85

Topic: Group Behaviour.
Text: Adolescence—its Social Psychology—Fleming.

	Whole Book	Chapters	Pages
1. Personal and Social Development		XI	141–63
2. Group membership		XII	164–77

Topic: Group Behaviour.
Text: Social Psychology of Education—Fleming.

	Whole Book	Chapters	Pages
General Discussion	X		
1. Individuals can modify groups		V	22–6
2. Groups can modify individuals		VI	27–9

Topic: Group Behaviour.
Text: Teaching—a Psychological Analysis—Fleming.

	Whole Book	Chapters	Pages
General Discussion	X		
1. The concept of self		IV	44–66
2. The pupil in the school situation		IX	140–9
3. The study of groups		XIV	218–24

Topic: Group Behaviour.
Text: Education and Society—Ottoway.

	Whole Book	Chapters	Pages
1. Social interraction		VIII	145–66
2. The school as a social unit		IX	167–89
3. Understanding human behaviour		X	190–207

GROUPS
(References to selected bibliography)

COMMUNITY BEHAVIOUR

Basic to the approach being elaborated here is the idea that the community is partially the cause of the problem, as well as being responsible for its solution. It is therefore necessary to consider the community in several of its aspects.

1. In so far as it forms or affects the social attitudes and so the behaviour of the unattached.

2. In so far as it offers services that are either accepted and used, or rejected.

3. In so far as it has the resources necessary to the provision of a more adequate network of services and opportunities.

4. In so far as it is the role of the detached worker to recognise and use these potentials and limitations in helping the community achieve more adequate youth work provision.

The discussion in the text on the accompanying chart offers some guidance in thinking about these matters.

Topic: Community Behaviour.
Text: The Social Purposes of Education—Collier.

	Whole Book	Chapters	Pages
General Discussion	X		
1. Increase in scale of modern communities		II	11–21
2. The resources of our community		IV	39–52
3. The creation of a tradition		V	53–60
4. Educational objectives		VI	61–85

Topic: Community Behaviour.
Text: Adolescence—its Social Psychology—Fleming.

	Whole Book	Chapters	Pages
1. The School in the Community		XIII	178–84

Topic: Community Behaviour.
Text: The Social Psycholgy of Education—Fleming.

	Whole Book	Chapters	Pages
1. Community Influences		XI	49–54

Topic: Community Behaviour.
Text: Teaching—a Psychological Analysis—Fleming.

	Whole Book	Chapters	Pages
1. Community resources		XVII	260–5

Topic: Community Behaviour.
Text: Total Education—Jacks.

	Whole Book	Chapters	Pages
1. The Community		VII	96–112

Topic: Community Behaviour.
Text: Education and Society—Ottoway.

	Whole Book	Chapters	Pages
1. The School as a Social Club		IX	167–89

COMMUNITY
(References to selected bibliography)

Anderson 4
Clinard 15
Du Sautoy 21
Ellis 22
'Education' 23
Jones 51
Kuenstler 56

Martin 68
Mulloy 80
'Neighbourhood' 82
Nicholson 83
Nisbet 84
'Our Neighbourhood' 89
Ponsioen 97

'Responsibility, 101
Rogers 104
'Self help' 105
Wilson 128
Woodroofe 130
Young 131

THE ROLE OF THE WORKER

A central concern of this kind of work must be the role of the worker, who is at once the representative of the community and agency offering the opportunities (and hence of its values and standards), the agent through and by which the opportunities are offered, as well as the individual person whose work is concerned with offering these things in such a way that the recipient is willing and able to understand and accept them. The role of the worker then is central, and so requires considerable care and attention. The discussions of the role of the teacher in the following texts when extended as background material for a discussion of the role of the worker in youth work might therefore be helpful.

Topic: The role of the worker.
Text: The Social Purposes of Education—Collier.

	Whole Book	*Chapters*	*Pages*
1. Authority and Discipline		XI	161–70
2. Authority and Participation		XII	171–85
3. Integrity		XIV	194–21

Topic: The role of the worker.
Text: Adolescence—its Social Psychology—Fleming.

	Whole Book	*Chapters*	*Pages*
1. The class looks at the teacher		I	1–3
2. Teachers as persons		XII & XIII Part II	67–78
3. Educational function		XIV	79–83
4. Treatment		XV	84–91

Topic: The role of the worker.
Text: Teaching—a Psychological Analysis—Fleming.

	Whole Book	*Chapters*	*Pages*
1. Self-observation and the study of groups		XIV	218–24

Topic: The role of the worker.
Text: Total Education—Jacks.

	Whole Book	*Chapters*	*Pages*
1. Teaching		VI	86–95

Topic: The role of the worker.
Text: Education and Society—Ottoway.

	Whole Book	*Chapters*	*Pages*
1. The role of the teacher		IX	167–89

THE ROLE OF THE WORKER
(*References in selected bibliography*)

SOCIAL CHANGE

Basic to this whole discussion has been the idea that most of the problems now arising in youth work and hence in work with the unattached are problems attendant upon the social change in contemporary society. The question of the values and standards in this discussion is, we believe, directly related to the kind, pace and quality of social change as it has affected the family, neighbourhood, community and the social institutions with which we are here concerned. The discussion in the following texts indicates some of the most relevant areas of change and point up some of the implications of those changes for practical work in the field.

Topic: *Social Change.*
Text: *Comparative Education—Nans.*

	Whole Book	Chapters	Pages
General Discussion	X		
1. Democracy and Education		XII	235–53
2. Education and Social Change			324–5

Topic: *Social Change.*
Text: *Total Education—Jacks.*

	Whole Book	Chapters	Pages
1. Analysis and Synthesis		I	1–12
2. Future education		II	13–28
3. Education and Social Change		VIII	113–26

Topic) *Social Change.*
Text) *Education and Society—Ottoway.*

	Whole Book	Chapters	Pages
General Discussion	X		
1. The sociology of education		I	1–20
2. The culture concept		II	21–40
3. Social forces and cultural change		III	41–59
4. The educational needs of future society		V	78–102
5. Education and Social Structure		VI	103–24
6. Beyond sociology		XI	208–15

Topic: Social Change.
Text: The Social purposes of Education—Collier.

	Whole Book	Chapters	Pages
General Discussion	X		
1. An evolving society		I	3–9
2. The increase in scale of the modern community		II	11–21
3. Changing attitudes of authority and tradition		III	22–36

Topic: Social Change.
Text: Adolescence—its Social Psychology—Fleming.

	Whole Book	Chapters	Pages
1. Reactions towards adolescence		III	21–33
2. Theories about adolescence		IV	34–44

Topic: Social Change.
Text: Crowther.

	Whole Report	Chapters	Pages
1. 60 years of growth		I	3–15
2. Pattern of Secondary Education		II	16–27
3. Population changes and their educational consequences		III	28–35
4. Changing social needs		IV	36–44
5. The pressures of educational change		V	45–53
6. Neglected educational territory		XXVIII	313–17
7. Changing patterns in Organisation		XXXVI	407–26

Topic: Social Change.
Text: Albemarle.

	Whole Report	Chapters	Pages
1. The youth service yesterday and today		I	4–12
2. Young people today —the changing scene —the world of young people		II	13–28
3. The youth service and society—a new focus		IX	102–7

Topic: Social Change.
Text: Newsom.

		Whole Report	*Chapters*	*Pages*
1.	Education for all		I	3–9
2.	The pupils, the schools and the problems		II	10–16
3.	Education in the slums		III	17–26
4.	Objectives		IV	27–31
5.	Finding approaches		V	32–40
6.	Spiritual and moral development		VII	52–9
7.	Going out into the world		IX	72–9

SOCIAL CHANGE
(*References in selected bibliography*)

Carstairs 12
Cohen 16
'Communities' 18
Edwards 24
Fyvel 33

Goldsmidt 38
Hoggart 47
Jones 50
Mead 73
'Social' 108

Sprott 115
Vereker 124
Wickwar 126
'Youth' 134

SELECTED BIBLIOGRAPHY

1. ACLAND, Sir Richard, "What's Wrong With Critics of What's Wrong?", *Challenge*, National Association of Boys' Clubs, Summer 1964.
2. ACLAND, Sir Richard, "What's Wrong", *Challenge*, Winter 1964.
3. *The Adolescent* (Subject of the Year, 1959–60), The British Medical Association, March, 1961.
4. ANDERSON, F. and BURKE, B., "Some Observations on a Non-Directive Approach to Community Self Study", *International Review of Community Development*, No. 4, 1959.
5. *Attitude Change in Inter group Relations*, Report on a Meeting of Experts, January 2–6, 1962, U.N.E.S.C.O. Youth Institute, Gauting, Munich.
6. BAKER, Paul and LITTLE, Alan, "The Margate Offenders—A Survey", *New Society*, No. 96, July 30, 1964.
7. BAPTIE, Tom, "The Self Programming Group—Principles Involved", *The Youth Officer*, No. 43, National Association of Youth Officers, July, 1960.
8. BATTEN, T. R., *Training for Community Development, A Critical Study of Method*, Oxford University Press, 1962.
9. BEAMAN, T. E., "From Teaching to Living", *New Society*, No. 92, July 2, 1964.
10. BENJAMIN, Joe, *In Search of Adventure: A Study of the Junk Playground*, The National Council of Social Service, 1961.
11. BREW, J. Macalister, *Youth and Youth Groups*, Faber and Faber, 1957.
12. CARSTAIRS, G. M., "This Island Now", The Reith Lectures, *The Listener*, November 15, 22, 29, December 6, 13, 20, 1962.
13. *Children and Young People: A guide to Studies*, National Council of Social Service, 1956.
14. *Citizens of Tomorrow: A Study of the Influences Affecting the Upbringing of Young People*, King George's Jubilee Trust, Odhams Press, 1955.
15. CLINARD, M. B., "Evaluation and Research in Urban Community Development", *International Review of Community Development*, No. 12, 1963.
16. COHEN, Emmeline E., *English Social Services, Methods and Growth*, George Allen and Unwin, 1949.
17. COLLIER, K. G., *The Social Purposes of Education, Personal and Social Values in Education*, International Library of Sociology and Social Reconstruction, Routledge and Kegan Paul, 1962.
18. *Communities and Social Change: Implications for Social Welfare*, A Guide to Studies For the 5th British National Conference on Social Welfare. The National Council of Social Service, 1964.
19. *Committees Work in This Way*, National Association of Youth Clubs, 1960.
20. DAVIES, Bernard, "The Practice of Social Group Work", *The Youth Leader*, Vol. 10 (New Series), No. 1, Spring, 1962.
21. DU SAUTOY, Peter, *The Organisation of a Community Development Programme*, Oxford University Press, 1962.

22. ELLIS, Lionel F., *Toynbee Hall and The University Settlements*. Paper read before the Royal Society of Arts. George Barber and Son, 1937.

23. *Education for Social Action*, Report of the Proceedings of the 26th National Conference of the National Federation of Community Associations. The National Federation of Community Association, 1959.

24. EDWARDS, Elvvyns, "Man and Technology", *New Society*, No. 65, December 26, 1963.

25. "Faults in the Youth Employment Service", *New Society*, No. 28, April 11, 1963.

26. *15 to 18* (The Crowther Report), Report of the Central Advisory Council for Education (two volumes), Ministry of Education, H.M.S.O., 1960.

27. FLEMING, C. M., *Adolescence, its social Psychology*, International Library of Sociology and Social Reconstruction, Routledge and Kegan Paul, 1963.

28. FLEMING, C. M., *Social Psychology of Education, an introduction and guide to its study*. International Library of Sociology and Social Reconstruction, Routledge and Kegan Paul, 1959.

29. FLEMING, C. M. (Ed.), *Studies in the Social Psychology of Adolescence*, International Library of Sociology and Social Reconstruction, Routledge and Kegan Paul, 1951.

30. FLEMING, C. M., *Teaching—a Psychological Analysis*, University Paper Backs, Methuen, 1964.

31. FREEGARD, Margaret, "Five Girls Against Authority", *Welfare Casework*, Vol. 3, No. 72, February 13, 1964.

32. FRENCH, Roderick S., "Youth Work—A theological Reflection on its Collapse", *The Ecumenical Review*, Vol. XV, No. 2, January, 1963, pp. 137–43.

33. FYVEL, T. R., *The Insecure Offenders: Rebellious Youth in the Welfare State*, Chatto and Windus, 1961.

34. GARDINER, R. K. and JUDD, H. O., *The Development of Social Administration*, Oxford University Press, Second Edition, 1959.

35. GIBBENS, T. C. N., "The Teenage Riots Round the World", *New Society*, No. 97, August 6, 1964.

36. GINSBERG, Morris, *On the Diversity of Morals: Essays in Sociology and Social Philosophy*, William Heinemann, 1956.

37. GINSBERG, Morris, *Sociology*, Oxford University Press, 1959.

38. GOLDSCHMIDT, Walter, *Understanding Human Society*, International Library of Sociology and Social Reconstruction, Routledge and Kegan Paul, 1960.

39. GROOMBRIDGE, Brian (Ed.), *Popular Culture and Personal Responsibility: A Study Outline*, National Union of Teachers, Pamphlet No. 221, 1961.

40. GOSLING, Ray, *Lady Albemarle's Boys*, A Young Fabian Publication, 1961.

41. *Group Discussion—In Educational, Social and Working Life*, Central Council for Health Education, 1957.

42. GRUNFELD, Dr. D. I. and HARDWICKE, Rev. Owen T. Alan, Bob, PIERSSENE, A.S.D. and CADBURY, Sir Egbert, Articles and Readers' Letters, *Challenge*, Spring 1964.

43. *Half our Future* (The Newsom Report), A report on the Central Advisory Council for Education, H.M.S.O., 1963.

44. HANMER, Jalna, *Girls at Leisure,* Published by the London Union of Youth Clubs, and the London Young Women's Christian Association, 1964.

45. HANS, Nicholas, *Comparative Education, A Study of Educational Factors and Traditions,* International Library of Sociology and Social Reconstruction, Routledge and Kegan Paul, 1961.

46. HERFORD, M. E. M., *Youth at Work: A Study of Adolescents in Industry by an appointed Factory Doctor,* Max Parrish, 1957.

47. HOGGART, Richard, *The uses of Literacy* (Aspects of working-class life with special reference to publications and entertainments), Penguin Books in Association with Chatto and Windus, 1958.

48. HYDE, Alice, "Social Casework and Social Groupwork", *Case Conference,* Vol. 10, No. 1, Association of Social Workers and Case Conference, May, 1963.

49. JACKS, M. L., *Total Education) A Plea for synthesis,* International Library of Sociology and Social Reconstruction, Routledge and Kegan Paul, 1955.

50. JONES, Havard, "The Future of the Approved Schools", *New Society,* No. 107, October 15, 1964.

51. JONES, Kathleen, "Community, Mental Care", *New Society,* No. 74, February 27, 1964.

52. KEEBLE, R. W. J., *A Life Full of Meaning,* Pergamon Press, Oxford, 1965.

53. KLEIN, Josephine, *The Study of Groups,* Routledge and Kegan Paul, 1958.

54. KLEIN, Josephine, *Working with Groups,* Hutchinson, 1961.

55. KLEIN, Josephine, *Samples from English Cultures,* Vols. I and II, Routledge and Kegan Paul, 1965.

56. KUENSTLER, Peter (Ed.), *Community Organisation in Great Britain,* Faber and Faber, 1961.

57. KUENSTLER, Peter, *Gangs, Groups and Clubs,* The eighth Charles Russell Memorial Lecture given in London, October 19, 1960. National Council of Social Service, 1960.

58. KUENSTLER, Peter (Ed.), *Social Groupwork in Great Britain,* Faber and Faber, 1951.

59. KUENSTLER, Peter, "Youth Groups and Group Work: a Comment on Some Training Problems", *Case Conference,* Vol. 9, No. 2, Association of Social Workers and Case Conference, June, 1962.

60. LAUFER, M., "The Help of an Adult: Welfare and Work", *New Society,* No. 64, December 19, 1963.

61. LEOPER, R. A. B., "The Relevance of Groups", *The Youth Leader,* Vol. 10 (New Series), No. 1, Spring 1962.

62. Lyndhurst Hall, "A New Start in a club for young people in Kentish Town", *Christian Teamwork,* No. 2, 1962.

63. MACGUIRIE, Alec, "Emancipated and reactionaries, *New Society,* Vol. 3, No. 87, May 28, 1964.

64. MACKENZIE, Norman (Ed.), *Conviction,* MacGibbon and Kee, 1958.

65. MACKINNON, D. M., WILLIAMS, H. A., VIDLER, A. R. and BESSANT, J. S., *Objections to Christian Belief,* Constable, 1963.
66. MADGE, Charles, *Society in the Mind: Elements of Social Eidos,* Faber and Faber, 1964.
67. MARSHALL, W. A., MILLER, Dereck and LOVELL, Kenneth, "The Seven ages of Man: the Body, Personality, Ability", *New Society,* No. 111, November 12, 1964.
68. MARTIN, D. V., "Problems in developing a Community Approach to Mental Hospital Treatment", *British Journal of Psychiatric Social Work,* Vol. 5, No. 2, Association of Psychiatric Social Workers, 1959.
69. MATTHEWS, Joan E., *Professional Skill: Functions of Club Organisers in Social Group Work,* National Association of Youth Clubs, 1960.
70. MATTHEWS, Joan, "Social Group Work in Youth Work", *New Society,* No. 69, January 9, 1964.
71. MAYS, John Barron, *Education and the Urban Child,* Social Research Series, Liverpool University Press, 1962.
72. MAYS, John Barron, *On the Threshold of Delinquency,* Social Research Series, Liverpool University Press, 1959.
73. MEAD, Margaret, *Cultural Patterns and Technical Change,* Tension and Technology Series, U.N.E.S.C.O., 1953.
74. MILLER, Derek, "Psychology of the Delinquent Boy", *New Society,* No. 95, July 23, 1964.
75. MORRIS, Cherry, *Social Casework in Great Britain,* Faber and Faber, 1954.
76. MORRIS, Mary, *Voluntary Organisations and Social Progress,* Victor Gollancz, 1955.
77. MORRIS, Sir Philip, *Welfare and Responsibility,* The Second Charles Russell Memorial Lecture given in London, October 15, 1953. National Council of Social Service, 1953.
78. MORRIS, Terence, "The Teenage Criminal", *New Society,* No. 28, April 11, 1963.
79. MASSIE, Peter, *An Experiment in Youth Welfare,* Privately Circulated, September, 1959.
80. MULLOY, P. N. "Training Local Leaders in Community Associations", *International Review of Community Development,* No. 3, 1959.
81. *The Nature and Role of Conformity,* Report on a meeting of experts, June 18–22, 1963. U.N.E.S.C.O. Youth Institute.
82. *Neighbourhood and Community: Social Relationships on a Housing Estate,* Liverpool University Press, 1954.
83. NICHOLSON, J. H., *New Communities in Britain: Achievements and Problems,* The National Council of Social Service, 1961.
84. NISBET, R. H., "Moral Values and Community", *International Review of Community Development,* No. 5, 1960.
85. *Notes on Education in Personal Relationships to Youth Leaders,* Published by the Church of England Moral Welfare Council, 1939.
86. OESER, O. A. and HAMMOND, S. B. (Ed.), *Social Structure and Personality in a City,* Routledge and Kegan Paul, 1954.
87. *Open Youth Centres and the Problems of the Social Maladjustment of Youth,* Report on a Meeting of Experts, October 4–8, 1960, U.N.E.S.C.O. Youth Institute.

88. OTTOWAY, A. U. C., *Education and Society—an Introduction to the Sociology of Education,* International Library of Sociology and Social Reconstruction, Routledge and Kegan Paul, 1962.

89. *Our Neighbourhood) A Handbook of Information For Community Centres and Associations,* The National Council of Social Service, 1950.

90. PACKER, Edwin, "The Probation Officer", A day in social work III, *New Society,* No. 19, February 7, 1963.

91. Papers on the teaching of personality development. *The Sociological Review,* Monograph No. 2, Keele University College, September, 1959.

92. Papers on the Teaching of Personality Behaviour, *The Sociological Review,* Monograph, No. 1, Keele University College, July, 1958.

93. PARKINSON, Geoffrey, "The Challenge of the Borstal Boy", *New Society,* No. 109, October 26, 1964.

94. PEAR, T. H., *Personality, Appearance and Speech,* George Allen and Unwin, 1957.

95. PHILP, A. F. and TIMMS, Noel, *The Problem of the Problem Family,* Family Service Units, 1962.

96. PILKINGTON, Sir Harry, *The Boy in Industry,* The Seventh Charles Russell Memorial Lecture, given in Liverpool, March 11, 1958. National Council of Social Service, 1958.

97. PONSIOEN, J. A., *Social Welfare Policy, Second Collection.* Contributions to Methodology, Institute of Social Studies, Mouton and Co., The Hague, 1963.

98. *The Principles and Practice of Group Work.* Report, European Seminar, Leicester, England, IM-31-July, 1956, United Nations, Geneva, UN/TAA/SEM/1956/Rep. 1.

99. *Report of the Committee on Children and Young Persons,* H.M.S.O., October, 1960.

100. *Report of the Juvenile Employment Service,* H.M.S.O., 1960.

101. *Responsibility in the Welfare State, A Study of Relationships Between the Social Services and the Churches in a City Suburb,* A Report of the Birmingham Social Responsibility Project, Published by the Birmingham Council of Christian Churches, 1961.

102. ROBINSON, John A. T., *Honest to God,* S.C.M. Press, 1963.

103. ROBINSON, John A. T. and EDWARDS, David L., *The Honest to God Debate,* S.C.M. Press, 1963.

104. ROGERS, W. C., "Voluntary Association and Urban Community Development", *International Review of Community Development,* No. 7, 1961.

105. *Self-Help in Social Welfare,* Proceedings of the Seventh International Conference of Social Work, Toronto, June, July, 1954. The South East Asia Regional Office, International Conference of Social Work, Bombay, India.

106. SEWELL, Lesley, *Looking at Youth Clubs,* National Association of Youth Clubs, 1955.

107. SMITH, Dr. C. S., "The Task Before the Youth Service", *The Youth Leader,* Vol. 10 (New Series), No. 1, Spring 1962.

108. *The Social Impact of Work Life on Young People,* Report on a Meeting of Experts, June 10-15, 1963, U.N.E.S.C.O. Youth Institute, March, 1964.

109. *The Social Worker and the Group Approach*—A Report of the Conference, May 28–29, 1954, The Association of Social Workers.

110. SPENCER, John, TUXFORD, Joy, and DENNIS, Norman, *Stress and Release in an Urban Estate: A Study in Action Research,* Tavistock Publications, 1964.

111. SPICER, "Talking to Delinquents", Welfare Conference Work, *New Society,* No. 120, January 14, 1965.

112. *Sport and the Community,* The Report of the Wolfenden Committee on Sport, The Central Council of Physical Recreation, September, 1960.

113. SPROTT, W. J. H., *The Problem of self respect.* The Fourth Charles Russell Memorial Lecture given at Nottingham on July 17, 1955, National Council of Social Service, 1955.

114. SPROTT, W. J. H., *Human Groups,* Penguin Books, 1958.

115. SPROTT, W. J. H., *Sociology,* Hutchinson University Library, 1959.

116. STEWARD, B. W., "Camping with Probationers", Welfare and Work, *New Society,* No. 99, August 20, 1964.

117. STOTT, D. H., *Present Needs in Our Work Among Youth,* The sixth Charles Russell Memorial Lecture, given in London, October 14, 1957. National Council of Social Service, 1957.

118. *The Teen Canteen at the Dulwich College Mission—A Report,* The Dulwich College Mission, 1960.

119. Training for Community Development (European Seminar), Athens, Greece, September, 1961. Report—S.O.A./E.S.W.P./1961/2. 1962.

120. Training for Social Work, 3rd International Survey, United Nations, Department of Economic and Social Affairs, New York, U.S.A., 1958. E/CN/331/St/S.O.A./37, 1958.

121. *The Training of Part-Time Youth Leaders and Assistants,* (Bessey Report) Report of the Working Party Appointed by the Ministry of Education, July, 1961—H.M.S.O., 1962.

122. TRIST, E. L. and SOFER, C., *Exploration in Group Relations,* Leicester University Press, 1959.

123. TURNER, Merfyn, *Safe Lodging,* Hutchinson, 1961.

124. VEREKER, C., MAYS, J. B., GITTUS, Elizabeth and BROADY, Maurice, *Urban Redevelopment and Social Change,* Liverpool University Social Research Series, Liverpool University Press, 1961.

125. *Volunteers, you, you and You,* Y.W.C.A. Area Office, London, 1963.

126. WICKWAR, Hardy and Margaret, *The Social Services, an Historical Survey,* Bodley Head, 1949.

127. *Widening Horizon,* Social Education in a Specialist Age, Workers' Educational Association, 1964.

128. WILSON, Roger, *Difficult Housing Estates,* Tavistock Pamphlet No. 5, Tavistock Publications, 1963.

129. WIRTH, Louis, *Community Life and Social Policy,* The University of Chicago Press, 1956.

130. WOODROOFE, Kathleen, *From Charity to Social Work,* Routledge and Kegan Paul, 1962.

131. YOUNG, Michael and WILLMOTT, Peter, *Family and Kinship in East London,* Institute of Community Studies, Routledge and Kegan Paul, 1957.

132. YOUNG, Michael, "How can Parents and Teachers work Together", *New Society*, Vol. 4, No. 104, September 24, 1964.

133. *The Youth Service in England and Wales,* (Albemarle Report), Report of the Committee Appointed by the Ministry of Education in November, 1958, H.M.S.O., 1960.

134. *Youth, The Church and the Changing World,* Background Information for Church and Society, Department on Church and Society Division of Studies, World Council of Churches, Geneva, November, 1964.

INDEX